AMAZON LAW LIBRARY

AMAZON LAW LIBRARY

Volume 1

CJ ROSENBAUM
LAWYERS FOCUSED ON AMAZON SELLERS

CJ Rosenbaum

ISBN: 0692762221
ISBN 13: 9780692762226

Amazon Sellers Law Book – An Introduction

This book has been put together by myself and my team here at The Amazon Sellers Lawyer, and is intended to be a "bible" of all the legal issues surrounding Amazon and the use of its online platform. The book contains summaries of nearly every case Amazon has litigated within the past several years. The book is broken down into three sections, all of which have been written in everyday or "layman's" terms in order to make the material accessible to anyone, whether they have a legal background or not. The first section is the Table of Contents; it provides a list of each legal category this book addresses. Section two is the Annotations Section; essentially this section defines what each category from section one will cover and also provides shorter, concise summaries of each case found in its respective section. The third and final section contains full case summaries and breaks down each case by its issue, rule, facts, analysis, and Conclusion.

Amazon.com, Inc. (Amazon) is the largest internet based retailer on the planet in terms of total sales and market capitalization. The content available on the Amazon platform includes a wide range of both products and services that are made easily accessible to almost any consumer. The products sold on the Amazon platform include merchandise and content that Amazon itself purchases from vendors, as well as products offered for sale by third party sellers. Amazon's corporate structure is divided into three segments: North America; International; and Amazon Web Services. Amazon's business operates on a global level; the Amazon platform has consumer websites operating in North America, Germany, France, Japan, and the United Kingdom.

Anyone who wishes to become a seller on the Amazon platform must agree to Amazon's conditions of use. The conditions for sellers are extremely strict, and Amazon takes their enforcement very seriously. The terms of this agreement are complex, but Amazon has put them in place in order to promote the maintenance of a safe marketplace for consumers, sellers, and manufacturers alike. The conditions of use govern everything from Intellectual Property (IP) violations to seller's late shipment rates. However, Amazon often reacts harshly towards sellers who violate this agreement in order to protect themselves. For example, Amazon will suspend a seller's account even if they are merely accused of an IP violation, whether it is baseless or not. This is because IP statutes generally will not assign liability to a hosting website *unless* that website is made aware of the infringement. This book contains countless other examples of situations where having a legal background will prove advantageous to anyone looking to resolve an issue within the Amazon platform.

When writing this book, I explained my vision to the team. Our goal was to create the go to source for legal research relating to Amazon and the use of the Amazon platform. The Amazon platform is unpredictable in the way it handles issues with sellers, so it is important to be prepared. When a seller has been suspended by Amazon, their reinstatement is handled on a case by case basis. What truly makes this book useful is how quickly and efficiently it allows the reader to research their issue. By starting with the Table of Contents, the reader will be able to quickly identify which section of the book their issue will fall under. Next, a reader can use the annotations section in order to identify which cases will be the most useful in supporting their position. Finally, the full summaries will allow the reader to identify typical patterns and procedures that arise in situations similar to their own. By purchasing this book, you are already taking a step towards bettering your Amazon business and / or understanding the complex issues surrounding the Amazon platform. Amazon has been involved in far more legal issues than many people realize. Our team at the Amazon Seller's Lawyer has been actively documenting each and every lawsuit involving Amazon since we have launched. This book provides case summaries of complete court opinions ranging from

Amazon's earliest days to the present. I hope this book helps anyone involved with the Amazon platform to educate themselves, avoid problems, and maximize their success as an online entrepreneur.

About the Author

CJ ROSENBAUM: THE GO-TO AMAZON ATTORNEY

"As an Amazon seller, your e-commerce success depends on your cooperation with the rules and regulations set by Amazon. When you are conducting an online business through Amazon, an account suspension brings your entire operation to a halt. Suspensions can happen at any time – even with just one complaint from a buyer. Amazon sellers don't need to live in fear of policy violations, buyer complaints, and account suspensions any longer. Amazon sellers now have a lawyer on their side to address these issues from a legal perspective, utilizing the law to pursue lost profit caused by an account suspension." – CJ

FOCUSED ON AMAZON SELLERS

Before CJ's law firm was founded, Amazon sellers had only one option for assistance in getting their account reinstated: non-lawyers who lack the education, expertise, and resources needed to defend a client against Amazon policies. These consultants also lack the X factor that CJ provides as a licensed attorney: the legal obligation to maintain your privacy.

C. J.'S BACKGROUND AND EXPERIENCE IN LAW AND E-COMMERCE

CJ's tech background includes membership in the New York New Media Association (NYNMA), a group of young entrepreneurs who recognized the commercial power of the web. It was founded in 1994 to support and promote the 'new media' industry in New York City. In 1996, CJ bought shares of Apple for $22 and $24 a share.

Since starting his practice in 1994, CJ has represented entrepreneurs who operate both online & brick & mortar businesses. CJ is also a courtroom lawyer and litigator. CJ has represented people across the United States, has taken countless depositions and tries more cases each year than most lawyers do during their entre careers.

- CJ has successfully litigated cases against some of the largest corporations in the world including McDonalds, Sears, Kentucky Fried Chicken, many insurance companies. In NYC, CJ has successfully obtained redress for his clients against the NYPD, the NYC Housing Department, the NYC Health and Hospitals Corp., and other behemoths. CJ has represented clients in the internet, finance, health and entertainment industries.
- CJ is admitted to practice law in state and federal courts.
- CJ holds executive and leadership roles in the NYS Bar Association and the National American Association for Justice.
- CJ has delivered lectures to other lawyers in New York, Chicago, Montreal, Maryland, Florida and this summer is scheduled to speak on several topics in Los Angeles.

In writing this book CJ combined his vast years of legal experience with his knowledge of the Amazon platform in order to deliver a resource for any Amazon seller that will help avoid issues that might compromise their account.

Special Contributions

The Amazon Law Library would not have come to fruition without the assistance of my team here at the Amazon Seller's Lawyer. Our staff, comprising of other attorney's, paralegals, and account analysts have contributed countless hours or research, writing, and editing in order to make this project a reality. Without the drive and determination of these amazing people, this valuable resource would not be possible.

NICOLE KULAGA

Paralegal

Nicole is a second year law student at Maurice A. Deane School of Law with a Bachelor's Degree in English from New Paltz University. She believes her experience as a fashion journalist has set the foundation needed to prepare her for a future in practicing Intellectual Property Law, specifically, Fashion Law. Nicole is a paralegal with Amazon Sellers Lawyer and spent her summer assisting in writing, editing, and organizing this volume. Nicole has assisted in and been a part of researching, writing, and organizing all sections of the Amazon Law Library.

ROBERT SEGALL

Paralegal

Robert is a second year law student at Maurice A. Deane School of Law with a Bachelor's degree in Finance from Long Island University at CW Post. Robert's business background provides him with key insight into the needs of everyday entrepreneurs, and he is passionate about fighting the injustices that occur on the Amazon platform. Robert was a key contributor in the writing and research that went into the Amazon Law Library, and additionally was responsible for editing this volume.

ANTHONY FAMULARO

Managing Attorney

Anthony has been with the Amazon Seller's Lawyer since its inception and has been an essential member of the team. According to Anthony, "I became passionate about representing Amazon sellers once I saw how frequently larger corporations use false legal claims to sabotage smaller Amazon sellers." Anthony now devotes his time to resolving these complex legal issues so that our clients can get back to selling on the Amazon platform as soon as possible. Anthony's made sure my vision of what this book should be became a reality. Anthony has supported and managed our team throughout this entire process and also devoted countless hours towards researching, writing, and editing this book.

Part I
Table of Contents

CJ ROSENBAUM
LAWYERS FOCUSED ON AMAZON SELLERS

Part II
Case Annotations

CJ ROSENBAUM

LAWYERS FOCUSED ON AMAZON SELLERS

Amazon Dismissed from All Claims

When a party believes they are wrongfully joined in a lawsuit, they can file a motion to dismiss for failure to state a claim pursuant to Federal rule 12. It is essential to state the claim you may have against Amazon clearly and sufficiently so that the court can see that there is a clear dispute. The complaint must be written according to Federal Rule of Civil Procedure 12(f) and must clearly state a claim. It is important to note that a motion to dismiss is different than a motion for summary judgment as it is done prior to discovery and is based solely on the pleadings.

In the cases that we have seen, Amazon is typically dismissed when they file a motion to dismiss and properly show that the plaintiff has failed to state a claim against them. The plaintiff must plead adequate facts to establish any harm, otherwise the case will be dismissed as it was in *Hard 2 Find Accessories, Inc. v. Amazon.com Inc.*[1] When plaintiff fails to state a proper claim with facts, courts find there to be no case in controversy, such as in *Brown Younger v. Lulu. com*[2], where a hearing revealed that Amazon never sold the product at issue nor was it ever listed on their website. Additionally, if there is an arbitration clause in an agreement with Amazon, they may have the case dismissed claiming the issue should be resolved in arbitration, such as in *Nicosia v. Amazon.com Inc.*[3]

---

1. *Hard 2 Find Accessories, Inc. v. Amazon.com, Inc.* Case No. C14-0950 RSM. United States District Court for the Western District of Washington, November 17, 2014.
2. *Brown-Younger v. Lulu.com,* No. 12 C 1979, 2012 U.S. Dist. LEXIS 91574 (N.D. Ill. July 3, 2012).
3. *Nicosia v. Amazon.com,* Case No. 14-cv-4513 (SLT) (MDG). United States District Court, E.D. New York, February 2015.

- ***Brown-Younger v. Lulu.com*, 2012 U.S. Dist. LEXIS 91574, 2012 WL 2576214 (N.D. Ill. July 3, 2012).**
  This case involves a copyright claim in which Amazon.com Inc. was improperly joined as a defendant, and plaintiff also filed frivolous ARDC charges against Amazon attorneys. The court found that it would be unfair to allow the charges to be left uncorrected because they contained no truth and Amazon never sold the book at issue. Plaintiff was ordered to retract and withdraw her ARDC charge.
- ***Del Vecchio v. Amazon.com Inc.*, 2011 U.S. Dist. LEXIS 138314, 2011 WL 6325910 (W.D. Wash. Nov. 30, 2011).**
  Amazon.com was a defendant in a case filed by Del Vecchio. Del Vecchio represented a class action against Amazon seeking relief under the Computer Fraud and Abuse act. Amazon motioned to dismiss and the court concluded that the defendant's motion to dismiss should be granted because the plaintiffs failed to plead adequate facts to establish any harm.
- ***Hard 2 Find Accessories, Inc. v. Amazon.com, Inc.*, 2014 U.S. Dist. LEXIS 160980, 2014-2 Trade Cas. (CCH) P78,968 (W.D. Wash. Nov. 17, 2014).**
  This was a case involving the defendant Apple Inc.'s motion to dismiss for failure to state a claim. Plaintiff was a former Amazon seller who was removed because Apple claimed plaintiff was selling counterfeit Apple products on the Amazon platform. Apple's motion to dismiss was granted because plaintiffs could not show that Apple's letter demanding the cease and desist of the infringing product sales was unfounded.
- ***Nicosia v. Amazon.com, Inc.*, 84 F. Supp. 3d 142, 2015 U.S. Dist. LEXIS 13560 (E.D.N.Y. 2015)**
  Amazon.com is a defendant in a case brought by Dean Nicosia for the selling of a controlled substance in a weight loss supplement. Amazon.com motioned to dismiss claiming that the issue should be settled in arbitration due the arbitration clause. The court agreed and granted Amazon's motion.

- ***Shive v. Amazon.Com, Inc.* Cv 15-406 Jb/Wpl, United States District Court for The District of New Mexico.**
  This case involved a court order to show cause directing the Plaintiff, James Shive, to move the case forward. However, because Shive did not respond to the order, Amazon.com was dismissed without prejudice.
- ***Switzer v. Litex Indus.* Case No. 11-cv-01174-REB. D. Colo., May 3, 2011.**
  This is a case involving patent infringement and a briefing schedule to resolve matters. The court orders that the parties shall file a joint claim construction statement of the patents at issue, limited to fifteen pages, to be filed thirty days after the statement is filed, deadlines for filing a response brief and reply shall be followed, a response brief shall be limited to twenty pages, and the parties shall convene a telephone motions hearing within ten days after the reply brief is filed to set a time for a hearing.
- ***Switzer v. Litex Indus.* Case No. 11-cv-01174-REB. D. Colo., August 23, 2011.**
  This is a case involving a stipulation for dismissal of the defendant, Amazon.com. The court grants the stipulation for dismissal of Amazon.com.
- ***Nomura Tetsuya v. Amazon.com, Inc.*, 2011 U.S. Dist. LEXIS 66443, 2011 WL 2472557 (N.D. Cal. June 22, 2011).**
  Plaintiff, Joe Nomura Tetsuya sued Amazon.com for patent infringement of patent 622. Amazon.com moved to dismiss the complaint pursuant to Federal Rules of Civil Procedure 12(f). The court found that the complaint filed by the defendant failed to state a claim because Tetsuya failed to allege which claims of the '622 patent had been infringed and what Amazon products or services infringed them and how. Thus the court granted Amazon's motion to dismiss.

Antitrust Law Violations

Antitrust laws outline the types of unlawful business mergers and unlawful business practices in general terms, and give the courts discretion to decide whether the conduct of each case is illegal based on each cases individual facts. Antitrust Laws serve a number of fundamental purposes: they protect the competitive process, consumer welfare, and total welfare. It battles behavior that reduce both competition and consumer welfare. The court can dismiss an antitrust claim if the moving party does not provide evidence of the violations or of suffering and injury as a result.

In *Bookhouse of Stuyvesant Plaza Inc. v. Amazon.com*[1], Amazon was accused of antitrust violations due to the nature of its Kindle, e-book reader. The software used on the Kindle only allowed books to be downloaded from Amazon if the user wanted to read the book on the kindle. The court found that plaintiff failed to show that there was a significant difference in the market for e-books versus traditional print books. We will also see that in *Gerlinger v. Amazon.com*[2], the plaintiff did not state the ways in which Amazon violated antitrust laws or show any harm suffered. There was also no actual evidence of injury provided by the plaintiff for the antitrust claim or the unfair competition claim, which resulted in the case being dismissed. Similarly, in *Joseph v. Amazon.com, Inc.*[3] the plaintiff failed to allege that Amazon made continuing violations or that Amazon coerced a business arrangement to support their action.

---

1. *Bookhouse of Stuyvesant Plaza, Inc. v. Amazon.com, Inc.*, 985 F. Supp. 2d 612, 2013 U.S. Dist. LEXIS 171871, 2013-2 Trade Cas. (CCH) P78,608, 2013 WL 6311202 (S.D.N.Y. 2013).
2. *Gerlinger v. Amazon.com*, Inc., 2005 U.S. Dist. LEXIS 26019, 2005-2 Trade Cas. (CCH) P75,004, 34 Media L. Rep. 1509 (N.D. Cal. Oct. 31, 2005).
3. *Joseph v. Amazon.com, Inc.*, 46 F. Supp. 3d 1095, 2014 U.S. Dist. LEXIS 121050, 42 Media L. Rep. 2496 (W.D. Wash. 2014).

- ***Bookhouse of Stuyvesant Plaza, Inc. v. Amazon.com, Inc.*, 985 F. Supp. 2d 612, 2013 U.S. Dist. LEXIS 171871, 2013-2 Trade Cas. (CCH) P78,608, 2013 WL 6311202 (S.D.N.Y. 2013).**
  This case involved an anti-trust claim against Amazon. Book publishers had brought suit because per Amazon's e-book platform, if a consumer owns a Kindle and wants to read an e-book on the Kindle that was published by any of the publishers in this action, then they must buy the book from Amazon. The court granted the Defendants' Motion to Dismiss, as they determined that the plaintiff's complaint failed to state a plausible claim.
- ***BookLocker.com, Inc. v. Amazon.com, Inc.*, 650 F. Supp. 2d 89, 2009 U.S. Dist. LEXIS 76352, 2009-2 Trade Cas. (CCH) P76,729 (D. Me. 2009).**
  In this case plaintiffs brought suit against Amazon, claiming anti-trust violations under the Sherman Act. Plaintiffs claimed a violation exists because if a consumer who owns a Kindle e-reader wishes to purchase an e-book produced by one of the plaintiff publishers, then that consumer *must* purchase the e-book from Amazon. The court denies Amazon's motion to dismiss because it found that plaintiff had made a plausible claim for relief.
- ***Gerlinger v. Amazon.com, Inc.*, 311 F. Supp. 2d 838, 2004 U.S. Dist. LEXIS 4604, 2004-1 Trade Cas. (CCH) P74,363 (N.D. Cal. 2004).**
  Plaintiff could not succeed on antitrust claim when the alleged violation was a price-fixing agreement that actually provided customers with lower prices.
- ***Gerlinger v. Amazon.com,* Inc., 2005 U.S. Dist. LEXIS 26019, 2005-2 Trade Cas. (CCH) P75,004, 34 Media L. Rep. 1509 (N.D. Cal. Oct. 31, 2005).**
  This case involved plaintiff claiming the defendants violated antitrust laws through their store agreement with Amazon, as well as the defendants' motion to dismiss. The court granted the motion to dismiss the antitrust claims and the unfair competition claim because it found that the plaintiff provided no actual evidence of the alleged injuries.

- ***Gerlinger v. Amazon.com, Inc.*, 526 F.3d 1253, 2008 U.S. App. LEXIS 11237, 2008-1 Trade Cas. (CCH) P76,161 (9th Cir. Cal. 2008).**
  This case involves the appellant challenging a judgment in a lower court that dismissed his antitrust claim against the defendants. The court affirmed the judgment of the district court because it agreed with the district court that plaintiff provided no evidence of the alleged injuries.
- ***Hard 2 Find Accessories, Inc. v. Amazon.com, Inc.*, 2014 U.S. Dist. LEXIS 160980, 2014-2 Trade Cas. (CCH) P78,968 (W.D. Wash. Nov. 17, 2014).**
  This is a case involving the defendant Apple Inc.'s motion to dismiss for failure to state a claim. Plaintiff was a former Amazon seller who was removed because Apple claimed plaintiff was selling counterfeit Apple products on the Amazon platform. Apple's motion to dismiss was granted because plaintiffs could not show that Apple's letter demanding the the cease and desist of the infringing product sales was unfounded.
- ***IPXL Holdings, L.L.C. v. Amazon.com, Inc.*, 333 F. Supp. 2d 513, 2004 U.S. Dist. LEXIS 19909, 72 U.S.P.Q.2D (BNA) 1469 (E.D. Va. 2004).**
  In this case, plaintiff claimed that Amazon violated their patent for a "one click" ordering system. The court granted the defendant's motion for summary judgment because plaintiff improperly claimed that Amazon's "one click" system violated both the system and method for using the system.
- ***Joseph v. Amazon.com, Inc.*, 46 F. Supp. 3d 1095, 2014 U.S. Dist. LEXIS 121050, 42 Media L. Rep. 2496 (W.D. Wash. 2014).**
  Plaintiff-publishing company could not bring anti-trust claim as the statute of limitations had passed on the alleged "tying" committed by Amazon.
- ***Lasoff v. Amazon.com, Inc.*, 2016 U.S. Dist. LEXIS 9878, 2016 WL 355076 (D.N.J. Jan. 28, 2016).**
  In this case, plaintiff Amazon seller was suing Amazon.com, in New jersey, for trademark infringement, anti-trust violations, and unfair business

practices because Amazon allowed other sellers to sell similar products to those of plaintiff. All sellers using the Amazon platform are subject to Amazon's terms of use, which contains a forum selection clause requiring litigation in a Washington court. The court ordered a venue transfer to Washington because it found that there were no public or local interests weighing strongly against the transfer.

Attempted Monopolization

Monopolization results when a seller becomes the only available resource in the market, and is therefore able to drive prices up because of the markets dependency on that seller. Amazon is a very powerful buyer in multiple markets and exerts a countervailing power that strongly influences both supply and demand chains. Amazon is sometimes engaged in predatory pricing as evidence suggests that Amazon sells popular products below their cost in order to raise their sales. However, it is likely that Amazon is taking actual loss rather than engaging in predatory pricing, and loss is pro-competition.

In *Bookhouse of Stuyvesant Plaza Inc. v. Amazon.com Inc.*[1], Bookhouse asserted claims against Amazon because e-books produced by certain publishers could not be read on the Kindle software if the e-books were not purchased from Amazon. Amazon filed a motion to dismiss and it was granted as the plaintiff failed to state a plausible claim to relief and was unable to prove the alleged claims. Bookhouse did not succeed in their suit as they were not able to satisfy the elements of monopolization.

---

1. *Bookhouse of Stuyvesant Plaza, Inc. v. Amazon.com, Inc.*, 985 F. Supp. 2d 612, 2013 U.S. Dist. LEXIS 171871, 2013-2 Trade Cas. (CCH) P78,608, 2013 WL 6311202 (S.D.N.Y. 2013).

- ***Bookhouse of Stuyvesant Plaza, Inc. v. Amazon.com, Inc.*, 985 F. Supp. 2d 612, 2013 U.S. Dist. LEXIS 171871, 2013-2 Trade Cas. (CCH) P78,608, 2013 WL 6311202 (S.D.N.Y. 2013).**

  This case involved an anti-trust claim against Amazon. Book publishers have brought suit because per Amazon's e-book platform, if a consumer owns a Kindle and wants to read an e-book on the Kindle that was published by any of the publishers in this action, they must buy the book from Amazon. The court granted the Defendants' Motion to Dismiss, as they determined that the plaintiff's complaint failed to state a plausible claim.

Attorney Client Privilege

According to the Bouvier Law Dictionary, "A client's privilege to bar introduction or evidence given to the client's attorney. The attorney-client privilege bars introduction or evidence provided by a client to an attorney in the attorney's performance of legal services for the client. Services eligible for the privilege include counseling, preparation, or the representation (or preparation for the representation) of the client in litigation, administrative matters, negotiations with other parties, or related matters. In some states, the privilege extends also to the attorney's communications with the client, although in other states such communications are only privileged when they reflect the client's own statements or information. The privilege is the client's, who may waive it, though it is of no application in a dispute between the client and the attorney. The privilege extends to communications with the attorney's agents, including paralegals and secretaries, but applies only to information provided to the attorney or the attorney's agents that is related to the representation of the client. The privilege is qualified, and an attorney is not barred by the privilege from disclosing information required: (a) to avert reasonably certain death or injury to the client, to the lawyer, or other others; (b) to prevent, mitigate, or rectify a serious crime or fraud by the client; (c) to secure advice about the extent of the privilege; (d) to defend the attorney from charges or claims arising from the representation; or (e) to comply with a court order. The privilege is to be narrowly construed, and doubts as to its applicability are to be resolved in favor of disclosure." Bouvier Law Dictionary Attorney - Client Privilege.

In *Soverain Software LLC v. The Gap, Inc.*[1], a business alleged there was a transfer of attorney client privilege when the business was taken over. Amazon argues that plaintiff cannot assert attorney- client privilege as Soverain is not the corporate successor of the companies. The court in this case was not convinced that the transfer of the Transact business amounted to just a transfer of assets and focused on whether the attorney- client privilege transfers when a business is taken over. Soverain not only acquired certain asserts but also has continues to operate the business.

---

1. *Soverain Software LLC v. Gap, Inc.*, 340 F. Supp. 2d 760 (E.D. Tex. 2004).

- ***Soverain Software LLC v. Gap, Inc.*, 340 F. Supp. 2d 760 (E.D. Tex. 2004).**
  In this case, the dispute arose over whether Soverain could claim attorney-client privilege with regard to documents that contained communications between Open Market, Inc. and Divine, Inc., who were the former owners of the patents asserted in the case. The Court here finds that Soverain is a successor to the "Transact" software business at issue here and the attorney-client privilege that attended that business – therefore, Soverain may assert the privilege as to communication between Open Market, Divine and their respective attorneys. Amazon's motion was denied.

Attorney's Fees

Occasionally, one party may against the other party in order to recover their attorney's fees. This typically occurs when the other party has filed motion or acted in bad faith or when they have wasted the court's time. The court usually awards attorney's fees when it believes the other party has acted in a way that is inappropriate and as a result, harmful to the case presented and or the court. Dismissal of plaintiff's action may cause the court to decide that defendant is entitled to recover attorneys' fees or costs as a prevailing party.

In the cases addressed in this section, we often see Amazon filing to recover attorney's fees. Amazon asserts that these plaintiffs acted in bad faith by not sufficiently stating their case in controversy and therefore should cover Amazon's attorney's fees. However, the party requesting reimbursement for attorney's fees must meet a high burden of proof or the court must impose sanctions in order for there to be an award to recover any attorney's fees.

- ***A'lor Int'l v. Tappers Fine Jewelry, Inc.*, 605 F. App'x 662 (9th Cir. 2015).** This is a copyright infringement case in which A'lor International, Ltd. appeals a summary judgment order that ruled in favor of its competitors who are producers, distributors, and retailers of jewelry. The Court vacated the attorneys' fees award because defendants were not prevailing parties with respect to the two designs that the district court dismissed without prejudice.
- ***IPXL Holdings, L.L.C. v. Amazon.com, Inc.*, 333 F. Supp. 2d 513, 2004 U.S. Dist. LEXIS 19909, 72 U.S.P.Q.2D (BNA) 1469 (E.D. Va. 2004).** Amazon could not collect Attorneys' Fees and Costs when it did not file its motion within the allotted time frame allowed by law.

- ***SmartData, S.A. v. Amazon.com, Inc.*, 2015 U.S. Dist. LEXIS 152606, 2015 WL 6955000 (N.D. Cal. Nov. 10, 2015).**
  In this case, the court denied Amazon's request for attorney's fees because they did not find the plaintiff acted in bad faith in bringing this suit.

Breach of Contract

A breach of contract occurs when one party fails to perform a promise previously bargained-for or interferes with another party's performance. A breach of contract claim must state the existence of a contract, the specifications of the parties' performance under the contract, the defendant's actions that breached the contract, and the harm that resulted from the breach to state a cause of action. The contract must be valid and fair for both parties, it cannot be one-sided, both parties have to freely enter into the agreement, and the terms have to be in the best interest of the public. If all parties agree to the contract without any coercion involved and the terms are clear and understandable, each party is bound by the terms of the agreement.

Amazon has acquired such a large share of many different markets, and thus enters into many different types of contracts. Typical issues that arise in the cases of this section include shipping contract disputes[1], membership contract disputes[2], employment contract disputes[3], and Amazon seller's contract disputes[4]. In the Amazon cases, the court usually grants summary judgment when there are no facts provided to show Amazon's conduct was unfair, deceptive, or the conduct negatively affected public interest. The only way for a claim to survive is by stating relevant facts that provide proof of breach. If there is no genuine issue of material fact, summary judgment will be granted in favor of the party that brings the motion.

---

1. *Amazon.com v. Coyote Logistics* Case No. C11-1015 RSL, United States District Court Western District of Washington at Seattle, December 11, 2013.
2. *Ekin v. Amazon Servs., LLC*, 84 F. Supp. 3d 1172 (W.D. Wash. 2014).
3. *Amazon.com, Inc. v. Powers*, No. C12-1911RAJ, 2012 U.S. Dist. LEXIS 182831 (W.D. Wash. Dec. 27, 2012).

4. *Peters v. Amazon Servs., LLC*, 2 F. Supp. 3d 1165, 2013 U.S. Dist. LEXIS 185964 (W.D. Wash. 2013).

- ***Amazon.com v. Coyote Logistics* Case No. C11-1015 RSL, United States District Court Western District of Washington at Seattle, December 11, 2013.**
  In this case, plaintiff, Amazon alleged that CP Transport was hired to transport a container of Amazon Kindles from Washington to Delaware in November 2009. Amazon alleged that the driver left the shipment unattended at a truck stop, resulting in the theft of the truck, container, and goods. The court awarded damages in favor of Amazon.
- ***Ekin v. Amazon Servs., LLC*, 84 F. Supp. 3d 1172 (W.D. Wash. 2014).**
  This case stems from the use of Amazon Prime Services by the Plaintiffs and the alleged breach of contract claims directed at Amazon Services LLC. The Plaintiffs disputed the price changes for Amazon Prime membership and claimed that Amazon unlawfully changed the terms and agreements of their Amazon Prime membership. Defendant's Motion to Compel Arbitration was granted. The court found the price dispute here to be within the scope of the arbitration agreement.
- ***Hammer v. Amazon.com*, 392 F. Supp. 2d 423, 2005 U.S. Dist. LEXIS 33398 (E.D.N.Y. 2005).**
  In this case Amazon was involved in an action where plaintiff, Jeffrey Hammer raised a number of claims including breach of contract, defamation, violation of copyright laws. Plaintiff claimed that Amazon breached their contract because they failed to remove negative reviews of his book from the Amazon platform. The court granted Amazon's motion for a permanent injunction preventing plaintiff from bringing any future action against Amazon.
- ***Huong Hoang v. Amazon.com, Inc.*, 2012 U.S. Dist. LEXIS 45498, 2012 WL 1088165 (W.D. Wash. Mar. 28, 2012).**
  Here, plaintiff paid a fee to sign up for the IMBD Pro service in order to connect with casting directors and obtain roles. Plaintiff claimed the service took her personal information and added it to her profile without

her authorization and thus harmed her career. The court granted in part and denied in part the defendant's motion to dismiss for failure to state a claim. Plaintiff's breach of contract claim survived the motion to dismiss because there was a valid contract, there may have been a breach of duty and plaintiff has proven that she suffered damage. Plaintiff's fraud claim fails because there is no specific evidence provided to support it.

- ***In re Zappos.com, Inc.*, 2013 U.S. Dist. LEXIS 128155, 2013 WL 4830497 (D. Nev. Sept. 9, 2013).**
  Amazon.com and Zappos.com are defendant's in a suit brought by Zappos customers following a security breach on the Zappos website. This document is a motion to dismiss by Amazon.com and Zappos. The court granted in part and denied in part the motions. The court found that the Plaintiffs had "sufficiently alleged that they have had to pay money to monitor their credit scores and secure their financial information due to the increased risk of criminal fraud against them which was caused by defendant's negligent loss of their personal information.
- ***Amazon.com, Inc. v. Powers*, No. C12-1911RAJ, 2012 U.S. Dist. LEXIS 182831 (W.D. Wash. Dec. 27, 2012).**
  Mr. Daniel Powers is a former Amazon Web Services employee. When Mr. Powers started working at Amazon, he signed a "Confidentiality, Noncompetition and Invention Assignment Agreement." Google, Inc., hired Mr. Powers in September 2012 to work as its Director of Global Cloud Platform Sales at its Mountain View, California headquarters. Amazon sued Mr. Powers for breach of the Agreement and violation of Washington's version of the Uniform Trade Secrets Act. The court ultimately granted an injunction that defendant may not assist in cloud computing services to any current, former, or prospective customer of Amazon about whom he learned confidential information while working at Amazon.
- ***Peters v. Amazon Servs., LLC*, 2 F. Supp. 3d 1165, 2013 U.S. Dist. LEXIS 185964 (W.D. Wash. 2013).**
  Plaintiffs are former third-party Amazon.com sellers. They sued Amazon alleging breach of contract, breach of fiduciary duty, violations of

Washington's Consumer Protection Act, and unjust enrichment. The Court found a valid agreement to arbitrate. Because the parties agreed to arbitration and Plaintiffs' claims clearly fall within the scope of that arbitration provision, the Court granted Amazon's motion to compel arbitration. The Court stayed the case for a period of 6 months or until arbitration is complete, whichever comes first, so that Plaintiffs can pursue their claims in arbitration.

- ***Singleton v. Amazon.com*, 2015 Cal. App. Unpub. LEXIS 1962 (Cal. App. 4th Dist. Mar. 20, 2015).**
  This case involved an appeal of a lower court confirming an arbitration award. The court affirmed the judgment of the lower court. Plaintiff, Stanley Singleton sued defendants, Amazon.com and Evan James, for breach of contract and fraudulent misrepresentation, over their disputes regarding the Amazon Services Business Solutions Agreement that Singleton has signed to enable him to sell merchandise on Amazon's website. The arbitrator ruled in favor of Amazon. Here, the Court of Appeals affirmed the trial court's decision finding that the arbitrator did not err in confirming the arbitrator's award.
- ***Spears v. Amazon*, 2013 U.S. Dist. LEXIS 18384, 34 I.E.R. Cas. (BNA) 1783, 27 Am. Disabilities Cas. (BNA) 1430 (E.D. Ky. Feb. 12, 2013).**
  Amazon.com was a defendant in a negligent misrepresentation suit. Amazon motioned for summary judgment. Plaintiff claimed that Amazon "fraudulently induced him to accept a position of employment in the company, or in the least negligently misrepresented the nature of compensation of the employment; that Amazon inappropriately terminated him on the basis of his disability in retaliation for a worker's compensation claim, and in transgression of public policy." The United States District Court denied Amazon's motion for summary judgment for the fraud claims in the inducement, negligent misrepresentation, and workers' compensation. The court granted Amazon's motion for summary judgment for the claims of wrongful discharge on the basis of disability and in violation of public policy. The court found that Spears had created a genuine issue of material fact as to

whether or not Amazon made the offer to Spears in reckless disregard of its falsity.

- ***Toysrus.com, LLC v. Amazon.Com Kids,* No. A-0292-04T5, 2005 N.J. Super. Unpub. LEXIS 811 (Super. Ct. App. Div. Apr. 12, 2005).**
The court here, on appeal was deciding whether to reverse the trial court's order granting a preliminary injunction against defendants from using new "one to one" technology because defendants breached their contract with plaintiff. The court reversed the preliminary injunction because it found the trial court did not properly consider the contractual language or provide sufficient support for its findings.

Claim Construction

Claim construction is an issue that arises in patent infringement cases and is used to determine what the claim covers, the scope of the claim, and to interpret the meaning and intention of the authors of the patent. The court may define terms for parties that cannot agree on a definition or where the text is silent. Claim construction is determined by how a reasonable competitor would interpret the actual language of the claim, not how the inventor would see it. The language must be looked at in its entirety. Claim construction is an issue of law for the court to decide.

In the Amazon cases, courts have granted summary judgment in favor of the party that proves there is no patent claim. The courts in the Amazon cases have not adopted a party's claim construction if the definitions are too vague or are not the generally accepted definitions of ordinary people. The court has the final say on disputed terms and may accept or deny a proposed claim construction.

- ***Alcatel-Lucent USA, Inc. v. Amazon.com, Inc.*, 2011 U.S. Dist. LEXIS 61039, 2011 WL 2260276 (E.D. Tex. June 7, 2011).**
  The court here defined the disputed terms in the five patents that are in controversy.
- ***Discovery Patent Holdings, LLC v. Amazon.com, Inc.*, 769 F. Supp. 2d 662 (D. Del. 2011).**
  The court here was determining what construction of the parties disputed terms in the patent claim should be adopted by the court.
- ***KKG, LLC v. Rank Group, PLC*, 2013 U.S. Dist. LEXIS 54279 (E.D. Tex. Apr. 16, 2013).**
  The court here was defining the meaning of 6 terms in dispute by the parties.

- ***M-Edge Accessories LLC v. Amazon, Inc.*, 2013 U.S. Dist. LEXIS 165422 (D. Md. Nov. 21, 2013).**
  In this case the court determined the meaning of the patents in suit.
- ***Mobile Telcoms. Techs., LLC v. Amazon.com, Inc.*, 2014 U.S. Dist. LEXIS 156454 (E.D. Tex. Nov. 5, 2014)**
  While Amazon.com was a named defendant, this document deals specifically with the claim construction order of the disputed claims within the patents.
- ***Research Frontiers, Inc. v. E Ink Corp.*, 2016 U.S. Dist. LEXIS 38441 (D. Del. Mar. 24, 2016).**
  Here, the court was determining what definitions to apply to disputed terms of the patent at issue.
- ***SFA Sys., LLC v. Amazon.com, Inc.*, 2013 U.S. Dist. LEXIS 189807 (E.D. Tex. Apr. 11, 2013).**
  Amazon.com was a defendant in a case dealing with patent infringement. Amazon.com motioned for partial summary judgment. The court found that defendants failed to show by clear and convincing evidence that these claims are insoluble due to an impermissible mix of apparatus limitations and method steps. Ultimately, the court denied the motion for partial summary judgment.
- ***Sipco, LLC v. Amazon.com, Inc.*, 2012 U.S. Dist. LEXIS 150940 (E.D. Tex. Oct. 19, 2012).**
  While Amazon.com is a named defendant in this patent infringement case, the document at hand deals specifically with the construction of disputed terms.
- ***United Video Props. v. Amazon.com, Inc.*, 2012 U.S. Dist. LEXIS 86914 (D. Del. June 22, 2012).**
  The court determined the claim construction of the patents that were allegedly infringed.

Class Action Lawsuits

A class action is a lawsuit in which the court allows a single person or small group of people to represent the interests of a larger group. A class action lawsuit requires settlement through litigation for the convenience of the public or interested parties that may not have an opportunity to protect their interests by appearing personally. A class action must be so large that an individual suit would be impracticable, there must be legal or factual questions common to the class, the claims or defenses of the parties must relate to the class, and the representative of the class must protect the interests of the class to the best of their ability.

In the Amazon cases, courts have granted Amazon's motions to dismiss where the claims against them were invalid because of agreements signed by both parties binding them to the terms and conditions stated. Arbitration clauses were enforced where the court decided the terms of agreement were binding and where there was a class action waiver.[1] Some courts have found class action waivers unconscionable and unenforceable when a party's right to litigation is jeopardized by the unfair terms.[2] A court may decide a class action is the best method for resolving a controversy and will let the suit proceed with litigation.

---

1. *Fagerstrom v. Amazon.com, Inc.*, 141 F. Supp. 3d 1051, 2015 U.S. Dist. LEXIS 143295 (S.D. Cal. 2015).
2. *Scott v. Cingular Wireless*, 161 P.3d 1000, 160 Wn.2d 843 (Wash., 2007).

- ***Amazon.Com, Inc. v. Underwriters, Lloyd's of London, et al, Defendants.*** In this class action, plaintiff's alleged that Amazon's officers and directors made fraudulent statements to inflate the value of certain Amazon securities. A second class action was filed alleging that Amazon sold certain securities to plaintiffs at an inflated price. Here, the court was determining whether to grant defendants motions to dismiss for lack of personal jurisdiction and for failing to properly serve defendants.

The court denied both motions and held that personal jurisdiction was proper because defendants purposefully availed themselves to the state of Washington. Service was proper because it complied with the Washington statute and defendants had admitted that they did in fact receive service.

- ***Blagman v. Apple, Inc.*, 2014 U.S. Dist. LEXIS 45401, 2014 WL 1285496 (S.D.N.Y. Mar. 31, 2014).**
  Blagman had filed a motion to depose third parties from the U.K. and France. Amazon contended that the court had already ruled that extraterritorial evidence was not admissible in this case. The court disagreed and granted the motion to depose the third parties located internationally.
- ***Blagman v. Apple, Inc.*, 307 F.R.D. 107, 2015 U.S. Dist. LEXIS 51676, Copy. L. Rep. (CCH) P30,754 (S.D.N.Y. 2015).**
  Mr. Blagman filed to amend his complaint for a third time to limit the scope of his class. Amazon contended that he was doing so in bad faith by using it as a tactical advantage and making false allegations. The court allowed for the third amended complaint as it found that it was not requested in bad faith.
- ***BookLocker.com, Inc. v. Amazon.com, Inc.*, 650 F. Supp. 2d 89, 2009 U.S. Dist. LEXIS 76352, 2009-2 Trade Cas. (CCH) P76,729 (D. Me. 2009).**
  In this case plaintiffs brought suit against Amazon, claiming anti-trust violations under the Sherman Act. Plaintiffs claimed a violation existed because if a consumer who owns a Kindle e-reader wished to purchase an e-book produced by one of the plaintiff publishers, then that consumer needed to purchase the e-book on the Amazon platform. The court denied Amazon's motion to dismiss because it found that plaintiff had made a plausible claim for relief.
- ***Del Vecchio v. Amazon.com Inc.*, 2011 U.S. Dist. LEXIS 138314, 2011 WL 6325910 (W.D. Wash. Nov. 30, 2011).**
  Amazon.com was a defendant in a case filed by Del Vecchio. Del Vecchio represented a class action against Amazon seeking relief under the

Computer Fraud and Abuse Act. Amazon motioned to dismiss and the court concluded that the defendant's motion to dismiss should be granted because the plaintiffs failed to plead adequate facts to establish any harm.

- ***Fagerstrom v. Amazon.com, Inc.*, 141 F. Supp. 3d 1051, 2015 U.S. Dist. LEXIS 143295 (S.D. Cal. 2015).**

  In this case, consumers claimed there was a discrepancy between Amazon's prices and other retailer prices of products. When checking out on Amazon, each customer must agree to the conditions of use in order to complete their order. Amazon's conditions of use states any dispute will be resolved through binding arbitration. The court granted Amazon's motion to compel arbitration and dismissed this action because it found the terms of the agreement to be fair and beneficial to both parties.
- ***Nicosia v. Amazon.com, Inc.*, 84 F. Supp. 3d 142, 2015 U.S. Dist. LEXIS 13560 (E.D.N.Y. 2015)**

  Amazon.com was a defendant in a case brought by Dean Nicosia for the selling of a controlled substance in a weight loss supplement. Amazon.com motioned to dismiss claiming that the issue should be settled in arbitration due the arbitration clause. The court agreed and granted Amazon's motion.
- ***Scott v. Cingular Wireless*, 161 P.3d 1000, 160 Wn.2d 843 (Wash., 2007).**

  The court here was determining whether the class action waiver signed by plaintiffs was unconscionable because it undermined Washington's CPA to the extent that it was "injurious to the public." The court held that the class action waiver was unconscionable because it effectively denied many consumers protection under Washington's Consumer Protection Act (CPA) and because it effectively exculpated Cingular from liability for a whole class of wrongful conduct. It was therefore unenforceable.
- ***Supnick v. Amazon.com, Inc.*, 2000 U.S. Dist. LEXIS 7073, 2000 WL 1603820 (W.D. Wash. May 18, 2000).**

  Amazon.com was a defendant in a privacy violation suit brought by Supnick. Plaintiffs motioned for a federal class certification. The court concluded that because the class was maintainable under Rule 23, and that the class action was the best method for litigating the dispute, the plaintiff's motion was granted.

Consumer Protection Law

Consumer protection law is a state or federal statute designed to protect consumers against unfair trade practices involving consumer goods in addition to protecting consumers against damaged and dangerous goods. The laws are created to guarantee fair trade, competition, and accuracy throughout the consumer market. These laws are designed to prevent businesses from taking advantage of consumers with unfair practices or having an unfair competitive edge towards other businesses in the same market.

In the Amazon cases we have reviewed, courts have typically allowed claims to proceed when a party has plead an unfair or deceptive practice in trade or commerce that affects the interests of the public and there is a causal relationship between the deception and the harm suffered by the moving party. Motions to dismiss are denied when a party sufficiently states a claim with relevant facts proving the possibility of a consumer protection violation.

- ***Ranazzi v. Amazon.com, Inc.*, 2015-Ohio-4411, 46 N.E.3d 213, 2015 Ohio App. LEXIS 4277 (Ohio Ct. App., Lucas County 2015).**
  In this case the court stayed proceedings until the outcome of Arbitration which was an enforceable forum for the dispute under the agreement between Plaintiff and Amazon for use of its website.
- ***Dean Nicosia v. Amazon.com* Case No. 14-cv-4513 (SLT) (MDG). United States District Court, E.D. New York, February 2015.**
  In this case the court dismissed claims against Amazon and directed plaintiff to resolve its claim through arbitration as plaintiff agreed to before making a purchase on Amazon's website.
- ***Del Vecchio v. Amazon.com Inc.*, 2011 U.S. Dist. LEXIS 138314, 2011 WL 6325910 (W.D. Wash. Nov. 30, 2011).**
  Amazon.com was a defendant in a case filed by Del Vecchio. Del Vecchio represented a class action against Amazon seeking relief under

the Computer Fraud and Abuse act. Amazon motioned to dismiss and the court concluded that the defendant's motion to dismiss should be granted because the plaintiffs failed to plead adequate facts to establish any harm.

- ***Ekin v. Amazon Servs., LLC*, 84 F. Supp. 3d 1172, 2014 U.S. Dist. LEXIS 181912 (W.D. Wash. 2014).**
  This case stems from the use of Amazon Prime Services by the Plaintiffs and the alleged breach of contract claims directed at Amazon Services LLC. The Plaintiffs disputed the price changes for Amazon Prime Members and claimed that Amazon unlawfully changed the terms and agreements of their Amazon Prime membership. Defendant's Motion to Compel Arbitration was granted because the court found the price dispute here to be within the scope of the arbitration agreement.
- ***FTC v. Amazon.com, Inc.*, 2016 U.S. Dist. LEXIS 41500, 99 Fed. R. Evid. Serv. (Callaghan) 1443, 2016 WL 1221654 (W.D. Wash. Mar. 29, 2016).**
  In this case the FTC alleged that Amazon was involved in unfair business practices relating to in-app purchases. The FTC was seeking to exclude testimony of Amazon's expert witnesses. The court found that the testimonies of certain witnesses would be helpful in providing relevant evidence to the case, and that others would not. Thus the motion to exclude the testimonies was granted in part and denied in part.
- ***FTC v. Amazon.com, Inc.*, 2016 U.S. Dist. LEXIS 55569, 2016-1 Trade Reg. Rep. (CCH) P79,600 (W.D. Wash. Apr. 26, 2016).**
  This case claimed Amazon used unfair business practices because its software allowed "in-app purchases" that many consumers were not familiar with and thus many adults were not aware of charges incurred by their children. The court found that Amazon was liable for damages to the consumers for unfair practices, but that a permanent injunction was not warranted because there was no clear danger of Amazon making the same violation again.

- ***Gerlinger v. Amazon.com*, Inc., 2005 U.S. Dist. LEXIS 26019, 2005-2 Trade Cas. (CCH) P75,004, 34 Media L. Rep. 1509 (N.D. Cal. Oct. 31, 2005).**
  This case involved plaintiff's claims that defendants violated antitrust laws through their store agreement with Amazon, as well as the defendants' motion to dismiss. The court granted the motion to dismiss the antitrust claims and the unfair competition claim because it found that the plaintiff provided no actual evidence of the alleged injuries.
- ***Gerlinger v. Amazon.com, Inc.*, 526 F.3d 1253, 2008 U.S. App. LEXIS 11237, 2008-1 Trade Cas. (CCH) P76,161 (9th Cir. Cal. 2008).**
  This case involved the appellant challenging a judgment in a lower court that dismissed his antitrust claim against the defendants. The court affirmed the judgment of the district court because it agreed with the district court that plaintiff provided no evidence of the alleged injuries.
- ***Hart v. Amazon.com, Inc.*, 2015 U.S. Dist. LEXIS 164627, 117 U.S.P.Q.2D (BNA) 1584, 44 Media L. Rep. 1250 (N.D. Ill. Dec. 8, 2015).**
  In this case, plaintiff authored three books and chose not to publish them to the public. Plaintiff discovered one of the books was for sale on Amazon. Plaintiff sent a letter to Amazon asking for the books to be removed from the website. The court found that plaintiff did not prove Amazon's posting of titles directly copies any of their work and dismissed the claim. The plaintiff failed to make a claim that third-party sellers were liable for copyright infringement. The plaintiff failed to provide facts to support any of their claims.
- ***Peters v. Amazon Servs., LLC*, 2 F. Supp. 3d 1165, 2013 U.S. Dist. LEXIS 185964 (W.D. Wash. 2013).**
  Plaintiffs are former third-party Amazon.com sellers. They sued Amazon alleging breach of contract, breach of fiduciary duty, violations of Washington's Consumer Protection Act, and unjust enrichment. The Court found a valid agreement to arbitrate. Because the parties agreed to arbitration and Plaintiffs' claims clearly fall within the scope of that arbitration provision, the Court granted Amazon's motion to compel arbitration. The Court stayed the case for a period of 6 months or until

arbitration was complete, whichever comes first, so that Plaintiffs could pursue their claims in arbitration.

- ***Routt v. Amazon.com, Inc.*, 2012 U.S. Dist. LEXIS 170602, 105 U.S.P.Q.2D (BNA) 1089, Copy. L. Rep. (CCH) P30,334 (W.D. Wash. Nov. 30, 2012).**

  In this case, plaintiff claimed that Amazon violated her copyrights in certain photographs because certain Amazon Associate websites displayed her photographs without her permission. The court found Amazon was not responsible for the alleged violation committed by a third-party, and could not be vicariously liable as it had no control over the third-party's activities.

- ***Vecchio v. Amazon.com, Inc.* No. C11-366RSL, 2012 U.S. Dist. LEXIS 76536 (W.D. Wash. June 1, 2012).**

  The court here was determining whether the plaintiffs had alleged sufficient facts to plead a plausible claim for relief such that the court should not grant defendants motion to dismiss. The court granted the motion in part and found that as to the CFAA and trespass to chattels claims that because plaintiffs had already had 2 opportunities to amend their complaint that plaintiffs clearly lacked the requisite facts to plead a sufficient claim. As to the CPA and unjust enrichment claims the court granted plaintiffs' request for a "reasonable opportunity to present all the material that is pertinent to the motion." Fed. R. Civ. P. 12(d).

Copyright Infringement

Copyright infringement is violating an owner's exclusive rights to a work of art, granted by the federal Copyright Act, by the use of protected works without permission. The use of copyrighted works is unauthorized unless consent is given by the owner. A copyright owner has the right to reproduce the work, prepare imitations of their copyrighted work, distribute their work, and perform or display the work publicly. To demonstrate a valid copyright infringement, claim a plaintiff must show ownership of a copyright, and show the defendant has copied elements of the work that are original.

In the Amazon cases, courts have denied motions to dismiss when facts are clearly stated to prove the defendant is actually aware they are infringing on copyright laws or there is proof of complete disregard for whether they are infringing on copyrights or not. On the other hand, claims have been dismissed where insufficient facts have been pleaded to establish that the plaintiff possessed a valid copyright or that the defendants reproduced copyrighted work. A reasonable juror must be able to infer from the facts stated that the defendants may have violated copyright laws. In the *Milo & Gabby v. Amazon* case, the court made a seminal decision and held that Amazon could not be held liable for Amazon seller's listings that infringed on others copyrights because Amazon was not themselves "offering for sale" the infringing products.[1]

---

1. *Milo & Gabby LLC v. Amazon.com*. Case No. C13-1932 RSM. United States District Court Western District of Washington at Seattle, November 2015.

- ***Almeida v. Amazon.com, Inc., 456 F.3d 1316 (11th Cir. 2006).***
  This case is an appeal to the district court decision that granted summary judgment in favor of defendant Amazon. Plaintiff claimed that

Amazon's use of her image in furtherance of sale of a book on its website violated her right of publicity and she claimed invasion of privacy and theft as well. The court here affirmed the district court's decision because plaintiffs right of publicity claim based on Fla. Stat. § 540.08 would not withstand a motion to dismiss, it was unnecessary for the district court to determine whether the CDA preempts Almeida's state law right of publicity claim. As to the theft claim the court here held that plaintiff failed to present any evidence that Amazon misappropriated her image with actual knowledge that its used was unauthorized.

- ***A'lor Int'l v. Tappers Fine Jewelry, Inc.*, 605 Fed. Appx. 662, 2015 U.S. App. LEXIS 8548 (9th Cir. Cal. 2015).**

  This was a copyright infringement case in which A'lor International, Ltd. appealed a summary judgment order that ruled in favor of its competitors who are producers, distributors, and retailers of jewelry. The Court chose to uphold the district court's application of thin copyright protection because it agreed that plaintiff's designs contained a small number of elements and thus weighed against broad protection because there are few combinations that these elements could yield.

- ***Blagman v. Apple Inc.*, 2013 U.S. Dist. LEXIS 71280, 107 U.S.P.Q.2D (BNA) 1699, Copy. L. Rep. (CCH) P30,433, 2013 WL 2181709 (S.D.N.Y. May 20, 2013).**

  Here, plaintiff filed a class action claim stating the defendants failed to ensure the music consumers download on their sites is licensed before distribution. Defendants filed a motion to dismiss the class action complaint, the plaintiff's individual claim, and motion to strike class allegations. Defendant's motion to dismiss the plaintiff's individual claim is denied because the plaintiff states a valid claim of infringement. The class allegations properly state a claim on behalf of the proposed class. The court found that dismissing the claim in the complaint stage would not be proper without hearing all the evidence that would come up in discovery.

- ***Brickey v. Amazon.com, Inc.*, 2014 U.S. Dist. LEXIS 97479, 2014 WL 3566566 (W.D. Tex. July 18, 2014).**
  The court here was determining whether actionable copying occurred here in the form of unauthorized sales of plaintiff's CD, such that defendants motion for summary judgment would be proper. The court found that no actionable copying took place because under the "first sale doctrine," Amazon was the rightful owner of the CD and thus had the right to sell it. The court also found that plaintiff did not allege any facts to show sales that would not be subject to the "first sale doctrine." Defendants motion for summary judgment was granted.
- **Brickey v. Amazon.com, Inc., 2014 U.S. Dist. LEXIS 9297, 2014 WL 297979 (W.D. Tex. Jan. 27, 2014).**
  The court was determining whether to grant defendants motion to dismiss for failure to state a claim, where plaintiff was seeking punitive damages under the Copyright Act. The court found that both the Copyright Act and the case law that interprets it do not indicate that congress intended to authorize punitive damages and thus the claim was not "plausible on its face." The court therefore granted the motion to dismiss.
- ***Brickey v. Amazon.com*, Inc., 2014 U.S. Dist. LEXIS 22304 (W.D. Tex. Feb. 21, 2014).**
  Here, the court was determining whether plaintiff provided sufficient evidence of copyright infringement to establish that no genuine issue of material fact exists and that he was entitled to judgment as a matter of law. The court finds that there was an issue of material fact as to whether any copyright infringement actually occurred here. The court thus denied the motion for summary judgment.
- ***Carlin v. Bezos*, 2016 U.S. App. LEXIS 9372 (3d Cir. Pa. May 23, 2016).**
  In this case the court affirmed the lower court's grant of defendant's motion for summary judgment as plaintiff failed to provide evidence sufficient to state a claim for copyright infringement.

- ***Chambers v. Amazon.com Inc.*, 632 F. App'x 742 (4th Cir. 2015).**
  The court here was determining whether the court below erred in adopting the Magistrate's recommendation that this case be summarily dismissed because plaintiff did not state any facts in which it could be reasonably inferred that DMCA or Copyright Act violations were present. Here, the court found that the decision adopting the magistrate's recommendation was proper. Plaintiff failed to allege sufficient facts to support either a Copyright or DMCA claim against defendants. Thus, the court affirmed the court below issuing an order for summary judgment.
- ***Chambers v. Amazon.com Inc.*, Civil Action No. 3:14-cv-4890-MGL, 2015 U.S. Dist. LEXIS 85367 (D.S.C. July 1, 2015).**
  The court here is determining whether it should adopt the decision of the Magistrate judge below and summarily dismiss this case. The court, agreed with the Magistrate, and found that plaintiff's arguments failed to cast any doubt on the findings of the Magistrate. Plaintiff's evidence only provided evidence for plaintiff's alleged damages. The court thus entered an order to summarily dismiss this case.
- ***Chambers v. Amazon.com Inc.*, No. 3:14-4890-MGL-PJG, 2015 U.S. Dist. LEXIS 85596 (D.S.C. Feb. 5, 2015).**
  The court here was determining whether to summarily dismiss this case. The court found that although the it must liberally construe a pro se complaint, the plaintiff's allegations were found to be speculative and conclusory. Therefore, the claims were insufficient to show a violation of the Copyright Act or the Digital Millennium Copyright Act and the court recommended summarily dismissing the claims.
- ***Clark v. Amazon.com*, 2006 U.S. Dist. LEXIS 69278 (E.D. Cal. Sep. 25, 2006).**
  The court here was determining whether to recommend granting the plaintiff's motion for injunctive relief that would stop defendant from selling plaintiff's copyrighted book on its site. The court recommended denying injunctive relief. The court found that plaintiff had not demonstrated irreparable injury and that plaintiff delayed too long in

seeking injunctive relief. Thus the Magistrate recommended that the motion be denied.

- ***Clark v. Amazon.com,* No. 2:05-cv-2187-GEB-DAD-PS, 2006 U.S. Dist. LEXIS 78151 (E.D. Cal. Oct. 26, 2006).**
  Here the court was deciding whether to adopt the magistrate judge's recommendation to deny plaintiff's application for a temporary restraining order. The court denied the application because it found the recommendation to be supported by the facts as well as the magistrate's analysis.
- ***Clark v. Amazon.com,* No. 2:05-cv-2187-GEB-DAD-PS, 2007 U.S. Dist. LEXIS 28896 (E.D. Cal. Apr. 19, 2007).**
  Here, Plaintiff's claim was recommended to a magistrate judge who issued a recommendation to deny plaintiffs motion to dismiss. The magistrate recommendation contained notice that any objections to the recommendation be filed within 10 days. Here, plaintiff had filed objections to the recommendation. The court was thus determining whether to adopt the recommendation of the magistrate. The court held that the recommendation was supported by the record and the magistrate's analysis. The court ordered full adoption of the recommendation and a denial of the plaintiff's motion to dismiss.
- ***Clark v. Amazon.com,* No. CIV S-05-2187 GEB DAD PS, 2007 U.S. Dist. LEXIS 19679 (E.D. Cal. Mar. 20, 2007).**
  The court as determining whether to recommend granting plaintiff's motion to dismiss. The court found that because defendants had a pending motion for summary judgment and subsequently plaintiff's filed a counter motion for summary judgment, that plaintiff's motion for dismissal be denied. The court recommended that plaintiffs' notice, that was construed as a motion to dismiss, be denied.
- ***Clark v. Amazon.com,* No. CIV S-05-2187 GEB DAD PS, 2007 U.S. Dist. LEXIS 34314 (E.D. Cal. May 10, 2007).**
  The court here was determining whether the magistrate should recommend summary judgment where both parties have filed cross motions for summary judgment. The court recommended denial of the plaintiffs'

motion because they failed to allege that defendants had knowledge of any copyright infringement. The court recommended granting the defendants motion because the "first sale doctrine" applied and defendants had the legal right to sell the copyrighted material.

- ***Corbis Corp. v. Amazon.com, Inc.*, 351 F. Supp. 2d 1090, 2004 U.S. Dist. LEXIS 27155, 77 U.S.P.Q.2D (BNA) 1182 (W.D. Wash. 2004).**
  In this case plaintiff claimed to have copyright interests in two photographs that Amazon placed on it's website IMDb.com as well as hundreds of photographs that were being sold by vendors on Amazon.com without Plaintiff's permission. Amazon is protected from liability under the DMCA for copyright infringement occurring on its third party vendor platform because Amazon qualifies as an Internet Service Provider protected under DCMA, does not have an affirmative duty to police possible infringement, but must also take reasonable steps if is alerted to infringement.
- ***Crowley v. Cybersource Corp.*, 166 F. Supp. 2d 1263, 2001 U.S. Dist. LEXIS 17020 (N.D. Cal. 2001).**
  In this case, Amazon filed a motion to dismiss by challenging the claims and also filed a motion for improper venue on the basis of a forum selection clause. The court determined that the forum selection clause only applied to the agreement and not to the privacy claims that were brought up in this case and therefore denied the motion. However, the court granted Amazon's motion to dismiss because Crowley failed to state a claim under the Wiretap Act and the ECPA.
- ***Ricchio v. Amazon.com, Inc.*, 2012 U.S. Dist. LEXIS 147193, 40 Media L. Rep. 2481, 2012 WL 4865016 (E.D. Wis. Oct. 12, 2012).**
  In this case plaintiff was accusing Amazon of copyright infringement. Plaintiff authorized 365 copies of his book for sale on the Amazon platform, but subsequently found out that Amazon had eventually allowed third party sellers to sell his book on the platform as well. Plaintiff did not receive compensation for any of the third party sales. The court found that plaintiff failed to state a claim for copyright infringement.

Plaintiff alleged only that defendant was allowing third party sales of the book without authorization, but plaintiff did not claim that any of the books being sold on the Amazon platform were counterfeit.

- ***Felix The Cat Prods. v. Cal. Clock Co.,* 2007 U.S. Dist. LEXIS 25290, 2007 WL 1032267 (S.D.N.Y. Mar. 29, 2007).**

  This is a case alleging trademark and copyright infringement that the defendants motioned to dismiss for failing to state a claim of relief. Defendants are both manufacturers and sellers of Felix the Cat "Kit Kat Clock" products. The court granted the defendant's motion to dismiss based on failure to plead copyright infringement and denied all other claims. The plaintiff did not state specific facts about what acts and time the alleged infringement occurred. There has to be factual allegations to give the opposing party fair notice of the claims against them. The court denied defendants motion to dismiss claims against the probability of confusing the two products because the plaintiff may have been able to provide facts to support this claim for relief.

- ***Gibson v. Amazon.com,* 2011 U.S. Dist. LEXIS 102065, 2011 WL 4020187 (C.D. Cal. Sept. 8, 2011).**

  This is a case involving defendants' motion for summary judgment and plaintiffs' motion for summary judgment, involving the sale of plaintiff's book on the Amazon platform. The court granted defendants' motion and plaintiffs' motion as denied because there was no support for a claim of copyright infringement. Amazon had neither published nor sold the book in question, their only involvement is through third party sellers which was legal.

- ***Gusler v. Fischer,* 580 F. Supp. 2d 309, 2008 U.S. Dist. LEXIS 75454 (S.D.N.Y. 2008).**

  Amazon.com as one of the named defendants for a claim of copyright infringement. Amazon, along with other defendants, motioned for a dismissal, and in the alternative, a summary judgment. The court in finding that the product was not copyrightable, granted the summary judgment in favor of the corporate defendants.

- ***Hammer v. Amazon.com*, 392 F. Supp. 2d 423, 2005 U.S. Dist. LEXIS 33398 (E.D.N.Y. 2005).**
  Amazon is involved in an action where Jeffrey Hammer raised a number of claims including breach of contract, defamation, violation of copyright laws. The court granted Amazon's motion for a permanent injunction and denied the motion for civil contempt sanctions.
- **Hendrickson v. Amazon.com, Inc., 298 F. Supp. 2d 914, 2003 U.S. Dist. LEXIS 24498, 69 U.S.P.Q.2D (BNA) 1471 (C.D. Cal. 2003).**
  This is a copyright infringement case involving the owner to the rights of the movie "Manson" and the unauthorized sale of this movie on Amazon. The Court maintained that Amazon.com did not have control over the sale in question; therefore, summary judgment in favor of Amazon regarding the copyright infringement claim was appropriate and granted by the court.
- ***Hendrickson v. Amazon.com, Inc.*, 181 Fed. Appx. 692, 2006 U.S. App. LEXIS 12720, Copy. L. Rep. (CCH) P29,180 (9th Cir. Cal. 2006).**
  This is a case involving an appeal from a lower court decision, which granted attorney's fees to defendants. The court vacated and remanded the case to the lower court to analyze and determine whether the attorney services here contributed the the defendant's success.
- ***John Does 1-10*. Case No. 12 Civ. 5453 (ALC) (JCF). United States District Court Southern District of New York, May 19, 2014.**
  This was a copyright infringement case involving the plaintiff requesting to file an amended complaint to include a larger class of defendants who have not made sure music was properly licensed before distributing it. The court granted the motion to file a second amended complaint.
- ***Kousnsky v. Amazon.com, Inc.*, 2014 U.S. Dist. LEXIS 185880 (S.D.N.Y. May 13, 2014).**
  This case involved Amazon moving to dismiss for insufficient and untimely service of process. The court ordered the complaint to be dismissed.

- ***Kousnsky v. Amazon.Com, Inc.*, 631 Fed. Appx. 22, 2015 U.S. App. LEXIS 20380, Copy. L. Rep. (CCH) P30,849 (2d Cir. N.Y. 2015).**
Here, plaintiff alleged the defendants infringed his copyright by publishing, selling, and distributing works of art created by the plaintiff. The plaintiff had an agreement with a publisher to allow the reproduction of his images for customers and did not limit any sales. The use of the image was authorized by the copyright owner so there is no evidence to show the defendants are liable for any misconduct. The court granted the motion to dismiss the case because plaintiff did not provide evidence to survive a motion for judgment.
- ***Masck v. Sports Illustrated*, 2013 U.S. Dist. LEXIS 81677, 108 U.S.P.Q.2D (BNA) 1232, 2013 WL 2626853 (E.D. Mich. June 11, 2013).**
In this case, plaintiff took an iconic photo of Defendant Desmond Howard on November 23, 1991 at Michigan Stadium. Plaintiff found out that the image was being used by multiple defendants as well as in product listings on the Amazon platform. The court determined that the vicarious infringement claim must be dismissed for lack of factual allegation, while the contributory infringement claim survived dismissal, as Amazon was well aware of potential infringement. Plaintiff only stated that Amazon had the right and ability to supervise the content of its website Amazon.com. This did not meet the pleading requirement as there were no factual allegations from which it may determine that Amazon had the ability to supervise the infringing conduct. The product in question was not Amazon's website but the merchandise sold on its website. However, Amazon was well aware of the potential infringement because plaintiff requested the products be removed from Amazon's website.
- ***Masck v. Sports Illustrated*, 5 F. Supp. 3d 881, 2014 U.S. Dist. LEXIS 30254, 110 U.S.P.Q.2D (BNA) 1591 (E.D. Mich. 2014).**
In this case, plaintiff took an iconic photo of Defendant Desmond Howard on November 23, 1991 at Michigan Stadium. Plaintiff found out that the image was being used by multiple defendants as well as in product listings on the Amazon platform. The court here was determining

whether to grant defendants' motion for summary judgment where plaintiff had waited to register the copyright until after several violations of the copyright occurred. With respect to claims against Amazon.com the motion was denied because questions of fact remained that needed to be determined by a court of law / jury.

- ***Milo & Gabby LLC v. Amazon.com*. Case No. C13-1932RSM. United States District Court Western District of Washington At Seattle, April 2014.**
  Milo & Gabby sued Amazon.com for multiple infringement claims. Amazon.com motioned to dismiss claiming that the plaintiffs failed to state a claim. The District Court agreed with Amazon and granted the motion to dismiss the III, V, VII claims.
- ***Milo & Gabby, LLC v. Amazon.com, Inc.*, 2015 U.S. Dist. LEXIS 143252 (W.D. Wash. Oct. 21, 2015).**
  Milo & Gabby sued Amazon.com for multiple infringement claims. The defendant, Amazon.com motioned in Limine. The court granted in part and denied in part.
- ***Milo & Gabby, LLC v. Amazon.com*, 2015 U.S. Dist. LEXIS 149939 (W.D. Wash. Nov. 3, 2015).**
  Milo & Gabby sued Amazon.com for multiple infringement claims. Amazon.com motioned to dismiss claiming that the plaintiffs failed to state a claim. After a jury hearing, the court adopted the jury's finding that Amazon.com was not liable for "offering to sell" the alleged infringing products at issue in this matter. A judgment was placed in favor of Amazon.com and all claims against Amazon.com were dismissed. Amazon is immune from liability for infringement by third-party sellers under the DMCA.
- ***Okocha v. Amazon.com*, 153 Fed. Appx. 849, 2005 U.S. App. LEXIS 23788 (3d Cir. N.J. 2005).**
  Plaintiff, Okocha, was an author who appealed the order of the lower court that granted summary judgment in favor of Amazon.com in suit for copyright infringement, conspiracy, fraud, negligent/intentional infliction of emotional harm, and loss of future wages claims. The court of

appeals affirmed the district court's order and denied the plaintiff's motion to expedite. Additionally, the court granted the plaintiff's motion to file supplementary proof and a supplemental appendix. The court of appeals found that the author failed to show he owned a valid copyright of his book. Additionally, the plaintiff failed to show the bookseller copied the material. The court additionally found that the author failed to provide admissible evidence to show that Amazon and third party sellers had conspired to violate his copyrights.

- ***Perfect 10, Inc. v. Amazon.com, Inc.*, 508 F.3d 1146, 2007 U.S. App. LEXIS 27843 (9th Cir. Cal. 2007).**
  Amazon.com is a defendant in a copyright infringement case brought by Perfect 10. The district court preliminarily enjoined defendant, Google from creating and publicly displaying thumbnail versions of plaintiff copyright holder's images, but did not enjoin the search engine operator from linking to third-party websites that displayed infringing full-size versions of the images. Both Perfect 10 and Google appealed. The court of appeals reversed the district court's ruling and vacated the preliminary injunction regarding Google's use of the thumbnail images. Additionally, the court reversed the district court's rejection of the claims that Google and Amazon were secondarily liable. All other rulings were affirmed.
- ***Perfect 10, Inc. v. Amazon.com, Inc.*, 487 F.3d 701, 2007 U.S. App. LEXIS 11420, 99 U.S.P.Q.2D (BNA) 1746, Copy. L. Rep. (CCH) P29,380 (9th Cir. Cal. 2007).**
  Amazon did not directly infringe, nor was it vicariously liable for infringement of third parties when it did not have control over third parties' activities. Amazon's motion for summary judgment as to indirect liability was denied, though, as there was a question of fact for the jury as to whether Amazon could have taken steps to alleviate infringement, and whether it would have been immune under DMCA.
- ***Ricchio v. Amazon.Com, Inc.*, 2012 U.S. Dist. LEXIS 52088 (E.D. Wis. Apr. 13, 2012).**
  The court was determining whether plaintiff met the poverty requirements such that his motion to proceed in forma pauperis should be

granted. The court found that here, plaintiff met the poverty requirements found in 28 U.S.C. § 1915. Plaintiff here has an income of $778 per month of which $754.16 goes to fixed expenses.

- ***Ricchio v. Amazon.com, Inc.*, 2012 U.S. Dist. LEXIS 147193, 40 Media L. Rep. 2481, 2012 WL 4865016 (E.D. Wis. Oct. 12, 2012).**
  The court here was determining whether the court should grant plaintiff's motion to appoint counsel and defendants motion to dismiss. The court denied the plaintiff's motion because it found that the case was uncomplicated and the presence of counsel was unlikely to affect the outcome of the litigation. The court granted defendants motion to dismiss because plaintiffs claim did not properly allege facts sufficient to state a claim for relief.
- ***Roe v. Amazon.com*, 2016 U.S. Dist. LEXIS 33297, 118 U.S.P.Q.2D (BNA) 1070, 44 Media L. Rep. 1469, 2016 WL 1028265 (S.D. Ohio Mar. 15, 2016).**
  In 2014, Defendant Jane Doe wrote a book entitled *A Gronking to Remember* and had it published by the Defendants Amazon.com, Inc., Barnes & Noble, Inc., Apple, Inc. and Smashwords. The Corporate Defendants offered the book for sale on their websites in both digital formats (Nook, Kindle, iBooks) as well as in paperback. The cover of the book contains a photograph of Plaintiffs taken during their engagement prior to their wedding. The Court concluded that the Corporate Defendants including Amazon.com Inc. were not publishers, and the corporate defendants' motion for summary judgment was granted.
- ***Routt v. Amazon.com, Inc.*, 2012 U.S. Dist. LEXIS 170602, 105 U.S.P.Q.2D (BNA) 1089, Copy. L. Rep. (CCH) P30,334 (W.D. Wash. Nov. 30, 2012).**
  The court granted the defendant's motion to dismiss because plaintiff failed to state a valid claim and to allege factual allegations to support her claim. Amazon did not directly infringe, had no supervision over third-party's infringing activities to be vicariously liable, and did not induce or encourage the infringement to be contributorily liable.

- ***Routt v. Amazon.com, Inc.*, 2013 U.S. Dist. LEXIS 26265, Copy. L. Rep. (CCH) P30,388, 2013 WL 695922 (W.D. Wash. Feb. 26, 2013).**
  Amazon.com was a defendant in a suit where plaintiff, Sandy Routt alleged that Amazon.com's associates had used her copyrighted photographs on the website without her permission. Amazon.com motioned to dismiss the amended complaint. Finding that the amended complaint did not change the court's original analysis, the court granted the motion to dismiss.
- ***Sandybeachgifts.com v. Amazon.com,* Inc., 584 Fed. Appx. 713, 2014 U.S. App. LEXIS 16794, Copy. L. Rep. (CCH) P30,647, 2014 WL 4252287 (9th Cir. Wash. 2014).**
  This is an appeal from the United States District Court by plaintiff, Sandy Routt for the dismissal of her first amended complaint against Amazon.com. The court of appeals affirmed the lower court's decision.
- **Gibson v. Amazon.com, 2011 U.S. Dist. LEXIS 102065, 2011 WL 4020187 (C.D. Cal. Sept. 8, 2011).**
  This is a copyright infringement case involving Gibson, a self-published author, and Amazon.com. Plaintiff "demonstrate[d] a fundamental misunderstanding of the facts, the Internet, and the law." Amazon's motion for summary judgment was granted.
- ***Authors Guild v. Google Inc.*, 770 F. Supp. 2d 666, 2011 U.S. Dist. LEXIS 29126, 98 U.S.P.Q.2D (BNA) 1229, 79 Fed. R. Serv. 3d (Callaghan) 114, Copy. L. Rep. (CCH) P30,057, 2011-1 Trade Cas. (CCH) P77,387 (S.D.N.Y. 2011).**
  This is a motion for final approval of the proposed settlement of a class action. The initial lawsuit involved Google.com's digital library that collected over 12 million books. Amazon.com raised a number on antitrust concerns presented by the ASA. The motion for final approval was denied by the courts because they found the agreement had gone too far.
- ***Vivo Per Lei, Inc. v. Bruchim* Case No. 11cv05169 GW (JCGx). C.D. Cal., March 20, 2012.**
  This case involves a proposed stipulated protective order to keep documents confidential in a case where defendants are accused of both

copyright and trademark violations. The court found that Amazon would likely have had to provide information during discovery that would have been potentially harmful if it were made available to competitors. The court ultimately granted the protective order in order to keep the requested information confidential and required the parties to sign a non disclosure agreement.

Counterfeit Goods

Amazon.com allows many third-party sellers to use their platform to sell their product. Unfortunately, some of the sellers on the website illegally sell counterfeit goods. According to Black's Law Dictionary, counterfeit means, "to unlawfully forge, copy, or imitate an item, esp. money or a negotiable instrument (such as a security or promissory note) or other officially issued item of value (such as a postage stamp or a food stamp), or to possess such an item without authorization and with the intent to deceive or defraud by presenting the item as genuine. Counterfeiting includes producing or selling an item that displays a reproduction of a genuine trademark to deceive buyers into thinking they are purchasing genuine merchandise". *See* 18 U.S.C. §§ 470 et seq. It is within Amazon's policy to remove any sellers who decide to sell counterfeit products.

That is what happened in the *Tre Milano* case.[1] Amazon was made aware that one of its users had violated not just their terms of the agreement, but had broken the law. Once Amazon was informed of the infringement, they immediately took action. Therefore, when a lawsuit was brought by the seller and the company, Amazon was dismissed from the case because they were not contributorily liable.

Amazon.com has created many safe guards to prevent sellers from selling counterfeit goods. Once Amazon is notified of a seller listing counterfeit items, they can suspend the user or block the user. Any time a seller is blocked, they are prohibited from opening a new account. This is to avoid any liability on behalf of their sellers should a lawsuit arise. Amazon's argument against counterfeit goods lawsuits is typically that they established preventative measures, and that when Amazon becomes aware that a seller is offering to sell counterfeit goods, they immediately take action against the seller.

---

1. *TRE Milano, LLC v. Amazon.com, Inc.*, No. S205747, 2012 Cal. LEXIS 11039 (Nov. 28, 2012).

- ***TRE Milano, LLC v. Amazon.com, Inc.*, No. S205747, 2012 Cal. LEXIS 11039 (Nov. 28, 2012).**
  Plaintiff's case against Amazon was dismissed because Amazon was not responsible for the infringement of a third-party, and could also not be held contributorily liable since Amazon took immediate action once it was notified of the third-party's infringement.

Defamation

Amazon.com has been involved in multiple defamation lawsuits. Many of these cases arise because a third-party Amazon seller has sold an item, such as a book, through the Amazon platform, and that item defamed another party. The party who believes their rights were violated will often file suit against not just the seller, but Amazon.com as well because Amazon was the platform that allowed this content to be available. According to Black's Law Dictionary, defamation means:

1. Malicious or groundless harm to the reputation or good name of another by the making of a false statement to a third person. If the alleged defamation involves a matter of public concern, the plaintiff is constitutionally required to prove both the statement's falsity and the defendant's fault.
2. A false written or oral statement that damages another's reputation.

If a buyer finds content being sold on Amazon that is defamatory, they may go after Amazon. In *Berkery v. Estate of Lyle Stuart*[1], a book was published and sold on the Amazon website that allegedly defamed the plaintiff. Amazon successfully argued that there was no evidence that the website intentionally published the book with knowledge of the defamation and the court ordered summary judgment in favor of Amazon.

There have also been claims of defamation that occurred within the comment section of Amazon's website that allows customers to write reviews. When a seller finds themselves unhappy with the reviews, they contact Amazon. Amazon has the discretion whether to remove the comments or not. When Amazon does not remove the comments, some sellers have filed suit, claiming defamation. In *Hammer v. Amazon*[2], Hammer had received negative reviews and requested that

Amazon take action. The court granted Amazon's motion for permanent injunction because the reviews were mere opinions, not actual defamation. Amazon found itself in a similar situation in *Schneider v. Amazon*[3], but instead argued that the Communications Decency Act (CDA) barred the plaintiff from recovery. Similarly, in *Rosner v. Amazon*[4], Amazon did not remove a negative comment and the court dismissed the complaint finding the plaintiff failed to state a cause of action.

However, Amazon has also been caught up in litigation due to employees alleging defamation. In *Dobias-Davis v. Amazon*[5], Dobias filed suit-alleging defamation in addition to gender and age violation of the ADEA. Amazon moved to dismiss the claims, but the court found that there needed to be more factual development to decide whether the case should be dismissed.

---

1. *Berkery v. Estate of Stuart*, 412 N.J. Super. 76, 988 A.2d 1201 (Super. Ct. App. Div. 2010).
2. *Hammer v. Amazon.com*, 392 F. Supp. 2d 423 (E.D.N.Y. 2005).
3. *Schneider v. Amazon.com, Inc.*, 108 Wash. App. 454, 31 P.3d 37 (2001).
4. *Rosner v. Amazon.com*, 2015 NY Slip Op 07638, 132 A.D.3d 835, 18 N.Y.S.3d 155 (App. Div.).
5. *Dobias-Davis v. Amazon.com.kydc, LLC*, Civil Action No. 3:15-cv-00393-JAG, 2016 U.S. Dist. LEXIS 3396 (E.D. Va. Jan. 11, 2016).

- ***Berkery v. Estate of Stuart*, 412 N.J. Super. 76, 988 A.2d 1201 (Super. Ct. App. Div. 2010).**
  This is a case where plaintiff claimed that defendants deliberately acted with malice against him. The court held there is no clear evidence the defendants acted with malice because a reasonable juror would not be able to say the defendants acted with malice against the plaintiff. The plaintiff's criminal records were open to the public so he qualifies as a limited-purpose public figure. The defendant did not intentionally publish information about the plaintiff with knowledge of it being false or disregard if the published information was true or false. The evidence

that the plaintiff has provided did not show any proof the defendants acted knowing the information published was false.

- ***Dobias-Davis v. Amazon.com.kydc, LLC,* Civil Action No. 3:15-cv-00393-JAG, 2016 U.S. Dist. LEXIS 3396 (E.D. Va. Jan. 11, 2016).** Dobias-Davis was suing Hoffman, her supervisor, and Amazon, her employer, for defamation and retaliation claims under Title VII and the ADEA. Amazon filed a motion to dismiss the claims, which was granted in part in relation to retaliation, as the court determined it did not have enough factual information to dismiss and denied in part in relation to the defamation claim, as it determined she did not participate in the protected activity.
- ***Hammer v. Amazon.com,* 392 F. Supp. 2d 423 (E.D.N.Y. 2005).** Amazon was involved in an action where plaintiff, Jeffrey Hammer raised a number of claims including breach of contract, defamation, violation of copyright laws. The defamation claims focused on negative reviews posted on the Amazon platform regarding a book written by plaintiff. Plaintiff claimed that Amazon breached their contract because they failed to remove negative reviews of his book from the Amazon platform. The court granted Amazon's motion for a permanent injunction preventing plaintiff from bringing any future action against Amazon.
- ***Schneider v. Amazon.com, Inc.,* 108 Wn. App. 454, 31 P.3d 37, 2001 Wash. App. LEXIS 2086, 29 Media L. Rep. 2421 (Wash. Ct. App. 2001).** In this case, plaintiff had written many books on the topics of both taxation and asset protection. The books were for sale on the Amazon platform. The Amazon platform allows consumers to leave reviews for the products they have purchased. Amazon posted visitor's comments about plaintiff and his books. The comments were negative and one alleged plaintiff was a felon. The court found that Amazon is immune from liability for defamation by third-parties under the Communications Decency Act because Amazon is a provider of interactive computer services, plaintiff's claims treat Amazon as a publisher, and Amazon is not the information content provider.

Defense Shifted to Insurer

When Amazon.com finds itself in litigation, sometimes they are not in suit with the original offender, but rather their insurance company. These ligations are when the defense is shifted to the insurer. This occurred in *Amazon.com International v. American Dynasty Surplus Lines Insurance.*[1] This patent infringement case involved Amazon's two insurers, Atlantic Mutual Insurance Company and American Dynasty Surplus Lines Insurance Company. In this case, American Dynasty covered patent infringement, and when they refused to defend, Amazon brought suit.

---

1. *Amazon.com v. Am. Dynasty Ins. Co.*, 120 Wn. App. 610, 85 P.3d 974, 2004 Wash. App. LEXIS 379 (Wash. Ct. App. 2004).

- ***Amazon.com v. Am. Dynasty Ins. Co.*, 120 Wn. App. 610, 85 P.3d 974, 2004 Wash. App. LEXIS 379 (Wash. Ct. App. 2004).**
  In this patent infringement case, Amazon had two insurers, Atlantic Mutual and American Dynasty. Both companies refused to represent Amazon, and when Amazon brought a declaratory judgment action against American Dynasty, the parties settled and Amazon was reimbursed for costs in the patent infringement litigation. On appeal the court found that the factual allegations made by the plaintiff in the patent infringement litigation conceivably amounted to an advertising injury covered by the primary policy with Atlantic Mutual. Thus Atlantic Mutual had aduty to defend, and the court reversed the judgment and remanded the case for entry of a summary judgment in favor of Dynasty.

DMCA Violations

According the Black's Law Dictionary, the Digital Millennium Copyright Act is "A 1998 federal law harmonizing United States copyright protection with international law, limiting copyright liability for Internet service providers, and expanding software owner's' ability to copy programs. Among many other provisions, the statute extends copyright protection to computer programs, movies, and other audiovisual works worldwide; attempts to regulate cyberspace; forbids devices whose purpose is to evade digital anti-piracy tools; and bars the production or distribution of falsified copyright-management information. The statute also limits the liability of Internet service providers against claims of direct and indirect copyright infringement based on content provided by third parties." 17 U.S.C. §§ 1301–1332.

Amazon.com has been involved in multiple DMCA violation lawsuits. This typically occurs when an Amazon Seller is selling items without the copyrighted license. When the copyright holder discovers their copyrighted work is being sold without a license on Amazon, they often file suit against not just the seller, but Amazon as well because Amazon is the platform in which the item was being sold.

When alleging a DMCA violation, it is the plaintiff's job to provide sufficient facts that there was a violation. In order to successfully litigate against Amazon, the plaintiff must prove Amazon had knowledge of the violations. If the plaintiffs fail to do so, then the complaint will be dismissed. That is what occurred in *Chambers v. Amazon.com.*[1] Additionally, Amazon will be dismissed from DMCA violation claims because they are often immune from liability from third-party sellers. This is Amazon's strongest defense whenever there is a DMCA violation that occurs with one of their sellers.

---

1. *Chambers v. Amazon.com Inc.*, 632 F. App'x 742 (4th Cir. 2015).

- ***Chambers v. Amazon.com Inc.*, 632 F. App'x 742 (4th Cir. 2015).**
  The court here is determining whether the lower court erred in adopting the Magistrate's recommendation that this case be summarily dismissed because plaintiff did not state any facts in which it could be reasonably inferred that DMCA or Copyright Act violations were present. Here, the court found that the decision adopting the magistrate's recommendation was proper. Plaintiff failed to allege sufficient facts to support either a Copyright or DMCA claim against defendants. Thus, the court affirmed the lower court's decision to enter an order for summary judgment.
- ***Chambers v. Amazon.com Inc.*, Civil Action No. 3:14-cv-4890-MGL, 2015 U.S. Dist. LEXIS 85367 (D.S.C. July 1, 2015).**
  The court here was determining whether it should adopt the decision of the Magistrate judge below and summarily dismiss this case. The court agreed with the Magistrate, and found that plaintiff's arguments failed to cast any doubt on the findings of the Magistrate. Plaintiff's evidence only provided evidence for plaintiff's alleged damages. The court thus entered an order to summarily dismiss this case.
- ***Chambers v. Amazon.com Inc.*, No. 3:14-4890-MGL-PJG, 2015 U.S. Dist. LEXIS 85596 (D.S.C. Feb. 5, 2015).**
  The court here was determining whether to summarily dismiss this case. The court found that although it must liberally construe a pro se complaint, the plaintiff's allegations were speculative and conclusory. Therefore, the claims were insufficient to show a violation of the Copyright Act or the Digital Millennium Copyright Act and the court recommended summarily dismissing the claims.
- ***Corbis Corp. v. Amazon.com, Inc.*, 351 F. Supp. 2d 1090, 2004 U.S. Dist. LEXIS 27155, 77 U.S.P.Q.2D (BNA) 1182 (W.D. Wash. 2004).**
  In this case plaintiff claimed to have copyright interests in two photographs that Amazon placed on it's website IMDb.com as well as hundreds of photographs that were being sold by vendors on Amazon without Plaintiff's permission. Amazon is protected from liability under the DMCA for copyright infringement occurring on its third party vendor platform. O Amazon qualifies as an Internet Service Provider

protected under DCMA, does not have affirmative duty to police possible infringement, but must take reasonable steps if is alerted to infringement.

- ***Milo & Gabby, LLC v. Amazon.com,* 2015 U.S. Dist. LEXIS 149939 (W.D. Wash. Nov. 3, 2015).**

  Milo & Gabby sued Amazon.com for multiple infringement claims. Amazon.com motioned to dismiss claiming that the plaintiffs failed to state a claim. After a jury hearing, the court adopted the jury's finding that Amazon.com was not liable for "offering to sell" the alleged infringing products at issue in this matter. A judgment was placed in favor of Amazon.com and all claims against Amazon.com were dismissed. Amazon is immune from liability for infringement by third-party sellers under the DMCA.

Employee's Rights

Amazon.com has been involved in multiple lawsuits involving employee's rights. These cases are mostly litigated between Amazon and their employees. If a party employed by Amazon believes their rights have been violated, they may file suit against their employer. Amazon has found itself accused of violating the Age Discrimination in Employment Act (ADEA). This is when the employee believes they were discriminated against due to their age or gender. This occurred in *Dobias-Davis v. Amazon*[1], where Dobias believed she was terminated from her employment due to her age.

In employee's rights cases, Amazon's strongest defense is that the employee has failed to state a claim. Amazon has successfully been dismissed from certain employee's rights lawsuits because they are able to prove that the complaint against them was invalid. That is what occurred in *Arnold v. Amazon.com*[2] where Amazon successfully had their motion to dismiss granted.

---

1. *Dobias-Davis v. Amazon.com.kydc, LLC*, Civil Action No. 3:15-cv-00393-JAG, 2016 U.S. Dist. LEXIS 3396 (E.D. Va. Jan. 11, 2016).
2. *Arnold v. Amazon.com Inc.*, No. 4:13-cv-00168-SEB-WGH, 2014 U.S. Dist. LEXIS 102421 (S.D. Ind. July 28, 2014)

- ***Amazon.com, Inc. v. Powers*, 2012 U.S. Dist. LEXIS 182831, 34 I.E.R. Cas. (BNA) 1878 (W.D. Wash. Dec. 27, 2012).**

  Mr. Daniel Powers is a former Amazon Web Services employee. When Mr. Powers started working at Amazon, he signed a "Confidentiality, Noncompetition and Invention Assignment Agreement." Google, Inc., hired Mr. Powers in September 2012 to work as its Director of Global Cloud Platform Sales at its Mountain View, California headquarters. Amazon sued Mr. Powers for breach of the Agreement and violation of Washington's version of the Uniform Trade Secrets Act.

- ***Arnold v. Amazon.com Inc.*, No. 4:13-cv-00168-SEB-WGH, 2014 U.S. Dist. LEXIS 102421 (S.D. Ind. July 28, 2014).**
  Plaintiff Gary Arnold filed an employment discrimination complaint against Amazon alleging violations of the Age Discrimination in Employment Act and the Americans with Disabilities Act. Arnold also claimed harassment and assault by coworkers. Arnold did not defend the legal sufficiency of his complaint, and Amazon demonstrated that its motion to dismiss is valid. Therefore, the Court granted Amazon's motion to dismiss.
- ***Dobias-Davis v. Amazon.com.kydc, LLC*, Civil Action No. 3:15-cv-00393-JAG, 2016 U.S. Dist. LEXIS 3396 (E.D. Va. Jan. 11, 2016).**
  In this case, Dobias-Davis was suing Hoffman, her supervisor, and Amazon, her employer, for defamation and retaliation claims under Title VII and the ADEA. Amazon filed a motion to dismiss the claims, which was granted in part in relation to retaliation, as the court determined it did not have enough factual information to dismiss and denied in part in relation to the defamation claim, as it determined she did not participate in the protected activity.
- ***Kelley v. Amazon.com, Inc.*, 2013 U.S. Dist. LEXIS 166534, 15 Accom. Disabilities Dec. (CCH) P15-244, 2013 WL 6119229 (E.D. Wash. Nov. 21, 2013).**
  This was a wrongful termination and employee's rights case. Plaintiff Jodie Kelley alleged that her former employer, a subsidiary of Amazon.com, Inc., violated state and federal law by failing to accommodate her disabilities and relied upon her requests for medical leave as a reason for terminating her employment. Kelley's argument was found to be ineffective. As a threshold matter, the evidence of a causal relationship between Plaintiff's deficient performance and her disabilities was entirely speculative.

- ***Raya v. Amazon.com, LLC,* 2015 U.S. Dist. LEXIS 86006 (N.D. Cal. June 30, 2015).**
  In this case, plaintiff Raya filed suit alleging Amazon's California hourly non-exempt employees in its warehouse operations were "not provided Second Unpaid 30-minute Meal Periods for qualifying shifts ..." Raya filed a Motion to Remand in order to have the case heard in state court. However, the court denied this motion, as the amount in controversy exceeded the jurisdictional threshold and the case belonged in federal court.
- ***Whitsitt v. Amazon.com,* 2014 U.S. Dist. LEXIS 58780, 2014 WL 1671502 (E.D. Cal. Apr. 25, 2014).**
  In this case, the plaintiff alleged that he was hired as a temporary employee by defendant SMX Staffing Agency to perform services for defendant Amazon.Com. He asserted that he sought employment with defendant Amazon.Com as a direct hire/permanent employee but was not hired for such a position. Plaintiff alleged violation of employee's rights under the ADEA (Age Discrimination in Employment Act) and intentional invasion of privacy by defendant Amazon.com. The court recommended that this action be dismissed and ruled in favor of Amazon.com.
- ***Whitsitt v. Amazon.Com,* 2014 U.S. Dist. LEXIS 62652 (E.D. Cal. May 6, 2014).**
  Whitsitt filed suit against Amazon.com for a violation of the Age Discrimination in Employment Act (ADEA), for intentional infliction of emotional distress, and for invasion of privacy. The court found that plaintiff's complaint had conclusory allegations, which failed to state a claim. The action was dismissed in favor of Amazon.com.

Fair Credit Reporting Act

"The federal Fair Credit Reporting Act (FCRA) promotes the accuracy, fairness, and privacy of information in the files of consumer reporting agencies. There are many types of consumer reporting agencies, including credit bureaus and specialty agencies (such as agencies that sell information about check writing histories, medical records, and rental history records)." https://www.consumer.ftc.gov/articles/pdf-0096-fair-credit-reporting-act.pdf. The basic rights afforded under the FCRA are outlined below.

<u>You Must Be Told if Information in Your File Has Been Used Against You</u>

Any party who uses a credit report or any other type of consumer report to deny an application for credit, insurance, or employment – or to take another adverse action against another party – must tell that party, and provide the name, address, and phone number of the agency that provided the information.

<u>You Have the Right to Know What is in Your File</u>

One has the right to request and obtain all the information about oneself in the files of a consumer reporting agency.

<u>You Have the Right to Ask for Your Credit Score</u>

One may request a credit score from a consumer reporting agency, but generally the requesting party must pay for the report.

<u>You Have the Right to Dispute Incomplete or Inaccurate Information</u>

If you identify information in your file that is incomplete or inaccurate, and report it to the consumer reporting agency, the agency must investigate unless your dispute is frivolous.

Consumer Reporting Agencies Must Correct or Delete Inaccurate, Incomplete, or Unverifiable Information

Consumer reporting agencies must remove inaccurate incomplete, or unverifiable information, usually within 30 days.

Consumer Reporting Agencies May Not Report Outdated Negative Information

Generally, consumer reporting agencies may not report negative information that is more than seven years old, or bankruptcies that are more than 10 years old.

Access to Your File is Limited

The FCRA outlines what types of parties have a valid need for access to someone's file. The situations generally included an application with a creditor, insurer, employer, landlord, or other business.

You Must Give Your Consent for Reports to be Provided to Employers

A consumer reporting agency may not give out information about you to your employer, or a potential employer, without your written consent given to the employer.

You may limit "Prescreened" Offers of Credit and Insurance You Get Based On Information in Your Credit Report

Unsolicited "prescreened" offers for credit and insurance must include a toll-free phone number you can call if you choose to remove your name and address from the lists these offers are based on.

You May Seek Damages from Violators

If a consumer reporting agency, or, in some cases, a user of consumer reports or a furnisher of information to a consumer reporting agency violates the FCRA, you may be able to sue in state or federal court.

Amazon has begun to make loan services available to sellers. Amazon must comply with the FCRA and the general policies outlined above.

- ***Williams v. Amazon.com, Inc.*, 312 F.R.D. 497, 2015 U.S. Dist. LEXIS 163326, 93 Fed. R. Serv. 3d (Callaghan) 811 (N.D. Ill. 2015).**
  This is a case involving potential violations of the Fair Credit Reporting Act and Rule 68 of the Federal Rules of Civil Procedure. Rule 68 states that if a plaintiff declines an offer for settlement in a suit and the case proceeds to litigation, and the plaintiff must reimburse the defendant if the judgment is less than the declined offer. The court here denied the plaintiff's motion to strike the defendants offer.

False and Deceptive Advertising

When a consumer hears or sees an advertisement, whether the medium be internet, radio, television, or other, Federal law says that ad must be truthful, not misleading, and in certain situations, backed by scientific evidence. The Federal Trade Commission (FTC) enforces these "truth in advertising" laws. The same standards apply to all types of ads including those used in newspapers, magazines, online, in the mail, or on billboards, buses, cabs, etc. Special weight is given to advertising claims that can affect consumer's health or bank accounts. Claims regarding food, over the counter medicines, dietary supplements, alcohol, and tobacco and on conduct related to high-tech products and the internet all get special attention from the FTC. If the FTC does find a case of fraud, the agency will file actions in federal court for orders to stop scams, prevent future scams, freeze perpetrators assets, and get compensation for victims.

- ***Fagerstrom v. Amazon.com, Inc.*, 141 F. Supp. 3d 1051, 2015 U.S. Dist. LEXIS 143295 (S.D. Cal. 2015).**

  In this case, consumers claimed there was a discrepancy between Amazon's prices and other retailer prices of products. When checking out on Amazon, each customer must agree to the conditions of use in order to complete their order. Amazon states any dispute will be resolved through binding arbitration. The court here granted Amazon's motion to compel arbitration and dismissed this action because the terms of the agreement were fair and beneficial to both parties.
- ***M-Edge Accessories LLC v. Amazon.com Inc.*, 2015 U.S. Dist. LEXIS 10095 (D. Md. Jan. 29, 2015).**

  Plaintiff's claim for False Advertisement under the Lanham Act failed as Plaintiff did not provide admissible evidence nor did it show it was harmed by the alleged violation.

- ***Sanmedica Int'l, LLC v. Amazon.com, Inc.*, 2015 U.S. Dist. LEXIS 50470 (D. Utah Mar. 27, 2015).**
  In this case the court refused to grant Amazon's motion to dismiss where it found the use of Plaintiff's trademark may cause initial interest confusion and thus was a question for the jury.
- ***Sen v. Amazon.com, Inc.*, 2013 U.S. Dist. LEXIS 178447, 2013 WL 6730180 (S.D. Cal. Dec. 19, 2013).**
  The issue here was whether the court should grant defendant Amazon's Motion to Enforce the Settlement where both Amazon and plaintiff, Sen have signed the settlement, but plaintiff was attempting to add additional terms to the agreement. The court granted the motion because it found the agreement to be complete, unambiguous, and intentionally entered into, the agreement contains all material terms and plaintiff's additional concerns are unfounded, and because the agreement contains valid consideration.

Federal Trade Commission

The Federal Trade Commission (FTC) is a federal agency that handles complaints filed regarding unfair business practices. Some common issues that the FTC handles include consumer scams, deceptive and false advertising claims, and monopolistic practices. The FTC is also responsible for reviewing business mergers to ensure that they do not hurt competition and or harm consumers. Since the FTC is an administrative agency, its rulings are not directly enforceable, but agencies can go to the courts to have their rulings enforced.

The FTC has brought claims against Amazon, alleging that the billing of parents and other account holders for in-app purchases incurred by children "without having obtained the account holders' express informed consent" is unlawful under the FTC Act, and is an unfair billing practice.[1] The court denied Amazon's motion to dismiss because it found that Amazon had not shown evidence that the purchases by the children were authorized or that having authorization would make it fair to bill account holders.[2] There was not enough evidence presented to dismiss the claim. Amazon customers may not have known about in app purchases or the refund process or may have been deterred by having to get in contact with someone in order to get the refund, these factors all helped lead to the conclusion that the practice was in fact unfair.[3]

---

1. *FTC v. Amazon.com, Inc.,* 71 F. Supp. 3d 1158 (W.D. Wash. 2014).
2. *Id.*
3. *Id.*

- ***FTC v. Amazon.com, Inc.*, 71 F. Supp. 3d 1158 (W.D. Wash. 2014).**
  In this case, the federal trade commission was suing Amazon for holding parents liable for their children's "in app purchases." Amazon moved to

dismiss the case for failure to state a claim. The court denied the motion to dismiss because plaintiff alleged sufficient facts to create a claim for relief under section 5 of the FTC Act.

Financial and Tax Law

Amazon.com has been involved with litigation involving tax disputes. This typically occurs when Tax laws are amended and Amazon's policies are directly impacted by the change. This occurred in *Amazon.com v. New York State Department of Taxation and Finance,* where Amazon argued that the amended tax law was unconstitutional.[1] Other tax law disputes have arisen between Amazon and a government body because an amazon seller has violated current tax laws.

---

1. *Amazon.com LLC v. N.Y. State Dept. of Taxation & Fin.,* 2009 NY Slip Op 29007, 23 Misc. 3d 418, 877 N.Y.S.2d 842 (Sup. Ct.).

- ***Amazon.com LLC v. Lay,* 758 F. Supp. 2d 1154, 2010 U.S. Dist. LEXIS 113163, 73 A.L.R. Fed. 2d 501 (W.D. Wash. 2010).**
  Amazon.com LLC, plaintiff, moved for summary judgment in this North Carolina tax lawsuit regarding Defendant Kenneth R. Lay where, defendant secretary of the North Carolina department of labor was requesting detailed information regarding sales by Amazon to North Carolina customers. Amazon.com LLC and the North Carolina Department of Revenue ("DOR") have long disputed whether Amazon must collect and remit North Carolina sales and use taxes. The motion for summary judgment was granted because the DOR conceded that it had no legitimate need or use for having details as to North Carolina Amazon customers' literary, music, and film purchases the court found that the request is too broad.
- ***Amazon.com LLC v. New York State Dept. of Taxation & Fin.,* 877 N.Y.S.2d 842, 23 Misc. 3d 418, 2009 N.Y. Misc. LEXIS 28, 2009 NY Slip Op 29007, 241 N.Y.L.J. 12 (N.Y. Sup. Ct. 2009).**
  Amazon filed suit alleging that the commission-agreement provision, "violated the Commerce Clause of the United States Constitution, ...

because it imposed tax collection obligations on out-of-state entities who have no substantial nexus with New York." The court concluded that because Amazon failed to state a cause of action, the suit was dismissed.

- ***Amazon.com, LLC v New York State Dept. of Taxation & Fin.*, 81 A.D.3d 183, 913 N.Y.S.2d 129, 2010 N.Y. App. Div. LEXIS 7943, 2010 NY Slip Op 7823 (N.Y. App. Div. 1st Dep't 2010).**
  Amazon filed a complaint seeking declaratory and injunctive relief on the ground that the tax statute was unconstitutional. The court dismissed and Amazon appealed. The court concluded that they did not find the facial challenges to have merit, but found that further discovery was necessary before a determination can be rendered as to the as-applied Commerce Clause and Due Process Clause claims.
- ***Breuer v. American Express Bank*, FSB, 2014 N.Y. Misc. LEXIS 2931, 2014 NY Slip Op 31698(U) (N.Y. Sup. Ct. June 30, 2014).**
  Plaintiff used a credit card to which he owed debt to make a purchase via Amazon. He returned the items and requested a check from Amazon rather than credit towards his debt. The court ruled in favor of AMEX and the funds were applied to his debt.
- ***Overstock.com, Inc. v New York State Dept. of Taxation & Fin.*, 20 N.Y.3d 586, 987 N.E.2d 621, 965 N.Y.S.2d 61, 2013 N.Y. LEXIS 542, 2013 NY Slip Op 2102, 2013 WL 1234823 (N.Y. 2013).**
  Amazon.com was a plaintiff in this case involving the New York State Department of Taxation. The issue here as whether the amended tax law at issue violated the constitution. The District Court found the amended law to be constitutional. The court of appeals found that the plaintiffs failed to demonstrate that the statute was facially unconstitutional under either the Commerce or the Due Process Clause, and affirmed the lower court's decision.
- ***Zaretsky v. Maxi-Aids, Inc.*, 2012 U.S. Dist. LEXIS 84291, 2012 WL 2345181 (E.D.N.Y. June 18, 2012).**
  On October 28, 2011, plaintiffs filed a letter requesting additional time to file a completed RICO statement, which defendants had construed to

be untimely objections to the Report. Since there is no clear error on the face of the Report, plaintiffs' objections were overruled and the Report of Magistrate Judge Boyle was accepted in its entirety.

Forcible Use of Arbitration

All customers making purchases on the Amazon platform are required to complete their purchases by reviewing a final checkout page and clicking a "place your order" button located on that page. At the top of the checkout page, under the heading "Review Your Order," there is a notice to customers stating that "by placing your order you agree to Amazon.com's privacy notice and conditions of use." The words "privacy notice" and "conditions of use" are set off in blue text that "links" to the full texts of both the privacy notice and conditions of use. The conditions of use contain Amazon's arbitration agreement.

When Amazon cases result in litigation, there are often disputes amongst the parties as to what forum the proceedings will take place in. Many cases arise where a party is challenging Amazon's right to include an Arbitration clause and wishes to have the case tried in a traditional court setting. The court's generally side with Amazon, and hold that the arbitration clause is not "unconscionable," and thus is enforceable.[1]

Amazon litigation may also be complex; many cases involve multiple parties as well as multiple issues. In some cases, courts grant motions to stay (postpone) proceedings in order arbitrate certain issues prior to fully litigating others in a traditional court setting.[2] These types of orders are aimed at promoting judicial economy and maintaining proper enforcement of arbitration clauses, as well as maintaining clarity in the resolution of each issue.

---

1. *Andrew K. Ranazzi v. Amazon.com,* Inc., No. L-14-1217, Ct. of Appeals Ohio, 6th App. Dist. (2015).
2. *Id.*

- **Segal v. Amazon.com, Inc., 763 F. Supp. 2d 1367, 2011 U.S. Dist. LEXIS 11429 (S.D. Fla. 2011).**
  Plaintiff is an Amazon seller who sued Amazon in Florida court for unjust enrichment and tortious interference after Amazon allegedly did not release to Plaintiff the profits of its sales on Amazon's website. Relying on the "Participation Agreement" that sellers are required to enter in order to sell on Amazon's website, Amazon argued that the agreement specifically states that any such lawsuits are to be brought in Washington state courts, and asked the Florida court to dismiss the case or transfer it to Washington. The court here upheld the forum selection clause.
- ***Fagerstrom v. Amazon.com, Inc.*, 141 F. Supp. 3d 1051, 2015 U.S. Dist. LEXIS 143295 (S.D. Cal. 2015).**
  In this case, consumers claim there is a discrepancy between Amazon's prices and other retailer prices of products. When checking out on Amazon, each customer muse agree to the conditions of use in order to complete their order. Amazon's conditions of use states that any dispute must be resolved through binding arbitration. The court granted Amazon's motion to compel arbitration and dismisses this action because the terms of the agreement were both fair and beneficial to both parties.
- ***Ranazzi v. Amazon.com, Inc.*, 2015-Ohio-4411, 46 N.E.3d 213, 2015 Ohio App. LEXIS 4277 (Ohio Ct. App., Lucas County 2015).**
  In this case, the court stayed proceedings until the outcome of Arbitration which was an enforceable forum for the dispute under the agreement between plaintiff and Amazon for use of its website.
- ***Nicosia v. Amazon.com, Inc.*, 84 F. Supp. 3d 142, 2015 U.S. Dist. LEXIS 13560 (E.D.N.Y. 2015).**
  Arbitration was proper forum for plaintiff's issue where they agreed to arbitration prior to using Amazon's website to make a purchase.
- ***Lasoff v. Amazon.com, Inc.*, 2016 U.S. Dist. LEXIS 9878, 2016 WL 355076 (D.N.J. Jan. 28, 2016).**
  In this case, plaintiff Amazon seller was suing Amazon.com, in New jersey, for trademark infringement, anti-trust violations, and unfair business

practices because Amazon allowed other sellers to sell similar products to those of plaintiff. All sellers using the Amazon platform are subject to Amazon's terms of use, which contains a forum selection clause requiring litigation in a Washington court. The court ordered a venue transfer to Washington because it found that there were no public or local interests weighing strongly against the transfer.

Initial Interest Confusion

This section focuses on confusion a trademark may cause for potential customers. The court considers eight non-exhaustive factors whether a trademark use causes a likelihood of confusion: strength of the mark, proximity or relatedness of the goods, similarity of the marks, evidence of actual confusion, marketing channels, degree of consumer care, the defendants' intent and likelihood of expansion.

In the case involving Multi Time Machine Inc. the court determined that the question of fact existed as to the likelihood of confusion.[1] They determined that under Amazon's clear labeling of the products at issue with name, model and photograph, no reasonable consumer could possibly find that they were sincerely confused by the Amazon search results.[2] Therefore, there was no infringement under the Lanham Act.[3] Additionally, in *Sanmedica International, LLC v. Amazon.com Inc.*, the court determined that there was no likelihood of confusion since unauthorized use of the trademark at issue did not influence any sales.[4]

---

1. *Multi Time Mach., Inc. v. Amazon.com, Inc.*, 792 F.3d 1070 (9th Cir. 2015).
2. *Id.*
3. *Id.*
4. *Sanmedica Int'l, LLC v. Amazon.com, Inc.*, No. 2:13-cv-00169-DN, 2015 U.S. Dist. LEXIS 50470 (D. Utah Mar. 27, 2015)

- ***Multi Time Mach., Inc. v. Amazon.com, Inc.*, 792 F.3d 1070 (9th Cir. 2015).**

  Plaintiff argued Amazon confused customers – Plaintiff did not sell items on Amazon, but when customers searched for it, Amazon returned results with Plaintiff's trademark and listings from other sellers.

- ***Sanmedica Int'l, LLC v. Amazon.com, Inc.*, 2015 U.S. Dist. LEXIS 50470 (D. Utah Mar. 27, 2015).**
  Plaintiff had a viable argument where Amazon confused customers by using its trademark in listings when it was not authorized and the goods could not be purchased.

International Depositions

Federal Rule of Civil Procedure Rule 28 allows deposition of a third party to be taken in a foreign country "on appropriate terms after application and notice of it."[1] Fed. R. Civ. P. 28(b)(2)(A). The court can request letters of interrogatory in order to formally request a court in another country to lend its judicial assistance in obtaining evidence or performing some other judicial act. The party that is seeking the deposition bears the burden of demonstrating the relevance and that the information is relevant and reasonably calculated enough to be added into evidence.

In *Blagman v. Apple* we saw that this request was granted, even though plaintiff requested twice to seek discovery of customers outside the United States and was denied.[2] The ones he requested in this motion were distinguishable, as the plaintiff sought to depose certain entities concerning digital recordings.[3] The testimony may also support plaintiff's claims of commonality.[4]

---

1. *Blagman v. Apple, Inc.*, 2014 U.S. Dist. LEXIS 45401 (S.D.N.Y. Mar. 31, 2014).
2. *Id.*
3. *Id.*
4. *Id.*

- ***Blagman v. Apple, Inc.*, 2014 U.S. Dist. LEXIS 45401 (S.D.N.Y. Mar. 31, 2014).**
  Blagman had filed a motion to depose third parties from the U.K. and France. Amazon contended that the court had already ruled that extraterritorial evidence was not admissible in this case. The court disagreed and granted the motion to depose the third parties located internationally.

Lanham Act Violations

The Lanham act is a Federal statute that was passed in 1946 by President Harry Truman. The Lanham act governs trademarks, service marks, and unfair competition. A trademark is a word, phrase, symbol, and/or design that identifies and distinguishes the source of the goods of one party from those of others. A service mark is essentially that same thing as a trademark, except a service mark identifies and distinguishes the source of a service rather than goods. Some examples of trademarks include Toyota (Cars and Trucks), Nike (Apparel), and Microsoft (Software). The Lanham act outlines the procedure for federally registering trademarks, states when owners of trademarks may be entitled to federal judicial protection against trademark infringement, and sets forth other guidelines and remedies for trademark owners.

Claims for Lanham Act violations are extremely prevalent in relation to the Amazon platform. There are two common situations that arise involving Amazon and the Lanham Act: (1) When a manufacturer sues Amazon directly, or an Amazon seller for a listing that used a trademark without the permission of the manufacturer, and (2) When a manufacturer sues Amazon, or an Amazon seller for selling items that are inauthentic or counterfeit and thus violate the Lanham Act for trademark infringement.

In recent litigation, it has been held that Amazon can not be held liable for infringement when other companies sell infringing products on the Amazon platform.[1] The court in *Milo* held that Amazon could not be held liable when a third party sold infringing goods on the Amazon platform because Amazon itself did not directly offer to sell infringing goods or engage in any other infringing acts. [2]

---

1. *Milo & Gabby, LLC v. Amazon.com*, No. C13-1932RSM, 2015 U.S. Dist. LEXIS 149939 (W.D. Wash. Nov. 3, 2015).
2. *Id.*

- ***Amazon.com, Inc. v. Nat'l Ass'n of College Stores, Inc.*, 826 F. Supp. 2d 1242, 2011 U.S. Dist. LEXIS 135880 (W.D. Wash. 2011).**
  The court denied NACS's Motion to Dismiss as it determined the court did have jurisdiction over the claims and the case and the complaint was valid and presented a controversy.
- ***Corbis Corp. v. Amazon.com, Inc.*, 351 F. Supp. 2d 1090, 2004 U.S. Dist. LEXIS 27155, 77 U.S.P.Q.2D (BNA) 1182 (W.D. Wash. 2004).**
  Court dismissed plaintiff's claim under Lanham Act as it was duplicative of their copyright infringement claim for which the Court already decided in favor of Amazon.
- ***M-Edge Accessories LLC v. Amazon.com Inc.*, 2015 U.S. Dist. LEXIS 10095 (D. Md. Jan. 29, 2015).**
  Plaintiff could not successfully argue False Advertising where it only produced a print out of Amazon's website without further authentication, and also did not show it suffered any harm by the alleged false advertising.
- ***Milo & Gabby, LLC v. Amazon.com, Inc., 12 F. Supp. 3d 1341 (W.D. Wash. 2014)***
  Milo & Gabby sued Amazon.com for multiple infringement claims. Amazon.com motioned to dismiss claiming that the plaintiffs failed to state a claim. The District Court agreed with Amazon and granted to motion to dismiss the III, V, VII claims.
- ***Milo & Gabby, LLC v. Amazon.com, Inc.*, 2015 U.S. Dist. LEXIS 143252 (W.D. Wash. Oct. 21, 2015)**
  Milo & Gabby sued Amazon.com for multiple infringement claims. The defendant, Amazon.com motioned in Limine. The court granted in part and denied in part.
- ***Milo & Gabby, LLC v. Amazon.com, 2015 U.S. Dist. LEXIS 149939 (W.D. Wash. Nov. 3, 2015).***
  Milo & Gabby sued Amazon.com for multiple infringement claims. Amazon.com motioned to dismiss claiming that the plaintiffs failed to state a claim. After a jury hearing, the court adopted the jury's finding that Amazon.com was not liable for "offering to sell" the alleged

infringing products at issue in this matter. A judgment was placed in favor of Amazon.com and all claims against Amazon.com were dismissed.

- ***Multi Time Mach., Inc. v. Amazon.com, Inc.*, 792 F.3d 1070 (9th Cir. 2015).**
  Court denied Amazon's motion to dismiss the case and found that Plaintiff raised a triable issue of fact as to whether Amazon infringed on plaintiff's trademark and confused customers in violation of the Lanham Act.
- ***Roe v. Amazon.com*, 2016 U.S. Dist. LEXIS 33297, 118 U.S.P.Q.2D (BNA) 1070, 44 Media L. Rep. 1469, 2016 WL 1028265 (S.D. Ohio Mar. 15, 2016).**
  In 2014, Defendant Jane Doe wrote a book entitled *A Gronking to Remember* and had it published by the Defendants Amazon.com, Inc., Barnes & Noble, Inc., Apple, Inc. and Smashwords. The Corporate Defendants offered the book for sale on their websites in both digital formats (Nook, Kindle, iBooks) as well as in paperback. The cover of the book contains a photograph of Plaintiffs taken during their engagement prior to their wedding. The Court concluded that the Corporate Defendants including Amazon.com Inc. were not publishers, and the corporate defendants' motion for summary judgment was granted.
- ***Routt v. Amazon.com, Inc.*, 2012 U.S. Dist. LEXIS 170602, 105 U.S.P.Q.2D (BNA) 1089, Copy. L. Rep. (CCH) P30,334 (W.D. Wash. Nov. 30, 2012).**
  The court granted the defendant's motion to dismiss as plaintiff failed to state a valid claim in the complaint and allege factual allegations to support her claim. Amazon did not directly infringe, had no supervision over third-party's infringing activities to be vicariously liable, and did not induce or encourage the infringement to be contributorily liable.
- ***Routt v. Amazon.com, Inc.*, 2013 U.S. Dist. LEXIS 26265, Copy. L. Rep. (CCH) P30,388, 2013 WL 695922 (W.D. Wash. Feb. 26, 2013).**
  Amazon.com was a defendant in this suit where plaintiff, Sandy Routt alleged that Amazon.com's associates had used her copyrighted photographs on the website without her permission. Amazon.com motioned

to dismiss the amended complaint. Finding that the amended complaint did not change the court's original analysis, the court granted the motion to dismiss.

- ***Sandybeachgifts.com v. Amazon.com,* Inc., 584 Fed. Appx. 713, 2014 U.S. App. LEXIS 16794, Copy. L. Rep. (CCH) P30,647, 2014 WL 4252287 (9th Cir. Wash. 2014).**
  This is an appeal from the United States District Court by plaintiff, Sandy Routt for the dismissal of her first amended complaint against Amazon.com. The court of appeals affirmed the lower court's decision.
- ***Sanmedica Int'l, LLC v. Amazon.com, Inc.,* 2015 U.S. Dist. LEXIS 50470 (D. Utah Mar. 27, 2015).**
  Court refused to grant Amazon's motion to dismiss where it found the use of Plaintiff's trademark may cause initial interest confusion and thus was a question for the jury.
- ***Sellify Inc. v. Amazon.com, Inc.,* 2010 U.S. Dist. LEXIS 118173 (S.D.N.Y. Nov. 3, 2010).**
  The court here was determining whether to grant defendants motion for summary judgment. The court granted the motion. The claims at issue here required direct action by Amazon in order to state a claim and no evidence existed as to this point. Further the court found that the damages requested by the plaintiff were too speculative to survive a motion to dismiss. The court therefore granted the motion.
- ***Video Professor, Inc. v. Amazon.com, Inc.,* Civil Action No. 09-cv-00636-REB-KLM, 2010 U.S. Dist. LEXIS 29414 (D. Colo. Mar. 8, 2010).**
  The court here was determining whether to grant plaintiff's motion to modify the discovery schedule. The motion was denied and the court held that plaintiff had not shown good cause for amendment of the deadline for discovery. Plaintiff's efforts to pursue discovery were less than diligent, and plaintiff had not shown evidence that additional discovery was relevant to claims as they were stated in the complaint.

Motion to Transfer

A motion to transfer is a request to transfer the case to another district or county because the original venue is improper under the relevant venue rules or because of local bias. Title 28, Section 1404(a) of the United States Code states a motion to transfer venue may be granted when the transfer is convenient for all parties and witnesses to a venue where the action may have been brought. A district court has broad discretion in deciding whether to order a transfer. The convenience of witnesses is weighed heavily in deciding whether to transfer venue or not.

In the Amazon cases, courts have granted motions when the transfer would be a more convenient venue than the original venue. A motion to transfer may be denied if the transfer is not valid and there are sufficient contacts within the original forum. Transfer may be granted when it is in the best interest of justice.

A motion to transfer is filed prior to the start of litigation of a case when a defendant wishes to change the venue of the trial to a different location. The Federal Rule for change of venue allows for the "convenience of parties and witnesses," and "in the interest of justice," a district court may transfer any civil action to any other district or division where it might have been brought or to any district or division to which all parties have consented.[1]

Motions to transfer are often brought in cases involving Amazon. Policies set forth by Amazon usually contain agreements requiring parties to consent forum selection clauses.[2] Courts typically enforce these agreements because their clear language implicates that the clause is binding.[3] Motions to transfer also arise in Amazon cases where the parties argue that another forum may be more convenient for litigation.[4] Because Amazon's business is so extensive, the differences in forum selection can heavily influence a case due to factors such as cost, travel, and availability of both evidence and witnesses.[5]

---

1. 28 U.S.C. § 1404(a)
2. *Appistry, Inc. v. Amazon.com, Inc.,* No. 4:13CV2547 HEA, 2015 U.S. Dist. LEXIS 24421 (E.D. Mo. Mar. 2, 2015).
3. *Id.*
4. *Amazon.com, Inc. v. Straight Path IP Grp., Inc.,* No. 5:14-cv-04561-EJD, 2015 U.S. Dist. LEXIS 69281 (N.D. Cal. May 28, 2015).
5. *Id.*

- ***Appistry, Inc. v. Amazon.com, Inc.,* No. 4:13CV2547 HEA, 2015 U.S. Dist. LEXIS 24421 (E.D. Mo. Mar. 2, 2015).**
  The Plaintiff, Appistry, Inc. brought suit against Amazon.com, Inc. and Amazon Web Services, Inc., for infringement of the following patents: the '746 Patent (U.S. Patent No. 8,200,746) and the "209 Patent (U.S. Patent No. 8,341,209). Defendants moved to transfer this action to the Western District of Washington based on a forum-selection clause contained in a "clickwrap" agreement between Plaintiff and Defendant Amazon.com.
- ***Amazon.com v. Cendant Corp.,* 404 F. Supp. 2d 1256, 2005 U.S. Dist. LEXIS 38855 (W.D. Wash. 2005).**
  This is a patent infringement case involving four software patents held by plaintiffs Amazon.com and A9.com, the assignee of one of the four patents at issue here. The plaintiffs alleged patent infringement via the company websites of defendants Cendant Corporation and its subsidiaries Trilegiant, Orbitz, Budget Rent-a-Car ("Budget"), and Avis Rent-a-Car Systems ("Avis"). The court granted the motion to transfer venues because the motion promoted the most convenience for the parties.

Negligence

In a negligence action, Amazon generally files suit against a party who negligently performs under a contract or agreement. In *Amazon.com v. Coyote Logistics*, Amazon alleged negligence among other claims due to a failed transport of Amazon Kindles that were left unattended.[1] The unattended goods resulted in theft.[2] Amazon alleged this negligence and the court agreed that Amazon was entitled to damages amounting to $1,447,023.20.[3] According to Black's Law Dictionary, negligence is defined as,

> The failure to exercise the standard of care that a reasonably prudent person would have exercised in a similar situation; any conduct that falls below the legal standard established to protect others against unreasonable risk of harm, except for conduct that is intentionally, wantonly, or willfully disregardful of others' rights; the doing of what a reasonable and prudent person would not do under the particular circumstances, or the failure to do what such a person would do under the circumstances. The elements necessary to recover damages for negligence are (1) the existence of a duty on the part of the defendant to protect the plaintiff from the injury complained of, and (2) an injury to the plaintiff from the defendant's failure.

However, parties have also filed suit against Amazon. In these situations, Amazon often motions to dismiss the claim or for summary judgment for failure to state claim.

---

1. *Amazon.com v. Coyote Logistics* Case No. C11-1015 RSL, United States District Court Western District of Washington at Seattle, December 11, 2013.
2. *Id.*

3. *Id.*
4. *Spears v. Amazon*, No. 10-325-GFVT, 2013 U.S. Dist. LEXIS 18384 (E.D. Ky. Feb. 12, 2013).

- ***Amazon.com v. Coyote Logistics* Case No. C11-1015 RSL, United States District Court Western District of Washington at Seattle, December 11, 2013.**
  In this case, plaintiff, Amazon alleged that CP Transport was hired to transport a container of Amazon Kindles from Washington to Delaware in November 2009. Amazon alleged that the driver left the shipment unattended at a truck stop, resulting in the theft of the truck, container, and goods. The court awarded damages for negligence in favor of Amazon.
- ***Cox v. Brand 44, LLC*, 2015 U.S. Dist. LEXIS 143120, 2015 WL 6182469 (D. Mass. Oct. 21, 2015).**
  This is a negligence and wrongful death suit brought by the estate of MJ Cox following his death due to a zip line accident. Defendants' Motion to Dismiss is granted in part, and denied in part. The court denied the motion to dismiss pain and suffering, breach of warranties and loss of consortium but granted in regards to punitive damages and strict liability.
- ***Hinton v. Dick's Sporting Goods, Inc.*, 2013 U.S. Dist. LEXIS 172245, 2013 WL 6384601 (S.D. Miss. Dec. 6, 2013).**
  In this case, plaintiff filed against defendants alleging that they sold her hunting equipment that had been recalled by the Consumer Product Safety Commission (CPSC). She decided to buy the hunting equipment subject to recall. Her son had subsequently died in a hunting accident. The court denied the Motion for Immediate Hearing for Permanent Injunction as the Plaintiff failed to prove that her case would be an actual success on the merits and merely showed a likelihood of success.
- ***Hinton v. Dick's Sporting Goods, Inc.*, 2014 U.S. Dist. LEXIS 24426 (S.D. Miss. Feb. 26, 2014).**
  In this case, plaintiff filed against defendants alleging that they sold her hunting equipment that had been recalled by the Consumer Product Safety Commission (CPSC). She decided to buy the hunting equipment

subject to recall. Her son had subsequently died in a hunting accident. The court granted the Motion for Additional Time to Respond to the Motion for Sanctions and Motion for Summary Judgment as it was found to be brought with good cause and was filed in a timely manner.

- ***Hinton v. Dick's Sporting Goods, Inc.*, 2014 U.S. Dist. LEXIS 137243 (S.D. Miss. Sept. 29, 2014).**
  In this case, plaintiff filed against defendants alleging that they sold her hunting equipment that had been recalled by the Consumer Product Safety Commission (CPSC). She decided to buy the hunting equipment subject to recall. Her son had subsequently died in a hunting accident. The court denied the Plaintiff's Motion to Strike and Motion in Limine, as it determined it will simply not consider the Report Plaintiff intended to strike and the Motion in Limine was done prematurely. The court granted her Motion for Permission to File Surrebuttal Brief as it determined that the court could consider the competing arguments and position in the Motion for Summary Judgment filed by the other defendants.
- ***Hobbs v. Rui Zhao*, 2014 U.S. Dist. LEXIS 161533 (N.D. Okla. Nov. 17, 2014).**
  Zhao was a commercial driver in the U.S. for four weeks when he drove to an Amazon distribution center in Kentucky to pick up cargo. Plaintiff got into an accident and the plaintiff suffered serious injuries. The court denied the Plaintiff's Motion to Amend his Complaint to add two more defendants, as the deadline has passed and he had not shown why he did not add these defendants at a prior time. Therefore, the court is lead to believe that he did so in bad faith, and therefore did not allow this amendment.
- ***Hobbs v. Rui Zhao*, 2015 U.S. Dist. LEXIS 11762 (N.D. Okla. Feb. 2, 2015).**
  Zhao was a commercial driver in the U.S. for four weeks when he drove to an Amazon distribution center in Kentucky to pick up cargo. Zhao got into an accident and as a result, plaintiff suffered serious injuries. The court granted summary judgment to Amazon in relation to the negligent entrustment claim, as Plaintiff failed to prove that the cargo was

a dangerous instrumentality and that Amazon owed plaintiff a duty of care. Additionally, summary judgment was granted to the negligent hiring claim, as Amazon did not select Zhao to perform the task. Amazon was dismissed from the case.

- ***Spears v. Amazon*, 2013 U.S. Dist. LEXIS 18384, 34 I.E.R. Cas. (BNA) 1783, 27 Am. Disabilities Cas. (BNA) 1430 (E.D. Ky. Feb. 12, 2013).** Amazon.com was a defendant in a negligent misrepresentation suit. Amazon motioned for summary judgment. Plaintiff claimed that Amazon "fraudulently induced him to accept a position of employment in the company, or in the least negligently misrepresented the nature of compensation of the employment; that Amazon inappropriately terminated him on the basis of his disability in retaliation for a worker's compensation claim, and in transgression of public policy." United States District Court denied Amazon's motion for summary judgment for the fraud claims in the inducement, negligent misrepresentation, and workers' compensation. The court granted Amazon's motion for summary judgment for the claims of wrongful discharge on the basis of disability and in violation of public policy. The court found that Spears had created a genuine issue of material fact as to whether or not Amazon made the offer to Spears in reckless disregard of its falsity.

Patent Infringement

Amazon.com often finds themselves in lawsuits relating to Patent Infringement. This typically occurs when a third-party Amazon Seller is selling a patented product without the proper license. According to Black's Law Dictionary, direct infringement for Patents is defined as, "The act of making, using, selling, offering for sale, or importing into the United States, without the patentee's permission, a product that is covered by the claims of a valid patent."[1]

However, Amazon themselves have been accused of infringing on certain patents with their own products such as computer systems or the technology behind their products. These products include the Amazon Kindle or the Amazon Instant Video service. That is what occurred in *Adaptix, Inc. v. Amazon.*[2]

Amazon's strongest defenses against patent infringement cases are first to prove the alleged patent is patent ineligible. That is what occurred in, *Appistry, Inc. v. Amazon.com.*[3] Amazon successfully showed that the patents in suit were invalid under 35 U.S.C. Section 101 and were granted judgment on the pleadings.[4] Amazon will then question the validity of the complaint, meaning, did the plaintiff meet its burden of proof of stating a cause of action? If Amazon can successfully show that the complaint is invalid, they will often receive judgment in their favor.

Amazon is not always on the defense. There are certain cases where Amazon believes their patents were infringed upon. That is what occurred in *Amazon.com v. Barnes and Noble.com*; Amazon believed that Barnes and Noble were infringing on their 411 patent.[5]

---

1. 35 USCA § 271(a).
2. *Adaptix, Inc. v. Amazon.com*, Inc., No. 5:14-cv-01379-PSG, 2015 U.S. Dist. LEXIS 111933 (N.D. Cal. Aug. 21, 2015).

3. *Appistry, Inc. v. Amazon.com, Inc.*, No. 4:13CV2547 HEA, 2015 U.S. Dist. LEXIS 24421 (E.D. Mo. Mar. 2, 2015).
4. *Id.*
5. *Amazon.com, Inc. v. Barnesandnoble.com, Inc.*, 239 F.3d 1343 (Fed. Cir. 2001).

- ***Adaptix, Inc. v. Amazon.com, Inc.*, 2015 U.S. Dist. LEXIS 111933 (N.D. Cal. Aug. 21, 2015).**
  This was a patent infringement case brought by Adaptix Inc. against Amazon.com and other named defendants. The court concluded that the 4 cases, in which Amazon was a defendant, must be dismissed because they were barred by the doctrine against claim splitting.
- ***Adaptix, Inc. v. Amazon.com, Inc.*, 2016 U.S. Dist. LEXIS 33521 (N.D. Cal. Mar. 14, 2016).**
  Adaptix asked the court to revisit this last set of decisions in their previous set of cases alleging patent infringement. The court had previously granted summary judgment on the claims in favor of defendants. The court concluded that because Adaptix made similar arguments that were already dismissed, the court denied the plaintiff's request.
- ***Affinity Labs of Tex., LLC v. Amazon.com, Inc.*, 2015 U.S. Dist. LEXIS 77411 (W.D. Tex. June 12, 2015).**
  In this case, the court was deciding whether to grant Amazon's motion to dismiss based solely on the pleadings (early in the legal process). Here, plaintiff's claim that Amazon was infringing their patent for "wirelessly communicating selective information to an electronic device." The court granted the motion because the patent infringement claim would inhibit the "abstract idea" that made the technology possible from growing and developing.
- ***Alcatel-Lucent USA, Inc. v. Amazon.com, Inc.*, 2011 U.S. Dist. LEXIS 61039, 2011 WL 2260276 (E.D. Tex. June 7, 2011).**
  The court here defined the disputed terms in the five patents that were in controversy.

- **Amazon. Com Int'l, Inc. v. Am. Dynasty Surplus Lines Ins. Co., 2004 Wash. LEXIS 864, 152 Wn.2d 1030, 103 P.3d 200 (Wash. 2004).**
Amazon.com International alleged that defendant American Dynasty Surplus Lines infringed upon its patents by misappropriating the software used on Amazon's website. The court concluded that "because the allegations conceivably amounted to an advertising injury covered by Amazon's policy with Atlantic Mutual Insurance Company, Atlantic Mutual had a duty to defend" and revered the summary judgment in favor of Atlantic Mutual. The court remanded for entry of summary judgment in favor of Amazon's excess carrier, American Dynasty Surplus Line. The court states that the duty is upon the primary insurer regarding any infringement of patents.
- **Amazon.com, Inc. v. Barnesandnoble.com, Inc., 73 F. Supp. 2d 1228, 1999 U.S. Dist. LEXIS 18660, 53 U.S.P.Q.2D (BNA) 1115 (W.D. Wash. 1999).**
Defendants may continue to offer an "Express Lane" feature if the feature is modified to avoid infringement of the '411 patent in a manner that is consistent with the applicable conclusion of law.
- ***Amazon.com, Inc. v. Barnesandnoble.com, Inc.*, 239 F.3d 1343, 2001 U.S. App. LEXIS 2163, 57 U.S.P.Q.2D (BNA) 1747 (Fed. Cir. 2001).**
The Court vacated the lower court's preliminary injunction and remanded the case for further proceedings based on BarnesandNoble.com's ability to raise substantial questions as to the validity of the '411 patent, which was not considered in the lower court.
- ***Amazon.com v. Cendant Corp.*, 404 F. Supp. 2d 1256, 2005 U.S. Dist. LEXIS 38855 (W.D. Wash. 2005).**
This was a patent infringement case involving four software patents held by plaintiffs Amazon.com and A9.com, the assignee of one of the four patents at issue here. The plaintiffs alleged patent infringement via the company websites of defendants Cendant Corporation and its subsidiaries Trilegiant, Orbitz, Budget Rent-a-Car ("Budget"), and Avis Rent-a-Car Systems ("Avis"). The court granted the motion to transfer venues. The

motion to transfer was granted here because the motion was backed by the convenience of the parties.

- ***Amazon.com, Inc. v. Straight Path IP Grp., Inc.*, 2015 U.S. Dist. LEXIS 69281 (N.D. Cal. May 28, 2015).**
  This was a patent infringement case involving the sale of Internet-enabled devices with pre-installed video streaming applications – Amazon Instant Video streaming service. The court denied defendant's motion to dismiss, and granted the motion to transfer venue.
- ***Appistry, Inc. v. Amazon.com, Inc.*, 2015 U.S. Dist. LEXIS 90004, 2015 WL 4210890 (W.D. Wash. July 9, 2015).**
  Amazon.com was a defendant in this patent infringement case. Amazon motioned for judgment on the pleadings. The court concluded that because the patents-in-suit were invalid under, 35 U.S.C. Section 101, the defendant's motion for judgment on the pleadings was granted.
- ***Appistry, Inc. v. Amazon.com, Inc.*, 2015 U.S. Dist. LEXIS 24421 (E.D. Mo. Mar. 2, 2015).**
  Amazon.com was a defendant in this patent infringement case. Amazon.com motioned to transfer pursuant to a clause within an agreement signed by both parties. The court granted the motion finding that the "clear language of the forum selection clause includes this action because it related to the Service Offerings." The court denied Amazon's motion for partial summary judgment as it found that there was a genuine issue of material fact when looking at the record in the light most favorable to the nonmoving party.
- ***B.E. Tech., LLC v. Amazon Digital Servs.*, 2013 U.S. Dist. LEXIS 101204, 2013 WL 3807820 (W.D. Tenn. July 19, 2013.)**
  Amazon Digital Services was a defendant in this patent infringement case. Amazon filed a motion to transfer. The court, after looking at the convenience of the witnesses, convenience of the parties, and the interest of justice, found that these factors did not weigh in favor of a transfer and denied the motion.

- ***Big Baboon Corp. v. Dell, Inc.*, 723 F. Supp. 2d 1224, 2010 U.S. Dist. LEXIS 80289 (C.D. Cal. 2010).**
  This was a patent infringement case involving a Motion to Compel, which the court granted in part and denied in part. The court ordered Big Baboon to provide Amazon with specific infringement claims charts with citations, so that Amazon could understand exactly what it was being accused of infringing.
- ***Bovino v. Amazon.com, Inc.*, 2014 U.S. Dist. LEXIS 32016 (D. Colo. Mar. 12, 2014).**
  Bovino filed a motion to amend his complaint to include an additional 100 products that Amazon allegedly infringed. The court granted this motion as it found no bad faith argument against this amendment and found Amazon's arguments to be without merit and therefore, invalid.
- ***Bovino v. Amazon.com, Inc.*, 2015 U.S. Dist. LEXIS 71772, 2015 WL 3523218 (D. Colo. June 1, 2015).**
  Amazon filed a Motion for Summary Judgment claiming that they did not infringe the patent as a result of the patent's meaning and that the patent is invalid. The court granted the Motion for Summary Judgment as Mr. Bovino did not adequately show a claim that the products infringed on the patent.
- ***Bovino v. Amazon.com, Inc.*, 2016 U.S. Dist. LEXIS 32368, 2016 WL 943780 (D. Colo. Mar. 14, 2016).**
  Amazon filed a Motion for Attorney's Fees and Mr. Bovino filed a Motion to Enforce Settlement Agreement. The court held that the Motion for Attorney's Fees was denied, as the case did not rise to the "exceptional" level required. Additionally, the court could not enforce a settlement agreement, after a judgment by a court had been entered.
- ***Celebrate Int'l, LLC v. LeapFrog Enters.*, 2015 U.S. Dist. LEXIS 114407, 2015 WL 5092611 (D. Del. Aug. 28, 2015).**
  This was a patent infringement case filed by Celebrate International LLC against Leapfrog Enterprises, an Amazon-owned e-reader for kids,

regarding the '398 Patent and the '776 Patent. The court stated that the parties were to submit a proposed order that was consistent with the terms agreed upon in the opinion.

- ***Cloud Satchel, LLC v. Amazon.com, Inc.*, 76 F. Supp. 3d 553, 2014 U.S. Dist. LEXIS 174715 (D. Del. 2014).**
  This was a patent infringement case where Cloud Satchel could not successfully argue patent infringement against Amazon.com Inc. and Barnes & Noble, Inc. The court granted Amazon.com and Barnes & Noble's request for summary judgment for invalidity.
- ***Clouding IP, LLC v. amazon.com, Inc.*, 2013 U.S. Dist. LEXIS 73655, 2013 WL 2293452 (D. Del. May 24, 2013).**
  Clouding IP filed suit against Amazon.com for patent infringement. The court addressed the issue of Direct Infringement, Induced Infringement, Willful Infringement, and a motion for a more definite statement. The court granted the motions in part and denied them in part.
- ***Content Guard Holdings, Inc. v. Amazon.com, Inc.*, 2015 U.S. Dist. LEXIS 39807 (E.D. Tex. Mar. 29, 2015).**
  Amazon filed a defense claiming that Content Guard Holdings had failed to plead a case upon which relief could be granted. After observing all of the relevant documents, pleadings, and briefs, the court found that Content Guard Holdings had pled a case upon which relief can be granted. Amazon's motion to dismiss was denied.
- ***Content Guard Holdings, Inc. v. Amazon.com, Inc.*, 2015 U.S. Dist. LEXIS 33881 (E.D. Tex. Mar. 19, 2015).**
  Amazon, along with other named defendants, found that the joinder was improper in this case and motioned to sever pursuant to Rule 21 of the Federal Rules of Civil Procedure. The court denied all motions to sever finding that the parties were properly joined.
- ***Content Guard Holdings, Inc. v. Amazon.com, Inc.*, 2015 U.S. Dist. LEXIS 34667 (E.D. Tex. Mar. 20, 2015).**
  While Amazon.com was a named defendant in this patent infringement suit, this document deals specifically with the court construing disputed terms.

- ***ContentGuard Holdings, Inc. v. Amazon.com, Inc.*, 2015 U.S. Dist. LEXIS 53687 (E.D. Tex. Apr. 23, 2015).**
  While Amazon.com was a named defendant in this case, this particular document involved a motion to transfer filed by defendant, Apple. The court denied the motion to transfer and found that venue was proper.
- ***Cordance Corp. v. Amazon.com, Inc.*, 730 F. Supp. 2d 333, 2010 U.S. Dist. LEXIS 74368 (D. Del. 2010).**
  Here, Plaintiff sued Amazon for patent infringement by use of its website's "1-click" purchase feature. Plaintiff claimed Amazon's information storage and way of collecting buyer and seller reviews violated plaintiff's patents. Amazon successfully argued against an order that would require them to permanently halt its infringing activities or pay an ongoing royalty to patent owners because plaintiff did not show irreparable harm that could not be rectified by monetary payment.
- ***Cordance Corp. v. Amazon.com, Inc.*, 855 F. Supp. 2d 244, 2012 U.S. Dist. LEXIS 51268 (D. Del. 2012).**
  Amazon.com was a defendant in this patent infringement case filed by plaintiff, Cordance. Judgment was entered in favor of Amazon.com. This document deals specifically with Amazon's request for costs. The court granted in part and denied in part. The court found that after looking to the evidence presented by Cordance, that they could not, "find that Amazon encumbered the record". Additionally, the court found that there should be a reduction in the amount of costs granted to Amazon
- ***CyberFone Sys., LLC v. Cellco P'ship*, 885 F. Supp. 2d 710, 2012 U.S. Dist. LEXIS 115740, 2012 WL 3528115 (D. Del. 2012).**
  Amazon was one of the named defendants in this patent infringement case. Cyberfone Systems, LLC, sued 175 defendants for violating the 060 patent. Defendants filed a motion for summary judgment. The court found that because the content patent was ineligible for patent protection, that the motion for summary judgment should be granted.

- ***CyberFone Sys., LLC v. Cellco P'ship,* 2012 U.S. Dist. LEXIS 60045, 2012 WL 1509504 (D. Del. Apr. 30, 2012).**
  Amazon.com is a named defendant in a patent infringement case. Cyberfone Systems, LLC, sued 175 defendants for violating the 060 patent and the 382 patent. A number of defendants motioned to sever and dismiss. The court granted in part on the issue of contributory infringement motions and denied in part on the remaining grounds.
- ***CyberFone Sys., LLC v. ZTE (USA), Inc.,* 2014 U.S. Dist. LEXIS 13478, 2014 WL 490586 (D. Del. Feb. 4, 2014).**
  Amazon.com was a named defendant in this patent infringement case. Cyberfone Systems, LLC, sued multiple defendants for violating the 060 patent. The Court of Appeals agreed with the District Court in finding that the patent was invalid because the categorical data storage mentioned in the patent is an abstract idea that is not patent-eligible.
- ***Discovery Patent Holdings, LLC v. Amazon.com, Inc.,* 769 F. Supp. 2d 662 (D. Del. 2011).**
  The court here is determining what construction of the parties disputed terms in the patent claim should be adopted by the court.
- ***Droplets, Inc. v. Amazon.com, Inc.,* No. 2:11-CV-392, 2012 U.S. Dist. LEXIS 122978 (E.D. Tex. June 27, 2012).**
  The court here was determining whether to grant defendants motion to transfer venue where the majority of relevant documents and defendants' headquarters were located in the District of Northern California. The court found that the location of sources of proof, availability of compulsory process, the convenience for witnesses, and the local interest factors all favored transfer, and granted the motion.
- **EBAY Inc. and Microsoft Corporation v. Kelora Systems, LLC.**
  This patent infringement case concerned Kelora's US Patent No. 6,275,821, or the '821 Patent. The Court found that, without the assistance of expert testimony, Defendants had not met the standards required for summary judgment.

- ***Eolas Techs., Inc. v. Adobe Sys.*, 810 F. Supp. 2d 795 (E.D. Tex. 2011).**
  In this case the court was construing the meaning of the term "browser application" within the meaning of the patent at issue. Here the plaintiff and defendant disagreed upon the meaning of the term and the court applies its own definition. The court held that the term "browser application" as "a client program that displays and responds to user interaction with hypermedia documents."
- ***Eolas Techs. Inc. v. Adobe Sys.*, 891 F. Supp. 2d 803 (E.D. Tex. 2012).**
  In this case, the court as assessing the fairness of allowing the defendants to recover the costs of: (1) video depositions; (2) electronic discovery costs including document collection, processing, hosting, scanning and conversion; (3) photocopies; (4) CD and DVD copies; (5) graphics professional support at trial; and (6) demonstratives and exhibits for trial. The court provided guidance to the parties in how the costs can most fairly be assessed and ordered the defendants to resubmit their Bill of Costs to the court.
- ***EON Corp. IP Holdings, LLC v. T-Mobile United States, Inc.*, 2012 U.S. Dist. LEXIS 76467 (N.D. Cal. June 1, 2012).**
  In this case the court esd deciding whether or not to grant a subpoena for discovery of third party *Kineto*. The court found that the subpoena could be granted with two slight exceptions because plaintiff *Eon* modified the scope of the subpoena to limit its discovery to matters relating strictly to T-Mobile devices.
- ***Execware, LLC v. Staples, Inc.*, 2012 U.S. Dist. LEXIS 174885 (D. Del. Dec. 10, 2012).**
  In this case a Magistrate judge recommended that claims against defendant Staples, Inc. for both direct and willful infringement be dismissed because the complaint did not allege that Staples' customers actually used the accused software, or that Staples caused its customers to directly infringe the patent, and plaintiff's amended complaint relies solely on allegations that Staples was made aware of the patent by the filing of the original complaint in the present action.

- ***Girafa.com, Inc. v. Amazon.com, Inc.*, 2008 U.S. Dist. LEXIS 99196 (D. Del. Dec. 9, 2008).**
  Amazon.com was a defendant in this patent infringement case. Girafa, plaintiff filed a motion for preliminary injunction. The court concluded that there were substantial questions concerning the infringement claims and their validity and thus denied Girafa's motion for preliminary injunction.
- ***Golden Bridge Tech., Inc. v. Apple Inc.*, 2012 U.S. Dist. LEXIS 130286 (C.D. Cal. Sept. 11, 2012).**
  The court held that the motion to sever was granted, as the defendants' infringements were not related and did not stem from the same occurrence. Additionally, the court denied the motion to transfer for Amazon, as it found that it had enough connections with the forum and there were also procedural issues with granting both motions.
- ***Golden Bridge Tech., Inc. v. Apple Inc.*, 937 F. Supp. 2d 490 (D. Del. 2013).**
  The court set forth an interpretation of the claim language in the patents provided for the cases and denied collateral estoppel from the previous Texas court decision.
- ***Guardian Media Techs., Ltd. v. Amazon.com, Inc.*, 2013 U.S. Dist. LEXIS 171254 (C.D. Cal. Dec. 3, 2013).**
  The court was determining whether defendants were improperly joined where it was alleged that defendants conduct was part of the same transaction or occurrence. The court held that joinder was improper as to all defendants except Amazon.com, Inc. because there is no indication that the defendants acted in concert or was connected in any way.
- ***Hand Held Prods. v. Amazon.com, Inc.*, 2014 U.S. Dist. LEXIS 85345 (D. Del. June 24, 2014).**
  In order to infringe upon a patent, the actions taken must follow the same sequence or order of actions outlined in the patent. Amazon did not present any expert testimony but rather merely relied on attorney arguments, and therefore did not show that claims of a patent were indefinite or invalid.

- ***In re Amazon.com, Inc.*, 476 Fed. Appx. 738 (Fed. Cir. 2012).**
  Amazon had submitted a writ of mandamus to vacate an order denying a motion to transfer a case and directing to transfer to the United States District Court for the Western District of Texas. The court ordered Global Sessions LP et al. to respond no later than February 8, 2012.
- ***In re Amazon.com Inc.*, 478 Fed. Appx. 669 (Fed. Cir. 2012).**
  Amazon had submitted a writ of mandamus to vacate an order denying a motion to transfer a case and directing to transfer to the United States District Court for the Western District of Texas. The court denied Amazon's writ of mandamus; the transfer of venue would not have been more convenient.
- ***Infinite Data Llc v. Amazon.com Inc.*, 2014 U.S. Dist. LEXIS 8849 (D. Del. Jan. 23, 2014).**
  In this case the court was deciding whether to grant a motion to stay (temporarily postpone judicial proceedings). The court ultimately held that those defendants who agreed to be bound by the litigation decided during the stay would be granted that stay, and that those who wanted to litigate on their own would not be granted a stay. This decision favored fairness to all parties because plaintiff was not forced to re-litigate against any defendant, thus avoiding any tactical advantages.
- ***Innovative Office Prods. v. Amazon.com, Inc.*, 2012 U.S. Dist. LEXIS 59090 (E.D. Pa. Apr. 26, 2012).**
  This was a patent infringement case brought by Innovative Office Productions against Amazon.com. among other defendants. Plaintiffs voluntarily dismissed most of the defendants, Amazon.com included. This case dealt specifically with the remaining defendants.
- ***IPXL Holdings, L.L.C. v. Amazon.com, Inc.*, 333 F. Supp. 2d 513 (E.D. Va. 2004).**
  In this case, plaintiff claimed that Amazon violated their patent for a "one click" ordering system. The court granted the defendant's motion for summary judgment because plaintiff improperly claimed that Amazon's "one click" system violated both the system and method for using the system.

- ***IPXL Holdings, L.L.C. v. Amazon.com, Inc.*, 430 F.3d 1377 (Fed. Cir. 2005).**
  This was a case involving the appellant appealing summary judgment for a patent infringement claim awarded by the previous court. The court affirmed summary judgment and reversed the award of attorney fees. The district court erred in granting Amazon attorney fees, Amazon did not file a timely request. The district court properly granted Amazon summary judgment for the infringement claim.
- ***JVW Enters. v. Amazon.com, Inc.*, 175 Fed. Appx. 344 (Fed. Cir. 2006).**
  JVW previously sued a wholesaler for patent infringement and no infringement was found so JVW appealed. The district court's decision was reversed in part and remanded in part. The case here was on appeal. The district court's decision was affirmed.
- ***KKG, LLC v. Rank Group, PLC*, 2013 U.S. Dist. LEXIS 54279 (E.D. Tex. Apr. 16, 2013).**
  The court was defining the meaning of 6 terms in dispute by the parties.
- ***Lexington Luminance LLC v. Amazon.com, Inc.*, 6 F. Supp. 3d 179 (D. Mass. 2014).**
  Lexington sued Amazon.com and Amazon Digital Services alleging that the Kindle e-readers created by amazon were in violation of patent infringement of the 851 patent. This case dealt specifically with defendant, Amazon's motion for judgment on the pleadings. The court found that the claim failed to narrow the composition of the substrate to any degree of substantial certainty. Ultimately, the court found the claim 1 of the 851 patent to be indefinite. The District Court allowed Amazon's motion for judgment on the pleadings. Judgment was entered on Amazon's counterclaim for a declaration of invalidity in its favor and Lexington's complaint was dismissed.
- ***Lexington Luminance LLC v. Amazon.com Inc.*, 601 Fed. Appx. 963 (Fed. Cir. 2015).**
  Lexington sued Amazon.com and Amazon Digital Services alleging that the Kindle e-readers created by amazon violated the 851 patent. This is

an appeal from the United States District Court judgment in favor of Amazon.com. The Court of Appeals now reviewed the judgment and found that the district court erred in construing the claim and in holding the claim indefinite. The court remands.

- ***Lexington Luminance LLC v. Amazon Digital Servs.*, 2016 U.S. Dist. LEXIS 46023 (D. Mass. Apr. 4, 2016).**
  The court determined claim construction for the patents in suit by defining them in a way that most naturally aligns with the patent's description.
- ***M-Edge Accessories LLC v. Amazon.Com Inc.*, 2013 U.S. Dist. LEXIS 311 (D. Md. Jan. 2, 2013).**
  The court denied the Defendant's Motion to Dismiss, as it determined the plaintiff's complaint contained enough factual allegations to support the claims.
- ***M-Edge Accessories LLC v. Amazon.com Inc.*, 2015 U.S. Dist. LEXIS 10095 (D. Md. Jan. 29, 2015).**
  Amazon was able to get one of two patent infringement claims dismissed where the Court had no question that Amazon's book cover did not infringe upon Plaintiff's patent. Amazon's motion for Summary Judgment was denied where there was a question of fact as to whether one of its e-reader book covers infringed upon the Plaintiff's patent.
- ***Milo & Gabby, LLC v. Amazon.com, Inc., 12 F. Supp. 3d 1341 (W.D. Wash. 2014)***
  Milo & Gabby sued Amazon.com for multiple infringement claims. Amazon.com motioned to dismiss claiming that the plaintiffs failed to state a claim. The District Court agreed with Amazon and granted to motion to dismiss the III, V, VII claims.
- ***Milo & Gabby, LLC v. Amazon.com, Inc.*, 2015 U.S. Dist. LEXIS 143252 (W.D. Wash. Oct. 21, 2015)**
  Milo & Gabby sued Amazon.com for multiple infringement claims. The defendant, Amazon.com motioned in Limine. The court granted in part and denied in part.

- ***Milo & Gabby, LLC v. Amazon.com, 2015 U.S. Dist. LEXIS 149939 (W.D. Wash. Nov. 3, 2015).***
  Milo & Gabby sued Amazon.com for multiple infringement claims. Amazon.com motioned to dismiss claiming that the plaintiffs failed to state a claim. After a jury hearing, the court adopted the jury's finding that Amazon.com was not liable for "offering to sell" the alleged infringing products at issue in this matter. A judgment was placed in favor of Amazon.com and all claims against Amazon.com were dismissed.
- ***Mobile Telcoms. Techs., LLC v. Amazon.com, Inc.,* 2014 U.S. Dist. LEXIS 138786 (E.D. Tex. Aug. 26, 2014).**
  Amazon.com was a defendant in a patent infringement case brought by Mobile Telecommunications. Amazon.com motioned to dismiss the claims. The United States District Court denied the defendant's motion to dismiss because they found the claims brought by plaintiff, Mobile Telecommunications were sufficient.
- ***Mobile Telcoms. Techs., LLC v. Amazon.com, Inc.,* 2014 U.S. Dist. LEXIS 156454 (E.D. Tex. Nov. 5, 2014).**
  While Amazon.com was a named defendant, this patent infringement suit deals specifically with the claim construction order of the disputed claims within the patents.
- ***Nazomi Communs., Inc. v. Nokia Corp.,* 2013 U.S. Dist. LEXIS 85344 (N.D. Cal. June 14, 2013).**
  The court granted the motion for judgment on the pleadings, as Nazomi failed to show specific facts that support their allegations.
- ***Nazomi Communs., Inc. v. Microsoft Mobile Oy,* 597 Fed. Appx. 1075 (Fed. Cir. 2014).**
  The court affirmed the lower court's order for summary judgment for the defendants, as it did not find Nazomi's arguments persuasive enough to overturn the decision.
- ***Nomura v. YouTube, LLC,* 2012 U.S. Dist. LEXIS 174332 (N.D. Cal. Dec. 7, 2012).** The court found that the new evidence and modifications dud not unfairly prejudice Nomura and therefore denied the plaintiff's motion to strike the modifications and not admit the new evidence.

- ***Nomura v. YouTube, LLC,* 2013 U.S. Dist. LEXIS 18292 (N.D. Cal. Feb. 8, 2013)** The court determined the meaning of the patent terms that were disputed in the claim of patent infringement.
- ***Nomura v. Amazon.Com, Inc.,* 2013 U.S. Dist. LEXIS 122895 (N.D. Cal. Aug. 28, 2013).**
  The court determined that the documents Amazon requested to be sealed did not contain privileged information or trade secrets and therefore as not entitled to protection under the law and thus denied the motion to seal.
- ***OIP Techs., Inc. v. Amazon.com, Inc.,* 788 F.3d 1359 (Fed. Cir. 2015).**
  OIP Technologies alleged that Amazon.com infringed on their patents. The court of appeals agreed with the district court in that, "the patent-in-suit claimed no more than an abstract idea coupled with routine data-gathering steps and conventional computer activity."
- ***Olympic Devs. AG, LLC v. Barnesandnoble.com LLC (N.D. Cal., 2011).***
  The court here was ruling on the parties' stipulation to stay (temporarily postpone) the proceedings pending re-examination of the patent at issue in this claim. The court held that this action was stayed in its entirety pending completion of the reexamination of the patent at issue.
- ***On Demand Mach. Corp. v. Ingram Indus.,* 442 F.3d 1331 (Fed. Cir. 2006).** Amazon.com was a named defendant in a suit filed by On Demand Machine Corp. for Patent infringement. The United States District Court for the Eastern district of Missouri found Amazon to be liable. Amazon, along with other named defendants appealed the verdict and the court of appeals ultimately reversed the lower court's decision.
- ***Parallel Networks, LLC v. Abercrombie & Fitch Co.,* 704 F.3d 958 (Fed. Cir. 2013).**
  The court here, on appeal, was determining whether the district court erred in granting summary judgment for defendants. Plaintiff made challenges to the lower courts rulings on claim construction, its non-infringement rulings, and its denial of a Fed. R. Civ. P. 59(e) motion with respect to the severed defendants. The court affirmed the lower court because it agreed that plaintiff was attempting to

amend its infringement contentions in order to make arguments that could have and should have been made before the entry of summary judgment.

- ***PersonalWeb Techs., LLC v. NEC Corp. of Am.*, 2013 U.S. Dist. LEXIS 110046 (E.D. Tex. Aug. 5, 2013).**
  The court determined the claim language of the patent and determined what each term shall mean for the duration of the case. Additionally, the court denied Facebook's Motion for Summary Judgment and HP's Motion for Summary Judgment for Indefiniteness.
- ***Personalized Media Communs., LLC v. Amazon.com, Inc.*, 2015 U.S. Dist. LEXIS 104369 (D. Del. Aug. 10, 2015).**
  The court granted the Defendant's Motion for Judgment on the Pleadings, as none of the claims stated were eligible patent claims.
- ***Piao Shang Indus. Co. v. Acco Brands Corp.*, 2011 U.S. Dist. LEXIS 67417 (C.D. Cal. June 23, 2011).**
  In this case the court was determining whether to allow plaintiff's claim to move forward where it does not appear that plaintiff's claim against defendants arise out of the same transaction or occurrence. The court held that it was not clear that plaintiff's claims against defendants arose out of the same transaction or occurrence because each defendant sold a different device allegedly infringing on the patented invention. The court ordered plaintiff to show cause in writing why one or more parties should not be dropped from this case for improper joinder. The plaintiff, alternatively, may file separate actions against each of the defendants
- ***Pragmatus Mobile, LLC v. Amazon.Com, Inc.*, 2015 U.S. Dist. LEXIS 82256 (D. Del. June 17, 2015).**
  The court determined that the Motion to Stay Litigation was done as a tactical attempt by the defendants and therefore denied the motion.
- ***Premium Prods. v. Pro Performance Sports, LLC*, 997 F. Supp. 2d 433 (E.D. Va. 2014).**
  The court affirmed the disqualification of Spiegel as the attorney for Premium as it would violate Virginia's witness-advocate rule. The court

determined that Spiegel would be a necessary witness and the magistrate did not rule contrary to law or erroneously.

- ***Red Pine Point LLC v. Amazon.Com, Inc.* Case No. 14C 00274; 14C 00290. United States District Court Northern District of Illinois Eastern Division, July 2014.**
  The court determined the motion to transfer was reasonable and granted to have all consolidated and related cases transferred to the Northern District of California.
- ***RMail Ltd. v. Amazon.com, Inc.*, 2013 U.S. Dist. LEXIS 34912 (E.D. Tex. Mar. 11, 2013).**
  The court issued claim construction for the patents-in-suit.
- ***Robbins v. Unemployment Ins. Appeals Bd.*, 2016 Del. Super. LEXIS 31 (Del. Super. Ct. Jan. 25, 2016).**
  Robbins sought unemployment compensation from Amazon after termination of his employment. Robbins did not provide a doctor's note when he returned to work from a previous injury and subsequently left because he felt unable to perform. The Unemployment Insurance Appeals Board determined that Robins was not entitle to unemployment compensation benefits because he voluntarily quit without good cause. The court determined that the decision of the Board should be affirmed as Robbins did not meet his burden to show that he left Amazon with good cause.
- ***Schneider v. Amazon.com, Inc.*, 108 Wn. App. 454 (Wash. Ct. App. 2001).**
  The court here was determining whether the lower court erred in dismissing plaintiffs claim against Amazon where Amazon was the provider or user of interactive computer services, plaintiff treated Amazon as a publisher, and Amazon was not the information content provider. The court agreed that because these elements were satisfied that the trial court did not err in dismissing the claim.
- ***SFA Sys., LLC v. Amazon.com, Inc.*, 2013 U.S. Dist. LEXIS 189807 (E.D. Tex. Apr. 11, 2013).**
  Amazon.com was a defendant in a case dealing with patent infringement. Amazon.com motioned for partial summary judgment. The court

found that defendants failed to show by clear and convincing evidence that these claims were insoluble due to an impermissible mix of apparatus limitations and method steps. Ultimately, the court denied the motion for partial summary judgment.

- ***Sipco, LLC v. Amazon.com, Inc.*, 2012 U.S. Dist. LEXIS 150940 (E.D. Tex. Oct. 19, 2012).**
  While Amazon.com was a named defendant in this patent infringement case, the document at hand dealt specifically with the construction of the disputed terms in the patent.
- ***Sipco, LLC v. Amazon.com, Inc.*, 2013 U.S. Dist. LEXIS 137518 (E.D. Tex. Sept. 25, 2013).**
  While Amazon.com was a named defendant in a patent infringement case, the document at hand dealt specifically with another named defendant, Hawking's motion for leave to reconvene. The United States District Court granted the motion in part and denied it in part.
- ***Soverain Software LLC v. Gap, Inc.*, 340 F. Supp. 2d 760 (E.D. Tex. 2004).**
  Amazon.com was a named defendant in a patent infringement case. The document at hand dealt specifically with Amazon.com's motion to compel production of non-privileged documents. The court disagreed with Amazon's arguments and denied the motion.
- ***Soverain Software L.L.C. v. Amazon.com, Inc.*, 383 F. Supp. 2d 904 (E.D. Tex. 2005).**
  Amazon.com was a named defendant in an action brought by Soverain Software alleging patent infringement. This case dealt specifically with defendant's motion for summary judgment. The court denied the vendor's motion as to the patentee's personal compliance with marking statute but granted the motion in all other respects.
- ***Soverain Software LLC v. Amazon.com, Inc.*, 356 F. Supp. 2d 660 (E.D. Tex. 2005).**
  Amazon.com was a named defendant in an action brought by Soverain Software alleging patent infringement. Defendant, Amazon motioned to stay. After looking to the three determining factors, the court found that they did not weight in favor of a stay and denied the motion.

- ***Switzer v. Litex Indus.* Case No. 11-cv-01174-REB. D. Colo., May 3, 2011.**
  This was a case involving patent infringement and a briefing schedule to resolve matters. The court ordered that the parties shall file a joint claim construction statement of the patents at issue, limited to fifteen pages, shall be filed thirty days after the statement is filed, deadlines for filing a response brief and reply shall be followed, a response brief shall be limited to twenty pages, and the parties shall convene a telephone motions hearing within ten days after the reply brief is filed to set a time for a hearing.
- ***TainoApp, Inc. v. Amazon.com, Inc.*, 2014 U.S. Dist. LEXIS 177361 (D.P.R. Dec. 24, 2014).**
  Amazon.com is a defendant in a patent infringement case. Amazon.com motioned for transfer and the court granted the motion finding that the interest of justice was in favor of transfer.
- ***Tech. Innovations, LLC v. Amazon.com, Inc.*, 2013 U.S. Dist. LEXIS 115352 (D. Del. Aug. 15, 2013).**
  Amazon.com was a defendant in this patent infringement case. After reviewing the multiple motions made by the parties, the United States District Court ordered that plaintiff must show cause on or before September 12, 2013 for why the assertion of the 407 patent was proper under the requirements of Rule 11.
- ***Tech. Innovations, LLC v. Amazon.com, Inc.*, 2015 U.S. Dist. LEXIS 51415 (D. Del. Apr. 20, 2015).**
  Amazon.com was defendant in this patent infringement case. Amazon.com requested attorney fees for the claims against them filed by plaintiff. This document deals specifically with the courts order for plaintiff to pay a total of $51,046 in attorney fees to Amazon.
- ***Telebuyer, LLC v. Amazon.com, Inc.*, 2015 U.S. Dist. LEXIS 96391 (W.D. Wash. July 23, 2015).**
  Amazon.com was a defendant in this patent infringement case brought by Telebuyer. Amazon.com motioned for summary judgment claiming that the patents were invalid. The court, after applying the *Alice* framework, found that each of the representative claims were directed to

patent-ineligible subject matter. Therefore, the court granted the defendant's motion for summary judgment.

- ***Telebuyer, LLC v. Amazon.com, Inc.*, 2015 U.S. Dist. LEXIS 18200 (W.D. Wash. Feb. 13, 2015).**

  This patent infringement case was dismissed in favor of Amazon because the claims in plaintiff's patents were abstract, generic and indefinite, and therefore invalid.

- **Tompkins v. Able Planet Inc., 2011 U.S. Dist. LEXIS 153068 (E.D. Tex. Feb. 17, 2011).**

  The court here issued an order severing plaintiff's claims. The court found that because the claims are clearly distinguishable, it should exercise its discretion and sever the claims based on product manufacturer in order to promote judicial economy as well as fairness to the litigants.

- ***Tuxis Techs., LLC v. Amazon.com, Inc.*, 2014 U.S. Dist. LEXIS 122457 (D. Del. Sept. 3, 2014).**

  The court was determining whether to grant defendant Amazon.Com, Inc.'s, Motion to Dismiss for Failure to State a Claim. The court found that the concept of "upselling" in the field of marketing is "as old as the field itself," and thus that the claim involved patent ineligible subject matter. The court noted that the limitations set out in the claim do narrow its scope, but not enough to save the claim from invalidity.

- ***Tuxis Techs., LLC v. Amazon.com, Inc.*, 2015 U.S. Dist. LEXIS 37128 (D. Del. Mar. 25, 2015).**

  The court here was determining whether to grant defendant Amazon. Com, Inc.'s, (Amazon) motion to dismiss for failure to state a claim where Amazon claimed the patent, which deals with the concept of "upselling," is for ineligible subject matter. The court held that the patent claims clearly are drawn to patent ineligible subject matter. The concept of "upselling" is a longstanding commercial practice. Even though limitations narrow the scope of the claims, these limitations do not amount to an "inventive concept." Thus all of the claims of the patent are invalid.

- ***United Video Props. v. Amazon.com, Inc.*, 2012 U.S. Dist. LEXIS 86914 (D. Del. June 22, 2012).**
  The court determined the claim construction of the patents that were allegedly infringed.
- ***United Video Props., Inc. v. Amazon.com*, Inc., 561 Fed. Appx. 914 (Fed. Cir. 2014).**
  The court affirmed the lower court's claim construction and their judgment of non-infringement under these claims and their definitions.
- ***Univ. Press v. Amazon.com*, 2001 U.S. Dist. LEXIS 26987 (N.D. Cal. Nov. 29, 2001).**
  The defendant filed a motion to dismiss based on the forum selection clause in the agreement. The court determined that the forum selection clause was valid, as the plaintiff failed to show that it would be unreasonable.
- ***Vantage Point Tech., Inc. v. Amazon.com, Inc.*, 2015 U.S. Dist. LEXIS 675 (E.D. Tex. Jan. 6, 2015).**
  This as a patent infringement case involving a number of manufacturers and suppliers of chipsets. The Court decided that the chipset manufacturers' cases will proceed to trial first. Amazon's motion to stay was denied.
- ***Vantage Point Tech., Inc. v. Amazon.com, Inc.*, 2015 U.S. Dist. LEXIS 8335 (E.D. Tex. Jan. 26, 2015).**
  The court decided what the terms in the patent meant for purposes of the claims, through claim construction.
- ***Vivo Per Lei, Inc. v. Bruchim* Case No. 11cv05169 GW (JCGx). C.D. Cal., March 20, 2012.**
  This case involved a proposed stipulated protective order to keep documents confidential in a case where defendants were accused of both copyright and trademark violations. The court found that Amazon would likely have had to provide information during discovery that would have been potentially harmful if it were made available to competitors. The court ultimately granted the protective order in order to keep the requested information confidential and required the parties to sign a non disclosure agreement.

- ***Voltstar Techs., Inc. v. Amazon.com, Inc.*, 2015 U.S. App. LEXIS 6008 (Fed. Cir. 2015).**
  Amazon.com was a defendant in this patent infringement case filed by Voltstar Tech. Amazon filed a motion for summary judgment and the court granted the motion finding that there were sufficient differences between the patented device created by Voltstar and the device used by Amazon.
- ***Walker Digital, LLC v. Facebook, Inc.*, 852 F. Supp. 2d 559 (D. Del. 2012).**
  This case involved a defendant's motion to dismiss for lack of standing. The court granted the defendants motion to dismiss.
- ***Wax v. Amazon Techs., Inc.*, 500 Fed. Appx. 944 (Fed. Cir. 2013).**
  The Court determined that because Amazon Technologies Inc. is the dominant component for the trademarks utilizing this term, there is a high degree of similarity between Amazon.com and the Plaintiff's desired mark, Amazon Ventures. This indicated a likelihood of confusion. The Court ruled in favor of Amazon Technologies, Inc. on the grounds that Mr. Wax's arguments lacked merit.
- **Wireless Recognition Tech. v. A9.com, Inc., 2012 U.S. Dist. LEXIS 130159 (N.D. Cal. Sept. 11, 2012).**
  While Amazon.com was a named defendant, the main issues of this case were whether or not the court should stay the action for the 474 Patent. The court considered all factors within the case and granted the defendant's motion for a stay of this case.

Privacy Violation

Amazon.com has found itself within litigation resulting from privacy violations. These issues often arise when an amazon seller has a product that allegedly violates someone's privacy. This can occur with the sale of books or photographs. In *Roe v. Amazon.com*, a couple's engagement photo was taken without permission and placed on the cover of an erotic book, which was then sold through the Amazon.com platform.[1] In this situation, Amazon successfully argued that it was not the publisher and not liable for the privacy violation.[2]

When a party finds a product on Amazon.com that they believe is in violation of their private rights, the issue is primarily with the sellers themselves, not Amazon. Therefore, because Amazon has no control over a third-party's unauthorized use of a product that violations a person's privacy, they are often dismissed from the case.

---

1. *Roe v. Amazon.com*, No. 3:15-cv-111, 2016 U.S. Dist. LEXIS 33297 (S.D. Ohio Mar. 15, 2016)
2. *Id.*

- ***Almeida v. Amazon.com, Inc.*, 456 F.3d 1316 (11th Cir. 2006).**
  Plaintiff's case against Amazon was dismissed as Amazon had no control of a third-party's unauthorized use of plaintiff's image.
- ***Bowens v. Aftermath Entm't*, 254 F. Supp. 2d 629 (E.D. Mich. 2003).**
  The court held that the Defendants' Motion to Dismiss is denied, as plaintiff has made a sufficient claim. Additionally, they grant Plaintiffs Motion to Leave to Amend the First Amended Complaint, as doing so would not be in bad faith and the Defendants have failed to show how it would be futile. Finally, the court denied the Motion for Sanctions, as

the Plaintiffs' claims are well founded and therefore there is no need for the court to sanction plaintiff.

- ***Bowens v. Aftermath Entm't*, 364 F. Supp. 2d 641 (E.D. Mich. 2005).**
  Plaintiffs' filed a case based on newly discovered evidence and the Defendants' filed a Motion for Summary Judgment on the basis of res judicata and issue preclusion. The court held that the state court determination precludes the Plaintiffs from re-litigating the issue before the court. Additionally, the court denied each parties motion for sanctions.
- ***Bowens v. Aftermath Entm't*, 711 N.W.2d 751 (Mich. 2006).**
  The court denied the application for leave to appeal the judgment because the court was not persuaded that the questions presented should be reviewed by the court.
- ***Bowens v. Ary*, 2009 Mich. App. LEXIS 2000 (Mich. Ct. App. Sept. 24, 2009).**
  The court here reversed an order of summary judgment that dismissed all claims against defendants. The court held that in order to establish a claim for eavesdropping the court must remand in order to determine whether plaintiff intended and reasonably expected that the conversation at issue was private.
- ***Bowens v. ARY, Inc.*, 489 Mich. 851, 794 N.W.2d 842, 2011 Mich. LEXIS 456 (Mich. 2011).**
  Here, the court reversed the ruling of the appellate court and reinstated summary judgment in favor of the defendants; the evidence showed that "no reasonable juror could conclude that plaintiffs had a reasonably expectation of privacy in the recorded conversation." *Id.*
- ***Curran v. Amazon.com, Inc.*, 2008 U.S. Dist. LEXIS 12479, 86 U.S.P.Q.2D (BNA) 1784, 36 Media L. Rep. 1641 (S.D. W. Va. Feb. 19, 2008).**
  A T-shirt producer's own website service agreement was insufficient to establish it as only an interactive computer service for Communications Decency Act of 1996. The court further found that immunity on a National Guardsman's claim of an invasion of the right of privacy in using his picture, taken in a combat zone; dismissal was not warranted.

- ***Vecchio v. Amazon.com, Inc.*, 2012 U.S. Dist. LEXIS 125399 (W.D. Wash. Sept. 4, 2012).**
  The court here was determining whether to grant defendants Motion for Protective Order. The court found that plaintiffs' request fell outside the time from allowed by the court to conduct discovery and thus granted the defendants motion for protective order.
- ***Roe v. Amazon.com*, 2016 U.S. Dist. LEXIS 33297 (S.D. Ohio Mar. 15, 2016).**
  This lawsuit was commenced following an incident where the plaintiffs' engagement photo was taken without their permission, and placed on the cover of an erotic book. The plaintiffs filed suit against the author of the book, and the publishers of the book, one of them being Amazon. Amazon, along with other defendants motioned for summary judgment. The court, found that Amazon.com was not a publisher, and granted the motion for summary judgment.
- ***Supnick v. Amazon.com, Inc.*, 2000 U.S. Dist. LEXIS 7073 (W.D. Wash. May 18, 2000).**
  Amazon.com was a defendant in this privacy violation suit brought by Supnick. Plaintiffs motioned for a federal class certification. The court concluded that because the class was maintainable under Rule 23, and that a class action was the best method for litigating the dispute, the plaintiff's motion was granted.
- ***Whitsitt v. Amazon.com*, 2014 U.S. Dist. LEXIS 29887 (E.D. Cal. Mar. 6, 2014).**
  The plaintiff alleged that he was hired as a temporary employee by defendant SMX Staffing Agency to perform services for defendant Amazon. Com. He asserted that he sought employment with defendant Amazon. Com as a direct hire/permanent employee but was not hired for such a position. Plaintiff alleged violation of employee's rights under the ADEA (Age Discrimination in Employment Act) and intentional invasion of privacy by defendant Amazon.com. The court recommended that this action be dismissed and ruled in favor of Amazon.com.

Procedure

Procedure is typically one of the most complex areas in the legal realm; procedural requirements play a vital role in any litigation and also give parties options to change the nature of the litigation in the form of motions or requests to the courts. Amazon's business is vast and many motions and procedural challenges are found in almost every case involving Amazon. Some of the most common motions found in Amazon litigation are motions to dismiss, motions for new venue, motions for summary judgment, and motions to stay judgment pending arbitration. The details of the types of cases involving procedure are found in their respective sections throughout the remainder of this book.

- ***Affinity Labs of Tex., LLC v. Amazon.com, Inc.*, 2015 U.S. Dist. LEXIS 77411 (W.D. Tex. June 12, 2015).**
  In this case, the court was deciding whether to grant Amazon's motion to dismiss based solely on the pleadings (early in the legal process). Here, plaintiff's claim that Amazon was infringing their patent for "wirelessly communicating selective information to an electronic device." The court granted the motion because the patent infringement claim would inhibit the "abstract idea" that made the technology possible from growing and developing.
- ***Alcatel-Lucent USA, Inc. v. Amazon.com, Inc.*, 2011 U.S. Dist. LEXIS 61039 (E.D. Tex. June 7, 2011).**
  The court here defined the disputed terms of the five patents that were in controversy.
- ***Almeida v. Amazon.com, Inc.*, 456 F.3d 1316 (11th Cir. 2006).**
  This case was an appeal to the district court decision that granted summary judgment in favor of defendant Amazon. Plaintiff claimed that Amazon's use of her image in furtherance of sale of a book on its website

violated her right of publicity and claimed invasion of privacy and theft as well. The court here affirmed the district court's decision because plaintiffs right of publicity claim based on Fla. Stat. § 540.08 would not withstand a motion to dismiss, it was unnecessary for the district court to determine whether the CDA preempts Almeida's state law right of publicity claim. As to the theft claim the court here held that plaintiff failed to present any evidence that Amazon misappropriated her image with actual knowledge that its use was unauthorized.

- ***Amazon.com, Inc. v. Barnesandnoble.com, Inc.*, 239 F.3d 1343 (Fed. Cir. 2001).**
  The Court vacated the lower court's preliminary injunction and remanded the case for further proceedings based on BarnesandNoble.com's ability to raise substantial questions as to the validity of the '411 patent, which was not considered in the lower court.
- ***Amazon.com, Inc. v. CITI Servs.*, 2008 U.S. Dist. LEXIS 94885 (D. Del. Nov. 21, 2008).**
  The Court here as deciding whether to grant the defendants Motion to Set Aside Default Order and Judgment. The court denied the motion because the plaintiff would be prejudiced if the judgment as lifted, the defendants were culpable, and the defendants did not have a meritorious defense.
- ***Amazon.com, Inc. v. Kalaydjian*, 2001 U.S. Dist. LEXIS 26376 (W.D. Wash. Mar. 27, 2001).**
  The court here as determining whether defendant purposefully availed itself to the Washington forum such that a motion to dismiss for lack of personal jurisdiction would not be possible. The court found that defendants' acts did not amount to purposeful availment because the website at issue only gave guidance on purchasing the tanning products, and did not offer them for sale via the internet. Thus the court granted defendants motion to dismiss for lack of personal jurisdiction.
- ***Amazon.com LLC v. Lay*, 758 F. Supp. 2d 1154 (W.D. Wash. 2010).**
  In this case Amazon was granted summary judgment on its claim. The court found the state department of revenue's request for Amazon's

sales to state of North Carolina residents violated the First Amendment because the departments request for information included names and specific literary music, and film purchase information and also that the department admitted that it had no legitimate need or use for the detailed information relating to the purchases.

- ***Amazon.Com v. Magee*, 2006 Nev. LEXIS 5 (Nev. Jan. 11, 2006).**
  The court reversed the lower court's denial of review of the petition, as Magee should not have been granted temporary total disability benefits as she was still able to earn a wage.
- ***Amazon.com, Inc. v. Nat'l Ass'n of College Stores, Inc.*, 826 F. Supp. 2d 1242 (W.D. Wash. 2011).**
  The court denied NACS's Motion to Dismiss as it determined the court did have jurisdiction over the claims and the case and the complaint was valid and presented a controversy.
- ***Amazon.com, Inc. v. Powers*, 2012 U.S. Dist. LEXIS 182831 (W.D. Wash. Dec. 27, 2012).**
  The court here was deciding whether it should grant Amazon's preliminary injunction against defendant past employee from disclosing trade secrets. The court granted in part and denies in part the injunction, holding that there as no evidence that defendant had or intended to recruit Amazon employees. The court also found it could not impose an injunction requiring defendant to return all amazon property because there was no evidence at all that he took anything from Amazon when he left. The court found that on the record Amazon was likely to succeed on the merits only if its clam was based on the Agreement's restriction on working with former customers.
- ***Amazon.Com, Inc. v. Underwriters, Lloyds's of London, et al, Defendants*:**
  Here, the court was determining whether to grant defendants motions to dismiss for lack of personal jurisdiction and for failing to properly serve defendants. The court denied both motions and held that personal jurisdiction was proper because defendants purposefully availed themselves to the state of Washington. Service was proper because it

complied with the Washington statute and defendants have admitted that they did in fact receive service.

- ***Apple Inc. v. Amazon.com Inc.,* et al. Case No. C11-1327 PJH (JSC). United States District Court for the Northern District of California, August 20, 2012.**

  This was a discovery case ordering the clarification by the defendant that the requested information to be sealed is confidential.

- ***Apple Inc. v. Amazon.com Inc.,* et al. Case No. C11-1327 PJH (JSC). United States District Court for the Northern District of California, August 23, 2012.**

  This was a discovery case granting plaintiff's motion to seal the file portions the defendant requested to be confidential.

- ***Apple Inc. v. Amazon.com, Inc.,* 2013 U.S. Dist. LEXIS 47124 (N.D. Cal. Apr. 1, 2013).**

  This was a discovery case ordering Apple to produce information from their testifying expert's assistants in limited depositions.

- ***Area 55, Inc. v. Amazon.com, Inc.,* 2012 U.S. Dist. LEXIS 191163 (S.D. Cal. May 3, 2012).**

  The court denied Amazon's motion for partial summary judgment as it found that there was a genuine issue of material fact when looking at the record in the light most favorable to the nonmoving party.

- ***Baghdasarian v. Amazon.com, Inc.,* 2009 U.S. Dist. LEXIS 115265 (C.D. Cal. Dec. 9, 2009).**

  The court here was determining whether it should grant defendant Amazon's motion for summary judgment where plaintiff claimed fraud for Amazon's shipping "holdback" fees. The court found that summary judgment was proper because plaintiff admitted in his own deposition that he chose to shop on Amazon.Com for price and security reasons, and thus did not rely on Amazon's shipping policy even if he was harmed by it.

- ***Baghdasarian v. Amazon.Com, Inc.,* 258 F.R.D. 383 (C.D. Cal. 2009).**

  Here, the court was deciding whether to grant plaintiff's motion for class certification The court ultimately granted plaintiff's motion. The court found that plaintiff had standing to bring his claim, and satisfied the requirements of Rule 23(a) for numerosity, commonality, typicality, and adequacy, as well as the rule 23(b) requirements of predominance and superiority.

- ***Baghdasarian v. Amazon.Com Inc.*, 458 F. App'x 622 (9th Cir. 2011).**
  Here, the court was determining on appeal whether the district court erred in granting summary judgment for plaintiff's reliance claims in favor of defendant Amazon.Com Inc. (Amazon), where plaintiff claims his decision to purchase books on the Amazon market place was based on total cost and security. The court affirmed the district court and found that because plaintiff testified that he made purchases based on comparative shopping to find the best price based on price and security, that he had not shown that he relied on Amazon's misrepresentation.
- ***Blagman v. Apple, Inc.*, 307 F.R.D. 107 (S.D.N.Y. 2015).**
  Mr. Blagman filed to amend his complaint for a third time to limit the scope of his class. Amazon contended that he was doing so in bad faith by using it as a tactical advantage and using false allegations. The court allowed plaintiff to submit a third amended complaint as it was not found to be requested in bad faith.
- ***Bookhouse of Stuyvesant Plaza, Inc. v. Amazon.com, Inc.*, 985 F. Supp. 2d 612 (S.D.N.Y. 2013).**
  This case involved an anti-trust claim against Amazon. Book publishers have brought suit because per Amazon's e-book platform, if a consumer owns a Kindle and wants to read an e-book on the Kindle that was published by any of the publishers in this action, they must buy the book from Amazon. The court granted the Defendants' Motion to Dismiss, as they determined that the plaintiff's complaint failed to state a plausible claim.
- ***Bovino v. Amazon.com, Inc.*, 2014 U.S. Dist. LEXIS 32016 (D. Colo. Mar. 12, 2014).**
  Bovino filed a motion to amend his complaint to include an additional 100 products that Amazon allegedly infringed. The court

granted this motion as it found no bad faith argument against this amendment and found Amazon's arguments to be without merit and therefore, invalid.

- ***Bovino v. Amazon.com, Inc.*, 2015 U.S. Dist. LEXIS 71772 (D. Colo. June 1, 2015).**
  Amazon filed a Motion for Summary Judgment claiming that they did not infringe the patent as a result of the patent's meaning and that the patent was invalid. The court granted the Motion for Summary Judgment as Mr. Bovino did not adequately show a claim that the products infringed on the patent.
- ***Bovino v. Amazon.com, Inc.*, 2016 U.S. Dist. LEXIS 32368 (D. Colo. Mar. 14, 2016).**
  Amazon filed a Motion for Attorney's Fees and Mr. Bovino filed a Motion to Enforce Settlement Agreement. The court held that the Motion for Attorney's Fees was denied, as the case did not rise to the "exceptional" level required. Additionally, the court could not enforce a settlement agreement, after a judgment by a court had already been entered.
- ***Bowens v. Aftermath Entm't*, 364 F. Supp. 2d 641 (E.D. Mich. 2005).**
  Plaintiffs' filed a case based on newly discovered evidence and the Defendants' filed a Motion for Summary Judgment on the basis of res judicata and issue preclusion. The court held that the state court determination precluded the Plaintiffs from re-litigating the issue before the court. Additionally, the court denied each parties motion for sanctions.
- ***Bowens v. Aftermath Entm't*, 711 N.W.2d 751 (Mich. 2006).**
  The court denied the application for leave to appeal the judgment because the court was not persuaded that the questions presented should be reviewed by the court.
- ***Bowens v. ARY, Inc.*, 489 Mich. 851, 794 N.W.2d 842, 2011 Mich. LEXIS 456 (Mich. 2011).**
  The court here denied motion for reconsideration because it did not appear that the order was entered erroneously.

- **Brickey v. Amazon.com, Inc., 2014 U.S. Dist. LEXIS 9297, 2014 WL 297979 (W.D. Tex. Jan. 27, 2014).**
  The court was determining whether to grant defendants motion to dismiss for failure to state a claim, where plaintiff is seeking punitive damages under the Copyright Act. The court found that both the Copyright Act and the case law that interprets it do not indicate that congress intended to authorize punitive damages and thus the claim was not "plausible on its face." The court granted the motion to dismiss.
- ***Brickey v. Amazon.com,* Inc., 2014 U.S. Dist. LEXIS 22304 (W.D. Tex. Feb. 21, 2014).**
  Here, the court was determining whether plaintiff provided sufficient evidence of copyright infringement to establish that no genuine issue of material fact existed and that he was entitled to judgment as a matter of law. The court found that there was an issue of material fact as to whether any copyright infringement actually occurred here. The court thus denied the motion for summary judgment.
- ***Brickey v. Amazon.com, Inc.,* 2014 U.S. Dist. LEXIS 97479, 2014 WL 3566566 (W.D. Tex. July 18, 2014).**
  The court here was determining whether actionable copying occurred here in the form of unauthorized sales of plaintiff's CD, such that defendants motion for summary judgment would be proper. The court found that no actionable copying took place because under the "first sale doctrine," Amazon was the rightful owner of the CD and thus had the right to sell it. The court also found that plaintiff did not allege any facts to show sales that would not be subject to the "first sale doctrine." Defendants motion for summary judgment was granted.
- ***Brown-Younger v. Lulu.com,* 2012 U.S. Dist. LEXIS 91574, 2012 WL 2576214 (N.D. Ill. July 3, 2012).**
  In this case plaintiff claimed copyright violation and falsely joined Amazon.com Inc. as a defendant despite the fact that Amazon.com Inc. never sold nor listed the copyrighted material. The court held that the appellate court may re-evaluate the sufficiency of plaintiff's claim

because the previous litigation revealed that she stated false claims and thus would not qualify as an in forma pauperis plaintiff.

- ***Carlin v. Bezos*, 2016 U.S. App. LEXIS 9372 (3d Cir. Pa. May 23, 2016).**
  The court affirmed the lower court's decision to grant defendant's motion for summary judgment as plaintiff failed to provide evidence sufficient to state a claim for copyright infringement.
- ***Chambers v. Amazon.com Inc.*, 632 Fed. Appx. 742 (4th Cir. S.C. 2015).**
  This case was an appeal to the grant of summary judgment dismissing plaintiffs claim. The court here affirmed the summary judgment because plaintiff's claim failed to provide factual support for the legal conclusions in his complaint.
- ***Chambers v. Amazon.com Inc.*, 2015 U.S. Dist. LEXIS 85367 (D.S.C. July 1, 2015).**
  The court here followed the Magistrate's recommendation that a motion to dismiss Amazon from a copyright infringement claim for failure to state a sufficient claim by plaintiff be granted. Here, Amazon was accused of copyright violations, however the complaint made conclusory statements with no factual support. This failed to meet the legal standards of a sufficient complaint and thus the motion was granted.
- ***Clark v. Amazon.com*, 2007 U.S. Dist. LEXIS 28896 (E.D. Cal. Apr. 19, 2007).**
  Here, Plaintiff's claim was recommended to a magistrate judge who issued a recommendation to deny plaintiffs motion to dismiss. The magistrate recommendation contained notice that any objections to the recommendation be filed within 10 days. Here, plaintiff had filed objections to the recommendation. The court was thus determining whether to adopt the recommendation of the magistrate. The court held that the recommendation was supported by the record and the magistrate's analysis. The court ordered full adoption of the recommendation and a denial of the plaintiff's motion to dismiss.

- **Clark v. Amazon.com, 2007 U.S. Dist. LEXIS 19679 (E.D. Cal. Mar. 20, 2007).**
  The court here was determining whether to recommend granting plaintiff's motion to dismiss. The court found that because defendants had a pending motion for summary judgment and subsequently plaintiff's filed a counter motion for summary judgment, that plaintiff's motion for dismissal be denied. The court recommended that plaintiffs' notice, that was construed as a motion to dismiss, should be denied.
- ***Clouding IP, LLC v. amazon.com, Inc.*****, 2013 U.S. Dist. LEXIS 73655 (D. Del. May 24, 2013).**
  Clouding IP filed suit against Amazon.com for patent infringement. The court addressed the issue of Direct Infringement, Induced Infringement, Willful Infringement, and a motion for a more definite statement. The United State District Court held that the Direct Infringement Claims were sufficient; the Induced Infringement claims should be dismissed; the Willful Infringement claims were sufficient, and the motion for a more definite statement should be denied.
- ***Content Guard Holdings, Inc. v. Amazon.com, Inc.*****, 2015 U.S. Dist. LEXIS 33881 (E.D. Tex. Mar. 19, 2015).**
  Amazon, along with other named defendants, found that joinder was improper in this case and motioned to sever pursuant to Rule 21 of the Federal Rules of Civil Procedure. The court denied all motions to sever finding that the parties were properly joined because there were common questions of fact; there were actual links between those facts; and that the "same transaction, occurrence, or series of transactions or occurrences" was accused.
- ***Content Guard Holdings, Inc. v. Amazon.com, Inc.*****, 2015 U.S. Dist. LEXIS 39807 (E.D. Tex. Mar. 29, 2015).**
  Amazon.com was a named defendant in this patent infringement suit, in this case the court defined disputed terms of the patent at issue in a claim construction proceeding.

- ***ContentGuard Holdings, Inc. v. Amazon.com, Inc.*, 2015 U.S. Dist. LEXIS 109743 (E.D. Tex. Aug. 19, 2015).**
  ContentGuard Holdings filed seven motions to exclude portions of testimony during their suit against Amazon and other named defendants for patent infringement. Amazon.com along with defendant Google, Inc. filed motions to strike. The court granted some motions, and denied others. The decisions of what testimony to exclude were based on their relevance to the case.
- ***ContentGuard Holdings, Inc. v. Amazon.com, Inc.*, 2015 U.S. Dist. LEXIS 139947 (E.D. Tex. Oct. 14, 2015).**
  While Amazon.com is a named defendant within the suit, the document at hand involves other named defendant, Apple's request of a continuance of the trial date until after the completion of post-trial briefing. The court denied this motion.
- ***Deuss v. Siso*, 2014 U.S. Dist. LEXIS 121464 (N.D. Cal. Aug. 29, 2014).**
  Duess filed a motion to subpoena Siso's records, including her Amazon account information. Amazon gave a 6-page document of her records. Siso then filed a motion to quash these subpoenas and a motion for sanctions, both of which were granted by the court.
- **Device Enhancement LLC v. Amazon.com, Inc., 2016 U.S. Dist. LEXIS 64600 (D. Del. May 17, 2016).**
  The court here was determining whether to grant defendants motion to dismiss a claim for patent infringement. The court granted the motion because it found that the patent claimed methods comprising of nothing more specific than the underlying idea itself.
- ***Dobias-Davis v. Amazon.com.kydc, LLC*, 2016 U.S. Dist. LEXIS 3396 (E.D. Va. Jan. 11, 2016).**
  Dobias-Davis was suing Hoffman, her supervisor, and Amazon, her employer, for defamation and retaliation claims under Title VII and the ADEA. Amazon filed a motion to dismiss the claims, which was granted in part in relation to retaliation, as the court determined it did not have enough factual information to dismiss and denied in part in relation to

the defamation claim, as it determined she did not participate in the protected activity.

- ***Droplets, Inc. v. Amazon.com, Inc.*, 2012 U.S. Dist. LEXIS 122978 (E.D. Tex. June 27, 2012).**
  The court here was determining whether to grant defendants motion to transfer venue where the majority of relevant documents and defendants' headquarters are located in the District of Northern California. The court found that the location of sources of proof, availability of compulsory process, the convenience for witnesses, and the local interest factors all favored transfer, and granted the motion.
- ***Gibson v. Amazon.com* Case No. 3-13-1136. United States District Court, M.D. Tennessee, Nashville Division, October 29, 2013.**
  This case involved the court ordered the parties to meet before their scheduled case management conference. The court orders the counsel to e-file the proposed order prior to the initial case management conference and bring their calendars and take into account everyone's schedule in determining a date for the case.
- ***Golden Bridge Tech., Inc. v. Apple Inc.*, 937 F. Supp. 2d 490 (D. Del. 2013).**
  The court set forth an interpretation of the claim language in the patents provided for the cases and denied collateral estoppel from the previous Texas court decision.
- ***Guardian Media Techs., Ltd. v. Amazon.com, Inc.*, No. CV 13-8369 PSG (PLAx), 2013 U.S. Dist. LEXIS 171254 (C.D. Cal. Dec. 3, 2013).**
  The court here was determining whether defendants were improperly joined where it is alleged that defendants conduct was part of the same transaction or occurrence. The court held that joinder was improper as to all defendants except Amazon.com, Inc. because there was no indication that the defendants acted in concert or were connected in any way.
- ***Hamilton v. Amazon.com, Inc.*, 2002-Ohio-7377 (Ohio Ct. App., Montgomery County Dec. 31, 2002).**
  The court here, was determining whether the court could recognize plaintiff's claim on appeal where he has failed to comply with Civ. R.

53(E)(3)(b). The court held that because plaintiff failed to comply with the rules of civil procedure by objecting to the magistrate's report, that the errors he assigned on appeal were not cognizable by the court.

- ***Hickman v. Amazon Fullfilment*, 2015 U.S. Dist. LEXIS 168782 (W.D. Pa. Dec. 17, 2015).**
  The court granted the defendant's motion to dismiss as the complaint provided by the plaintiffs had failed to state a claim.
- ***Hickman v. Amazon Fullfilment*, 2016 U.S. Dist. LEXIS 45937 (W.D. Pa. Apr. 5, 2016).**
  The court granted the defendant's motion to dismiss as the complaint provided by the plaintiffs had failed to state a claim. Additionally, the court did not grant leave to amend as it determined plaintiff had been awarded enough opportunities to do so.
- ***Higgins ex rel. Underwriters at Lloyd's v. Amazon.com, Inc.*, 2002 U.S. Dist. LEXIS 23670 (S.D.N.Y. Dec. 4, 2002).**
  The court granted the motion to transfer to the Western District of Washington, as it was more convenient and in the interests of justice.
- ***Hinton v. Amazon.com.DEDC, LLC*, 72 F. Supp. 3d 685 (S.D. Miss. 2014).**
  While Amazon.com Inc. is a named defendant in this case; the document at hand dealt specifically with defendant, eBay's motion to dismiss. The Court granted eBay's motion to dismiss.
- **Hinton v. Dick's Sporting Goods, Inc., 2014 U.S. Dist. LEXIS 24426 (S.D. Miss. Feb. 26, 2014).**
  The court granted the Motion for Additional Time to Respond to the Motion for Sanctions and Motion for Summary Judgment as it was with good cause and was filed in a timely manner.
- ***Hinton v. Dick's Sporting Goods, Inc.*, 2014 U.S. Dist. LEXIS 137243 (S.D. Miss. Sept. 29, 2014).**
  The court denied the Plaintiff's Motion to Strike and Motion in Limine, as it determined it will simply not consider the Report Plaintiff intended to strike and the Motion in Limine was done prematurely. The court granted her Motion for Permission to File Surrebuttal Brief as it

determined that the court could consider the competing arguments and position in the Motion for Summary Judgment filed by the other defendants.

- ***Hobbs v. Rui Zhao*, 2014 U.S. Dist. LEXIS 161533 (N.D. Okla. Nov. 17, 2014).**

  The court denied the Plaintiff's Motion to Amend his Complaint to add two more defendants, as the deadline has passed and he had not shown why he did not add these defendants at a prior time. Therefore, the court was lead to believe that he did so in bad faith, and therefore did not allow this amendment.
- ***Hobbs v. Rui Zhao*, 2015 U.S. Dist. LEXIS 11762 (N.D. Okla. Feb. 2, 2015).**

  The court granted summary judgment to Amazon in relation to the negligent entrustment claim, as Plaintiff failed to prove that the cargo was a dangerous instrumentality and that Amazon owed Plaintiff a duty of care. Additionally, summary judgment was granted to the negligent hiring claim, as Amazon did not select Zhao to perform the task. Amazon was dismissed from the case.
- ***Huong Hoang v. Amazon.com, Inc.*, 2012 U.S. Dist. LEXIS 191386 (W.D. Wash. July 2, 2012).**

  The court here was determining whether it should grant defendants motion to dismiss plaintiff's fraud claims. The court found that plaintiff failed to allege the circumstances of fraud with particularity as required by the federal rules and also did not state the elements of a fraud claim under Washington law. Thus the court dismissed plaintiff's fraud claim.
- ***H-W Tech., L.C v. Amazon.com, Inc.*, 2013 U.S. Dist. LEXIS 87043 (N.D. Tex. June 20, 2013).**

  The court here was issuing an order stating that it agrees with the findings, conclusions and recommendation of the Magistrate Judge. The court, based on the magistrates reasoning, denied the defendants renewed motion to dismiss.

- **H-W Tech., L.C. v. Amazon.Com, Inc., 2012 U.S. Dist. LEXIS 121273 (N.D. Tex. Aug. 27, 2012).**
  This case is the courts order accepting the magistrate findings and recommendation as to defendant Google Inc.'s motion to strike supplemental infringement contentions and corrected memorandum in support, are correct and they are accepted as the findings and conclusions of the court. The court granted googles motion to strike in part and denied it in part.
- ***In re Amazon.com, Inc.*, 2014 U.S. Dist. LEXIS 100716 (W.D. Ky. July 23, 2014).**
  This was a multidistrict class action that consolidated several proceedings brought by Amazon.com fulfillment center employees. The court found that "a blanket equitable tolling of all current and prospective opt-in plaintiffs was unjustified and premature". The court denied the plaintiff's motion for an equitable tolling.
- ***In re Amazon.com, Inc.*, 2016 U.S. Dist. LEXIS 48650 (W.D. Ky. Mar. 30, 2016)**
  This case dealt specifically with the court deciding whether the Supreme Court's ruling in Integrity Staffing Solutions, Inc. v. Busk, 135 S. Ct. 513 (2014) also resolved their state law claims. The court found that it did and granted a judgment on the pleadings in favor of the defendants.
- ***In re Grand Jury Subpoena to Amazon.com* dated Aug. 7, 2006, 246 F.R.D. 570 (W.D. Wis. 2007).**
  The court here was determining whether the grand jury decision to withdraw the subpoena to Amazon.com was proper. The court held that a grand jury does not need court permission to withdraw a subpoena. The court held that although the court granted a motion to quash the subpoena, that the grand jury withdrawal is still proper because it was a "logical and prudent" decision under the circumstances.
- ***In re Grand Jury Subpoena (Amazon.com)*, 246 F.R.D. 570 (W.D. Wis. 2007).**
  The court here was determining whether it should grant defendant Amazon.Com's motion to quash part of a subpoena requesting

information regarding the identifying the customers who purchased books from a certain seller who was under criminal investigation. The court ultimately held that finding volunteer witnesses from the pool of customers who bought books from the seller would be the best way to satisfy the governments needs without violating first amendment rights of the customers. Amazon would send letters that would allow any used book buyer who chose to cooperate with the investigation to contact the government and arrange an interview.

- ***In re Grand Jury Subpoena to Amazon.com, Inc.*, 246 F.R.D. 570 (W.D. Wis. 2007):** The court here was determining whether it should grant defendants motion to unseal the record of the subpoena dispute between Amazon and the Grand Jury where there has been an indictment against the criminal seller of used books on Amazon.Com. The court granted the motion to unseal because it found that since the grand jury removed the challenged sections of its subpoena, that the court's sealed orders did not result in the production of any evidence to the grand jury. Thus, unsealing the orders would not disclose any information obtained and used as part of the investigation.
- ***In Re Zappos.com Inc.* Case No. 3:12-CV-003250-RCJ-VCP. United States District Court District of Nevada, September 2012.**
  While Amazon was a named defendant in this suit involving a security breach, the document at hand dealt specifically with defendant Zappos.com's motion to compel arbitration. The court denied the motion to compel arbitration and stay action.
- ***In re Zappos.Com, Inc.* Case No. 3:12-CV-00325-RCJ-VPC. United States District Court District of Nevada, June 2015.**
  Amazon.com and Zappos.com were defendant's in a suit brought by Zappos customers following a security breach on the Zappos website. This case was a motion to dismiss filed by Amazon.com; a motion to strike Prayers for Punitive Damages and Restitution, and a motion for leave to file excess pages filed by Zappos. The court here specifically mentions Zappos' motions and granted the motion to dismiss and denied the motion to strike.

- ***Innovative Office Prods. v. Amazon.com, Inc.*, 2012 U.S. Dist. LEXIS 59090 (E.D. Pa. Apr. 26, 2012).**
  This was a patent infringement case brought by Innovative Office Productions against Amazon.com. among other defendants. Plaintiffs voluntarily dismissed most of the defendants, Amazon.com included. This case dealt specifically with the remaining defendants.
- ***Int'l Game Tech., Inc. v. Second Judicial Dist. Court*, 122 Nev. 132 (Nev. 2006).**
  In this case the court was determining whether the District Court (lower court) abused its discretion by improperly refusing to dismiss defendants action. The court held that the motions should be granted and discretion was abused by the lower court because no party demonstrated that the Attorney General acted improperly in moving to dismiss the underlying actions; therefore, the district courts manifestly abused their discretion when they refused to dismiss the underlying tax-based false claims actions for good cause.
- ***Kabbaj v. Google, Inc.*, 2014 U.S. Dist. LEXIS 47425 (D. Del. Apr. 7, 2014).**
  In this case, the court was deciding whether to grant defendants motion to dismiss where defendants, including Amazon had hosted defamatory content about plaintiff created by a third party. Ultimately the court found the amended complaint did not state, nor would it ever be able to state, any viable claims against defendants with respect to their decision to publish third party statements. The defendants motion to dismiss was granted.
- ***Koeckritz v. Amazon.com Inc.*, 2013 U.S. Dist. LEXIS 47776 (W.D. Wash. Apr. 2, 2013).**
  This was specifically an order by the United States District Court Judge. While Amazon.com is a named defendant, this document relatd to the plaintiff's motion to appoint counsel. The motion was denied.
- ***Lexington Luminance LLC v. Amazon.com Inc.*, 601 Fed. Appx. 963 (Fed. Cir. 2015).**
  Lexington sued Amazon.com and Amazon Digital Services alleging that the Kindle e-readers created by amazon were in violation of patent

infringement of the 851 patent. This was an appeal from the United States District Court judgment in favor of Amazon.com. The Court of Appeals now reviewed the judgment and found that the district court erred in construing the claim and in holding the claim indefinite. The court remanded for further proceedings.

- ***Lexington Luminance LLC v. Amazon Digital Servs.,* 2016 U.S. Dist. LEXIS 46023 (D. Mass. Apr. 4, 2016).**

  The court determined claim construction for the patents in suit by defining them in a way that most naturally aligns with the patent's description.

- ***Masck v. Sports Illustrated,* 2013 U.S. Dist. LEXIS 81677 (E.D. Mich. June 11, 2013).**

  In this case, plaintiff took an iconic photo of Defendant Desmond Howard on November 23, 1991 at Michigan Stadium. Plaintiff found out that the image was being used by multiple defendants as well as in product listings on the Amazon platform. The court determined that the vicarious infringement claim must be dismissed for lack of factual allegation, while the contributory infringement claim survived dismissal, as Amazon was well aware of potential infringement. Plaintiff only stated that Amazon had the right and ability to supervise the content of its website Amazon.com. This did not meet the pleading requirement as there are no factual allegations from which it may determine that Amazon had the ability to supervise the infringing conduct. The product in question was not Amazon's website but the merchandise sold on its website. However, Amazon was well aware of the potential infringement because plaintiff requested the products be removed from Amazon's website.

- ***Masck v. Sports Illustrated,* 5 F.Supp.3d 881 (E.D. Mich., 2014).**

  In this case, plaintiff took an iconic photo of Defendant Desmond Howard on November 23, 1991 at Michigan Stadium. Plaintiff found out that the image was being used by multiple defendants as well as in product listings on the Amazon platform. The court here was determining whether to grant defendants' motion for summary judgment where plaintiff has waited to register the copyright until after several violations of the copyright occurred. With respect to claims against Amazon.com the motion was denied because questions of fact remain that needed to be determined by a court of law / jury.

- ***McGee v. Amazon.com*, 2013 Del. Super. LEXIS 33 (Del. Super. Ct. Jan. 31, 2013).**
  The court determined that the decision of UIAB should be affirmed as Amazon had substantial evidence to show that violation of the company policy should constitute denial of worker's compensation benefits. As an employee was on notice that he needed to improve his attendance record or risk losing his job, and as the employee received a third warning within a 12-month period in violation the employer's policy, the employee was terminated for just cause; thus, he was not entitled to unemployment benefits under Del. Code Ann. tit. 19, § 3314(2).
- ***M-Edge Accessories LLC v. Amazon.Com Inc.*, 2013 U.S. Dist. LEXIS 311 (D. Md. Jan. 2, 2013).**
  The court denied the Defendant's Motion to Dismiss, as it determined the plaintiff's complaint contained enough factual allegations to support the claims.
- ***Mobile Telcoms. Techs., LLC v. Amazon.com, Inc.*, 2014 U.S. Dist. LEXIS 138786 (E.D. Tex. Aug. 26, 2014).**
  Amazon.com was a defendant in this patent infringement case brought by Mobile Telecommunications. Amazon.com motioned to dismiss the claims. The United States District Court denied the defendant's motion to dismiss because they found the claims brought by plaintiff, Mobile Telecommunications were sufficient to state a cause of action
- ***Mobile Telecomms. Techs., LLC v. Amazon.com, Inc.*, 2014 U.S. Dist. LEXIS 137542 (E.D. Tex. Sept. 29, 2014).**
  This was a report filed by a Magistrate Judge on August 26, 2014. The Magistrate Judge recommended the denial of Amazon's motion to dismiss Mobile Telecommunication's Indirect and Willful Infringement Claims. The motion was denied.

- ***Nazomi Communs., Inc. v. Nokia Corp.*, 2013 U.S. Dist. LEXIS 85618 (N.D. Cal. June 18, 2013).**
  The court granted the motion for judgment on the pleadings, as Nazomi failed to show specific facts that supported their allegations.
- ***Nazomi Communs., Inc. v. Microsoft Mobile Oy*, 597 Fed. Appx. 1075 (Fed. Cir. 2014).**
  The court affirmed the lower court's order for summary judgment for the defendants, as it did not find Nazomi's arguments persuasive enough to overturn the decision.
- ***Nomura v. YouTube, LLC*, 2012 U.S. Dist. LEXIS 174332 (N.D. Cal. Dec. 7, 2012).**
  The court found that the new evidence and modifications do not unfairly prejudice Nomura and therefore denied the plaintiff's motion to strike the modifications and not admit the new evidence.
- ***Nomura v. YouTube, LLC*, 2013 U.S. Dist. LEXIS 18292 (N.D. Cal. Feb. 8, 2013).**
  The court determined the meaning of the patent terms that were disputed in the claim of patent infringement.
- ***Nomura v. Amazon.Com, Inc.*, 2013 U.S. Dist. LEXIS 122895 (N.D. Cal. Aug. 28, 2013).**
  The court determined that the documents Amazon requested to be sealed did not contain privileged information or trade secrets and therefore was not entitled to protection under the law and therefore denied the motion to seal.
- ***OIP Techs., Inc. v. Amazon.com, Inc.*, 788 F.3d 1359 (Fed. Cir. 2015).**
  In this case, the court granted the parties' joint motion to stay pending its final disposition of CLS Bank International. The parties were directed to inform the court within 14 days of the issuance of the mandate in CLS Bank International how they believed this appeal should proceed.
- ***Olympic Devs. AG, LLC v. Barnesandnoble.com LLC* (N.D. Cal., 2011).**
  The court here was ruling on the parties' stipulation to stay (temporarily postpone) the proceedings pending re-examination of the patent at

issue in this claim. The court held that this action was stayed in its entirety pending completion of the reexamination of the patent at issue.

- ***Okocha v. Amazon.com*, 153 Fed. Appx. 849 (3d Cir. N.J. 2005).**
  Plaintiff, Okocha, was an author who appealed the order of the lower court that granted summary judgment in favor of Amazon.com in suit for copyright infringement, conspiracy, fraud, negligent/intentional infliction of emotional harm, and loss of future wages claims. The court of appeals affirmed the district court's order and denied the plaintiff's motion to expedite. Additionally, the court granted the plaintiff's motion to file supplementary proof and a supplemental appendix.
- ***Parallel Iron LLC v. Acknowledge Inc.* (D. Del., 2012).**
  The court was deciding whether to grant defendant EMC Corporation's motion for attorney's fees where plaintiff had wrongfully brought suit due to a terminal disclaimer. The court denied the motion for attorney's fees, holding that plaintiff did not act in bad faith by bringing suit because an honest mistake was made in violating the terminal disclaimer.
- ***PersonalWeb Techs., LLC v. NEC Corp. of Am.*, 2013 U.S. Dist. LEXIS 110046 (E.D. Tex. Aug. 5, 2013).**
  The court determined the claim language of the patent and determined what each term shall mean for the duration of the case. Additionally, the court denied Facebook's Motion for Summary Judgment and HP's Motion for Summary Judgment for Indefiniteness.
- ***Personalized Media Communs., LLC v. Amazon.com, Inc.*, 2015 U.S. Dist. LEXIS 104369 (D. Del. Aug. 10, 2015).**
  The court granted the Defendant's Motion for Judgment on the Pleadings, as none of the claims stated were eligible patent claims.
- ***Phila. Contributionship Ins. Co. v. Neoteric Solutions,* Inc., 2016 U.S. Dist. LEXIS 23673 (D.N.J. Feb. 24, 2016).**
  The court in this case, was making a recommendation as to whether to grant third party defendants' motion to dismiss. The magistrate recommended that the motion should not be granted because plaintiffs claims

raise the possibility that defendant's products were sold in New Jersey which would subject defendants to personal jurisdiction there.

- ***Piao Shang Indus. Co. v. Acco Brands Corp.*, 2011 U.S. Dist. LEXIS 67417 (C.D. Cal. June 23, 2011).**
  In this case the court was determining whether to allow plaintiff's claim to move forward where it does not appear that plaintiff's claim against defendants arose out of the same transaction or occurrence. The court held that it as not clear that plaintiff's claims against defendants arose out of the same transaction or occurrence because each defendant sold a different device allegedly infringing on the patented invention. The court ordered plaintiff to show cause in writing why one or more parties should not be dropped from this case for improper joinder. The plaintiff, alternatively, may file separate actions against each of the defendants.
- ***Power Play Mktg. Group v. Treasure Transp., Inc.*, 2014 U.S. Dist. LEXIS 93597 (D.S.D. July 10, 2014).**
  In this case plaintiff moved for default judgment because some of the defendants have not responded. The court denied the plaintiff's motion for default judgment.
- ***Pragmatus Mobile, LLC v. Amazon.Com, Inc.*, 2015 U.S. Dist. LEXIS 82256 (D. Del. June 17, 2015).**
  The court determined that the Motion to Stay Litigation was done as a tactical attempt by the defendants and therefore denied the motion.
- ***Premium Prods. v. Pro Performance Sports, LLC*, 997 F. Supp. 2d 433 (E.D. Va. 2014).**
  The court affirmed the disqualification of Spiegel as the attorney for Premium as it would violate Virginia's witness-advocate rule. The court determined that Spiegel would be a necessary witness and the magistrate did not rule contrary to law or erroneously.
- ***Pullins v. Amazon.com.indc*, LLC, 2015 U.S. Dist. LEXIS 137272 (S.D. Ind. Oct. 8, 2015).**
  Pullins alleged that Amazon had discriminated against him when he was terminated from employment for not meeting industry standards.

Amazon was able to prove that he repeatedly failed to meet the standards when he received three warnings, and was even retrained. Therefore, the court granted summary judgment to Amazon, as Pullins failed to establish that Amazon had unreasonably discriminated against him.

- ***Raya v. Amazon.com, LLC*, 2015 U.S. Dist. LEXIS 86006 (N.D. Cal. June 30, 2015).**
  Raya filed a Motion to Remand in order to have the case heard in state court. However, the court denied this motion, as the amount in controversy exceeded the jurisdictional threshold and the case belonged in federal court.
- ***Raya v. Amazon.com, LLC*, 2015 U.S. Dist. LEXIS 85997 (N.D. Cal. July 1, 2015).**
  The court denied Amazon's motion to dismiss or stay as it determined that the cases are substantially dissimilar and do not meet the first-to-file requirements necessary.
- ***Red Pine Point LLC v. Amazon.Com, Inc.* Case No. 14C 00274; 14C 00290. United States District Court Northern District of Illinois Eastern Division, July 2014.**
  The court determined the motion to transfer was reasonable and granted to have all consolidated and related cases transferred to the Northern District of California.
- ***Robbins v. Unemployment Ins. Appeals Bd.*, 2016 Del. Super. LEXIS 31 (Del. Super. Ct. Jan. 25, 2016).**
  Robbins sought unemployment compensation from Amazon after termination of his employment. Robbins did not provide a doctor's note when he returned to work from a previous injury and subsequently left because he felt unable to perform. The Unemployment Insurance Appeals Board determined that Robins was not entitle to unemployment compensation benefits because he voluntarily quit without good cause. The court determined that the decision of the Board should be affirmed as Robbins did not meet his burden to show that he left Amazon with good cause.

- ***Rosner v Amazon.com*, 132 A.D.3d 835 (N.Y. App. Div. 2d Dep't 2015).**
The court affirmed the lower court's decision to dismiss the amended complaint, as the plaintiff failed to meet the elements of a defamation claim.
- ***Routt v. Amazon.com, Inc.*, 2012 U.S. Dist. LEXIS 170602, 105 U.S.P.Q.2D (BNA) 1089, Copy. L. Rep. (CCH) P30,334 (W.D. Wash. Nov. 30, 2012).**
In this case, plaintiff claimed that Amazon violated her copyrights in certain photographs because certain Amazon Associate websites displayed her photographs without her permission. The court found Amazon was not responsible for the alleged violation committed by a third-party, and could not be vicariously liable as it had no control over the third-party's activities.
- ***Schnall v. AT&T Wireless Servs., Inc.*, 2010 Wash. LEXIS 61 (Wash. 2010).**
This case dealt specifically with a class action against AT&T wireless for billing practices. The plaintiffs sought a nationwide class certification, which was denied. The Court of appeals reversed. The Supreme Court affirmed in part and denied in part.
- ***Schnall v. AT&T Wireless Servs., Inc.*, 171 Wn.2d 260 (Wash. 2011).**
This case dealt specifically with a class action against AT&T wireless for billing practices. The plaintiffs sought a nationwide class certification, which was denied. The Court of appeals reversed and the Supreme Court affirmed in part and denied in part.
- ***Script Sec. Solutions L.L.C. v. Amazon.com, Inc.*, 2016 U.S. Dist. LEXIS 34259 (E.D. Tex. Mar. 16, 2016).**
The court here is determining whether to grand defendants motions to dismiss for improper venue and for insufficient pleading of indirect infringement and willfulness. The court denied the motions because the definition of "resides" found in 28 U.S.C § 1391 also applied to § 1400, and because plaintiff had pleaded sufficient facts to satisfy claims for both indirect infringement and willfulness.

- ***Segal Co. (Eastern States), Inc. v. Amazon.Com,* 280 F. Supp2d (W.D. Wash., 2003).**
  The court here was deciding whether to grant defendants motions to dismiss because plaintiff's claims failed to plead facts sufficient to state a cause of action. The court held that that in this case, plaintiff failed to specify the identities of the alleged fraud perpetrators, the time and place the fraudulent statements were made, and exactly what statements were fraudulent. Therefore, the complaint did not state the circumstances of fraud with sufficient particularity to satisfy the requirements of Rule 9(b).
- ***Segal v. Amazon.com, Inc.,* 2011 U.S. Dist. LEXIS 29183 (W.D. Wash. Mar. 7, 2011).**
  The court here was deciding whether to grant plaintiffs motion to stay (temporarily delay) this case pending resolution of their petition for a writ of mandamus to the Eleventh Circuit Court of Appeals. The court denied the motion because there was no likely success for appellants, there would be no irreparable harm absent a stay, and a stay would prejudice Amazon.
- ***Shulman v. Amazon.com.kydc, LLC, 2015* U.S. Dist. LEXIS 51291 (E.D. Ky. Apr. 20, 2015).**
  The court granted Defendants' Motion to Dismiss, as Shulman failed to state a claim in his complaint for the alleged discrimination.
- ***Shulman v. Amazon,* 2014 U.S. Dist. LEXIS 113506 (E.D. Ky. Aug. 15, 2014).**
  The defendants' Motion for Sanctions was denied for lack of evidence of plaintiff's reckless conduct or intent to thwart the proceedings.
- ***Site Update Solutions, LLC v. Accor North America, Inc.,* 2013 U.S. Dist. LEXIS 72765 (N.D. Cal. May 21, 2013).**
  The court here was determining whether to grant defendant Newegg's motion to declare case exceptional and for an award of attorney's fees. The court conducted a "meta-analysis" of the parties' claim construction positions, as well as their other positions in this case and found that the case was not exceptional and so did not warrant an award of attorneys'

fees to Newegg. Plaintiff may have been on the losing side of several arguments, but losing is not sufficient for a finding of objective baselessness and subjective bad faith.

- ***SmartData, S.A. v. Amazon.com, Inc.*, 2015 U.S. Dist. LEXIS 152606 (N.D. Cal. Nov. 10, 2015).**
  The court here was determining whether to grant defendant Amazon. Com, Inc.'s (Amazon) motion for attorney's fees where Amazon claims that plaintiff acted in bad faith coupled with the improper purpose of manipulating the proceedings. The court denied the motion, found that plaintiff's conduct does not rise to the level of bad faith and declined to issue sanctions.
- ***Smartflash LLC v. Apple Inc.*, 621 Fed. Appx. 995 (Fed. Cir. 2015).**
  The court here was determining whether Amazon.com. Inc.'s (Amazon) motion to stay would be granted pending review of the asserted patents at issue. The court granted Amazon's motion to stay. The court here found that the Amazon case is in its very early stages. Substantial opportunities were still available for cost saving and issue simplification. Plaintiff would not be unduly prejudiced by a stay. There was no evidence that Amazon knew if its alleged infringement for more than a few months.
- ***Smartflash LLC v. Apple, Inc.*, 2015 U.S. Dist. LEXIS 18419 (E.D. Tex. Jan. 21, 2015).**
  This case was an appeal to the District Court's denial of appellant defendants Apple Inc., Samsung Telecommunications America, LLC, HTC Corporation, HTC America, Inc., and Exeda, Inc. motions to stay patent infringement litigation pending covered business method (CBM) review of the asserted claims. The court affirmed the district court's order as to Apple, but reversed as to Samsung. Amazon was granted their motion to stay at the District Court, and no notable issues arose in this case relating to Amazon.
- ***Spears v. Amazon.com.kydc, LLC* Case No. C12-1922 RAJ. United States District Court Western District of Washington at Seattle, June 2013.**
  The court determined this was not a stock grant and in fact was an illusory promise and dismissed the contact and promissory estoppel claims.

The court allowed the fraud and misrepresentation claims to continue as they were properly pled.

- ***Star Fabrics, Inc. v. Amazon.com Inc.* Case No. 2:14-CV-09190. United States District Court C.D. California, May 2015.**
  The court granted a protective order awarding material in the case special protection from public disclosure or use for any purpose other than prosecuting this matter.
- ***Supnick v. Amazon.com, Inc.*, 2000 U.S. Dist. LEXIS 7073 (W.D. Wash. May 18, 2000).**
  Amazon.com was a defendant in a privacy violation suit brought by Supnick. Plaintiffs motioned for a federal class certification. The court concluded that because the class was maintainable under Rule 23, and that the class action was the best method for litigating the dispute, the plaintiff's motion was granted.
- ***TainoApp, Inc. v. Amazon.com, Inc.*, 2014 U.S. Dist. LEXIS 177361 (D.P.R. Dec. 24, 2014).**
  Amazon.com was a defendant in a patent infringement case. Amazon.com motioned for transfer and the court granted the motion finding that the interest of justice was in favor of transfer.
- ***TainoApp, Inc. v. Amazon.Com Inc.*, 2015 U.S. Dist. LEXIS 153490 (N.D. Cal. Nov. 12, 2015).**
  Amazon.com was a defendant in a patent infringement case. This document dealt specifically with Amazon.com's file for costs. The court awarded the costs to Amazon.com because they were the prevailing party and the costs were reasonable.
- ***Tech. Innovations, LLC v. Amazon.com, Inc.*, 2013 U.S. Dist. LEXIS 115352 (D. Del. Aug. 15, 2013).**
  Amazon.com is a defendant in a patent infringement case. After reviewing the multiple motions made by the parties, the United States District Court ordered that TI must show cause on or before September 12, 2013 for why the assertion of the 407 patent was proper under the requirements of Rule 11.

- ***Tech. Innovations, LLC v. Amazon.com, Inc.*, 35 F. Supp. 3d 613 (D. Del. 2014).** Amazon.com was a defendant in this patent infringement case. Amazon.com motioned for summary judgment of invalidity and non-infringement of the 965 patent, and a motion to exclude the testimony and evidence of Dr. Conte and Mr. McCourt. The District Court granted Amazon.com's motion for summary judgment of invalidity and denied TI's motion for partial summary judgment of no invalidity. Amazon's motions for summary judgment of non-infringement and to exclude testimony and evidence were denied as moot.
- ***Tech. Innovations, LLC v. Amazon.Com, Inc.*, 2014 U.S. Dist. LEXIS 100061 (D. Del. July 23, 2014).**
  Amazon.com was a defendant in this patent infringement case. Amazon.com requested attorney fees for the claims against them filed by TI. The court found that attorney fees should be awarded to Amazon for the claims against them relating to the 407 patent. The court denied Amazons request that TI and its counsel be held jointly liable for any fees awarded.
- ***Tech. Innovations, LLC v. Amazon.com, Inc.*, 2015 U.S. Dist. LEXIS 51415 (D. Del. Apr. 20, 2015).**
  Amazon.com was a defendant in this patent infringement case. Amazon.com requested attorney fees for the claims against them filed by TI. This document deals specifically with the courts order for TI to pay a total of $51,046 in attorney fees to Amazon.com.
- ***Telebuyer, LLC v. Amazon.com, Inc.*, 2014 U.S. Dist. LEXIS 147794 (W.D. Wash. Oct. 16, 2014).**
  Amazon.com was a defendant in this patent infringement case brought by Telebuyer. Amazon.com motioned to limit the number of patent claims. Plaintiffs brought nearly 800 patent claims against Amazon. The court held that Telebuyer should limit the number of asserted claims to "not more than ten claims to limit each patent and not more than a total of 32 claims within ten days of the date of the order." Additionally, the court found that the appointment of a technical advisor was appropriate in the case.

- ***Telebuyer, LLC v. Amazon.com, Inc.*, 2015 U.S. Dist. LEXIS 18200 (W.D. Wash. Feb. 13, 2015).**
  In this case the court was determining whether to grant defendant Amazon.Com, Inc.'s, motion to redact portions of the transcript from a technology tutorial held in December of 2014. The court here granted the motion because the transcripts disclosed "trade secrets" of Amazon, and might harm Amazon's competitive standing.
- ***Telebuyer, LLC v. Amazon.com, Inc.*, 2015 U.S. Dist. LEXIS 96391 (W.D. Wash. July 23, 2015).**
  Amazon.com was a defendant in this patent infringement case brought by Telebuyer. Amazon.com motioned for summary judgment claiming that the patents were invalid. The court, after applying the Alice framework, found that each of the representative claims were directed to patent-ineligible subject matter. Therefore, the court granted the defendant's motion for summary judgment.
- ***Tompkins v. Able Planet Inc.*, 2011 U.S. Dist. LEXIS 153068 (E.D. Tex. Feb. 17, 2011).**
  The court here issued an order severing plaintiff's claims. The court found that because the claims were clearly distinguishable, it should exercise its discretion and sever the claims based on product manufacturer in order to promote judicial economy as well as fairness to the litigants.
- ***Tuxis Techs., LLC v. Amazon.com, Inc.*, 2015 U.S. Dist. LEXIS 37128 (D. Del. Mar. 25, 2015).**
  The court here was determining whether to grant defendant Amazon. Com, Inc.'s, Motion to Dismiss for Failure to State a Claim. The court found that the concept of "upselling" in the field of marketing is "as old as the field itself," and thus that the claim involved patent ineligible subject matter. The court noted that the limitations set out in the claim do narrow its scope, but not enough to save the claim from invalidity. Even though limitations narrow the scope of the claims, these limitations do not amount to an "inventive concept." Thus all of the claims of the patent were held to be invalid.

- ***Unicolors, Inc. v. Shoreline Wear, Inc.*, 2016 U.S. Dist. LEXIS 72508 (C.D. Cal. May 24, 2016).**
  The court granted the protective order as the discovery process would likely reveal privileged information that should be protected by law.
- ***United Pet Grp., Inc. v. Doe* (E.D. Mo., 2013).**
  The court was determining whether to grant Plaintiff's motion for expedited discovery which would force Amazon.Com, Inc. (Amazon) to release the identity of sellers accused of trademark violations. The court found that plaintiff had demonstrated good cause because it has shown potential irreparable harm from infringement, no prejudice to defendants, and limited availability of information sought and thus granted the motion for expedited discovery and ordered that plaintiff may serve subpoenas on Amazon.com to obtain information necessary to identify the John Doe defendants.
- ***United Video Props. v. Amazon.com, Inc.*, 2012 U.S. Dist. LEXIS 86914 (D. Del. June 22, 2012).**
  The court determined the claim construction of the patents that were allegedly infringed.
- ***United Video Props., Inc. v. Amazon.com, Inc.*, 561 Fed. Appx. 914 (Fed. Cir. 2014).**
  The court affirmed the lower court's claim construction and their judgment of non-infringement under these claims and their definitions.
- ***Univ. Press v. Amazon.com*, 2001 U.S. Dist. LEXIS 26987 (N.D. Cal. Nov. 29, 2001).**
  Defendant, Amazon filed a motion to dismiss based on the forum selection clause in the agreement. The court determined that the forum selection clause was valid, as the plaintiff failed to show that it would be unreasonable.
- ***Vance v. Amazon.com, Inc. (In re Amazon.com, Inc.)*, 2016 U.S. Dist. LEXIS 48650 (W.D. Ky. Mar. 30, 2016).**
  The court here was determining whether to grant defendants motion to dismiss. The court found that the plaintiffs do not have a sufficient claim under Kentucky law. Even though Kentucky has its own wage

and hour law, the state statute closely resembles the FLSA. Neither the statute of the FLSA defines the word "work." The court finds that in order to define the term "work," that Kentucky courts will look to federal cases interpreting the FLSA to decide what activities constitute "work." In the *Busk* case, the Supreme Court held that the the Portal-to-Portal Act excludes post-shift security checks, and Kentucky courts will use *Busk* to fill the state's statutory void. Therefore, the court granted the defendants motion for judgment on the pleadings.

- ***Vantage Point Tech., Inc. v. Amazon.com, Inc.*, 2015 U.S. Dist. LEXIS 8335 (E.D. Tex. Jan. 26, 2015).**
  The court decided what the terms in the patent meant for purposes of the claims, through claim construction.
- ***Vantage Point Tech., Inc. v. Amazon.com, Inc.*, 2015 U.S. Dist. LEXIS 675 (E.D. Tex. Jan. 6, 2015).**
  The court denied Amazon's and Sharps' Motion to Stay as it did not fit the consumer-suit exception of the first-to-file rule.
- ***Vecchio v. Amazon.com, Inc.*, 2012 U.S. Dist. LEXIS 76536 (W.D. Wash. June 1, 2012).**
  The court here was determining whether the plaintiffs have alleged sufficient facts to plead a plausible claim for relief such that the court should not grant defendants motion to dismiss. The court granted the motion in part and found that as to the CFAA and trespass to chattels claims that because plaintiffs had already had 2 opportunities to amend their complaint that plaintiffs clearly lacked the requisite facts to plead a sufficient claim. As to the CPA and unjust enrichment claims the court granted plaintiffs' request for a "reasonable opportunity to present all the material that is pertinent to the motion. Fed. R. Civ. P. 12(d).
- ***Vecchio v. Amazon.com, Inc.*, 2012 U.S. Dist. LEXIS 125399 (W.D. Wash. Sept. 4, 2012).**
  The court here was determining whether to grant defendants Motion for Protective Order. The court found that plaintiffs' request fell outside the time from allowed by the court to conduct discovery and thus granted the defendants motion for protective order.

- ***Voltstar Techs., Inc. v. Amazon.com, Inc.*, 2015 U.S. App. LEXIS 6008 (Fed. Cir. 2015).**

  This was a case involving an appeal from a lower court judgment. The court affirmed the lower court judgment.
- ***Walker Digital, LLC v. Facebook, Inc.*, 852 F. Supp. 2d 559 (D. Del. 2012).**

  This case involved defendant's motion to dismiss for lack of standing. The court granted the defendants motion to dismiss.
- ***Walker Digital, LLC v. Expedia, Inc.*, 2013 U.S. Dist. LEXIS 148983 (D. Del. Oct. 16, 2013).**

  The court here as determining whether to grant defendants' motions for attorney fees and dismissal. The court denied the motions because this case was resolved originally on a motion to dismiss, based on disputed ownership of the patents in suit, the court can use its discretion under Fed. R. Civ. P. 54(b) and deny defendant's motions pending appeal.
- ***Warner Bros. Home Entertainment Inc. v. Amazon.com*. Case No. CV 12-9148 R (AGRx). United States District Court Central District Of California, March 2013.**

  While Amazon.com as a named defendant, this document dealt specifically with the order of an injunction.
- ***Warner Bros. Home Entm't v. Jimenez*, 2013 U.S. Dist. LEXIS 97139 (C.D. Cal. July 8, 2013).**

  Jimenez was an Amazon seller who allegedly violated Warner Bros. copyrighted material. Warner Bros. filed a complaint and Jimenez never responded. The court concluded that a judgment should be entered in favor of plaintiff Warner Bros. and awarded damages in the amount of $66,000.00.
- ***Westermajer v. Nutrex Research, Inc.*, 2015 U.S. Dist. LEXIS 167245 (D.N.J. Dec. 15, 2015).**

  The court here was deciding whether defendant Vitamin Shoppe was fraudulently joined in an effort to destroy diversity jurisdiction such that the case should NOT be remanded to state court. The court found that Vitamin Shoppe was not fraudulently joined because plaintiff plead facts sufficient to raise a question of material fact as to whether plaintiff purchased a product containing DMAA from Vitamin Shoppe.

- ***Whitsitt v. Amazon.com,* 2014 U.S. Dist. LEXIS 58780, 2014 WL 1671502 (E.D. Cal. Apr. 25, 2014).**
  The plaintiff alleged that he was hired as a temporary employee by defendant SMX Staffing Agency to perform services for defendant Amazon. Com. He asserted that he sought employment with defendant Amazon. Com as a direct hire/permanent employee but was not hired for such a position. Plaintiff alleged violation of employee's rights under the ADEA (Age Discrimination in Employment Act) and intentional invasion of privacy by defendant Amazon.com. The court recommended that this action be dismissed and rules in favor of Amazon.com.
- ***Whitsitt v. Amazon.Com,* 2014 U.S. Dist. LEXIS 62652 (E.D. Cal. May 6, 2014).**
  Whitsitt filed suit against Amazon.com for a violation of the Age Discrimination in Employment Act (ADEA), for intentional infliction of emotional distress, and for invasion of privacy. The court found that plaintiff's complaint had conclusory allegations, which failed to state a claim. The action was dismissed in favor of Amazon.com.
- ***Wireless Recognition Tech. v. A9.com, Inc.,* 2012 U.S. Dist. LEXIS 130159 (N.D. Cal. Sept. 11, 2012).**
  This case was an alternative dispute resolution case that involved the extension of a mediation completion deadline. The court ordered the mediation deadline to be modified to the requested date.
- ***Worldslide, LLC v. Amazon.com, Inc.* Case No. 2:11-cv-03352-GEB-CKD. United States District Court Eastern District of California, March, 2012.**
  This case was a motion to consolidate cases to be heard together because they were both similar and related. The court granted the motion and combined the four different lawsuits that Worldslide filed against four different defendants.

- ***Wreal LLC v. Amazon.com, Inc.*, 2015 U.S. Dist. LEXIS 176382 (S.D. Fla. Feb. 3, 2015).** The court here held that expert testimony used by plaintiff solely during the preliminary injunction faze of trial did not entitle Amazon to subpoena that expert, unless the testimony was designated for use at trial.

Product Liability

Product liability suits arise against Amazon.com when third-party sellers are caught in litigation due to an issue with their products. Amazon.com is often a named defendant because they are the platform where the products are being sold. According to Black's Law Dictionary, products liability means,

> "1. A manufacturer's or seller's tort liability for any damages or injuries suffered by a buyer, user, or bystander as a result of a defective product. Products liability can be based on a theory of negligence, strict liability, or breach of warranty. 2. The legal theory by which liability is imposed on the manufacturer or seller of a defective product. 3. The field of law dealing with this theory."

When Amazon.com is involved with a product liability dispute, they will often motion to dismiss, or motion to stay proceedings pending arbitration. This is because Amazon will argue that they are not the party who is liable for the defected product, the seller is the party who is liable.

- ***Westermajer v. Nutrex Research, Inc.*, 2015 U.S. Dist. LEXIS 167245 (D.N.J. Dec. 15, 2015).**
  Defendants could not sufficiently prove that Westermajer did not buy any cans of Lipo 6 that contained DMAA during the time period in question. The Plaintiff's motion to remand was granted by the Court.
- ***Ranazzi v. Amazon.com, Inc.*, 2015-Ohio-4411 (Ohio Ct. App., Lucas County 2015).**
  This case involves an appellant bringing a motion to review a lower court's finding. The court affirmed the lower courts judgment to stay the action pending arbitration.

Property and Real Estate Law

Property and Real Estate law deals with lawsuits that arise between parties who are in a dispute over situations ranging from breach of contracts in lease agreements, to disputes between neighbors. Amazon was involved in a legal dispute over property when Amazon wanted to rent commercial space. This is what occurred in *DOLP v. Amazon Corporate.*[1] When Amazon did not follow through on a Letter of Intent agreement, DOLP Properties filed suit.[2] Amazon.com's greatest argument in this situation was to claim that the plaintiffs failed to state a claim.[3]

---

1. *DOLP 1133 Props. II LLC v Amazon Corporate, LLC*, 2015 N.Y. Misc. LEXIS 3019 (N.Y. Sup. Ct. Aug. 17, 2015).
2. *Id.*
3. *Id.*

- ***DOLP 1133 Props. II LLC v Amazon Corporate, LLC,* 2015 N.Y. Misc. LEXIS 3019 (N.Y. Sup. Ct. Aug. 17, 2015).**
  This was a property infringement claim between Amazon Corporate, LLC and Plaintiff DOLP 1133 Properties II LLC. The court denied Plaintiff punitive damages and attorneys' fees, dismissed breach of good faith claim, and upheld the fraud claim.

Rico Violations

RICO stands for Racketeer Influenced and Corrupt Organizations Act. According to Black's Law Dictionary, RICO is the "1970 federal statute designed to attack organized criminal activity and preserve marketplace integrity by investigating, controlling, and prosecuting persons who participate or conspire to participate in racketeering."[1] Amazon finds themselves in litigation involving RICO violations when their sellers are liable for RICO violations. As a result, Amazon is typically, not liable for the violation.

---

1. 18 USCA §§ 1961–1968.

- ***Zaretsky v. Maxi-Aids, Inc.*, 2012 U.S. Dist. LEXIS 84291 (E.D.N.Y. June 18, 2012).**
  Amazon.com, Inc. was a named defendant in this case, yet the issues at hand do not deal directly with Amazon.com, Inc. This was a motion to dismiss from the additionally named defendants, Citibank, European American Bank; and JP Morgan Chase Bank. N.A. Amazon.com Inc. was a defendant to an action brought by plaintiff pursuant to the Racketeer Influenced and Corrupt Organizations Act.
- ***Zaretsky v. Maxi-Aids, Inc.*, 529 Fed. Appx. 97 (2d Cir. N.Y. 2013).**
  The court held that the lower court did not abuse its discretion in dismissing appellants' complaint for failure to prosecute and for failure to comply with a court order and thus affirmed the lower courts judgment. Here, the parties failed to file within a timely manner as required by the court which barred an appeal.

Sale of Controlled Substances

A controlled substance is defined by Black's Law Dictionary as, "A drug that is illegal to possess or use without a doctor's prescription; specifically, any type of drug whose manufacture, possession, and use is regulated by law, including a narcotic, a stimulant, or a hallucinogen." Amazon finds themselves to be in litigation over the sale of controlled substances when an Amazon seller uses the Amazon platform to sell these products. It is Amazon's responsibility to remove these items that could potentially cause harm to customers.

In *Nicosia v. Amazon.com*, there was a weight-loss supplement being sold on Amazon that contained a controlled substance.[1] However, Amazon was successfully dismissed from all claims because the claims were governed by mandatory arbitration. [2]

---

1. *Nicosia v. Amazon.com, Inc.*, 84 F. Supp. 3d 142, 2015 U.S. Dist. LEXIS 13560 (E.D.N.Y. 2015)
2. *Id.*

- ***Westermajer v. Nutrex Research, Inc.*, 2015 U.S. Dist. LEXIS 167245 (D.N.J. Dec. 15, 2015).**

  Defendants could not sufficiently prove that Westermajer did not buy any cans of Lipo 6 that contained DMAA during the time period in question. The Plaintiff's motion to remand was granted by the Court.
- ***Nicosia v. Amazon.com, Inc.*, 84 F. Supp. 3d 142, 2015 U.S. Dist. LEXIS 13560 (E.D.N.Y. 2015)**

  Amazon.com was a defendant in a case brought by Dean Nicosia for the selling of a controlled substance in a weight loss supplement. Amazon.com motioned to dismiss claiming that the issue should be settled in arbitration due the arbitration clause. The court agreed and granted Amazon's motion.

Settlement Agreements

Sometimes, Amazon.com will not proceed to trial and create a settlement agreement with the parties in dispute. A settlement agreement is when the parties in dispute come to an agreement on their own terms. This can be performed in writing or even though an e-mail exchange. For example, in *Basis Technology v. Amazon*, the court held that the email was sufficiently complete and both parties were bound by the e-mail agreement.[1]

---

1. *Basis Tech. Corp. v. Amazon.com, Inc.*, 71 Mass. App. Ct. 29, 878 N.E.2d 952, 2008 Mass. App. LEXIS 8 (Mass. App. Ct. 2008).

- ***Basis Tech. Corp. v. Amazon.com, Inc.*, 71 Mass. App. Ct. 29, 878 N.E.2d 952, 2008 Mass. App. LEXIS 8 (Mass. App. Ct. 2008).**
  Basis Technology filed suit against Amazon.com alleging breach of fiduciary duty, quantum meruit, and G.L. c. 93A violations for non-payment for "out of scope work". The parties via e-mail agreed to a settlement, the judge held that settlement to be enforceable and Amazon appealed. The court found that the judge correctly ruled that the e-mail was a sufficiently complete and unambiguous statement as a matter of law, and that both parties were to be bound by this agreement.
- ***Sen v. Amazon.com, Inc.*, 2013 U.S. Dist. LEXIS 178447, 2013 WL 6730180 (S.D. Cal. Dec. 19, 2013).**
  The issue here was whether the court should grant defendant Amazon. Com, Inc.'s Motion to Enforce the Settlement where both defendant and plaintiff, Sen have signed the settlement, but plaintiff was attempting to add additional terms to the agreement. The court granted the motion because it found the agreement to be complete, unambiguous, and

intentionally entered into, the agreement contained all material terms and plaintiff's additional concerns are unfounded, and because the agreement contained valid consideration.

Theft

Theft is defined by Black's Law Dictionary as, "1. The wrongful taking and removing of another's personal property with the intent of depriving the true owner of it; larceny. 2. Broadly, any act or instance of stealing, including larceny, burglary, embezzlement, and false pretenses."

When Amazon.com uses a service to transport goods, and those goods are stolen, Amazon will file suit to collect damages. That is what occurred in *Amazon.com v. Coyote Logistics and CP Transport LLC*, when the party responsible to transport goods negligently left the shipment unattended, and that shipment was stolen. Amazon.com filed suit against the negligent party and was able to collect damages.[1] However, Amazon has also been in litigation involving theft due to third party sellers using the platform. In the past, Amazon successfully been dismissed from these claims because they have argued they had no control over the third party's unauthorized use of an image.

---

1. *Amazon.com v. Coyote Logistics* Case No. C11-1015 RSL, United States District Court Western District of Washington at Seattle, December 11, 2013.

- ***Amazon.com v. Coyote Logistics* Case No. C11-1015 RSL, United States District Court Western District of Washington at Seattle, December 11, 2013.**

  In this case, plaintiff, Amazon alleged that CP Transport was hired to transport a container of Amazon Kindles from Washington to Delaware in November 2009. Amazon alleged that the driver negligently left the shipment unattended at a truck stop, resulting in the theft of the truck, container, and goods. The court awarded damages in favor of Amazon.

- ***Almeida v. Amazon.com, Inc.,* 456 F.3d 1316 (11th Cir. 2006).**
This case was an appeal to the district court decision that granted summary judgment in favor of defendant Amazon. Plaintiff claimed that Amazon's use of her image in furtherance of sale of a book on its website violated her right of publicity and claimed invasion of privacy and theft as well. The court here affirmed the district court's decision because plaintiffs right of publicity claim based on Fla. Stat. § 540.08 would not withstand a motion to dismiss, it was unnecessary for the district court to determine whether the CDA preempts Almeida's state law right of publicity claim. As to the theft claim the court here held that plaintiff failed to present any evidence that Amazon misappropriated her image with actual knowledge that its used was unauthorized.

Tortious Interference

Tortious interference is tort that allows a party to claim damages against a defendant who wrongfully interferes with the plaintiff's contractual or business relationships. The essential requirements for a tortious interference claim are: (1) a valid contract or expectancy between plaintiff and a third person; (2) knowledge of the contract or expectancy by the defendant; (3) intent by the defendant to interfere with the contract or expectancy; (4) actual interference; (5) the interference is improper; and (6) the plaintiff suffers actual damage.

Amazon is sometimes accused of tortious interference due to contractual relationships between manufacturers and their authorized sellers because per Amazon's policy, they do not enforce authorized sale agreements. Minimum Advertised Price (MAP) agreements may also be the subject of tortious interference claims for the same reason; Amazon's policy does not enforce MAP agreements.

- **Segal v. Amazon.com, Inc., 763 F. Supp. 2d 1367, 2011 U.S. Dist. LEXIS 11429 (S.D. Fla. 2011).**
  Plaintiff was an Amazon seller suing Amazon in Florida court for unjust enrichment and tortious interference after Amazon allegedly did not release to Plaintiff the profits of its sales on Amazon's website. Relying on the "Participation Agreement" that sellers are required to enter to sell on Amazon's website, Amazon argued that the agreement specifically states that any such lawsuits are to be brought in Washington state courts, and asked the Florida court to dismiss the case or transfer it to Washington. The court here upheld the forum selection clause.
- ***Parisi v. Sinclair*, 774 F. Supp. 2d 310 (D.D.C. 2011).**
  Daniel Parisi alleged that Amazon.com was liable for tortious acts following the sale of the book *Barack Obama & Larry Sinclair: Cocaine, Sex,*

Lies & Murder. Amazon.com motioned for summary judgment and the District Court granted the motion because the court found that the plaintiffs had failed to provide evidence that supports their claim that B&N and Amazon.com did play a role in the creation or development of the promotional statements for the book. As a result, the court found that the defendants, B&N and Amazon.com were entitled to summary judgment for the claims of defamatory promotional statements appearing on their websites.

- ***Schneider v. Amazon.com, Inc.*, 108 Wn. App. 454, 31 P.3d 37, 2001 Wash. App. LEXIS 2086, 29 Media L. Rep. 2421 (Wash. Ct. App. 2001).** In this case, plaintiff had written many books on the topics of both taxation and asset protection. The books were for sale on the Amazon platform. The Amazon platform allows consumers to leave reviews for the products they have purchased. Amazon posted visitor's comments about plaintiff and his books. The comments were negative and one alleged plaintiff was a felon. The court found that Amazon is immune from liability for defamation by third-parties under the Communications Decency Act because Amazon is a provider of interactive computer services, plaintiff's claims treat Amazon as a publisher, and Amazon is not the information content provider.

Trademark Infringement

A trademark is any word, name, symbol, or design, or any combination thereof, used in commerce to identify and distinguish the goods of one manufacturer or seller from those of another and to indicate the source of the goods.[1] Often, a manufacturer will sue both the Amazon seller and Amazon.com for trademark infringement; usually in cases where a seller is accused of selling items that are inauthentic, counterfeit, or are sold by an unauthorized reseller. In a 2015 decision, the court held that Amazon could not be held liable for a seller's trademark violation because Amazon itself was not "offering for sale" the infringing items at issue.[2]

---

1. 15 U.S.C § 1127.
2. *Milo & Gabby, LLC v. Amazon.com*, 2015 U.S. Dist. LEXIS 149939 (W.D. Wash. Nov. 3, 2015).

- ***Amazon.com, Inc. v. Kalaydjian*, 2001 U.S. Dist. LEXIS 4924 (W.D. Wash. Feb. 20, 2001).**

  The court here was determining whether defendant purposefully availed itself to the Washington forum such that a motion to dismiss for lack of personal jurisdiction would not be possible. The court found that defendants' acts did not amount to purposeful availment because the website at issue only gave guidance on purchasing the tanning products here, and did not offer them for sale via the internet. Thus the court granted defendants motion to dismiss for lack of personal jurisdiction.
- ***Apple, Inc. v. Amazon.Com, Inc.*, 2011 U.S. Dist. LEXIS 72271 (N.D. Cal. July 6, 2011).**

  This was a trademark infringement case denying Apple's preliminary injunction motion to keep Amazon from using the mark "App Store"

- **Apple Inc. v. Amazon.Com Inc., 915 F. Supp. 2d 1084 (N.D. Cal. 2013).** This was a trademark infringement case alleging Amazon has improperly used the term "APP STORE" while selling apps for Android devices and Amazon's tablet computer. The court granted Amazon's motion for partial summary judgment.
- ***Fandino v. Amalgam Entm't, LLC,* 2010 U.S. Dist. LEXIS 14684 (S.D.N.Y. Feb. 18, 2010).**
  This as a case involving the defendant's motion to dismiss or to transfer the action in favor of the first filed action. The court granted defendant's motion to transfer.
- ***Free Kick Master LLC v. Apple Inc.,* 140 F. Supp. 3d 975 (N.D. Cal. 2015).**
  This was a trademark infringement case determining if the plaintiff had stated a claim against Amazon in order to proceed with litigation. The court granted the defendant's motion to dismiss for failure to state a claim.
- ***Free Kick Master LLC v. Apple Inc.,* 2016 U.S. Dist. LEXIS 25478 (N.D. Cal. Feb. 29, 2016).**
  This was a case involving trademark infringement, the defendants filed a motion to dismiss an amended complaint for lack of providing evidence to state a claim. The court granted the motion to dismiss the amended complaint.
- ***Lasoff v. Amazon.com, Inc.,* 2016 U.S. Dist. LEXIS 9878, 2016 WL 355076 (D.N.J. Jan. 28, 2016).**
  In this case, plaintiff Amazon seller was suing Amazon.com, in New jersey, for trademark infringement, anti-trust violations, and unfair business practices because Amazon allowed other sellers to sell similar products to those of plaintiff. All sellers using the Amazon platform are subject to Amazon's terms of use, which contains a forum selection clause requiring litigation in a Washington court. The court ordered a venue transfer to Washington because it found that there were no public or local interests weighing strongly against the transfer.

- ***Milo & Gabby LLC v. Amazon.com.* Case No. C13-1932RSM. United States District Court Western District Of Washington At Seattle, April 2014.**
  Milo & Gabby sued Amazon.com for multiple infringement claims. Amazon.com motioned to dismiss claiming that the plaintiffs failed to state a claim. The District Court agreed with Amazon and granted to motion to dismiss the III, V, VII claims.
- ***Milo & Gabby LLC v. Amazon.com.* Case No. C13-1932RSM. United States District Court Western District of Washington At Seattle, October 2015.**
  Milo & Gabby sued Amazon.com for multiple infringement claims. The defendant, Amazon.com motioned in Limine. The court granted in part and denied in part.
- ***Milo & Gabby, LLC v. Amazon.com,* 2015 U.S. Dist. LEXIS 149939 (W.D. Wash. Nov. 3, 2015).**
  Milo & Gabby sued Amazon.com for multiple infringement claims. Amazon.com motioned to dismiss claiming that the plaintiffs failed to state a claim. After a jury hearing, the court adopted the jury's finding that Amazon.com was not liable for "offering to sell" the alleged infringing products at issue in this matter. A judgment was placed in favor of Amazon.com and all claims against Amazon.com were dismissed.
- ***Multi Time Mach., Inc. v. Amazon.com, Inc.,* 792 F.3d 1070 (9th Cir. 2015).**
  Plaintiff argued Amazon confused customers – Plaintiff did not sell items on Amazon, but when customers searched for it, Amazon returned results with Plaintiff's trademark and listings from other sellers.
- ***Sanmedica Int'l, LLC v. Amazon.com, Inc.,* 2015 U.S. Dist. LEXIS 50470 (D. Utah Mar. 27, 2015).**
  Court refused to grant Amazon's motion to dismiss where it found the use of Plaintiff's trademark may cause initial interest confusion and thus was a question for the jury.

- ***Sellify Inc. v. Amazon.com, Inc.*, 2010 U.S. Dist. LEXIS 118173 (S.D.N.Y. Nov. 3, 2010).**

  The court here was determining whether to grant defendants motion for summary judgment. The court granted the motion. The claims at issue here required direct action by Amazon in order to state a claim and no evidence existed as to this point. Further the court found that the damages requested by the plaintiff were too speculative to survive a motion to dismiss. The court therefore granted the motion.
- ***Sen v. Amazon.com, Inc.*, 2013 U.S. Dist. LEXIS 178447, 2013 WL 6730180 (S.D. Cal. Dec. 19, 2013).**

  The issue here was whether the court should grant defendant Amazon. Com, Inc.'s Motion to Enforce the Settlement where both defendant and plaintiff, Sen had signed the settlement, but plaintiff was attempting to add additional terms to the agreement. The court granted the motion because it found the agreement to be complete, unambiguous, and intentionally entered into, the agreement contained all material terms and plaintiff's additional concerns were unfounded, and because the agreement contained valid consideration.
- ***TRE Milano, LLC v. Amazon.com, Inc.*, No. S205747, 2012 Cal. LEXIS 11039 (Nov. 28, 2012).**

  Plaintiff's case against Amazon was dismissed because Amazon was not responsible for the infringement of a third-party, and could also not be held contributorily liable since Amazon took immediate action once it was notified of the third-party's infringement.
- ***United Pet Grp., Inc. v. Doe* (E.D. Mo., 2013).**

  The court was determining whether to grant Plaintiff's motion for expedited discovery which would force Amazon.Com, Inc. (Amazon) to release the identity of sellers accused of trademark violations. The court found that plaintiff had demonstrated good cause because it had shown potential irreparable harm from infringement, no prejudice to defendants, and limited availability of information sought. The court thus granted the motion for expedited discovery and ordered that plaintiff may serve subpoenas on Amazon.com to obtain information necessary to identify the John Doe defendants.

- ***Vallavista Corp. v. Amazon.com, Inc.*, 657 F. Supp. 2d 1132 (N.D. Cal. 2008).**

  This case involved a defendant's motion for summary judgment claiming there was no dispute of material facts. The court granted in part and denied in part Target Corporation's motion for summary judgment.
- ***Video Professor, Inc. v. Amazon.com, Inc.*, Civil Action No. 09-cv-00636-REB-KLM, 2010 U.S. Dist. LEXIS 29414 (D. Colo. Mar. 8, 2010).**

  The court here was determining whether to grant plaintiff's motion to modify the discovery schedule. The motion was denied and the court held that plaintiff had not shown good cause for amendment of the deadline for discovery. Plaintiff's efforts to pursue discovery were less than diligent, and plaintiff had not shown evidence that additional discovery is relevant to claims as they were stated in the complaint.
- ***Video Professor, Inc. v. Amazon.com, Inc.*, 2010 U.S. Dist. LEXIS 39103 (D. Colo. Apr. 21, 2010).**

  Here the court was determining whether to grant defendant Amazon. Com Inc.'s motion for summary judgment. The court granted the motion because the conduct alleged as wrongful was allowed by the parties Vendor agreement.
- ***Wax v. Amazon Techs., Inc.*, 500 Fed. Appx. 944 (Fed. Cir. 2013).**

  The Court determined that because Amazon Technologies Inc. was the dominant component for the trademarks utilizing this term, there was a high degree of similarity between Amazon.com and the Plaintiff's desired mark, Amazon Ventures. This indicated a likelihood of confusion. The Court ruled in favor of Amazon Technologies, Inc. on the grounds that Mr. Wax's arguments lacked merit.
- ***Wreal, LLC v. Amazon.com, Inc.*, 2014 U.S. Dist. LEXIS 160160 (S.D. Fla. Nov. 14, 2014).**

  Amazon filed a discovery motion to have Wreal reveal the identities of their non-testifying experts. The court granted this discovery motion, as they determined that Amazon had demonstrated good cause for this type of discovery.

- ***Wreal LLC v. Amazon.com, Inc.*, 2015 U.S. Dist. LEXIS 176382 (S.D. Fla. Feb. 3, 2015).** The court here held that expert testimony used by plaintiff solely during the preliminary injunction faze of trial did not entitle Amazon to subpoena that expert, unless the testimony was designated for use at trial.

Unfair Business Practices

Unfair business practices generally cover acts of fraud, misrepresentation, or oppressive and unethical practices committed by businesses against consumers or other businesses. Most courts adopt a broad definition of what constitutes unfair business practices. Some examples of what courts have held to constitute an unfair business practice include: deceptive or misleading advertising, conspiracy to fix prices, monopolization attempts, and price discrimination.

In *United States v. Apple Inc.*, Apple and five book publishers were found to be engaging in the unfair business practice of conspiracy to fix prices and capture the market.[1] The court found that by acting collectively, Apple and the five publishers illegally pressured Amazon to change its pricing strategy.[2]

---

1. *United States v. Apple Inc.*, 952 F. Supp. 2d 638 (S.D.N.Y. 2013).
2. *Id.*

- ***Baghdasarian v. Amazon.Com Inc.*, 458 F. App'x 622 (9th Cir. 2011).**
  Here, the court was determining on appeal whether the district court erred in granting summary judgment for plaintiff's reliance claims in favor of defendant Amazon.Com Inc. (Amazon), where plaintiff claims his decision to purchase books on the Amazon market place was based on total cost and security. The court affirmed the district court and found that because plaintiff testified that he made purchases based on comparative shopping to find the best price based on price and security, that he had not shown that he relied on Amazon's misrepresentation.
- ***Fagerstrom v. Amazon.com, Inc.*, 141 F. Supp. 3d 1051, 2015 U.S. Dist. LEXIS 143295 (S.D. Cal. 2015).**
  In this case, consumers claimed there was a discrepancy between Amazon's prices and other retailer prices of products. When checking

out on Amazon, each customer must agree to the conditions of use in order to complete their order. Amazon states any dispute will be resolved through binding arbitration. The court granted Amazon's motion to compel arbitration and dismissed this action because the terms of the agreement were fair and beneficial to both parties.

- ***Lasoff v. Amazon.com, Inc.*, 2016 U.S. Dist. LEXIS 9878, 2016 WL 355076 (D.N.J. Jan. 28, 2016).**
  In this case, plaintiff Amazon seller was suing Amazon.com, in New jersey, for trademark infringement, anti-trust violations, and unfair business practices because Amazon allowed other sellers to sell similar products to those of plaintiff. All sellers using the Amazon platform are subject to Amazon's terms of use, which contains a forum selection clause requiring litigation in a Washington court. The court ordered a venue transfer to Washington because it found that there were no public or local interests weighing strongly against the transfer.
- ***Ranazzi v. Amazon.com, Inc.*, 2015-Ohio-4411, 46 N.E.3d 213, 2015 Ohio App. LEXIS 4277 (Ohio Ct. App., Lucas County 2015).**
  In this case, the court stayed proceedings until the outcome of Arbitration which was an enforceable forum for the dispute under the agreement between Plaintiff and Amazon for use of its website.
- ***Sellify Inc. v. Amazon.com, Inc.*, 2010 U.S. Dist. LEXIS 118173 (S.D.N.Y. Nov. 3, 2010).**
  The court here is determining whether to grant defendants motion for summary judgment. The court grants the motion. The claims at issue here require direct action by Amazon in order to state a claim and no evidence exists as to this point. Further the court finds that the damages requested by the plaintiff are too speculative to survive a motion to dismiss. The court therefore grants the motion.
- ***Sen v. Amazon.com, Inc.*, 2013 U.S. Dist. LEXIS 178447, 2013 WL 6730180 (S.D. Cal. Dec. 19, 2013).**
  The issue here was whether the court should grant defendant Amazon. Com, Inc.'s Motion to Enforce the Settlement where both defendant and plaintiff, Sen had signed the settlement, but plaintiff was attempting to

add additional terms to the agreement. The court granted the motion because it found the agreement to be complete, unambiguous, and intentionally entered into, the agreement contained all material terms and plaintiff's additional concerns were unfounded, and because the agreement contains valid consideration.

- ***State ex rel. Beeler, Schad & Diamond, P.C. v. Ritz Camera Ctrs., Inc.,* 377 Ill. App. 3d 990, 316 Ill. Dec. 128, 878 N.E.2d 1152 (2007).**
  In this case Plaintiff law firm, acting on behalf of the State of Illinois, filed a complaint alleging that defendant retailers had violated the Illinois Whistleblower Reward and Protection Act as to use tax. The defendants filed a joint motion to dismiss, but it was denied. The court here on interlocutory appeal is answering six certified questions directed to this court by the Illinois Supreme Court. The court here answered the six certified questions from the Illinois Supreme Court and then remanded for further proceedings consistent with those answers.
- ***Vecchio v. Amazon.com, Inc.* No. C11-366RSL, 2012 U.S. Dist. LEXIS 76536 (W.D. Wash. June 1, 2012).**
  The court here was determining whether the plaintiffs had alleged sufficient facts to plead a plausible claim for relief such that the court should not grant defendants motion to dismiss. The court granted the motion in part and found that as to the CFAA and trespass to chattels claims that because plaintiffs had already had 2 opportunities to amend their complaint that plaintiffs clearly lacked the requisite facts to plead a sufficient claim. As to the CPA and unjust enrichment claims the court granted plaintiffs' request for a "reasonable opportunity to present all the material that is pertinent to the motion. Fed. R. Civ. P. 12(d).
- ***Video Professor, Inc. v. Amazon.com, Inc.,* Civil Action No. 09-cv-00636-REB-KLM, 2010 U.S. Dist. LEXIS 29414 (D. Colo. Mar. 8, 2010).**
  The court here was determining whether to grant plaintiff's motion to modify the discovery schedule. The motion was denied and the court held that plaintiff had not shown good cause for amendment of the deadline for discovery. Plaintiff's efforts to pursue discovery were less

than diligent, and plaintiff had not shown evidence that additional discovery is relevant to claims as they were stated in the complaint.

- ***Video Professor, Inc. v. Amazon.com, Inc.*, 2010 U.S. Dist. LEXIS 39103 (D. Colo. Apr. 21, 2010).**

  Here the court was determining whether to grant defendant Amazon. Com Inc.'s motion for summary judgment. The court granted the motion because the conduct alleged as wrongful was allowed by the parties Vendor agreement.

Unfair Competition

Unfair competition laws aim to prevent economic injury to businesses through wrongful and/or deceptive practices. There are two general categories regarding unfair competition: (1) to refer only to torts that are meant to confuse consumers as to the source of the product; and (2) "unfair trade practices." Some common examples of unfair competition include trademark infringement, misappropriation, false advertising, "bait and switch" sales techniques, use of confidential information from a former employee, theft of trade secrets, trade libel, and false representations of products or services.

Amazon litigation dealing with unfair competition is commonly found in the laws of intellectual property. It is common for manufacturers to accuse Amazon and its sellers of violations of copyrights, trademarks, and/or patents. Claims often include copyright violations for use of an image in a product detail listing, trademark violations and accusations of inauthentic or counterfeit products, as well as similar products claiming patent violations.

- ***A'lor Int'l v. Tappers Fine Jewelry, Inc.*, 605 F. App'x 662 (9th Cir. 2015).** This was a copyright infringement case in which A'lor International, Ltd. appealed a summary judgment order that ruled in favor of its competitors who were producers, distributors, and retailers of jewelry. The Court vacated the attorneys' fees award because Defendants were not prevailing parties with respect to the two designs that the district court dismissed without prejudice.
- ***Baghdasarian v. Amazon.Com Inc.*, 458 F. App'x 622 (9th Cir. 2011).** Here, the court was determining on appeal whether the district court erred in granting summary judgment for plaintiff's reliance claims in favor of defendant Amazon.Com Inc. (Amazon), where plaintiff claims his decision to purchase books on the Amazon market place was based on

total cost and security. The court affirmed the district court and found that because plaintiff testified that he made purchases based on comparative shopping to find the best price based on price and security, that he had not shown that he relied on Amazon's misrepresentation.

- ***Baghdasarian v. Amazon.Com, Inc.*, 258 F.R.D. 383 (C.D. Cal. 2009).** Here, the court was deciding whether to grant plaintiff's motion for class certification The court ultimately granted plaintiff's motion. The court found that plaintiff had standing to bring his claim, and satisfied the requirements of Rule 23(a) for numerosity, commonality, typicality, and adequacy, as well as the rule 23(b) requirements of predominance and superiority.
- ***Corbis Corp. v. Amazon.com, Inc.*, 351 F. Supp. 2d 1090, 2004 U.S. Dist. LEXIS 27155, 77 U.S.P.Q.2D (BNA) 1182 (W.D. Wash. 2004).** In this case plaintiff claimed to have copyright interests in two photographs that Amazon placed on it's website IMDb.com as well as hundreds of photographs that were being sold by vendors on Amazon without Plaintiff's permission. Amazon is protected from liability under the DMCA for copyright infringement occurring on its third party vendor platform because Amazon qualifies as an Internet Service Provider protected under DCMA, does not have affirmative duty to police possible infringement, but must take reasonable steps if is alerted to infringement.
- ***Gerlinger v. Amazon.com, Inc.*, 311 F. Supp. 2d 838, 2004 U.S. Dist. LEXIS 4604, 2004-1 Trade Cas. (CCH) P74,363 (N.D. Cal. 2004).** Plaintiff could not succeed on antitrust claim when the alleged violation was a price-fixing agreement that actually provided customers with lower prices.
- ***M-Edge Accessories LLC v. Amazon.Com Inc.*, 2013 U.S. Dist. LEXIS 311 (D. Md. Jan. 2, 2013).** The court denied the Defendant's Motion to Dismiss, as it determined the plaintiff's complaint contained enough factual allegations to support the claims.

- ***Sanmedica Int'l, LLC v. Amazon.com, Inc.*, 2015 U.S. Dist. LEXIS 50470 (D. Utah Mar. 27, 2015).**
  Court refused to grant Amazon's motion to dismiss where it found the use of Plaintiff's trademark may cause initial interest confusion and this was a question for the jury.
- ***Sellify Inc. v. Amazon.com, Inc.*, 2010 U.S. Dist. LEXIS 118173 (S.D.N.Y. Nov. 3, 2010).**
  The court here was determining whether to grant defendants motion for summary judgment. The court granted the motion. The claims at issue here required direct action by Amazon in order to state a claim and no evidence existed as to this point. Further the court found that the damages requested by the plaintiff were too speculative to survive a motion to dismiss. The court therefore granted the motion.
- ***Sen v. Amazon.com, Inc.*, 2013 U.S. Dist. LEXIS 178447, 2013 WL 6730180 (S.D. Cal. Dec. 19, 2013).**
  The issue here was whether the court should grant defendant Amazon. Com, Inc.'s Motion to Enforce the Settlement where both defendant and plaintiff, Sen had signed the settlement, but plaintiff was attempting to add additional terms to the agreement. The court granted the motion because it found the agreement to be complete, unambiguous, and intentionally entered into, the agreement contained all material terms and plaintiff's additional concerns were unfounded, and because the agreement contained valid consideration.
- ***Video Professor, Inc. v. Amazon.com, Inc.*, Civil Action No. 09-cv-00636-REB-KLM, 2010 U.S. Dist. LEXIS 29414 (D. Colo. Mar. 8, 2010).**
  The court here was determining whether to grant plaintiff's motion to modify the discovery schedule. The motion was denied and the court held that plaintiff had not shown good cause for amendment of the deadline for discovery. Plaintiff's efforts to pursue discovery were less than diligent, and plaintiff had not shown evidence that additional discovery was relevant to the claims as they were stated in the complaint.

Unjust Enrichment

Unjust enrichment is the "retention of a benefit conferred by another, that is not intended as a gift, and is not legally justifiable, without offering compensation in circumstances where compensation is reasonably expected." Recovery for unjust enrichment typically occurs where the parties did not have a contract, or when the contract is found to be invalid. The requirements for a claim of unjust enrichment are: (1) the enrichment of the party accused of unjust enrichment; that the enrichment was at the expense of the party seeking damages; (3) the circumstances are such that compensation would be the only way to restore equity and good conscience; and sometimes (4) that the party accused must know of the benefit received by the other party.

Amazon is often dismissed from claims of unjust enrichment made by manufacturers who accuse Amazon of intellectual property violations.[1] Amazon can usually escape liability for these types of claims because they are not themselves "offering products for sale," and the law currently goes after the individual sellers rather than Amazon.[2]

---

1. *Milo & Gabby, LLC v. Amazon.com*, 2015 U.S. Dist. LEXIS 149939 (W.D. Wash. Nov. 3, 2015)
2. **Id.**

- ***Nicosia v. Amazon.com, Inc.*, 84 F. Supp. 3d 142, 2015 U.S. Dist. LEXIS 13560 (E.D.N.Y. 2015)**
  Amazon.com was a defendant in a case brought by Dean Nicosia for the selling of a controlled substance in a weight loss supplement. Amazon.com motioned to dismiss claiming that the issue should be settled in arbitration due the arbitration clause. The court agreed and granted Amazon's motion.

- ***Gerlinger v. Amazon.com, Inc.*, 311 F. Supp. 2d 838, 2004 U.S. Dist. LEXIS 4604, 2004-1 Trade Cas. (CCH) P74,363 (N.D. Cal. 2004).**
  Plaintiff could not succeed on antitrust claim when the alleged violation was a price-fixing agreement that actually provided customers with lower prices.
- ***Gusler v. Fischer*, 580 F. Supp. 2d 309, 2008 U.S. Dist. LEXIS 75454 (S.D.N.Y. 2008).**
  Amazon.com was one of the named defendants for a claim of copyright infringement. Amazon, along with other defendants, motioned for a dismissal, and in the alternative, a summary judgment. The court in finding that the product was not copyrightable, granted the summary judgment in favor of the corporate defendants.
- ***Del Vecchio v. Amazon.com Inc.*, 2011 U.S. Dist. LEXIS 138314, 2011 WL 6325910 (W.D. Wash. Nov. 30, 2011).**
  Amazon.com was a defendant in a case filed by Del Vecchio. Del Vecchio represented a class action against Amazon seeking relief under the Computer Fraud and Abuse act. Amazon motioned to dismiss and the court concluded that the defendant's motion to dismiss should be granted because the plaintiffs failed to plead adequate facts to establish any harm.
- ***Peters v. Amazon Servs., LLC*, 2 F. Supp. 3d 1165, 2013 U.S. Dist. LEXIS 185964 (W.D. Wash. 2013).**
  Plaintiffs were former third-party Amazon.com sellers. They sued Amazon alleging breach of contract, breach of fiduciary duty, violations of Washington's Consumer Protection Act, and unjust enrichment. The Court found a valid agreement to arbitrate. Because the parties agreed to arbitration and Plaintiffs' claims clearly fall within the scope of that arbitration provision, the Court granted Amazon's motion to compel arbitration. The court stayed the case for a period of 6 months or until arbitration is complete, whichever comes first, so that Plaintiffs could pursue their claims in arbitration.
- **Segal v. Amazon.com, Inc., 763 F. Supp. 2d 1367, 2011 U.S. Dist. LEXIS 11429 (S.D. Fla. 2011).**
  Plaintiff was an Amazon seller suing Amazon in Florida court for unjust enrichment and tortious interference after Amazon allegedly did not

release to Plaintiff the profits of its sales on Amazon's website. Relying on the "Participation Agreement" that sellers are required to enter to sell on Amazon's website, Amazon argued that the agreement specifically stated that any such lawsuits are to be brought in Washington state courts, and asked the Florida court to dismiss the case or transfer it to Washington. The court here upheld the forum selection clause.

Unlawful Use of Images

When one does not have a copyright for an image, one can stop a website's use of their image for three reasons: invasion of privacy, violation of right of publicity, or defamation. Invasion of privacy occurs when a party is falsely portrayed in an offensive manner, and also when a party is intruded on and a photo is taken in a situation where that party has a reasonable expectation of privacy.

Right of publicity is another claim that can be made in order to stop a website's use of a party's image. Right of publicity violations occur when the image is used for commercial purposed, like to sell and/or endorse products.

Also defamation claims can be made to stop a website from unlawfully displaying someone's image. Defamation occurs when a false impression that is damaging to one's reputation is created. The photo must *falsely* defame the person and must cause most people in the community to think less of you.

In some cases, Amazon is accused of unlawfully using images to display products on an item's product listing case. In *Roe v. Amazon.com*, plaintiffs' engagement photo was used on the cover of an erotic book without their permission.[1] Plaintiffs sued the publisher of the book as well as Amazon. The court held that Amazon could not be held liable because they did not publish the book.[2]

---

1. *Roe v. Amazon.com*, 2016 U.S. Dist. LEXIS 33297, 118 U.S.P.Q.2D (BNA) 1070, 44 Media L. Rep. 1469, 2016 WL 1028265 (S.D. Ohio Mar. 15, 2016).
2. *Id.*

- ***Bowens v. Aftermath Entm't*, 254 F. Supp. 2d 629 (E.D. Mich. 2003).** The court held that the Defendants' Motion to Dismiss was denied, as plaintiff had made a sufficient claim. Additionally, they granted Plaintiffs Motion to Leave to Amend the First Amended Complaint, as doing so would not be in bad faith and the Defendants had failed to show how it would be futile. Finally, the court denied the Motion for Sanctions, as the Plaintiffs' claims were well founded and therefore there was no need for the court to sanction plaintiff.

- ***Bowens v. Aftermath Entm't*, 364 F. Supp. 2d 641 (E.D. Mich. 2005).**
  Plaintiffs' filed a case based on newly discovered evidence and the Defendants' filed a Motion for Summary Judgment on the basis of res judicata and issue preclusion. The court held that the state court determination precludes the Plaintiffs from re-litigating the issue before the court. Additionally, the court denied each parties motion for sanctions.
- ***Bowens v. Aftermath Entm't*, 711 N.W.2d 751 (Mich. 2006).**
  The court denies the application for leave to appeal the judgment because the court was not persuaded that the questions presented should be reviewed by the court.
- ***Bowens v. Ary*, 2009 Mich. App. LEXIS 2000 (Mich. Ct. App. Sept. 24, 2009).**
  The court here reversed an order of summary judgment that dismissed all claims against defendants. The court held that in order to establish a claim for eavesdropping the court must remand in order to determine whether plaintiff intended and reasonably expected that the conversation at issue was private.
- ***Bowens v. ARY*, Inc., 489 Mich. 851, 794 N.W.2d 842, 2011 Mich. LEXIS 456 (Mich. 2011).**
  Here, the court reversed the ruling of the appellate court and reinstated summary judgment in favor of the defendants; the evidence showed that "no reasonable juror could conclude that plaintiffs had a reasonably expectation of privacy in the recorded conversation." *Id.*
- ***Roe v. Amazon.com*, 2016 U.S. Dist. LEXIS 33297, 118 U.S.P.Q.2D (BNA) 1070, 44 Media L. Rep. 1469, 2016 WL 1028265 (S.D. Ohio Mar. 15, 2016).**
  In 2014, Defendant Jane Doe wrote a book entitled *A Gronking to Remember* and had it published by the Defendants Amazon.com, Inc., Barnes & Noble, Inc., Apple, Inc. and Smashwords. The Corporate Defendants offered the book for sale on their websites in both digital

formats (Nook, Kindle, iBooks) as well as in paperback. The cover of the book contains a photograph of Plaintiffs taken during their engagement prior to their wedding. The Court concluded that the Corporate Defendants including Amazon.com Inc. were not publishers, and thus the corporate defendants' motion for summary judgment was granted.

- **Yasin v Q-Boro Holdings, LLC, 27 Misc. 3d 1214(A) (N.Y. Sup. Ct. 2010).**
  The Plaintiff, Tasleema Yasin, alleged unlawful use of her photo without her consent on the cover of a book published by Q-Boro Holdings, LLC and Urban Books, LLC entitled Baby Doll. Yasin's motion for a permanent injunction was granted and the defendants were prohibited from further selling, displaying, or using her image.

Vendor's Infringement

Vendor infringement cases typically fall under the other sections of this book for infringement discussed in the respective section topics for IP violations. It is important to note that Amazon is often dismissed from vendor infringement cases because courts generally hold that Amazon is immune from liability from third party vendors.[1]

---

1. *Perfect 10, Inc. v. Amazon.com, Inc*, No. CV 05-4753 AHM (SHx), 2009 U.S. Dist. LEXIS 42341 (C.D. Cal. May 12, 2009).

- ***Corbis Corp. v. Amazon.com, Inc.*, 351 F. Supp. 2d 1090, 2004 U.S. Dist. LEXIS 27155, 77 U.S.P.Q.2D (BNA) 1182 (W.D. Wash. 2004).**
  In this case, plaintiff claimed to have copyright interests in two photographs that Amazon placed on it's website IMDb.com as well as hundreds of photographs that were being sold by vendors on Amazon without Plaintiff's permission. Amazon is protected from liability under the DMCA for copyright infringement occurring on its third party vendor platform. Amazon qualifies as an Internet Service Provider protected under DCMA, does not have affirmative duty to police possible infringement, but must take reasonable steps if is alerted to infringement.
- ***Milo & Gabby, LLC v. Amazon.com, Inc.*, NO. C13-1932RSM, U.S. Dist. Ct., W.D. of Wash., 2015.**
  Amazon won this infringement case under defense of DMCA – Amazon is immune from liability for infringement by third-party vendors.
- ***Perfect 10, Inc. v. Amazon.com, Inc.*, 508 F.3d 1146, 2007 U.S. App. LEXIS 27843 (9th Cir. Cal. 2007).**
  Amazon.com was a defendant in this copyright infringement case brought by Perfect 10. The district court preliminarily enjoined

defendant, Google from creating and publicly displaying thumbnail versions of plaintiff copyright holder's images, but did not enjoin the search engine operator from linking to third-party websites that displayed infringing full-size versions of the images. Both Perfect 10 and Google appealed. The court of appeals reversed the district court's ruling and vacated the preliminary injunction regarding Google's use of the thumbnail images. Additionally, the court reversed the district court's rejection of the claims that Google and Amazon were secondarily liable. All other rulings were affirmed.

- ***Routt v. Amazon.com, Inc.*, 2012 U.S. Dist. LEXIS 170602, 105 U.S.P.Q.2D (BNA) 1089, Copy. L. Rep. (CCH) P30,334 (W.D. Wash. Nov. 30, 2012).**

  In this case, plaintiff claimed that Amazon violated her copyrights in certain photographs because certain Amazon Associate websites displayed her photographs without her permission. The court found Amazon was not responsible for the alleged violation committed by a third-party, and could not be vicariously liable as it had no control over the third-party's activities.
- ***TRE Milano, LLC v. Amazon.com, Inc.*, No. S205747, 2012 Cal. LEXIS 11039 (Nov. 28, 2012).**

  Plaintiff's case against Amazon was dismissed because Amazon was not responsible for the infringement of a third-party, and could also not be held contributorily liable since Amazon took immediate action once it was notified of the third-party's infringement.

Violations of Computer Fraud and Abuse Act

The Computer Fraud and Abuse Act went into effect in 1986. The act essentially states that anyone who intentionally accesses a computer without authorization or exceeds authorized access, and thereby obtains information from any protected computer if the the conduct involved an interstate or foreign communication shall be punished under the act. A 1994 amendment to the act allowed civil actions to be brought under the statute as well. In 1996 the CFAA was again amended and the term "federal interest computer" was replaced with the term "protected computer.

- ***Del Vecchio v. Amazon.com Inc.*, 2011 U.S. Dist. LEXIS 138314, 2011 WL 6325910 (W.D. Wash. Nov. 30, 2011).**
  Amazon.com was a defendant in a case filed by Del Vecchio. Del Vecchio represented a class action against Amazon seeking relief under the Computer Fraud and Abuse act. Amazon motioned to dismiss and the court concluded that the defendant's motion to dismiss should be granted because the plaintiffs failed to plead adequate facts to establish any harm.
- ***Vecchio v. Amazon.com, Inc.* No. C11-366RSL, 2012 U.S. Dist. LEXIS 76536 (W.D. Wash. June 1, 2012).**
  The court here was determining whether the plaintiffs had alleged sufficient facts to plead a plausible claim for relief such that the court should not grant defendants motion to dismiss. The court granted the motion in part and found that as to the CFAA and trespass to chattels claims that because plaintiffs had already had 2 opportunities to amend their complaint that plaintiffs clearly lacked the requisite facts to plead a sufficient claim. As to the CPA and unjust enrichment claims the court granted plaintiffs' request for a "reasonable opportunity to present all the material that is pertinent to the motion." Fed. R. Civ. P. 12(d).

Violations of the Sherman Act

The Sherman Act is a federal anti-monopoly and antitrust statute passed in 1890 and codified as 15 U.S.C §§ 1-7. In a 2013 case, Apple, in an effort to compete with the Amazon platform for sale of digital books, was found liable for violations of the Sherman Act.[1] The court held that Apple conspired to restrain trade with 5 individual publishers because they attempted to force Amazon to change its selling practices by acting collectively to pressure Amazon to change its pricing strategy.[2]

---

1. *United States v. Apple Inc.*, 952 F. Supp. 2d 638 (S.D.N.Y. 2013)
2. *Id.*

- ***Bookhouse of Stuyvesant Plaza, Inc. v. Amazon.com, Inc.*, 985 F. Supp. 2d 612, 2013 U.S. Dist. LEXIS 171871, 2013-2 Trade Cas. (CCH) P78,608, 2013 WL 6311202 (S.D.N.Y. 2013).**
  This case involved an anti-trust claim against Amazon. Book publishers had brought suit because per Amazon's e-book platform, if a consumer owned a Kindle and wanted to read an e-book on the Kindle that was published by any of the publishers in this action, they must buy the book from Amazon. The court granted the Defendants' Motion to Dismiss, as they determined that the plaintiff's complaint failed to state a plausible claim.
- ***Gerlinger v. Amazon.com, Inc.*, 311 F. Supp. 2d 838, 2004 U.S. Dist. LEXIS 4604, 2004-1 Trade Cas. (CCH) P74,363 (N.D. Cal. 2004).**
  Plaintiff could not succeed on antitrust claim when the alleged violation was a price-fixing agreement that actually provided customers with lower prices.

- ***Authors Guild v. Google Inc.*, 770 F. Supp. 2d 666, 2011 U.S. Dist. LEXIS 29126, 98 U.S.P.Q.2D (BNA) 1229, 79 Fed. R. Serv. 3d (Callaghan) 114, Copy. L. Rep. (CCH) P30,057, 2011-1 Trade Cas. (CCH) P77,387 (S.D.N.Y. 2011).**
  This was a motion for final approval of the proposed settlement of a class action. The initial lawsuit involved Google.com's digital library that collected over 12 million books. Amazon.com raised a number on anti-trust concerns presented by the ASA. The motion for final approval was denied by the courts because they found the agreement had gone too far.
- ***United States v. Apple Inc., 952 F. Supp. 2d 638 (S.D.N.Y. 2013).***
  The court here was determining whether defendants Apple Inc. (Apple), and five book publishing companies conspired to raise, fix, and stabilize the retail price for newly released and bestselling trade e-books in violation of the Sherman Anti-Trust Act. The court found that Apple conspired to restrain trade in violation of Section 1 of the Sherman Act. Apple and the publishers are both separate economic entities that worked together to restrain trade.

Workers' Compensation

Workers compensation is a form of insurance providing pay and medical benefits to employees who are injured while they are at work, in exchange for mandatory relinquishment of the employee's right to sue his or her employer for negligence. Any large scale business, such as Amazon will be subject to numerous worker's compensation claims throughout its existence. Amazon has employees worldwide who all perform vastly different tasks, including, warehouse employees, customer service representatives, technical analysts, etc. Most of the litigation regarding workers' compensation and Amazon takes place first in an administrative setting and then is brought to a court of law for the decision to be challenged and/or enforced.

- ***Amazon.Com v. Magee*, 2006 Nev. LEXIS 5 (Nev. Jan. 11, 2006).**
  The court reversed the lower court's denial of review of the petition, as Magee should not have been granted temporary total disability benefits as she was still able to earn a wage.
- ***Amazon.com v. Magee*, 121 Nev. 632 (Nev. 2005).**
  The court concluded that a worker released to work with restrictions is only temporarily partially disabled; therefore, her position and salary need not comport with NRS 616C.475, which sets forth standards regarding when an employer, by offering modified employment, can cease making temporary total disability payments.
- ***Amazon.com v. Workers' Comp. Appeal Bd. (Davidson)*, 2015 Pa. Commw. Unpub. LEXIS 592 (Pa. Commw. Ct. 2015).**
  Amazon.com filed a petition to review an order of the Workers' Compensation Appeal Board that affirmed the decision of a workers' compensation judge denying Employer's termination petition and

granting the review and reinstatement petitions filed by Leon Davison. The court concluded that because the findings showed no legal error, they affirmed the judgment.

- ***Boyd v. Review Bd.*, 13 N.E.3d 950 (Ind. Ct. App. 2014).**
  The court here was determining whether there was sufficient evidence to support the Indiana Department of Workforce Development Board's (the board) determination that Plaintiff, Boyd was ineligible for unemployment compensation benefits because she was discharged for just cause. The court affirmed the decision and found that plaintiff was discharged for just cause because plaintiff was aware of the attendance policy at issue as well as the fact that her actions would violate the policy. The court found this to be just cause for termination.
- ***Gillette v. Amazon.com*, 2016 Del. Super. LEXIS 168 (Del. Super. Ct. Jan. 22, 2016).**
  Amazon.com was the employer of plaintiff, Gillette. Gillette petitioned to the Industrial Accident Board to determine compensation due for her back injuries that allegedly began at work. The Board denied the petition and Gillette appealed. On appeal, the District Court affirmed the Boards decision to deny the petition to determine compensation due. The court found there was no legal error on behalf of the board.
- ***Gribbins v. Amazon.com*, Case No. 2003-CA-002208-WC. Court of Appeals of Kentucky, March 2004.**
  Ina Barnett Gribbins was an employee at Amazon. She alleged that she sustained injuries at work. The Workers' Compensation Board found she was only at a 5% impairment. She appealed the order. The court, finding that the evidence did not fall in favor of Gribbins, affirmed the order of the Workers' Compensation Board.
- ***Gribbins v. Amazon.Com*, 2005 Ky. Unpub. LEXIS 67 (Ky. Apr. 21, 2005).**
  Ina Barnett Gribbins was an employee at Amazon. She alleged that she sustained injuries at work. She now appeals the Court of Appeals decision to affirm the Workers' Compensation Boards' affirming of the

Administrative Law Judge's award. The Supreme Court of Kentucky affirmed the opinion of the Court of Appeals.

- ***Hickman v. Amazon Fullfilment*, 2015 U.S. Dist. LEXIS 168782 (W.D. Pa. Dec. 17, 2015).**
  The court granted the defendant's motion to dismiss as the complaint provided by the plaintiffs had failed to state a claim.
- ***Hickman v. Amazon Fullfilment*, 2016 U.S. Dist. LEXIS 45937 (W.D. Pa. Apr. 5, 2016).**
  The court granted the defendant's motion to dismiss as the complaint provided by the plaintiffs had failed to state a claim. Additionally, the court did not grant leave to amend as it determined plaintiff had been awarded enough opportunities to do so.
- ***Kelley v. Amazon.com, Inc.*, 2013 U.S. Dist. LEXIS 166534, 15 Accom. Disabilities Dec. (CCH) P15-244, 2013 WL 6119229 (E.D. Wash. Nov. 21, 2013).**
  This was a wrongful termination and employee's rights case. Plaintiff Jodie Kelley alleged that her former employer, a subsidiary of Amazon.com, Inc., violated state and federal law by failing to accommodate her disabilities and relying upon her requests for medical leave as a reason for terminating her employment. Kelley's argument was found to be ineffective. As a threshold matter, the evidence of a causal relationship between Plaintiff's deficient performance and her disabilities was entirely speculative.
- ***McGee v. Amazon.com*, 2013 Del. Super. LEXIS 33 (Del. Super. Ct. Jan. 31, 2013).**
  The court determined that the decision of UIAB should be affirmed as Amazon had substantial evidence to show that violation of the company policy should constitute denial of worker's compensation benefits. As an employee was on notice that he needed to improve his attendance record or risk losing his job, and as the employee received a third warning within a 12-month period in violation the employer's policy, the employee was terminated for just cause; thus, he was not entitled to unemployment benefits under Del. Code Ann. tit. 19, § 3314(2).

- ***Shulman v. Amazon.com, Inc.*, 2013 U.S. Dist. LEXIS 20984 (E.D. Wis. Feb. 15, 2013).** This was a case involving plaintiff's request for relief from a sanctions judgment. The court denied the motion for relief of judgment.
- ***Shulman v. Amazon.com.kydc, LLC*, 2015 U.S. Dist. LEXIS 51291 (E.D. Ky. Apr. 20, 2015).**
  The court granted Defendants' Motion to Dismiss, as Shulman failed to state a claim in his complaint for the alleged discrimination.
- ***Shulman v. Amazon.com, Inc.*, 2013 U.S. Dist. LEXIS 76975 (W.D. Wash. May 30, 2013).**
  This case involved defendants' motion to dismiss a complaint for not being filed in a timely manner and failing to state a claim under the family medical leave act. The court granted the motion to dismiss the complaint and action.
- ***Shulman v. Amazon*, 2014 U.S. Dist. LEXIS 113506 (E.D. Ky. Aug. 15, 2014).**
  The defendants' Motion for Sanctions is denied for lack of evidence of plaintiff's reckless conduct or intent to thwart the proceedings.
- ***Stevenson v. Amazon.Com, Inc.*, 2016 U.S. Dist. LEXIS 21172 (D. Mass. Feb. 22, 2016).**
  This was a case involving plaintiff's claim that her constitutional rights were violated by her employer. The court dismissed the claims against Amazon and Security Industry Specialists, Inc., that stemmed from the alleged constitutional rights violations.
- ***Stout v. Hartford Life & Accident Ins. Co.*, 2012 U.S. Dist. LEXIS 172088 (N.D. Cal. Dec. 4, 2012).**
  This case involved a plaintiff's motion to seal documents from being published to the public. The court granted the plaintiff's motion to seal confidential documents in part and denies in part.
- ***Vance v. Amazon.com, Inc. (In re Amazon.com, Inc.)*, 2016 U.S. Dist. LEXIS 48650 (W.D. Ky. Mar. 30, 2016).**
  The court here was determining whether to grant defendants motion to dismiss. The court found that the plaintiffs did not have a sufficient

claim under Kentucky law. Even though Kentucky has its own wage and hour law, the state statute closely resembles the FLSA. Neither the statute of the FLSA defines the word "work." The court finds that in order to define the term "work," that Kentucky courts will look to federal cases interpreting the FLSA to decide what activities constitute "work." In the *Busk* case, the Supreme Court held that the the Portal-to-Portal Act excludes post-shift security checks, and Kentucky courts will use *Busk* to fill the state's statutory void. Therefore, the court granted the defendants motion for judgment on the pleadings.

Wrongful Death

A wrongful death action takes place when a claim exists against someone who can be liable for the death of another. The decedents heirs and other beneficiaries are entitled to file a wrongful death action against those responsible for the decedents death. Wrongful death laws are typically based on statute and vary from state to state. There are generally two types of wrongful death claims, those for intentional wrongful death, and those for unintentional wrongful death.

- ***Cox v. Brand 44, LLC*, 2015 U.S. Dist. LEXIS 143120, 2015 WL 6182469 (D. Mass. Oct. 21, 2015).**
  This was a negligence and wrongful death suit brought by the estate of MJ Cox following his death due to a zip line accident. Defendants' Motion to Dismiss was granted in part, and denied in part. The court denied the motion to dismiss pain and suffering, breach of warranties and loss of consortium but granted in regards to punitive damages and strict liability.

Part III
Case Summaries

CJ ROSENBAUM

LAWYERS FOCUSED ON AMAZON SELLERS

Adaptix, Inc. v. Amazon.com, Inc.
Patent Infringement

Adaptix, Inc. v. Amazon.com, Inc., 2015 U.S. Dist. LEXIS 111933 (N.D. Cal. Aug. 21, 2015).

ISSUE

Should the court grant the defendants motion to dismiss?

RULE

Pursuant to 28 U.S.C. § 299, "No longer can unrelated accused infringers be bound in a single lawsuit 'based solely on allegations that they each have infringed the patent or patents in suit.' Except where there are 'questions of fact common to all," each defendant now gets its own complaint and case."

CASE DETAILS

Facts

Defendants Apple Inc., HTC America, Inc., HTC Corporation, AT&T Mobility LLC, Verizon Wireless, Amazon.com, Inc., Dell, Inc. and Sony Mobile Communications (USA), Inc. moved to dismiss the seven newest cases brought by Adaptix, Inc. for infringement of United States Patent Nos. 6,947,748 and 7,454,212 ('748 and '212 patents). The patents were titled, "OFDMA with adaptive subcarrier-cluster configuration and selective loading." Both patents describe methods for "subcarrier selection for wireless communication systems." Adaptix filed 35 cases alleging infringement of the patents. These cases were filed in certain waves. The court granted the defendant's motion for summary judgment on the wave 1 cases for non-infringement and invalidity.

Defendants, Amazon.com included, within wave 3 and 4, argued that the nine cases are duplicative of others against them and are therefore barred by claim preclusion, issue preclusion, the doctrine against claim splitting and the *Kessler* doctrine.

Analysis

The court found that claim splitting bared Adaptix's claims against Sony and Amazon in the Wave 4 cases. The court held that the, "main purpose behind the rule preventing claim splitting is `to protect the defendant from being harassed by repetitive actions based on the same claim.'"

CONCLUSION

The court concluded that the wave 4 cases, which Amazon.com was a defendant, must be dismissed because they were barred by the doctrine against claim splitting.

Affinity Labs of Tex., LLC v. Amazon.Com, Inc.
Patent Infringement; Procedure

***Affinity Labs of Tex., LLC v. Amazon.com, Inc.*, 2015 U.S. Dist. LEXIS 77411 (W.D. Tex. June 12, 2015).**

ISSUE

Should the court grant the defendants' motion for judgment on the pleadings?

RULE

Section 101 of the Patent Act defines patentable subject matter as "whoever invents or discovers any new and useful process, machine, manufacture, or composition of matter, or any new and useful improvement thereof, may obtain a patent therefor, subject to the conditions and requirements of this title." 36 U.S.C. § 101.

Under the Federal Rules of Civil Procedure 12(c), a party can move for a judgment on the pleadings after the pleadings are close but early enough not to delay trial. Fed. R. Civ. P. 12(c).

CASE DETAILS

Facts

Affinity Labs of Texas, LLC, is the owner of large portfolio of technology-based patents. Defendants are Amazon.Com and Amazon Digital Services. Affinity filed suit against Amazon alleging patent infringement for "wirelessly communication selective information to an electronic device."

Analysis

Affinity argues that Defendants' Motion is premature because: (1) claim construction has not occurred yet, (2) Amazon has not met its burden to prove all underlying factual disputes by clear and convincing evidence, (3) because the motion is incomplete in its effort to invalidate all twenty claims. Denying the Defendants' Motion as premature, only because claim preclusion had not occurred is unwarranted. The court only needs to review the patent itself in regards to a judgment on the pleadings and there is no clear mandate from the courts as to whether the clear and convincing evidentiary standard should be applied in a challenge to patent's eligibility under §101. The court decided that allowing the claims to survive would curb any innovation related to the implementation of the abstract idea on potentially any portable device that utilizes the internet and therefore grants the defendants' motion.

CONCLUSION

The court granted the Defendants' Motion for judgment on the pleadings.

Alcatel- Lucent USA, Inc. v. Amazon.com, Inc.
Patent Infringement; Procedure; Claim Construction

***Alcatel-Lucent USA, Inc. v. Amazon.com, Inc.*, 2011 U.S. Dist. LEXIS 61039, 2011 WL 2260276 (E.D. Tex. June 7, 2011).**

ISSUE

What definitions should the court apply to the terms in dispute in the patents at issue in this claim?

RULE

The claims of a patent define the invention to which the patentee is entitled the right to exclude. *Phillips v. AWH Corp.*, 415 F.3d 1303, 1312 (Fed. Cir. 2005). In claim construction, the court can examine the patent's intrinsic evidence to define the patented invention's scope.

CASE DETAILS

Facts:

Alcatel- Lucent USA, Inc. was suing for patent infringement against defendants. Amazon.com, Inc. counterclaimed that ALU infringed on its U.S. Patents. All five patents are before the court for claim construction.

Analysis:

The court used its ability for claim construction to define the terms of the '131, '656, and '507 Patents. They defined the following as:

- Identifier- a unique label assigned to identity
- Transmitting to said device- transmitting information directly to the device without first downloading the information to an intermediate processor
- Terminal device- computing device such as a data terminal, workstation, portable computer, or smart phone that enables a user to communicate with a host processor.

- Host processor- computer that communicate with one or more users to provide services such as transaction processing or database access.
- Input object type- kinds of displayable graphical symbol that is suitable for display on a user's terminal device and that generates particular input when touched or manipulated by a user.
- Choice- an input object type that may be selected by a user when displayed
- Entry- an input object type that solicits information from a user when displayed
- Text- an input object type that provides textual information to a user when displayed
- Image-an input object type that displays a graphic image
- Script- a series of commands that are interpreted by a program in order to accomplish

CONCLUSION

The court interprets the claim language in the case in the matter set forth above.

Almeida v. Amazon.com, Inc., 456 F.3d 1316 (11th Cir. 2006)
Copyright; Procedure

Almeida v. Amazon.com, Inc., 456 F.3d 1316 (11th Cir. 2006)

ISSUE

Whether the Communications Decency Act (CDA) immunizes an interactive service provider such as Amazon.com from a state law right of publicity claim.

RULE

The majority of federal circuits have interpreted the CDA to establish broad "federal immunity to any cause of action that would make service providers liable for information originating with a third-party user of the service." *Zeran v. Am. Online, Inc.*, 129 F.3d 327, 330 (4th Cir. 1997).

Subsection 230(c) of the CDA provides:

1) Treatment of publisher or speaker

   No provider or user of an interactive computer service shall be treated as the publisher or speaker of any information provided by another information content provider.

(2) Civil liability

   No provider or user of an interactive computer service shall be held liable on account of--(A) any action voluntarily taken in good faith to restrict access to or availability of material that the provider or user considers to be obscene, lewd, lascivious, filthy, excessively violent, harassing, or otherwise objectionable, whether or not such material is constitutionally protected; or (B) any action taken to enable or make available to information content providers or others the technical means to restrict access to material described in paragraph (1). 47 U.S.C. § 230(c).

To maintain a cause of action under the civil theft statute, Almeida must show by "clear and convincing evidence" an injury caused by the defendant's violation of one or more of the provisions of the criminal theft laws found in Fla. Stat. §§ 812.012-037. *Palmer v. Gotta Have It Golf Collectibles, Inc.*, 106 F. Supp. 2d 1289, 1303 (S.D. Fla. 2000).

CASE DETAILS

Facts

Plaintiff, Almeida brought suit against Amazon because they displayed her image on their website in furtherance of sale of the book "Anjos Proibidos." Plaintiff claimed theft, violations under the right of publicity statute, and invasion of privacy. The image was a picture of plaintiff as a 10-year-old child and was displayed on the cover and inside second edition of the book whose title translates to "Forbidden Angels." Plaintiff claims that Amazon should not display her image to promote the sale of the book because she did not consent and did not receive just compensation for the use of her image.

Timeline

At the district court, summary judgment was entered in favor of Amazon for all claims. The district court held as to the right of publicity and invasion of privacy claims, that plaintiff may not recover because her claims were preempted by the CDA. As to the theft claim, the court held that plaintiff failed to establish felonious intent on behalf of Amazon with clear and convincing evidence. This case involves plaintiffs appeal to the district court's decision.

Analysis

The court here holds that it was not necessary to address the difficult issues of application of the CDA under the facts of this case. Because plaintiffs right of publicity claim based on Fla. Stat. § 540.08 would not withstand a motion to dismiss, it was unnecessary for the district court to determine whether the CDA preempts Almeida's state law right of publicity claim.

As to the theft claim the court here held that plaintiff failed to present any evidence that Amazon misappropriated her image with actual knowledge that its use was unauthorized.

CONCLUSION

The court here affirmed the district court's grant of summary judgment in favor of defendant Amazon.

A'lor Int'l v. Tappers Fine Jewelry, Inc.
Copyright Infringement, Attorney's Fees, Unfair Competition

***A'lor Int'l v. Tappers Fine Jewelry, Inc.*, 605 Fed. Appx. 662, 2015 U.S. App. LEXIS 8548 (9th Cir. Cal. 2015).**

ISSUE

Whether the court below erred in holding that defendants did not infringe upon plaintiff's copyright to certain jewelry designs.

CASE DETAILS

Facts

This is a copyright infringement case in which A'lor International, Ltd. appeals a summary judgment order that ruled in favor of its competitors who are producers, distributors, and retailers of jewelry. A'lor owns the copyrights to 24 jewelry designs and maintains that the defendants infringed upon these copyrights. A'lor asserts an unfair competition claim under a theory of misappropriation. A'lor also requests reversal of the attorneys' fees awarded to defendants.

Analysis

The Court finds the existence of contested issues of material fact as to whether A'lor's twenty-four jewelry designs are virtually identical to Lau International, Inc.'s designs, which could infringe A'lor's copyrights, the Court chooses to reverse and remand for trial.

While the district court did not recognize the inverse ratio rule, nor provide its analysis as to each of the twenty-four designs in finding a thin copyright, the Court agrees that the small number of elements in the A'lor designs weighed against applying broad protectability because there are relatively few combinations these elements can yield.

CONCLUSION

The Court chooses to uphold the district court's application of thin copyright protection. The Court grants the dismissal of A'lor's unfair competition claim under a theory of misappropriation. The Court vacates the attorneys' fees award because Defendants were not prevailing parties with respect to the two designs that the district court dismissed without prejudice.

Amazon.com v. American Dynasty Surplus Lines Insurance *Patent Infringement*

***Amazon.com v. Am. Dynasty Ins. Co.*, 120 Wn. App. 610, 85 P.3d 974, 2004 Wash. App. LEXIS 379 (Wash. Ct. App. 2004).**

ISSUE

Did defendant, American Dynasty Surplus Lines Insurance (American Dynasty) have a duty to defend Amazon for injury relating to advertising?

RULE

"Only if the alleged claim is clearly not covered by the policy is the insurer relieved of its duty to defend. If the complaint is ambiguous, it will be liberally construed in favor of triggering the insurer's duty to defend."

CASE DETAILS

Facts

Intouch, the holder of patents for interactive music preview technology, alleged that Amazon used its patents. Amazon.com International alleged that Amazon infringed upon its patents by misappropriating the software used on Amazon's website. Amazon had two insurers, Atlantic Mutual Insurance Company and American Dynasty Surplus Lines Insurance Company. American Dynasty covers patent infringement. Both of the insurers refused to defend, and Amazon filed a declaratory judgment action against Dynasty. This eventually settled and American Dynasty reimbursed Amazon for costs in the Intouch litigation. American Dynasty then brought action alleging that Atlantic Mutual should have provided a defense "because Intouch's allegations amounted to an adverse injury." The court granted summary judgment for Atlantic Mutual and American Dynasty appealed.

Analysis

The court found that Atlantic Mutual had a duty to defend Amazon "unless the injuries alleged by Intouch were clearly not covered by the policy." The injuries were covered and Intouch's complaint triggered Atlantic Mutual's duty to defend. As Amazon's assignee, "American Dynasty was entitled to summary judgment in its favor."

CONCLUSION

The court concluded that "because the allegations conceivably amounted to an advertising injury covered by Amazon's policy with Atlantic Mutual Insurance Company, Atlantic Mutual had a duty to defend" and reversed the summary judgment in favor of Atlantic Mutual. The court remanded for entry of summary judgment in favor of Amazon's excess carrier, American Dynasty Surplus Line.

Amazon.com, Inc. v. Barnesandnoble.com
Patent Infringement

***Amazon.com, Inc. v. Barnesandnoble.com, Inc.*, 73 F. Supp. 2d 1228, 1999 U.S. Dist. LEXIS 18660, 53 U.S.P.Q.2D (BNA) 1115 (W.D. Wash. 1999).**

ISSUE

Whether the court should grant the injunction restricting defendant BarnesandNoble.com from infringing on Amazon's patent for "one click" ordering technology.

RULE

To obtain a preliminary injunction, pursuant to 35 U.S.C. § 283, a party must establish a right thereto in light of four factors: (1) reasonable likelihood of success on the merits; (2) irreparable harm; (3) the balance of hardships tipping in its favor; and (4) the impact of the injunction on the public interest. "*Hybritech, Inc. v. Abbott Labs.*, 849 F.2d 1446, 1451 (Fed Cir. 1988).

CASE DETAILS

Facts

This is a patent infringement suit brought by Amazon.com, Inc. against barnesandnoble.com. The patent in question is United States Patent No. 5,960,411 (the'411 patent), which was issued on September 28, 1999.

The '411 patent describes a Method and System for "Placing a Purchase Order via a Communications Network." The '411 patent, in essence, describes a method and system in which a consumer can complete a purchase order for an item via the Internet using only a single action (such as a single click of a computer mouse button) once information identifying the item is displayed to the consumer.

Amazon.com alleges that Defendants' "Express Lane" ordering feature infringes various claims of the '411 patent. Concurrently with its complaint, Amazon.com filed a motion for a preliminary injunction to enjoin Barnesandnoble.com from infringing the '411 patent.

Analysis

It does not appear that Barnesandnoble.com has ever described the Express Lane ordering process as requiring more than one action, other than in the course of this litigation. The strong similarities between the Amazon.com 1-click feature and the Express Lane feature subsequently adopted by Barnesandnoble.com suggest that Barnesandnoble.com copied Amazon.com's feature. Barnesandnoble.com presented evidence that a number of other e-commerce retailers have offered single-action ordering to customers. The invention described in the '411 patent is of significant commercial value, as evidenced by the large number of customers who make use of single-action ordering available on the websites of both Amazon.com and Barnesandnoble.com. The harm Amazon.com would suffer if denied the benefit of using its invention to distinguish itself from its competitor Barnesandnoble.com could not easily be measured in dollars. Amazon.com would not be able to distinguish itself from a key competitor by offering single-action ordering and would likely lose market share and customers to Barnesandnoble.com. The Court finds that this loss would not be easily compensable in damages. Exclusive rights to the patented invention are important to Amazon.com's ability to differentiate the customer experience available at its site from that of competitor sites such as Barnesandnoble.com.

CONCLUSION

The Court finds that Plaintiff has demonstrated a reasonable likelihood of success on the merits at trial. The Court finds that Plaintiff has made a strong showing that the '411 patent is valid and that Defendants' Express Lane feature infringes the patent. Plaintiff is therefore entitled to a presumption of irreparable harm. Therefore, the Court ordered that defendants are enjoined from continuing to infringe United States Patent No. 5,960,411, including by continuing to make or use within the United States Defendants' Express Lane feature as currently configured or any other single-action ordering system that employs the methods or systems of the '411 patent, or by inducing others to make or use within the United States Defendants' Express Lane feature as currently configured or any other single-action ordering system that employs the methods of systems of the '411 patent. Defendants may continue to offer an Express Lane feature if the feature is modified to avoid infringement of the '411 patent in a manner that is consistent with the findings of fact and conclusions of law set forth above.

Amazon.com, Inc. v. Barnesandnoble.com, Inc.
Patent Infringement; Procedure

***Amazon.com, Inc. v. Barnesandnoble.com, Inc.*, 239 F.3d 1343, 2001 U.S. App. LEXIS 2163, 57 U.S.P.Q.2D (BNA) 1747 (Fed. Cir. 2001).**

ISSUE

Should the court grant Amazon's Motion for a Preliminary Injunction?

RULE

Preliminary injunction 35 U.S.C. § 283 (1994) is within the sound discretion of the district court. *Novo Nordisk of N. Am., Inc. v. Genentech, Inc.*, 77 F.3 1364, 1367 (Fed. Cir. 1996). "An abuse of discretion may be established by showing that the court made a clear error of judgment in weighing relevant factors or exercised its discretion based upon an error of law or clearly erroneous factual findings." *Id.*

CASE DETAILS

Facts

Amazon brought a patent infringement case on October 21, 1999, against barnesandnoble.com and moved for a preliminary injunction to prohibit BN's use of a feature of its web site called "Express Lane." Amazon's patent is directed to a method for "single action" ordering of items in a server environment such as the Internet.

Timeline

The United States District Court for the Western District of Washington rejected BarnesandNobles.com contentions that Express Lane feature did not infringe the claims of Amazon's patent. The district court held that Amazon had presented a case showing a likelihood of infringement by Barnes and Noble and their challenge to validity of the patent lacked merit. Barnes and Noble appeals.

Analysis

The moving party, Amazon, is entitled to a preliminary injunction if it can show a reasonable likelihood of success on the merits, irreparable harm if an injunction is not granted, a balance of hardships tipping in its favor, and the injunction's favorable impact on the public interest. *Reebok Int'l Ltd. v. J. Baker, Inc.*, 32 F.3d 1552, 1555, 31 (Fed. Cir. 1994). The court used its authority for claim construction to determine the meaning of the terms within the patent. The court also looked at the validity challenges that the district court dismissed. Amazon did not submit any evidence to show either that its commercial success was related to the "1-Click" ordering feature or that single-action ordering caused a reduction in the number of abandoned shopping carts. The court found that although Amazon has carried its burden of demonstrating the likelihood of success on infringement, BarnesandNoble.com has also raised substantial questions as to the validity of the '411 patent.

CONCLUSION

The court vacated the preliminary injunction and remanded the case for further proceedings.

Amazon.com, Inc. v. CITI Servs
Procedure

***Amazon.com, Inc. v. CITI Servs.*, 2008 U.S. Dist. LEXIS 94885 (D. Del. Nov. 21, 2008).**

ISSUE

Whether the court should grant should grant defendants Motion to Set Aside Default Order and Judgment.

RULE

When deciding whether to set aside a default judgment, the Third Circuit has prescribed three factors that a district court should consider: (1) whether lifting the default judgment will prejudice the plaintiff; (2) whether the defendant has a meritorious defense; and (3) whether the defendant's conduct in defaulting was culpable. See Harad v. Aetna Cas. & Sur. Co., 839 F.2d 979, 982 (3d Cir. 1988); Nationwide Mut. Ins. Co. v. Starlight Ballroom Dance Club, Inc., 175 Fed. Appx. 519, 522 (3d Cir. 2006).

CASE DETAILS

Facts

In August of 1999, plaintiff, Amazon.Com, Inc. (Amazon) filed suit against defendants claiming trademark infringement, unfair competition, and dilution. Amazon alleged that defendants wrongfully used amazon domain names and trademarks, and that defendants copied Amazon's copyrighted works. Defendants did not pay their legal bills and the defense's counsel withdrew. The court ordered defendants to respond to discovery requests and obtain new counsel, but defendants did not oblige. The lower court ultimately granted default judgment against the defendants.

Analysis

The court finds that here, the plaintiff will be prejudiced if the default judgment is lifted. The plaintiff has already been awarded injunctive relief, damages, and attorney's fees as part of the default judgment. Vacating this award and forcing the plaintiffs to re-litigate would be costly and certainly unfair to plaintiffs. The court next finds that here the defendants have not persuaded the court that they have a meritorious defense. The defendants offer no evidence or reason for the court to reconsider its findings. Finally, the court finds that the defendants conduct was certainly culpable (blameworthy). The defendants repeatedly failed to adhere to judicial orders and this case has been pending for over 6 years. If defendant wanted to raise any issues, they had plenty of time to do so.

CONCLUSION

For the foregoing reasons, the court denies defendants' Motion to Set Aside Default Order and Judgment.

Amazon.com Inc. v. Coyote Logistics
Theft, Breach of Contract, Negligence

***Amazon.com v. Coyote Logistics* Case No. C11-1015 RSL, United States District Court Western District of Washington at Seattle, December 11, 2013.**

ISSUE

Whether after the entry of default judgment, the court has reason to award damages.

RULE

Upon entry of default, the well-pleaded allegations of the complaint relating to defendant's liability are taken as true, and the defaulting party is deemed to have admitted all allegations in the complaint pertaining to liability. *Televideo System, Inc. v. Heidenthal*, 826 F.2d 915, 917-918 (9th Cir .1987).

CASE DETAILS

Facts

The parties allege that CP Transport was hired to transport a container of Amazon Kindles from Washington to Delaware in November 2009. Plaintiff alleges that the driver left the shipment unattended at a truck stop, resulting in the theft of the truck, container, and goods.

Amazon and Coyote Logistics have asserted claims of breach of contract, breach of bill of lading, loss under the Carmack Amendment, negligence, and/or equitable indemnification against CP Transport that is due to the loss of the Kindles.

In the First Amended Complaint, Amazon requested an award of lost market value in the amount of $1,454,346.00, plus the realistic costs of investigating, recovering, repairing, and shipping the recovered goods.

Although CP Transport was served in this action, it has not responded. Default was entered against it in October 2013.

Analysis

When there has been an entry of default judgment, the court does not need to make detailed findings of fact as long as the allegations contained in the pleasdings are sufficient to establish liability. After reviewing the case memorandum, declarations, and exhibits, the court found as follows below.

CONCLUSION

The court ruled in favor of Coyote Logistics, LLC, and against CP Transport, Inc., in the amount of $685,000.00. The court ruled in favor of Amazon.com, Inc., and Amazon Fulfillment Services, Inc., and against CP Transport, Inc., for a total amount of $1,447,023.20.

Amazon.com, Inc. v. Kalaydjian
Trademark Infringement

***Amazon.com, Inc. v. Kalaydjian*, 2001 U.S. Dist. LEXIS 4924 (W.D. Wash. Feb. 20, 2001).**

ISSUE

Whether defendant's acts constitute purposeful availment such that granting of defendant's motion to dismiss for lack of personal jurisdiction would not be proper.

RULE

In order to establish purposeful availment under the effects doctrine, the plaintiff must demonstrate the existence of "(1) intentional actions (2) expressly aimed at the forum state (3) causing harm, the brunt of which is suffered - and which the defendant knows is likely to be suffered - in the forum state." Core-Vent Corp. v. Nobel Indus. AB, 11 F.3d 1482, 1486(9thCir.1993).

CASE DETAILS

Facts

Plaintiff, Amazon.Com, Inc. (Amazon) sells many products, including suntan lotions and cosmetics. Amazon uses AMAZON.COM and other logos as marks to identify its goods and services. These marks are registered with the United States Patent and Trademark Office. Defendant Kalaydjian (defendant) makes and sells sun tanning products under the name Amazon Cosmetics and Tan Products (Amazon Tan). Amazon tan uses three marks in association with its tanning oil products: (1) AMAZONTAN.COM, Reg. No. 106216, a trademark for identification of skin tanning preparations; (2) AMAZON, Reg. No. 53218, a service mark used for "company advertising and producing sun skin tanning preparations;" and (3) AMAZON, Reg. No. 053218, a service mark used for "producing sun tanning preparations.

Defendant has sold about 100 bottles of tanning oil. Of these 100 bottles about 98 were sold at a flea market in California. The other bottles were sold to customers in Arizona and Canada. It is unclear whether the sales originated from AmazonTan.com. Defendant also mailed a free sample of the oil to a Washington resident, per the resident's request. Both parties have sent each other cease and desist letters asserting that they infringed each others marks. Amazon ultimately filed suit in the Western District of Washington, alleging that defendant infringed and diluted its trademarks. This motion to dismiss for lack of personal jurisdiction followed.

Analysis

The court finds defendants website is not sufficiently interactive to support a finding of personal availment. The site does not allow purchases via the internet, but merely provides information about Amazon Tan products and tells customers how to purchase the products through the mail. The court further finds that the fact that a single bottle was shipped to Washington does not warrant the conclusion that there was purposeful availment in this case.

CONCLUSION

The court finds that defendants acts do not establish purposeful availment and thus the court need not consider whether Amazon's claims arise out of defendant's forum related activities or whether jurisdiction would be reasonable. The court grants defendants motion to dismiss for lack of personal jurisdiction.

Amazon.com v. Lay
Finance and Tax Law

***Amazon.com LLC v. Lay*, 758 F. Supp. 2d 1154, 2010 U.S. Dist. LEXIS 113163, 73 A.L.R. Fed. 2d 501 (W.D. Wash. 2010).**

ISSUE

Whether the court should grant Amazon.Com LLC's (Amazon) motion for summary judgment where defendant secretary of the North Carolina department of labor is requesting detailed information regarding sales by Amazon to North Carolina customers.

RULE

Summary judgment is proper if the pleadings, depositions, answers to interrogatories, admissions on file, and affidavits show that there are no genuine issues of material fact for trial and that the moving party is entitled to judgment as a matter of law. Fed. R. Civ. P. 56(c). The First Amendment protects a buyer from having the expressive content of her purchase of books, music, and audiovisual materials disclosed to the government. Citizens are entitled to receive information and ideas through books, films, and other expressive materials anonymously. In the context of distribution of handbills, the Supreme Court held that anonymity "exemplifies the purpose behind the Bill of Rights, and of the First Amendment in particular." *McIntyre v. Ohio Elections Comm'n*, 514 U.S. 334, 357, 115 S. Ct. 1511, 131 L. Ed. 2d 426 (1995).

CASE DETAILS

Facts

Amazon and the North Carolina Department of Revenue (DOR) have long disputed whether Amazon must collect and remit North Carolina sales and use taxes. As part of an audit of Amazon, the DOR's secretary, defendant Lay, sent a request to Amazon for "all information for all sales to customers with a North Carolina shipping address by month in an electronic format for all dates between August 1, 2003 and February 28, 2010. Amazon provided the DOR with "detailed information about millions of purchases made by North Carolina customers during the relevant time period." Amazon provided the order ID number, seller, ship-to city, county, postal code, the non-taxable amount of the purchase, and the tax audit record identification. In addition, Amazon provided the Amazon Specific Identification Number ("ASIN") for every purchase, a number which permits access to the specific and detailed description of the product. Amazon identifies products in its catalog and maintains its sales records using ASIN numbers, rather than more generic product codes. Collectively, this information permits the DOR to learn of the "title and description of every book, DVD, music selection, or other item purchased by the customer." Amazon did not include the name, address, phone number, e-mail address or other personally identifiable information of any customer. On March 19, 2010, the DOR requested Amazon provide the "Bill to Name; Bill to Address (Street, City, State, and Zip); Ship to Name; Ship to Address (Street); [and] Product/item code or description."

Amazon claims: (1) That the First Amendment and Article 1, Sections 4 and 5 of the Washington State Constitution bar the revelation of the identities of its customers' purchases and any specifics as to the content of the purchases; and (2) that the Video Privacy Protection Act, 18 U.S.C. § 2710, bars compliance with the DOR's March 2010 request.

Analysis

The court finds that because the DOR's request implicates the First Amendment, the DOR must show "a compelling governmental interest warrants the burden, and that the restrictive means to achieve the government's ends are not available. Because the DOR conceded that it had no legitimate need or use for having details as to North Carolina Amazon customers' literary, music, and film purchases the court finds that the request is too broad.

CONCLUSION

The court grants Amazon's motion for summary judgment.

Amazon.com v. Magee
Workers' Compensation and Employees' Rights

***Amazon.com v. Magee*, 121 Nev. 632 (Nev. 2005).**

ISSUE

Whether an employee who is treated for injuries sustained on the job is considered temporarily totally disabled or temporarily partially disabled when she is able to return to work on a part-time basis.

RULE

NRS 616C.475(1) establishes the compensation owed to an employee who is classified as temporarily totally disabled and states that the employee "is entitled to receive for the period of temporary total disability, 66 2/3 percent of the average monthly wage." Under NRS 616C.475(5), however, temporary total disability benefits must cease when:

(a) A physician or chiropractor determines that the employee is physically capable of any gainful employment for which the employee is suited, after giving consideration to the employee's education, training and experience;
(b) The employer offers the employee light-duty employment or employment that is modified according to the limitations or restrictions imposed by a physician or chiropractor pursuant to subsection 7.

CASE DETAILS

Facts / Timeline

April 18, 2001: Dee Dee Magee injured her right wrist while working at her job with Amazon.com in Fernley, Nevada. Magee sought treatment at a local emergency room, and after an examination, the treating physician diagnosed her injury as possible carpal tunnel syndrome, placed her in a forearm splint and prescribed naproxen.

April 23, 2001: Magee sought further medical advice regarding the cause and extent of her injury. After an examination, the physician noted that Magee should be placed on restricted duty.

May 14 - June 10, 2001: Magee visited several physicians. Each physician recommended Magee keep her workload to light-duty work with some physical restrictions and limitations.

June 11, 2001: Magee was released to light-duty work with a four-hour-a-day work restriction after a doctors' appointment.

August 13, 2001: Magee underwent corrective surgery on her right wrist. Following the surgery, she experienced pain in her left hand and was diagnosed with carpal tunnel syndrome in her left wrist. Consequently, Magee underwent a second surgery to repair her left wrist.

October 30, 2001: Magee was released to full-duty work with no restrictions.

Analysis

Before the initial wrist injury, Magee worked approximately ten hours per day, four days a week, for a total of forty hours per week. She was paid $10.00 per hour for a gross weekly wage of $400.00. After her initial wrist injury, when Magee was restricted in the number of hours she could work, she still earned $10.00 an hour. The record indicates that her daily and weekly hours varied, but that she generally never worked more than four hours a day or sixteen hours a week.

Magee eventually submitted workers' compensation claims for the injuries to her wrists. Amazon.com never disputed Magee's diagnosis or that her condition was the result of her employment.

From May 5 through October 30, 2001, Amazon.com's insurer found that Magee was eligible for temporary partial disability benefits, with at least two periods when she was eligible for temporary total disability benefits.

The first period of Magee's temporary total disability, which began after the right-wrist surgery on August 13, 2001, was terminated on August 24, 2001, because she returned to light-duty work and collected temporary partial disability benefits. Temporary total disability benefits were reinstated on October 3, 2001, due to Magee's left-wrist surgery, but were terminated on October 16, 2001, after her physician released her to light-duty work.

Finally, based upon her release to full-duty work with no restrictions on October 30, 2001, all benefits ceased.

Magee administratively appealed the insurer's determinations to a workers' compensation hearing officer with the Nevada Department of Administration, asserting generally that under NRS 616C.475, she was entitled to temporary total disability benefits for the entire period of May 5, 2001, through October 30, 2001. The hearing officer disagreed and affirmed the insurer's previous determinations.

CONCLUSION

The court concluded that a worker released to work with restrictions is only temporarily partially disabled; therefore, her position and salary need not comport with NRS 616C.475, which sets forth standards regarding when an employer, by offering modified employment, can cease making temporary total disability payments.

The court chose to reverse the district court's order denying Amazon.com's petition for judicial review and remand for further proceedings consistent with this opinion.

Amazon.com v. Magee
Employer Rights; Procedural

***Amazon.Com v. Magee*, 2006 Nev. LEXIS 5 (Nev. Jan. 11, 2006).**

ISSUE

Whether an employee who is treated for injuries obtained on the job is considered temporarily disabled whether partial or totally when she is able to return to work on a part time schedule?

RULE

Under NRS 616C.475, an employer who provides a temporarily disabled employee with a post-injury job that is similar in hours, location and gross pay to the job the employee held pre-injury, and who gives adequate consideration to the employee's post-injury limitations, can cease paying the employee temporary total disability benefits.

CASE DETAILS

Facts:

On April 18, 2001, Magee injured her wrist at her job with Amazon.com. She was released to light-duty work subject to limitations. She continued to work four hour days, instead of her usual ten hours a day, and therefore sough workers' compensation. Magee filed suit alleging she was entitled to temporary total disability benefits for the entire period.

Timeline:

Employer petitions for the review of the decision from the Department of Administration that awarded Magee temporary total disability benefits for period when she could not return to work on a part-time schedule. The First Judicial District Court denied the petition. Amazon.com now appeals.

Analysis:

The court, on appeal, determined that Magee was only partially disabled. She was unable to earn her total pre-injury wages; however, her disability was partial not total. She was not entitled to temporary total disability benefits because the limitations, for the most part did not prevent her from earning wages. Therefore, the court determined that the appeals officer erroneously determined that Magee was entitled to temporary total compensation benefits and reverses the district court's denying the petition for judicial review and remand.

CONCLUSION

The court reversed the district court's denial for review and remanded the case for further proceedings.

Amazon.Com Inc. v. National Association of College Stores Inc.
Lanham Act; Procedural- Motion to Dismiss

***Amazon.com, Inc. v. Nat'l Ass'n of College Stores, Inc.*, 826 F. Supp. 2d 1242, 2011 U.S. Dist. LEXIS 135880 (W.D. Wash. 2011).**

ISSUE

Whether the court should grant the Defendant's Motion to Dismiss for lack of subject matter jurisdiction.

RULE

The burden of establishing subject matter jurisdiction rests upon the party-asserting jurisdiction. Federal Rule of Civil Procedure 12(b)(1) attacks on jurisdiction can be facial or factual. *Savage v. Glendale Union High Sch.*, Dist. No. 205, 343 F.3d 1036, 1039. (9th Cir. 2003).

CASE DETAILS

Facts:

Amazon is an online retailer that sells many things, including college textbooks. NACS is an association representing the campus retailing industry. On February 2, 2011, NACS sent a letter to Amazon expressing concern that Amazon was selling textbooks at a loss in order to take NACS customers. It requested that Amazon review its policies. Amazon alleges that it does not violate the Lanham Act and wants a declaration that its use of the three advertising claims is legitimate. Defendant Nation Association of College Stores, Inc.'s Motion to Dismiss Amazon's complaint is before the court. NACS alleges that the court lacks subject matter jurisdiction over Amazon's declaratory judgment complaint and the court lacks personal jurisdiction over NACS. Amazon opposes the motion.

Analysis:

Amazon's allegations that it intends to continue using the three advertising claims challenged by NACS, and NACS's conduct in requesting substantiation of Amazon's claims, filing a complaint with the NAD, and issuing a press release publicizing its dispute with Amazon, demonstrate that there is a substantial controversy between adverse parties and reality to warrant the issuance of declaratory judgment regarding Amazon's right to continue to use its advertising claims. Amazon has met its burden to establish that it satisfies the Declaratory Judgment Act's "actual controversy requirement." The court decided it does have jurisdiction over the matter and therefore denied NACS's motion to dismiss.

CONCLUSION

The court denied NACS's Motion to Dismiss.

Amazon.Com LLC V. New York State Department Of Taxation And Finance
Financial and Tax Law

***Amazon.com LLC v. New York State Dept. of Taxation & Fin.*, 877 N.Y.S.2d 842, 23 Misc. 3d 418, 2009 N.Y. Misc. LEXIS 28, 2009 NY Slip Op 29007, 241 N.Y.L.J. 12 (N.Y. Sup. Ct. 2009).**

ISSUE

Did Amazon.com sufficiently state a cause of action such that this case should not be dismissed for failure to state a claim?

RULE

In New York, "every vendor of tangible personal property" is required to collect sales tax (*see* Tax Law § 1131 [1]; § 1105).

"The commission-agreement provision thus requires collection of New York taxes from New Yorkers by out-of-state sellers that contractually agree to pay commissions to New York residents for referring potential customers to them, provided that more than $10,000 was generated from such New York referrals during the preceding four quarterly periods."

CASE DETAILS

Facts

Amazon created an "Associates Program" which allowed participants to maintain links to Amazon.com on the website. Along with this, Amazon has a Amazon Prime program which "paid them a $12 bounty for each new enrollee." Thousands of the associates in this program are New York residents. Amazon acknowledged that its "Associates Program generated more than $10,000 per year in sales to customers located in New York".

Amazon filed suit alleging that the commission-agreement provision, "violated the Commerce Clause of the United States Constitution, ... because it imposes tax collection obligations on out-of-state entities who have no substantial nexus with New York." Additionally, Amazon alleged that this "violates the Federal and State Constitutions' Due Process Clauses, both facially and as applied, because "it effectively creates an irrebuttable presumption of `solicitation' and is overly broad and vague"

Analysis

The court held, "The commission-agreement provision is carefully crafted to ensure that there is a sufficient basis for requiring collection of New York taxes and, if such a basis does not exist, it gives the seller an out." Therefore, the statue was facially valid.

Additionally, the court found that Amazon did not properly refute the Tax Law's presumed constitutionality. Ultimately, the court dismissed Amazon's first cause of action for declaratory relief based on violation of the Commerce Clause.

The court dismissed Amazon's second and third causes of action as well. The court found that Amazon failed to state a cause of action.

CONCLUSION

The court concluded that because Amazon failed to state a cause of action, the suit was dismissed.

Amazon.com v. New York State Department of Taxation and Finance
Financial and Tax Law

***Amazon.com, LLC v New York State Dept. of Taxation & Fin.*, 81 A.D.3d 183, 913 N.Y.S.2d 129, 2010 N.Y. App. Div. LEXIS 7943, 2010 NY Slip Op 7823 (N.Y. App. Div. 1st Dep't 2010).**

ISSUE

Is the amended Tax Law § 1101 (b) (8) (vi) Constitutional?

RULE

Tax Law § 1101 (b) (8) (vi) intended to force on-line retailers to collect a sales tax on purchases made by New York residents.

CASE DETAILS

Facts

Amazon created an "Associates Program" which allowed participants to maintain links to Amazon.com on the website. Along with this, Amazon has a Amazon Prime program which "paid them a $12 bounty for each new enrollee." Thousands of the associates in this program are New York residents. Amazon acknowledged that its "Associates Program generated more than $10,000 per year in sales to customers located in New York".

Amazon filed a complaint seeking declaratory and injunctive relief on the ground that the statute was unconstitutional. Amazon asserted claims for violation of the Commerce, Due Process and Equal Protection Clauses of the United States Constitution, as well as the Due Process and Equal Protection Clauses of the New York State Constitution. The court granted the State's motion to dismiss.

Amazon and co-plaintiff, Overstock.com appealed. Amazon raised three challenges to the statute. First, Amazon argued that the statute is unconstitutional because it lacks a substantial nexus within the state. Second, Amazon argued that the statute violated the Due Process Clause because, "facially and as applied, it enacts an irrational and irrebuttable presumption, and is also vague." Third,

Amazon argued that the statute violated the Equal Protection Clause because "it targets Amazon in bad faith."

Analysis

The court held that the facial challenge based upon the Commerce Clause must fail because, "there is a set of circumstances under which the statute would be valid, i.e., when a New York representative uses some form of proactive solicitation which results in a sale by Amazon and a commission to the representative, and the representative has an in-state presence sufficient to satisfy the substantial nexus test."

Additionally, the court found that "it would be premature to find that the due process challenges are unavailing, whether because the statute creates an illegal and irrebuttable presumption or because the language of the statute is so vague that plaintiffs cannot ascertain which transactions give rise to their obligations to collect the sales tax."

CONCLUSION

The court concluded that they did not find the facial challenges to have merit, but found that further discovery was necessary before a determination can be rendered as to the as-applied Commerce Clause and Due Process Clause claims. Additionally, the court found that, "the dismissal of the complaint on Commerce Clause and federal and state due process and equal protection grounds, should be modified, on the law and on the facts, to declare that the statute is constitutional on its face and does not violate the Equal Protection Clause either on its face or as applied and to reinstate the complaint for further proceedings with regard to the claims that, as applied, the statute violates the Commerce and Due Process Clauses, and otherwise affirmed, with costs."

Amazon.com, Inc. v. Powers
Procedure

***Amazon.com, Inc. v. Powers*, No. C12-1911RAJ, 2012 U.S. Dist. LEXIS 182831 (W.D. Wash. Dec. 27, 2012).**

ISSUE

Whether the court should grant Amazon's preliminary injunction against defendant past employee from disclosing trade secrets.

RULE

The court may issue a preliminary injunction where a party establishes (1) a likelihood of success on the merits, (2) that it is likely to suffer irreparable harm in the absence of preliminary relief, (3) that the balance of hardships tips in its favor, and (4) that the public interest favors an injunction. *Winter v. Natural Resources Defense Council, Inc.*, 555 U.S. 7, 20, 129 S. Ct. 365, 172 L. Ed. 2d 249 (2008). A party can also satisfy the first and third elements of the test by raising serious questions going to the merits of its case and a balance of hardships that tips sharply in its favor. *Alliance for the Wild Rockies v. Cottrell*, 632 F.3d 1127, 1131 (9th Cir. 2011).

CASE DETAILS

Facts

Amazon hired defendant to serve as vice president of its Amazon Web Services (AWS) division. This division focused on sales to businesses and dealt with cloud computing services. After roughly two years, defendant stopped working at Amazon.

When defendant began work defendant signed a "confidentiality, noncompetition and invention assignment agreement." Three moths after leaving work at Amazon, defendant began working or Google, Inc. (google). Google voluntarily restricted defendants cloud computing work, but these restrictions did not satisfy Amazon. Amazon here seeks a five-part injunction that would prohibit defendant from disclosing Amazon's confidential information or trade secrets. It would prevent him from engaging in "any activity that directly or indirectly supports any aspect of Google's cloud computing business that competes with Amazon's cloud computing business," including but not limited to the three specific Google products that allegedly compete with Amazon cloud products. *Id.* He would not be able to solicit "any customer or prospect of Amazon's cloud computing business with whom he had direct contact or regarding whom he received confidential information while employed by Amazon." *Id.* He would not be able to solicit or recruit any "current Amazon employees." *Id.* Finally, the injunction would require him to return anything that he took from Amazon.

<u>Analysis</u>

The court first dismisses the injunction requests prohibiting defendant form "soliciting or recruiting any current Amazon employees. The court finds that there is no evidence that defendant has or intends to recruit Amazon employees. The court also finds it cannot impose an injunction requiring defendant to return all amazon property because there is no evidence at all that he took anything from Amazon when he left.

The court finds that on the record Amazon is likely to succeed on the merits only on its clam based on the Agreement's restriction on working with former customers. The court ultimately enters the following injunction:

> Until March 19, 2013, unless the court orders otherwise, Defendant Daniel Powers may not directly or indirectly assist in providing cloud computing services to any current, former, or prospective customer of Amazon about whom he learned confidential information while working at Amazon. "Confidential information" has the definition the parties gave it in the Agreement.

<u>CONCLUSION</u>

The court grants in part and denies in part Amazon's motion for preliminary injunction.

***Amazon.com, Inc. v. Straight Path IP Grp., Inc.* Patent Infringement**

***Amazon.com, Inc. v. Straight Path IP Grp., Inc.*, 2015 U.S. Dist. LEXIS 69281 (N.D. Cal. May 28, 2015).**

ISSUE

Should the court grant the motion to dismiss? Should the court grant the motion to transfer?

RULE

Under *Rule 12(b)(1)*, a party may file a motion to dismiss for lack of subject matter jurisdiction.

Pursuant to 28 *U.S.C. 1404(a)*, "a district court may transfer any civil action to any other district or division where it might have been brought or to any district or division to which all parties have consented"

CASE DETAILS

Facts

Straight Path sued Amazon.com for patent infringement in the Eastern District of Virginia. In dispute was whether Amazon's technology infringed U.S. Patent Nos. 6,009,469 (the "'469 patent"), 6,108,704 (the "'704 patent"), and 6,131,121 (the "'121 patent"). The actions had been stayed pending "1) the outcome of a currently-pending appeal to the Court of Appeals for the Federal Circuit relating to the patentability of the patents-in-suit, and (2) three requests for *inter partes* review challenging the patentability of the patents-in-suit."

Defendant, Straight Path IP Group, Inc. motioned to dismiss for lack of subject matter jurisdiction over plaintiff, Amazon.com. In the alternative, the defendant requested to transfer to the Eastern District of Virginia.

Analysis

The court found that there was substantial controversy for Straight Path's infringement claims against LGE and VIZIO, and strongly support the conclusion that the Court has jurisdiction. Additionally, the court found that "Amazon's obligation to indemnify LGE and VIZIO alone creates a standing for jurisdiction." The court denied Straight Path's Motion to Dismiss for lack of subject matter jurisdiction.

The court looked to the convenience of the parties and found that this weighed in favor of transfer. The court looked to the plaintiff's choice in forum and found that this made a minimal difference. The court found that the location where relevant agreements negotiated and executed was neutral. The court found the respective parties' contacts with the forum to be neutral. For the differences in the costs of litigation in the two forums, the court found that this weighed in favor of transfer. For the convenience to the witnesses, the court weighed strongly in favor of transfer. Finally, for the interest of justice, the court found that this weighed in favor of transfer.

CONCLUSION

For the foregoing reasons, the court denied the motion to dismiss and granted the motion to transfer venue.

Amazon.Com, Inc. v. Underwriters, Lloyds's of London, et al, Defendants
Procedure; Class Action

Amazon.Com, Inc. v. Underwriters, Lloyds's of London, et al, Defendants

ISSUE

Whether the court should grant defendants' motions to dismiss for lack of personal jurisdiction and for failure to properly serve.

RULE

In relevant part, Washington's long arm statute states: (1) [a]ny person, whether or not a citizen or resident of this state, who in person or through an agent does any of the acts in this section enumerated, thereby submits said person, and, if an individual, his personal representative, to the jurisdiction of the courts of this state as to any cause of action arising from the doing of any said acts: ... (d) Contracting to insure any person, property or risk located within this state at the time of contracting. RCW 4.28.185.

Under Washington law, service of process for unauthorized alien insurers may be effectuated by serving duplicate copies of the summons on the state Insurance Commissioner via a person competent to serve a summons or by registered mail, along with payment of a $10 fee to the Commissioner. RCW 48.05.215.

CASE DETAILS

Facts

In Mach of 2001, a consolidated class action was filed in this court. Plaintiff's alleged that Amazon's officers and directors made fraudulent statements to inflate the value of certain Amazon securities. A second class action was filed alleging that Amazon sold certain securities to plaintiffs at an inflated price. Amazon purchased insurance for its directors and officers from both National Union and Underwriters at Lloyd's of London, as well as other companies for more supplemental insurance. Amazon claims that certain insurance companies are hampering Amazon's efforts in the class actions because the insurance companies are refusing that their policies cover the violations of those class action claims.

Amazon filed this action asking the court to grant it declaratory relief and find that the excess insurers have breached their contracts with Amazon. Defendant brings motions to dismiss for lack of personal jurisdiction and for failure to properly serve.

Analysis

The court finds that as to the motion to dismiss for lack of personal jurisdiction, that defendants have purposefully availed themselves to the state of Washington, such that jurisdiction is proper. By insuring a company in Washington, the defendants established ties that would make them "reasonably anticipate being haled to court there." *World-Wide Volkswagen Corp. v. Woodson,* 444 U.S. 286, 287,100 S.Ct. 559, 62 L.Ed.2d 490.

The court further finds that Amazon complied with the Washington statute regarding service on unauthorized, alien insurers. Service compliance focuses on whether the method of service was "reasonably calculated to provide notice the the defendant." Powell v. Sphere Drake Ins. P.L.C., 97 Wash. App. 890, 899, 988 P.2d 12 (1999).

CONCLUSION

For the foregoing reasons, the court denies both motions to dismiss.

Amazon.com v. Workers' Comp
Workers' Compensation; Employees' Rights

***Amazon.com v. Workers' Comp. Appeal Bd. (Davidson),* 2015 Pa. Commw. Unpub. LEXIS 592 (Pa. Commw. Ct. 2015).**

ISSUE

Should the court affirm the holding made by the Workers' Compensation Judge?

RULE

Pursuant to the holding in *Daniels v. Workers' Compensation Appeal Board,* "A decision is 'reasoned' for purposes of Section 422(a) if it allows for adequate review by the [Board] without further elucidation and if it allows for adequate review by the appellate courts under applicable review standards. A reasoned decision is no more, and no less."

CASE DETAILS

Facts

Amazon.com filed a petition to review an order of the Workers' Compensation Appeal Board that affirmed the decision of a workers' compensation judge denying Employer's termination petition and granting the review and reinstatement petitions filed by Leon Davison.

Leon Davison argued that he was diagnosed with a low back sprain and was required to attend physical therapy for months. Additionally, he received multiple epidural steroid injections and a lesioning procedure. He returned to work with the restrictions that he only perform light work, pushing and pulling "no more than fifteen pounds".

He further alleged that his employer requested him to go back to work, doing full performance, because the issue had been resolved.

Analysis

The court found that the WCJ's findings were supported by the record and reflected no legal error. Additionally, the WCJ's credibility determinations were "not made arbitrarily and capriciously and as his findings are supported by substantial evidence, the WCJ's decision cannot be disturbed on appeal."

CONCLUSION

The court concluded that because the findings showed no legal error, they affirmed the judgment.

Appistry, Inc. v. Amazon.com, Inc.
Patent Infringement; Procedure

***Appistry, Inc. v. Amazon.com, Inc.*, 2015 U.S. Dist. LEXIS 90004, 2015 WL 4210890 (W.D. Wash. July 9, 2015).**

ISSUE

Should the court grant the defendant's motion for judgment on the pleadings?

RULE

"After the pleadings are closed, a party may move for judgment on the pleadings. *Fed. R. Civ. P. 12(c).*

Pursuant to Milne ex rel., "A judgment on the pleadings is properly granted when, taking all the allegations in the pleadings as true, the moving party is entitled to judgment as a matter of law." *Milne ex rel. Coyne v. Stephen Slesinger, Inc., 430 F.3d 1036, 1042 (9th Cir. 2005).*

CASE DETAILS

Facts

Plaintiff, Appistry filed suit against defendant, Amazon.com for patent infringement. Plaintiff alleged that it had property rights to a "fabric computing technology". Plaintiff offered a license to the technology in 2004 and the parties entered into a non-disclosure agreement. During a course of meetings, plaintiffs discussed the technology behind the patented object to Amazon. Amazon eventually declined the offer made by the plaintiffs. Plaintiffs allege that Amazon had copied the technology for their own services and alleged two counts of infringement.

The defendant motioned to transfer the action to the Western District of Washington based on forum selection clause contained in an agreement between the parties. The motion was granted.

The defendant then motioned for judgment on the pleadings. Amazon argued that the patents were directed at the abstract idea of a project management.

<u>Analysis</u>

The court agreed that the asserted claims were directed to an abstract idea. The court held, "that the claims of the patents-in-suit amount to the recitation of an abstract idea with instructions to apply the idea with ordinary computers connected through ordinary networks. As such, the patents claim patent-ineligible subject matter."

CONCLUSION

The court concluded that because the patents-in-suit were invalid under 35 U.S.C. Section 101, the defendant's motion for judgment on the pleadings was granted.

Appistry, Inc. v. Amazon.com, Inc.
Patent Infringement

Appistry, Inc. v. Amazon.com, Inc., 2015 U.S. Dist. LEXIS 24421 (E.D. Mo. Mar. 2, 2015).

ISSUE

Should the court grant the motion to transfer?

RULE

Pursuant to the holding in *M.B. Rests v. CKE Rests,* "Forum selection clauses are prima facie valid and are enforced unless they are unjust or unreasonable or invalid for reasons such as fraud or overreaching." *M.B. Rests., Inc. v. CKE Rests., Inc., 183 F.3d 750, 752 (8th Cir.1999).*

CASE DETAILS

Facts

Plaintiff, Appistry filed suit against defendant, Amazon.com for patent infringement. Plaintiff alleged that it had property rights to a "fabric computing technology". Plaintiff offered a license to the technology in 2004 and the parties entered into a non-disclosure agreement. During a course of meetings, plaintiffs discussed the technology behind the patented object to Amazon. Amazon eventually declined the offer made by the plaintiffs. Plaintiffs allege that Amazon had copied the technology for their own services and alleged two counts of infringement.

Amazon motioned to transfer the action to the Western District of Washington based on forum selection clause contained in an agreement between the parties.

Analysis

The court held that the "clear language of the forum selection clause includes this action because it related to the Service Offerings."

CONCLUSION

The court granted the motion to transfer.

Apple Inc. v. Amazon.com Inc., et al.
Procedure

***Apple Inc. v. Amazon.com Inc.*, et al. Case No. C11-1327 PJH (JSC). United States District Court for the Northern District of California, August 20, 2012.**

ISSUE

Whether the information requested to be sealed is actually confidential.

RULE

The party stating information is confidential must clarify all information provided is necessary to be sealed by providing an explanation as to why.

CASE DETAILS

Facts

The plaintiff filed a motion to seal documents that the defendant listed as confidential. The court requires the defendant to file a declaration stating that the document is sealable, and if it is not the party must withdraw the information that should not be sealed and an explanation as to why or why not.

Analysis

The defendant must provide an explanation as to why the documents should be sealed, they cannot just state that they should be sealed without any other information about it.

CONCLUSION

The court ordered the defendants to provide explanations of why information should be sealed before it granted the seal, any information that should not have been sealed must be withdrawn.

Apple Inc. v. Amazon.com Inc., et al.
Procedure

***Apple Inc. v. Amazon.com Inc.,* et al. Case No. C11-1327 PJH (JSC). United States District Court for the Northern District of California, August 23, 2012.**

ISSUE

Whether the court will allow a seal of the information the defendant seeks to keep confidential.

RULE

The court has discretion to allow information to be sealed when the defendant clearly identifies the confidential documents and the plaintiff acknowledges the confidentiality as well.

CASE DETAILS

Facts

The plaintiff filed a motion to seal documents that the defendant listed as confidential. The defendant filed a declaration in favor of the plaintiff's motion stating the documents are indeed confidential.

Analysis

The court viewed the documents and determined that the documents may be sealed electronically except those stated by the defendant that need not be sealed. Another copy of the documents must be submitted in a redacted version for the public.

CONCLUSION

The court granted the plaintiff's motion to file portions of the defendant's reply in discovery under seal. The plaintiff is ordered to produce a redacted version for the public.

Apple Inc. v. Amazon.com Inc., et al.
Procedure

Apple Inc. v. Amazon.com, Inc., 2013 U.S. Dist. LEXIS 47124 (N.D. Cal. Apr. 1, 2013).

ISSUE

Whether the work of Apple's expert's assistants is discoverable and should be produced to Amazon.

RULE

Any documents worked on by non-testifying experts in relation to testifying experts work must be produced for discovery.

CASE DETAILS

Facts

Apple had two of their employees, Dragun and Hofman, conduct surveys as consulting experts who later were used to assist one of Apple's testifying experts. Amazon wants the survey information that the two assistants worked on to be produced in discovery. Apple's expert worked directly with the two assistants while working on some surveys. There are billing records that show the assistants worked on the survey for more hours than the expert.

Analysis

Apple should be obligated to produce any information from the expert's assistants that involved work that has to do with later survey's they directly worked with the expert on. Amazon would not violate any rules if they only deposed the assistants on the later survey they had a direct involvement with Apple's expert. Other cases have held non-testifying experts have assisted with information related to what the testifying expert has worked on so they must be produced. Any information the assistants helped with Apple's expert is considered discoverable.

CONCLUSIONS

The court holds that Apple must produce the expert's assistants if they are needed to testify about their work and any involvement with the work of Apple's expert. Amazon cannot seek information regarding any work the assistants worked on previous to the expert's work but may ask for additional discovery if they find the assistants' related work is discoverable.

Apple Inc. v. Amazon.com Inc., et al.
Trademark Infringement

***Apple, Inc. v. Amazon.Com, Inc.*, 2011 U.S. Dist. LEXIS 72271 (N.D. Cal. July 6, 2011)**

ISSUE

Whether the court will decide if Apple can stop Amazon from using the mark "App Store" with their products.

RULE

An injunction may be made as long as a party clearly shows the harm without it would be irreparable and it is in the interest of the public to do so.

CASE DETAILS

Facts

Apple filed an application to register "App Store" with the U.S. Patent and Trademark Office in July 2008. In July 2010 Apple was notified the mark was published in the Trademark Official Gazette and any party that thought they would be damaged by the registration of the mark could oppose. Microsoft opposed and said the word was generic. Apple demanded Amazon to stop using "App Store" but Amazon launched it for Android. The court finds Apple does not have evidence to support for infringement claims.

Analysis

Apple has not established "App Store" is a strong enough mark to not allow anyone else to use. Apple consumers cannot buy products from Amazon's "App Store," only Android consumers are allowed which makes the markets they target different. Apple is not likely to succeed on the confusion element of their infringement claim Even though Apple has spent great time and money advertising "App Store," other companies have also used it. There is no evidence Amazon intentionally used the mark to associate itself with Apple.

CONCLUSION

The court denies Apple's motion for a preliminary injunction against Amazon using the mark "App Store." There is no evidence Amazon will harm Apple's good name or the public.

Apple Inc. v. Amazon.com Inc.
Trademark Infringement

***Apple Inc. v. Amazon.Com Inc.*, 915 F. Supp. 2d 1084 (N.D. Cal. 2013)**

ISSUE

Whether Amazon made a false statement of fact in an advertisement about its own or another's product

RULE

Evidence of false advertisement must be shown to prove a party misrepresented or deceived consumers about a product in comparison to another if the false statement is not explicitly expressed.

CASE DETAILS

Facts

Apple has been selling application, also known as "apps" since July 2008 through its APP STORE service and tried to register APP STORE with the U.S. Patent and Trademark Office but was not successful. In September 2011 Amazon launched the Amazon APP STORE for Android. Apple has not presented any evidence that Amazon has copied their product or confused customers through advertisement.

Analysis

Other cases have found for the party claiming false advertisement who have shown evidence of confusion or copying of slogans and symbols, Amazon has not implied that the use of the word APP STORE is the same as Apple's products. Apple has not provided any information that Amazon is expressly or impliedly advertising that their products are the same in quality or features. The first element of the false advertising claim is not supported. There is no evidence that Amazon has deceived any of its customers or misrepresented any of its products.

CONCLUSION

The court grants Amazon's motion for summary judgment in relation to the fifth cause of action for false advertisement. Apple did not provide any evidence that Amazon has made false statements to mislead consumers about the use of APP STORE in comparison of Apple products and Amazon products.

Area 55 v. Amazon.com
Patent Infringement; Procedure

Area 55, Inc. v. Amazon.com, Inc., 2012 U.S. Dist. LEXIS 191163 (S.D. Cal. May 3, 2012).

ISSUE

Whether the court should grant defendant Amazon.com's motion for Summary Judgment?

RULE

The Federal Rules of Civil Procedure Rule 56 governs Summary Judgment and states summary judgment can be granted if the moving party demonstrates the absence of a genuine issue of material fact and entitlement to judgment as a matter of law.

CASE DETAILS

Facts

Plaintiffs are owners of patents, as they invented, designed and currently sell the Vinturi wine aerator, a product that utilizes the technology of Area 55 patents. Plaintiffs filed suit against Amazon for advertising, offering for sale and the sale of third-party products that infringe on the patents.

Timeline

Amazon filed a motion for partial summary judgment on third party sales. On April 16, 2012, Plaintiffs filed their response in opposition. Amazon filed its reply on April 23, 2012 and the court held a hearing on April 30, 2012.

Analysis

Amazon contends in its motion for summary judgment on third-party sales that it is not liable for direct or contributory infringement under 35 U.S.C. § 271 (a) and (c). Viewing the record in the light most favorable to the nonmoving party, the court concludes that a genuine question of fact exists as to whether the Amazon provided a service for a fee to the sellers or whether Amazon sold infringing products to buyers. Therefore, the court denies the defendant's motion for partial summary judgment on third party sales.

CONCLUSION

The court denies Amazon's motion for partial summary judgment.

Arnold v. Amazon.com, Inc.
Workers' Compensation, Employees' Rights

***Arnold v. Amazon.com Inc.,* No. 4:13-cv-00168-SEB-WGH, 2014 U.S. Dist. LEXIS 102421 (S.D. Ind. July 28, 2014).**

ISSUE

Whether the court should grant defendants motion to dismiss the complaint filed by plaintiff for its failure to state a claim upon which relief may be granted under Rule 12(b)(6).

RULE

To survive a motion to dismiss under Rule 12(b)(6), a complaint need only contain "a short and plain statement of the claim showing that [the plaintiff] is entitled to relief." Fed. R. Civ. P. 8(a)(2). But that short and plain statement must include allegations that "give the defendant fair notice of what the ... claim is and the grounds upon which it rests," and "raise a right to relief above the speculative level." *Pisciotta v. Old Nat'l Bancorp,* 499 F.3d 629, 633 (7th Cir. 2007). This means the complaint must plead factual content that enables the court to "draw the reasonable inference that the defendant is liable for the misconduct alleged." *Ashcroft v. Iqbal,* 556 U.S. 662, 678, 129 S. Ct. 1937, 173 L. Ed. 2d 868 (2009).

CASE DETAILS

Facts

Plaintiff Gary Arnold filed an employment discrimination complaint against Amazon alleging violations of the Age Discrimination in Employment Act and the Americans with Disabilities Act. Arnold also claimed harassment and assault by coworkers. Arnold reported the harassment and assault to his supervisor and to a Human Resources representative. *Arnold* alleges that Amazon's Human Resources representative failed to call the police to report the assault, and that his supervisor "seemed amused by the harassment."

Arnold's Statement of Legal Claim says that Amazon "failed to provide a safe working environment."

Analysis

The court finds that both plaintiff's age discrimination and disability discrimination claims should be dismissed because they failed to allege factual content as to all the foregoing elements of each claim. As to the age discrimination claim, plaintiff failed to even include his age. And as to the disability claim, plaintiff did not even allege that he is a disabled erson within the meaning of the Americans with Disabilities Act.

CONCLUSION

The court found that Arnold had not defended the legal sufficiency of his complaint, and Amazon had demonstrated that its motion to dismiss was valid. Therefore, the Court granted Amazon's motion to dismiss.

Sen v. Amazon.com, Inc.
Settlement Agreements, Trademark Infringement, Unfair Competition

---

***Sen v. Amazon.com, Inc.*, 2013 U.S. Dist. LEXIS 178447, 2013 WL 6730180 (S.D. Cal. Dec. 19, 2013).**

ISSUE

Whether the court should enforce the parties' settlement agreement where plaintiff opposes on the grounds that she did not understand the terms she signed on to and the agreement itself.

RULE

It is well settled that a district court has the equitable power to enforce summarily an agreement to settle a case pending before it. However, the district court may enforce only complete settlement agreements." *Callie v. Near*, 829 F.2d 888, 890 (9th Cir. 1987) (emphasis and citations omitted). Thus, to be enforced, a settlement agreement must meet two requirements. First it must be a complete agreement. *Maynard v. City of San Jose*, 37 F.3d 1396, 1401 (9th Cir. 1994). Second, both parties must have either agreed to the terms of the settlement or authorized their respective counsel to settle the dispute. *Harrop v. Western Airlines, Inc.*, 550 F.2d 1143, 1144-45 (9th Cir. 1977).

CASE DETAILS

Facts

This case is in regards to the enforceability of a disputed settlement agreement between Plaintiff, Sen and Amazon.com. Plaintiff sued Amazon for trademark infringement, unfair competition, and false advertising. During trial, the parties entered into a settlement agreement. The parties came to agreement in settlement conference, they were directed to put their agreement into more a formal format and then to submit it to the court. Plaintiff disputed their agreement prior to putting it into the proper format for the court.

Amazon filed motion to enforce their original agreement, and Plaintiff opposed saying they did not understand the terms of the agreement, that it lacked valid consideration and that it left out terms that were agreed upon in settlement conferences.

Analysis

The court found that the agreement was complete, unambiguous, and intentionally entered into, that it contained all of the material terms required, and that plaintiff's concerns were unfounded, and that it was supported by valid consideration.

CONCLUSION

For the foregoing reasons, the Court granted Amazon's motion to enforce the agreement as is.

Baghdasarian v. Amazon.com, Inc.
Procedure

***Baghdasarian v. Amazon.com, Inc.*, 2009 U.S. Dist. LEXIS 115265 (C.D. Cal. Dec. 9, 2009).**

ISSUE

Whether the court should grant defendant Amazon.Com. Inc.'s (Amazon) motion for summary judgment.

RULE

Summary judgment is appropriate only where the record, read in the light most favorable to the non-moving party, indicates that "there is no genuine issue as to any material fact and . . . the moving party is entitled to a judgment as a matter of law." Fed. R. Civ. P. 56(c); see also *Celotex Corp. v. Catrett*, 477 U.S. 317, 323-24, 106 S. Ct. 2548, 91 L. Ed. 2d 265 (1986).

The California Supreme Court recently clarified the standard that must be met by class representatives to maintain a claim under the fraud prong of the UCL. First, the representatives must establish that they have "suffered injury in fact and ha[ve] lost money or property as a result of [such] unfair competition." *In re Tobacco II Cases*, 46 Cal. 4th 298, 306, 93 Cal. Rptr. 3d 559, 207 P.3d 20 (2009). Second, "a class representative proceeding on a claim of misrepresentation as the basis of his or her UCL action must demonstrate actual reliance on the allegedly deceptive or misleading statements, in accordance with well-settled principles regarding the element of reliance in ordinary fraud actions." *Id.* at 306.

CASE DETAILS

Facts

Defendant Amazon operates an online marketplace. When a customer orders an item on the marketplace, defendant processes the order, but an independent seller delivers the goods to the buyer. Plaintiff purchased eight books from independent sellers on Amazon Marketplace. "Amazon.com charges Marketplace buyers a flat rate for shipping, and funds are passed to the seller to offset the costs of packaging and labor, as well as the postage required. The credit given to a seller will usually closely match what the seller pays to ship the item, using the option you have chosen (Standard or Expedited). However, there may be times when the credit a seller is given for a Marketplace order will be above and beyond what is actually paid for postage. Shipping costs are an inherent feature in any mail-order service, and we hope that you will understand." *Baghdasarian v. Amazon.com, Inc.*, No. CV 05-8060 AG (CTx), 2009 U.S. Dist. LEXIS 115265 (C.D. Cal. Dec. 9, 2009). Amazon charged a higher shipping rate than the estimated cost of shipping and handling. Defendants then retained any amount of shipping money leftover; this is known as a "holdback fee." Plaintiff then sued Amazon for violation of fraud under California's Unfair Competition Law.

Analysis

The court here finds that if the defendant had charged a shipping and handling fee that only reflected the seller's actual anticipated shipping costs, then plaintiff would have paid less, which demonstrates that he was damaged by defendants practice of inflating the shipping and handling fee. Plaintiff also has evidence that defendant retains the leftover shipping funds. The evidence supports at least a triable issue of fact that plaintiff would have paid less for the items he purchased if defendant didn't charge the excess shipping fee.

However, as to actual reliance, the court holds that plaintiff has not offered evidence to show that the shipping policy caused him to buy products from Amazon Marketplace. Plaintiff testified that he chose to use Amazon Marketplace because of price and security, showing that these were his primary causes for using the site. The court finds that there is no triable issue of fact concerning whether plaintiff can show actual reliance on the shipping policy of Amazon. Therefore, summary judgment is appropriate.

CONCLUSION

For the foregoing reasons the court grants defendant Amazon's motion to dismiss.

Baghdasarian v. Amazon.Com, Inc.
Unfair Competition; Procedure

***Baghdasarian v. Amazon.Com, Inc.*, 258 F.R.D. 383 (C.D. Cal. 2009)**

ISSUE

Whether the court should grant plaintiff's motion for class certification.

RULE

According to Federal Rule of Civil Procedure 23(a), one or more members of a class may sue or be sued as representative parties on behalf of all members only if:

(1) the class is so numerous that joinder of all members is impracticable;
(2) there are questions of law or fact common to the class;
(3) the claims or defenses of the representative parties are typical of the claims or defenses of the class; and
(4) the representative parties will fairly and adequately protect the interests of the class.

A class action may only be maintained if Rule 23(a) is satisfied and if one of the three subparts of Rule 23(b) is satisfied. Rule 23(b) provides:

(1) prosecuting separate actions by or against individual class members would create a risk of:
 (A) inconsistent or varying adjudications with respect to individual class members that would establish incompatible standards of conduct for the party opposing the class;
 (B) adjudications with respect to individual class members that, as a practical matter, would be dispositive of the interest of the other members not parties to the individual adjudications or would substantially impair or impede their ability to protect their interests;

(2) the party opposing the class has acted or refused to act on grounds that apply generally to the class, so that final injunctive relief or corresponding declaratory relief is appropriate respecting the class as a whole; or
(3) the court finds that the questions of law or fact common to class members predominate over any questions affecting only individual members, and that a class action is superior to other available methods for fairly and efficiently adjudicating the controversy.

California Business and Professions Code § 17204 addresses a plaintiff's standing to assert an unfair competition claim. A private individual may bring a claim under Section 17204 only if he has: (1) "suffered an injury in fact," and (2) "lost money or property as a result of such unfair competition." *Buckland v. Threshold Enterprises, Ltd.*, 155 Cal. App. 4th 798, 812, 66 Cal. Rptr. 3d 543 (Cal. Ct. App. 2007).

CASE DETAILS

Facts

Defendant Amazon.Com, Inc. (Amazon) provides a platform, called the Amazon Marketplace for buyers and sellers to engage in commerce. Amazon receives a sales commission and a percentage of the sales price for each item sold. Until 2005, Amazon also charged shipping and handling fees, but sellers took care of the actual packaging and shipping of the products. Amazon kept a portion of the shipping and handling, called a "holdback." Marketplace buyers were not made aware of these holdback practices. Here, plaintiff bought books from a marketplace seller and paid the shipping and handling fee.

Analysis

The court first addresses the plaintiff's standing to bring its claim. The court agrees with plaintiff's argument and finds that here, plaintiff and members of the class clearly paid more than they would have absent the extra commission hidden as a shipping and handling charge and thus plaintiff had standing to bring his UCL claim.

The court next finds that plaintiff meets the rule 23(a) requirements of numerosity, commonality, typicality, and adequacy. Here, numerosity is satisfied because the class consists of all marketplace buyers who were California residents during the class period. The commonality requirement is satisfied because there are common questions of law and fact among the class. The typicality requirement is satisfied because the claims are "reasonably co-extensive with those of absent class members." Here, plaintiff's and the class members' claims arise from the same scheme and challenge the same allegedly unlawful conduct. Finally, plaintiff satisfies the adequacy requirement because plaintiff has no conflicts of interest with other class members and the record shows that plaintiff's attorneys will adequately represent the class.

Finally, the court must address rule 23(b) requirements for class certification. The court finds the predominance requirement to be satisfied because the questions of fact are common to the entire class and no separate inquiry to the other class members is necessary. The court holds that superiority is satisfied because the facts show that there are thousands of potential class members, each with small claims. It would be difficult and expensive for most class members to successfully litigate this type of claim. Thus a class action is the best way for the class to succeed in a claim.

CONCLUSION

The court ultimately grants plaintiff's motion for class certification. The court finds that plaintiff has standing to bring his claim, and satisfies the requirements of Rule 23(a) for numerosity, commonality, typicality, and adequacy, as well as the rule 23(b) requirements of predominance and superiority.

Baghdasarian v. Amazon.Com Inc.
Procedure – Summary Judgment

***Baghdasarian v. Amazon.Com Inc.*, 458 F. App'x 622 (9th Cir. 2011)**

ISSUE

Whether the district court erred in granting summary judgment for plaintiff's reliance claims in favor of defendant Amazon.Com Inc. (Amazon), where plaintiff claims his decision to purchase books on the Amazon market place was based on total cost and security.

RULE

The UCL requires a plaintiff to have "lost money or property as a result of" the business practice or act at issue. Cal. Bus. & Prof. Code § 17204 (emphasis added). The UCL's "as a result of" language imposes an "actual reliance" requirement, thus, to prevail, a plaintiff must establish that the alleged misrepresentation was an "immediate cause" or "substantial factor" in the plaintiff's decision to engage in the injury-producing conduct. *In re Tobacco II Cases*, 46 Cal. 4th 298, 326-27, 93 Cal. Rptr. 3d 559, 207 P.3d 20 (2009).

CASE DETAILS

Facts

Plaintiff appeals the district court's grant of summary judgment in favor of amazon, and argues that the district court incorrectly found that there was no issue of material fact as to whether he established reliance as required by California's Unfair Competition Law (UCL).

Analysis

Plaintiff testified in his own deposition that his decision to purchase books through the Marketplace was driven by total cost and security, these are factors unrelated to Amazon's alleged misrepresentation. He also testified that had he been aware of Amazon's practices involving shipping and handling that he would still have made the purchases. Thus, the court holds that the existence of a hidden fee in Amazon's price was not a factor that could have affected plaintiff's decision to purchase on the Marketplace.

CONCLUSION

For the foregoing reasons the court here affirms the district court's decision and grants summary judgment.

Basis Technology Corporation v. Amazon.com Inc.
Settlement Agreement

***Basis Tech. Corp. v. Amazon.com, Inc.*, 71 Mass. App. Ct. 29, 878 N.E.2d 952, 2008 Mass. App. LEXIS 8 (Mass. App. Ct. 2008).**

ISSUE

The issue of this appeal is the enforceability of a disputed midtrial settlement agreement.

RULE

Following the holding in Demoulas v. Demoulas, "A finding is `clearly erroneous' only when, `although there is evidence to support it, the reviewing court on the entire evidence is left with the definite and firm conviction that a mistake has been committed.'"

CASE DETAILS

Facts

The plaintiff, Basis Technology and defendant, Amazon.com, were in a business relationship. Basis Technology, a company that creates software, entered into a "Services Agreement" with Amazon.com which provided Amazon with the services to create an "electronic commerce system in Japan for the sale of books and other products." Additionally, the parties entered into a "Series A Preferred Stock Purchase Agreement".

In May of 2003, Basis filed suit against Amazon for breach of fiduciary duty, quantum meruit, and G.L. c. 93A violations for nonpayment for "out of scope work".

During trial, both parties, via an electronic mail exchange, agreed upon settlement terms. This settlement was then spoken before the court and the trial ceased. After they were directed by the judge to file an agreement, the parties disagreed and Amazon.com refused to settle. The judge found that the email agreement was valid and entered judgment in favor of Basis for specific enforcement of the settlement terms. Amazon appealed claiming "(1) That the judge, as a matter of law, incorrectly ruled that the e-mail exchange created a complete and unambiguous agreement; and (2) that the judge, as a matter of fact finding, incorrectly determined that Amazon had intended to be bound by the e-mail terms at the time of their exchange."

Analysis

The court found that genuine ambiguity requires, "suscepti[bility] of more than one meaning [so that] reasonably intelligent persons would differ as to which meaning is the proper one." *Ins. Co.* v. *Gomez,* 426 Mass. 379, 381 (1998). Therefore, the court held that the stock conversion term was sufficiently definite for enforcement. When looking to the intentions of the parties to be bound as a matter of fact, the court found that because there was a report of a settlement, that this was reported during the progress of a trial, and that there was evidence in support of the parties' intention to settle.

CONCLUSION

The court found that the judge correctly ruled that the e-mail was a sufficiently complete and unambiguous statement as a matter of law, and that both parties are to be bound by this agreement.

B.E. Tech., LLC v. Amazon Digital Servs.
Patent Infringement

***B.E. Tech., LLC v. Amazon Digital Servs.*, 2013 U.S. Dist. LEXIS 101204, 2013 WL 3807820 (W.D. Tenn. July 19, 2013.)**

ISSUE

Should the court grant the defendant, Amazon Digital Services' motion to transfer?

RULE

Pursuant to *28 U.S.C. § 1404(a)*, "[f]or the convenience of the parties and witnesses, in the interest of justice, a district court may transfer any civil action to any other district or division where it might have been brought."

CASE DETAILS

Facts

Plaintiff, B.E. Tech., LLC, alleged that defendant, Amazon Digital Services infringed on their 290 patent by selling, using, and offering to sell tablet computer products. The products that were alleged to infringe on the patent included, "the Kindle, Kindle Touch, Kindle Touch 3G, Kindle Keyboard 3G, Kindle DX, and the Kindle Fire".

Amazon motioned to dismiss, then filed a motion to transfer venue. Amazon then filed a motion to stay pending resolution of its motion to transfer, which was granted, by the court.

Analysis

The court looked at (1) the convenience of the witnesses, being the party witnesses and non-party witnesses; (2) convenience of the parties, being the location of sources of proof and the financial hardships attendant to litigating in the chosen forum; and (3) the interest of justice, being the trial efficiency and local interest.

Amazon asserted, "The engineers most knowledgeable about the design, developments, and operation of the accused Kindle products work in Amazon's facility in Cupertino, California." The court found that this indicated that the witness-convenience factor did not weigh in favor of transfer. Additionally, the court found that, "Amazon is only able to estimate that it is "highly doubtful" that any of the non-party witnesses would be unwilling to testify in this District if asked to do so" Therefore, the factor weighed only slightly in favor of transfer.

The Court found the "considerations relevant to the convenience-of-the-parties factor are the location of the sources of proof and the parties' financial hardships due to litigation in the chosen forum."

The court looked to the location of sources of proof and found that this factor was not sufficient to require transfer. The court looked to the financial hardships attended to litigating in the chosen forum and found that the hardship to Amazon did not indicate transfer to be more convenient.

For the interest of justice, the court looked to trial efficiency and local interest. For trial efficiency, the court found that this factor was neutral. For the local interest, the court found that Amazon failed to show that the Northern District of California's local interest outweighs that of the Western District of Tennessee.

CONCLUSION

The court, after looking at the convenience of the witnesses, convenience of the parties, and the interest of justice, found that these factors did not weigh in favor of a transfer and denied the motion.

Berkery v. Estate of Lyle Stuart
Defamation

***Berkery v. Estate of Stuart,* 412 N.J. Super. 76, 988 A.2d 1201 (Super. Ct. App. Div. 2010).**

ISSUE

Whether the judge erred in concluding the plaintiff did not establish enough evidence showing malice on the part of the defendants in writing and distributing a book.

RULE

A limited purpose public figure must show evidence of actual malice by the defendant to recover in a defamation action.

CASE DETAILS

Facts

Plaintiff sued a journalist and publisher about statements made in a newspaper article about himself. Hornblum wrote a book about old gang members, the plaintiff was contacted to be a part of the book. The book was published and plaintiff filed a complaint to take his name out of the book because he was defamed. The lower court did not find any actual malice in the evidence provided by the plaintiff.

Analysis

A reasonable juror would not be able to say the defendants acted with malice against the plaintiff. The plaintiff's criminal records were open to the public so he qualifies as a limited-purpose public figure. The defendant did not intentionally publish information about the plaintiff with knowledge of it being false or disregard if the published information was true or false. The evidence that the plaintiff has provided does not show any proof the defendants acted knowing the information published was false. The defendants are not required to prove or disprove any information because the burden is on the plaintiff. No support is shown to prove Hornblum lied about dates or information in the book, even if he was not credible it does not prove malice. Hornblum relied on material he thought was credible and true at the time of writing the book.

CONCLUSION

The court held that the lower court did not err in finding no evidence of malice against the plaintiff by the defendants. Summary judgment should not have been granted.

Big Baboon Corporation v. Dell, Inc.
Patent Infringement

***Big Baboon Corp. v. Dell, Inc.*, 723 F. Supp. 2d 1224, 2010 U.S. Dist. LEXIS 80289 (C.D. Cal. 2010).**

ISSUE

Whether the court should grant Amazon's motion to compel Big Baboon Corp. to produce more detailed infringement charts.

RULE

Following the Northern District of California's Local Patent Rule 3-1, the party claiming patent infringement must serve on all parties, no later than 10 days after the Initial Conference, a "Disclosure of Asserted Claims and Preliminary Infringement Contentions." N.D. Cal. Local Patent Rule 3-1. This must include "separately for each claim, each accused apparatus, product, device, process, method, act, or other instrumentality of each opposing party in which the party is aware and a chart identifying specifically where each element of each claim is found within each Accused Instrumentality." *Id.* Courts usually decline to compel pinpoint citations in infringement contentions only when the plaintiff did not yet have the source code. However, once the source code has been provided, courts have required plaintiffs to supplement their infringement charges with pinpoint citations.

CASE DETAILS

Facts:

Amazon seeks infringement claims charts that set forth Big Baboon's infringement theory, showing each element of each asserted claim in each accused system with pinpoint citations to the source code and/or documents. Amazon requested Big Baboon to produce these infringement charts with citations by April 27, 2010. Big Baboon has failed to provide these contentions and Amazon seeks an order compelling them to provide these claims charts immediately.

Amazon's Arguments:

Amazon claims that Big Baboon fails to provide adequate infringement contentions, despite Amazon providing them with the source code, which would allow them to sufficiently analyze it. Amazon claims it is forced to build its defenses against allegations of patent infringement without having understanding of how exactly it is being accused of it. Amazon requests more detailed infringement charts showing where each element of each claim is found in each accused system. Amazon additionally argues that Big Baboon should be able to analyze the code without need to depose programmers or access to the environment in which it is normally run.

Big Baboon's Arguments:

Big Baboon contends that Amazon provided them with 60,000 source codes that they must now review. Amazon has not provided them with essential materials to understand the code, such as their source code encyclopedia or a system level map. Additionally, in searching the code, it has found references to six files that were not included in the source code production. Big Baboon further argues that it has not been able to analyze the code because it was not made available in the environment in which the programs are usually run and they need to depose Amazon Programmers to understand fully how the code works. They have provided Amazon with 82-page detailed claims charts; however, these charts do not contain citations to the source code. Big Baboon additionally claims that it will supplement its infringement contentions once discovery has had an opportunity to meaningfully progress.

CONCLUSION

The court grants the motion in part and denies in part. Big Baboon must produce infringement charts that clearly show where each element of each claim is found in each accused system with pinpoint citations to the source code. Big Baboon must move quickly to produce these contentions, as they have already had the source code for more than four months. Since Big Baboon has been provided with the source code for over four months, Big Baboon can no longer delay the production of infringement charts with citations to the source code. The court finds that Big Baboon has not demonstrated how producing the detailed infringement chart on Amazon's timeline would be unduly burdensome nor that its expert attempted to analyze Amazon's source code in a diligent or expeditious matter. In addition, Amazon agrees to provide Big Baboon with their source code encyclopedia, a system level map and the six files Big Baboon claims it requires to provide the infringement charts with pinpoint citations within 14 days of the June 22 hearing. The court determines that Big Baboon has been provided a reasonable opportunity to review Amazon's source code, and will have an additional 46 days to review and analyze the code, which would amount to 6 months of having access to the code, which the court determines a reasonable opportunity to analyze it.

Blagman v. Apple Inc., Amazon.com, Inc.
Copyright Infringement

***Blagman v. Apple Inc.*, 2013 U.S. Dist. LEXIS 71280, 107 U.S.P.Q.2D (BNA) 1699, Copy. L. Rep. (CCH) P30,433, 2013 WL 2181709 (S.D.N.Y. May 20, 2013).**

ISSUE

Whether the Plaintiff made a claim of copyright infringement such that the case should not be dismissed.

RULE

Cases may not be dismissed before the court learns more information that would come up after the complaint stage without proper evidence as to why it should be dismissed.

CASE DETAILS

Facts

Plaintiff filed a class action claim stating the defendants failed to ensure the music consumers download on their sites is licensed before distribution. Defendants filed a motion to dismiss the class action complaint, the plaintiff's individual claim, and motion to strike class allegations. The defendant has to actually be aware that they are infringing on copyright laws or completely disregard whether they are doing so or not in order for a plaintiff to prove copyright infringement.

Analysis

Defendant's motion to dismiss the plaintiff's individual claim is denied because the plaintiff states a valid claim of infringement. The class allegations properly state a claim on behalf of the proposed class. Dismissing the claim in the complaint stage would not be proper without hearing all the evidence that would come up in discovery.

CONCLUSION

The court held the defendant's motion to strike the class allegations is denied, the motion to dismiss individual claims is denied and the motion to dismiss the class action complaint is denied. The case proceeds to pre-trial and discovery stages.

Blagman v. Apple, Inc.
Class Action Lawsuits; Copyright Infringement; International Depositions

---

***Blagman v. Apple, Inc.*, 2014 U.S. Dist. LEXIS 45401, 2014 WL 1285496 (S.D.N.Y. Mar. 31, 2014).**

ISSUE

Mr. Blagman requests an order for six 3rd party witnesses in the United Kingdom and France to be deposed.

RULE

Pursuant to Rule 28 of the Federal Rules of Civil Procedure, a deposition of a third party may be taken in a foreign country "on appropriate terms after application and notice of it." Fed. R. Civ. P. 28(b)(2)(A). Letters of interrogatory are a way for court to formally request a court in another country to lend its judicial assistance in obtaining evidence or performing some other judicial act. The party seeking the discovery bears the burden of demonstrating the relevance and information must be relevant and "reasonably calculated to lead to the discovery of admissible evidence." *Chen-Oster v. Goldman, Sachs & Co.*, 293 F.R.D. 557, 571 (S.D.N.Y. 2013); Fed. R. Civ. P. 26(b)(1). The opposing party must justify any restrictions on discovery, such as where the information sought would be "unreasonably cumulative or duplicative" or "when the burden or expense of the proposed discovery outweighs its likely benefit." Fed R. Civ. P. 26(b)(2)(C)(i),(iii).

The Copyright Act gives owners of copyrights in non-dramatic music compositions the exclusive rights to reproduce and distribute their copyrighted songs and to authorize others to engage in such activity. 17 U.S.C. § 106(1), (3). When an individual who does not own the copyright to the composition wants to make and distribute their own recording, they must obtain a mechanical license from the owner of the copyright. These mechanical licenses can be obtained by negotiation or by the procedures provided by 17 U.S.C. §115.

CASE DETAILS

Facts

This is a class action alleging that defendants illegally reproduced and distributed musical compositions in United States based online stores without the necessary licenses. Mr. Blagman has been writing, producing, and recording music for over 50 years and is the composer and copyright owner of many compositions. He is the composer and copyright owner of three works that he now alleges have been illegally copied, distributed, sold and performed by the defendants. He is suing on behalf of himself and of a proposed class of all copyright owners of compositions that have been reproduced, distributed or sold by defendants. There are two groups of defendants: the major digital music retailers and those that supplied the recordings to the retailers. The letters of interrogatory relate to three topics: 1) mechanical licensing and whether 3rd parties obtained phone record delivery or mechanical licenses pursuant to U.S. Copyright Act, 2) Duplication of already fixed sound recordings and whether entity was granted authority to duplicate by copyright owners or any person who fixed the sound, and 3) whether entity obtained import authorization for recordings embodying copyrighted compositions.

Timeline

Prior to this request, the plaintiff requested twice to seek discovery regarding exportation and actions relating to customers outside the U.S. and both were denied.

CONCLUSION

The proposed letters of interrogatory are distinguishable from the prior requests in that here, the plaintiff seeks to depose certain entities concerning digital recordings that are distributed through the defendant's online music stores, despite being uploaded abroad. Additionally, testimony may support plaintiff's claims of commonality.

Blagman v. Apple, Inc.
Class Action Lawsuits; Copyright Infringement; Procedural

***Blagman v. Apple, Inc.*, 307 F.R.D. 107 (S.D.N.Y. 2015).**

ISSUE

Whether Mr. Blagman can successfully move for leave to file his third amended complaint?

RULE

Pursuant to Rule 15(a)(2) of the Federal Rules of Civil Procedure, courts should freely allow plaintiffs to amend "when justice so requires." Fed. R. Civ. P. 15(a)(2). They should only be denied for good reasons, such as undue delay, bad faith or dilatory motive, and the party opposing the amendment has the burden of establishing that amendment would be inappropriate. *Allison v. Close-ette Too, L.L.C.*, No. 14 Civ 1618 (S.D.N.Y. Jan. 9, 2015)

CASE DETAILS

Facts:

This is a class action alleging that defendants illegally reproduced and distributed musical compositions in United States based online stores without the necessary licenses. Mr. Blagman has been writing, producing, and recording music for over 50 years and is the composer and copyright owner of many compositions. He is the composer and copyright owner of three works that he now alleges have been illegally copied, distributed, sold and performed by the defendants. He is suing on behalf of himself and of a proposed class of all copyright owners of compositions. There are two groups of defendants: the major digital music retailers and those that supplied the recordings to the retailers. This is his third amended complaint request. He states there are three significant changes, two relating to the class definition and one related to the damages. This proposed complaint would limit the class by eliminating eleven record companies and provide more detailed allegations. Additionally, it would fix the damages award as the minimum statutory damages of $750 per infringement under the Copyright Act.

Timeline:

The first amended complaint, filed October 2012, three months after the original complaint identified the class as "including all persons who own all or part of registered copyrighted musical compositions that have been reproduced, distributed or sold by defendants." Nine and a half months later, the plaintiff moved to amend his complaint to narrow the scope of the class and limit it to composition copyright holders whose songs were provided to the Retailer Defendants by 69 allegedly unlawful record labels. This application was granted in May 2014.

Analysis:

The modification Mr. Blagman suggested appears to be calculated in addressing the concerns that the judge expressed after his second amended complaint. Additionally, the time between the length of the original complaint to this request is two and a half years, which is not completely out of bounds. The third complaint focuses the class explicitly by pairing the included labels with aggregators who supplied the works.

CONCLUSION

The court held that the motion to leave to file a third amended complaint is granted as a result of not being amended in bad faith.

Blagman v. Apple Inc., Amazon.com, Inc.
Copyright Infringement

Blagman v. Apple, Inc., 2014 U.S. Dist. LEXIS 69178, Copy. L. Rep. (CCH) P30,608 (S.D.N.Y. May 19, 2014).

ISSUE

Whether the court should grant plaintiff's motion for leave to file a second amended complaint.

RULE

Courts have the discretion to grant amended complaints where the delay is a significant amount of time depending on a reasonable explanation.

CASE DETAILS

Facts

The amended complaint is to include all parties that have reproduced, distributed, or sold music that came from the defendants. The defendants filed a motion to dismiss and strike the class allegations, which was denied. The plaintiff has had a significant period of time to amend their complaint but no showing of bad faith was provided.

Analysis

Amending new issues is not allowed unless there is some reason that was uncontrolled and a new issue arose. An amendment would also not be granted if it would not prevail on a motion to dismiss. The plaintiff's claim arises from the same course of conduct, based on the distributed music not licensed, and slight variation is allowed.

CONCLUSION

The court held the class certification motion may be amended. Class definition may be amended regardless if it is unknown to the defendant.

Bookhouse of Stuyvesant Plaza, Inc. v. Amazon.com, Inc.
Antitrust Law Violation; Violation of the Sherman Act; Procedural

---

***Bookhouse of Stuyvesant Plaza, Inc. v. Amazon.com, Inc.*, 985 F. Supp. 2d 612 (S.D.N.Y. 2013).**

ISSUE

Whether the court should grant the defendants' Motion to Dismiss?

RULE

"To survive a motion to dismiss, a complaint must contain sufficient factual matter, accepted as true, to state a claim to relief that is plausible on its face." *Ashcroft v. Iqbal*, 556 U.S. 662, 678 (2009). In deciding whether the motion to dismiss should be granted the court must accept all factual allegations in the plaintiff's complaint as true and draw reasonable inferences in their favor. *Kleinman v. Elan Corp., PLC*, 706 F.3d 145, 152 (2d. Cir. 2013).

CASE DETAILS

Facts:

The Bookhouse of Stuyvesant Plaza Inc., Fiction Addiction LLC, and Posnan Books at Grand Central Inc., three independent "brick-and-mortar" bookstores are asserting antitrust claims against Amazon.com and 6 book publishers in the U.S. Plaintiffs assert claims under of the Sherman Act. Plaintiffs sell print books and e-books, as does Amazon, one of the defendants. Amazon's e-book platform is a "closed ecosystem." If a consumer owns a Kindle and wants to read an e-book on the Kindle that was published by any of the publishers in this action, they must buy the book from Amazon.

Timeline:

Publishers have moved to dismiss the plaintiffs' restraint of trade claim. Amazon has moved to dismiss the First Amended Complaint.

Analysis:

Plaintiffs allege three kind of harm: (1) consumers are unable to purchase e-books at their local independent bookstore that are readable on the Kindle, (2) price competition is restricted because independent bookstores cannot sell e-books for the vast majority of consumers in the market because independent bookstores cannot sell the e-books for the kindle, (3) independent bookstores have been foreclosed from selling e-books by the publishers for Kindle devices. The court determined that the first and third harms are identical. The Court cannot reasonably infer that these two markets simultaneously are so different that e-books and print books are not acceptable substitutes and yet so similar that the publishers' market share is the same in both markets. Additionally, plaintiffs have failed to allege market power. The court then determined that Plaintiffs have failed to state a plausible claim to relief and therefore granted the Defendants'' motion to dismiss.

CONCLUSION

The court granted the Defendants' Motion to Dismiss.

Booklocker.com v. Amazon.com, Inc.
Class Action, Antitrust Law Violations

***BookLocker.com, Inc. v. Amazon.com, Inc.*, 650 F. Supp. 2d 89, 2009 U.S. Dist. LEXIS 76352, 2009-2 Trade Cas. (CCH) P76,729 (D. Me. 2009).**

ISSUE

Whether plaintiff alleged sufficient facts that Amazon violated antitrust laws by tying its book-selling services to the use of a specific printing service such that a motion to dismiss would not be proper.

RULE

"Federal Rule of Civil Procedure 8(a)(2) requires only a short and plain statement of the claim showing that the pleader is entitled to relief, in order to give the defendant fair notice of what the . . . claim is and the grounds upon which it rests." *Bell Atl. Corp. v. Twombly*, 550 U.S. 544, 555, 127 S. Ct. 1955, 167 L. Ed. 2d 929 (2007) (internal quotation omitted). Rule 12(b)(6), however, provides that a court may dismiss a complaint for "failure to state a claim upon which relief can be granted." Fed. R. Civ. P. 12(b)(6).

CASE DETAILS

Facts

Amazon offered the sale of "Print on Demand" (POD) books to its customers in two different ways. Consumers may purchase POD books directly from Amazon by clicking "Add to Cart," or through third party sellers in the Amazon Marketplace. Amazon acquired a company called BookSurge that provided printing services to POD publishers. Amazon subsequently informed POD publishers that Amazon would only continue to sell POD books through the Direct Amazon Sales Channel if the publisher agreed to print its books through BookSurge. Plaintiff's bought this suit alleging anti trust violations, and Amazon filed a motion to dismiss for failure to state a claim.

Analysis

The court found that it remained a matter of material fact whether Amazon was creating a monopoly here or simply engaging in efficiency enhancing, pro-competitive behavior. Because the court must make all reasonable inferences in favor of plaintiff, Booklocker's complaint raised a plausible right to relief.

CONCLUSION

The court denied Amazon's motion to dismiss and found plausible claim for Plaintiff

Bovino v. Amazon.com, Inc.
Patent Infringement; Procedure

***Bovino v. Amazon.com, Inc.*, 2014 U.S. Dist. LEXIS 32016 (D. Colo. Mar. 12, 2014).**

ISSUE

Whether the court will grant defendant Bovino's motion for summary judgment.

RULE

Pursuant to Fed. R. Civ. P. 15(a)(2), "the court should freely give leave to amend when justice so requires." Fed. R. Civ. P. 15(a)(2). The courts can refuse to amend only if the opposing party is able to show undue delay, undue prejudice, bas faith or dilatory motive. *Bylin v. Billings*, 568 F.3d 1224, 1229 (10th Cir. 2009) (quoting *Frank v. U.S. West, Inc.*, 3 F.3d 1357, 1365 (10th Cir. 1993)).

CASE DETAILS

Facts

Bovino is arguing that he discovered over 100 additional products that infringe his patent and that these products are sold by Amazon. He included an exhibit list to this order that outlines the alleged infringed products. It identified the accused product by manufacturer, product description, model number, Amazon Standard Identification Number, and application.

Analysis

The court finds no bad faith argument for the Plaintiff to amend his complaint. He includes the required exhibit list and the defendant's arguments against this order are without merit.

CONCLUSION

The court grants the Plaintiff's motion to amend his complaint.

Bovino v. Amazon.com, Inc.
Patent Infringement; Procedure

***Bovino v. Amazon.com, Inc.*, 2015 U.S. Dist. LEXIS 71772, 2015 WL 3523218 (D. Colo. June 1, 2015).**

ISSUE

Whether the court will grant Mr. Bovino's motion to amend his complaint?

RULE

Claim construction is interpreted by how a reasonable competitor would interpret the actual claim language, not what the inventor intended to claim. *Oakley Inc. v. Sunglass Hut International*, 316 F.3d 1331, 1340 (Fed. Cir. 2003). Rule 56 of the Federal Rules of Civil Procedure allows the court to enter a judgment only if it is determined that a trial is not needed. Summary judgment is authorized when there is no genuine dispute as to any material fact. Fed. R. Civ. P. 56(a).

CASE DETAILS

Facts:

Mr. Bovino owns a patent for "a portable computer having an integral case.. to protect the portable computer from wear and tear." He alleges Amazon infringed this patent by selling "cases for various versions of PC & Apple cellular phones, computers, and tablets." Amazon now moves for summary judgment stating that the accused products do not infringe the patent because they do not contain an integrated computer and do not contain "resilient ribs" on the exterior surface of the case and the patent is invalid as obvious.

Analysis:

The words in the patent are analyzed in their ordinary and customary meaning, as a person of ordinary skill in the art at the time of the invention would understand them to mean. *Phillips v. AWH Corp.*, 415 F.2d 1303, 1312-13 (Fed. Cir. 2005) (en banc). The court looks to sources available to the public to give meaning to the inventor's language, including: words of the claims, reminder of patent's specifications, the prosecution history of the patent, the extrinsic evidence concerning the scientific principles, the common meaning of the terms used, and the state of the art at the time of the invention. *Id.* The language must be construed in the entirety of the patent as well and must be read in conjunction with the more general and descriptive specification portion of the patent. *Id* at 1315.

CONCLUSION

The court held that the Motion for Summary Judgment is granted because Mr. Bovino did not adequately show a claim that any of the accused products infringed the patent. The court did not need to consider whether the patent is invalid as obvious.

Bovino v. Amazon.com, Inc.
Patent Infringement; Procedure

***Bovino v. Amazon.com, Inc.*, 2016 U.S. Dist. LEXIS 32368, 2016 WL 943780 (D. Colo. Mar. 14, 2016).**

ISSUE

Is Amazon entitled to attorney's fees and can Mr. Bovino enforce the settlement agreement?

RULE

A prevailing defendant is entitled to an attorney fee award for "exceptional" cases appropriate under 35 U.S.C. § 285. The court additionally, cannot enforce settlement agreements after the court has already ruled or entered judgment on a case.

CASE DETAILS

Facts:

Mr. Bovino alleged that Amazon was infringing upon his patent, which describes a computer with a case possessing "resilient ribs." The court previously granted summary judgment to Amazon. Amazon filed a motion seeking attorney's fees. Separately, Mr. Bovino moved to enforce the terms of a settlement offer from Amazon that he purported to accept. May of 2015, Amazon sent an email to Mr. Bovino offering a settlement if Mr. Bovino dismisses the infringement claims and Amazon would waive attorney's fees and would disclaim any further attempts to invalidate the patent. A few days later, the court entered summary judgment in favor of Amazon. A few hours later, Amazon emailed Mr. Bovino's counsel to discuss attorney's fees and said that there could be a "way to avoid all that."

Analysis:

An "exceptional case" that would allow the court to award attorney's fees to the prevailing party would be one that "stands out form others with respect to the substantive strength of the party's litigating position or the unreasonable manner in which the case was litigated." *Octane Fitness, LLC v. ICON Health Fitness,*

Inc., 134 S.Ct. 1749, 1756 (2014). The court cannot say that as a whole, the action rises to the "exceptional" case such that fees should be awarded to Amazon.

Additionally, the court states that although the offer stated that Mr. Bovino has a couple of days to reply with acceptance for the offer, it was intended that he accept prior to the court's ruling for summary judgment. Once the summary judgment motion was granted, Mr. Bovino could no longer dismiss his claims and therefore could not uphold his end of the deal.

CONCLUSION

The court denied Amazon's request for attorney's fees, as it did not rise to an "exceptional case" required, and also denies Mr. Bovino's request to enforce the settlement agreement, as a judgment has already been entered.

Bowens v. Aftermath Entertainment
Privacy Violation; Unlawful Use of Images

***Bowens v. Aftermath Entm't*, 254 F. Supp. 2d 629 (E.D. Mich. 2003).**

ISSUE

Whether the court should grant the Defendants' Motion to Dismiss, Plaintiff's Second Motion for Leave to Amend the First Amended Complaint, and Defendant's Motion for Sanctions.

RULE

Federal Rule of Civil Procedure 12(b)(6) authorizes the district court to dismiss any complaint that fails to state a claim. It gives the opportunity for a defendant to test whether the plaintiff is entitled to legal relief even if everything in the complaint is alleged as true. Federal Rule of Civil Procedure 15(a) gives the court the discretion to grant a motion to amend freely when justice requires so unless it is requested in bad faith. Fed. R. Civ. P. 15(a). Rule 10(c) of Federal Rules of Civil Procedure provides that "a copy of any written instrument which is an exhibit to a pleading is a part of thereof for all purposes." Under Rule 11 of the Federal Rules of Civil Procedure and 28 U.S.C. § 1927, sanctions can be issues by the court by determining "whether the individual attorney's conduct was reasonable under the circumstances." *Mann v. G & G Mfg., Inc.*, 900 F.2d 953, 958 (6th Cir. 1990).

CASE DETAILS

Facts:

On July 6, 2000, the "Up n Smoke" music tour, featuring performances by artists known as Dr. Dre, Eminem, Ice Cube and Snoop Dogg, prepared for a concert at Joe Louis Arena in Detroit. Several Detroit officials, including Bowen, a mayoral press secretary, Bridges, a Detroit Police Department spokesperson, and Brown a Detroit police commander (plaintiffs), arrived at the arena and sought a meeting with tour promoters (defendants). Plaintiffs were concerned that an eight-minute video introduction to performances by Dr. Dre and Snoop Dogg would violate city ordinances due to its explicitly. Ultimately, the defendants obtained footage of the conversations that took place between plaintiffs and defendant officials. The footage was used as "exclusive backstage footage" on a concert DVD. The DVD was subsequently sold on Amazon.

Timeline:

The plaintiffs filed the First Amended Complaint on April 24, 2002, adding individuals as defendants. In this complaint the plaintiffs alleged nineteen causes of action, only three of which remain in the court at this time, each of which arises under the Federal Wiretap Act.

Analysis:

Plaintiffs allege that defendants violated the Federal Wiretap Act intercepting disclosures and disclosing contents for purposes of producing, marketing and distributing and using the contents to produce, market and distribute. Plaintiffs want to amend the complaint as they did not include a copy of the Concert DVD in their First Amended Complaint. The court is not convinced that it may construe the DVD under Rule 10(c), as it does not fit in the categories of written instrument. The court concluded by stating that Plaintiffs have alleged facts sufficient to state a claim and therefore there is no need to dismiss and the amendment was granted. Additionally, the Defendants' moved for sanctions before the court's dismissal of Plaintiff's state law claims and two federal claims. Therefore, the only claims that the court examined are the Federal Wiretap Act claims and determined that these claims are well-founded, and therefore there is no need for sanctions.

CONCLUSION

The court denies Defendants' Motion to Dismiss, grants Plaintiff's Second Motion to Leave to Amend the First Amended Complaint, and denies Defendant's Motion for Sanctions.

Bowens v. Aftermath Entertainment
Privacy Violation; Unlawful Use of Images; Procedural

***Bowens v. Ary, Inc.*, 486 Mich. 962, 782 N.W.2d 779, 2010 Mich. LEXIS 1117 (2010)**

ISSUE

Whether the court should grant the Plaintiff's application for appeal?

CASE DETAILS

Facts:

On July 6, 2000, the "Up n Smoke" music tour, featuring performances by artists known as Dr. Dre, Eminem, Ice Cube and Snoop Dogg, prepared for a concert at Joe Louis Arena in Detroit. Several Detroit officials, including Bowen, a mayoral press secretary, Bridges, a Detroit Police Department spokesperson, and Brown a Detroit police commander (plaintiffs), arrived at the arena and sought a meeting with tour promoters (defendants). Plaintiffs were concerned that an eight-minute video introduction to performances by Dr. Dre and Snoop Dogg would violate city ordinances due to its explicitly. Ultimately, the defendants obtained footage of the conversations that took place between plaintiffs and defendant defendants. The footage was used as "exclusive backstage footage" on a concert DVD. The DVD was subsequently sold on Amazon.

Timeline:

The plaintiffs filed the First Amended Complaint on April 24, 2002, adding individuals as defendants. In this complaint the plaintiffs alleged nineteen causes of action, only three of which remain in the court at this time, each of which arises under the Federal Wiretap Act. The state court dismissed the state claims in an order for summary judgment. The court also went into judgment on April 19, 2005 in favor of the defendants.

Analysis:

The court determined that the questions presented should not be reviewed by this court at this time and therefore, determine that the application for appeal is denied.

CONCLUSION

The court held that the application for appeal is denied, as there is not enough proof to demonstrate that the questions should be reviewed by this court.

Bowens v. Ary
Privacy Violations; Unlawful Use of Images

***Bowens v. Ary*, 2009 Mich. App. LEXIS 2000 (Mich. Ct. App. Sept. 24, 2009).**

ISSUE

The issue here is whether plaintiff reasonably expected that the conversation taking place with defendant was intended to and was reasonably expected to be private such that the use of the conversation for profit would be unlawful.

RULE

Whether a conversation is private depends on whether the person conversing "intended and reasonably expected that the conversation was private." *Dickerson v Raphael*[, 461 Mich 851; 601 NW2d 108 (1999). Whether a conversation is private depends on the intent and reasonable expectation of the plaintiff, and "not whether the subject matter was intended to be private." *Id.*

CASE DETAILS

Facts

On July 6, 2000, the "Up n Smoke" music tour, featuring performances by artists known as Dr. Dre, Eminem, Ice Cube and Snoop Dogg, prepared for a concert at Joe Louis Arena in Detroit. Several Detroit officials, including Bowen, a mayoral press secretary, Bridges, a Detroit Police Department spokesperson, and Brown a Detroit police commander (plaintiffs), arrived at the arena and sought a meeting with tour promoters (defendants). Plaintiffs were concerned that an eight-minute video introduction to performances by Dr. Dre and Snoop Dogg would violate city ordinances due to its explicitly. Ultimately, the defendants obtained footage of the conversations that took place between plaintiffs and defendant defendants. The footage was used as "exclusive backstage footage" on a concert DVD. The DVD was subsequently sold on Amazon.

Timeline

At the trial level the court granted summary judgment in favor of defendants thus dismissing all claims. Here, on appeal, the court affirmed the summary judgment on all issues except for an eavesdropping claim.

Plaintiff's Argument

Plaintiffs claim that they had clearly and repeatedly requested that the portion of the meeting included on the DVD remain private, and that they did not give anyone permission to record the discussion. Defendant brown testified, that had the cameramen refused to shut off their cameras, that he "would not have had [the] meeting had [he] known the camera was on." *Bowens v. Ary*, No. 282711, 2009 Mich. App. LEXIS 2000 (Ct. App. Sep. 24, 2009). The conversation took place backstage in an area called "the referee's room." MTV as well as other media outlets had backstage access. *Id.* The area was busy with other people walking in and out as well. *Id.*

CONCLUSION

The court here explains that the location of a conversation, standing alone, does not automatically establish whether the parties to the conversation "reasonably intended" and expected that their interchange would remain private." *Id.*

In this case the parties both agree that a request by the plaintiffs for a private conversation was agreed upon by the defendants. *Id.* The court held that a jury must make the determination of whether plaintiffs' expectation of privacy "under the circumstances" presented here qualified as a reasonable one. *People v Stone*, 463 Mich 558, 563; 621 NW2d 702 (2001).

This court focused on the defendants' use of the footage for profit. "Although this suit demonstrates that there may be an occasional situation in which an anonymous scanner will risk criminal prosecution by passing on information without any expectation of financial reward or public praise, surely this is the exceptional case." *Bartnicki v Vopper*, 532 US 514; 121 S Ct 1753; 149 L Ed 2d 787 (2001). Based on this distinction the courts conclusion to remand the case is supported. When footage is used for profit, the First Amendment does not shield defendants from liability for a claim against them.

Bowens v. ARY
Privacy Violations; Unlawful Use of Images

***Bowens v. ARY*, Inc., 489 Mich. 851, 794 N.W.2d 842, 2011 Mich. LEXIS 456 (Mich. 2011).**

ISSUE

Whether a genuine issue of material fact exists to warrant a trial concerning whether the conversation recorded and used in the "Up in Smoke Tour" concert DVD constituted a "private conversation" such that eavesdropping laws were applicable.

RULE

Michigan's eavesdropping statute, MCL 750.539a *et seq.*, which prohibits "[a]ny person who is present or who is not present during a *private conversation* [from] willfully us[ing] any device to eavesdrop upon the conversation without the consent of all parties thereto...." MCL 750.539c (emphasis added). "'[P]rivate conversation' means a conversation that a person reasonably expects to be free from casual or hostile intrusion or surveillance." *People v Stone*, 463 Mich 558, 563 (2001). After considering all the evidence of record in the light most favorable to plaintiffs, the non-moving party, *Quinto v Cross & Peters Co*, 451 Mich 358, 362 (1996).

CASE DETAILS

Timeline

At the trial level the court granted summary judgment in favor of defendants thus dismissing all claims. At the court of appeals, the court affirmed the summary judgment on all issues except for an eavesdropping claim. Here, at the Supreme Court of Michigan, the court reverses the holding of the Court of Appeals, and reinstates the summary judgment in favor of the defendants on all claims.

Facts

On July 6, 2000, the "Up n Smoke" music tour, featuring performances by artists known as Dr. Dre, Eminem, Ice Cube and Snoop Dogg, prepared for a concert at Joe Louis Arena in Detroit. Several Detroit officials, including Bowen, a mayoral press secretary, Bridges, a Detroit Police Department spokesperson, and Brown a Detroit police commander (plaintiffs), arrived at the arena and sought a meeting with tour promoters (defendants). Plaintiffs were concerned that an eight-minute video introduction to performances by Dr. Dre and Snoop Dogg would violate city ordinances due to its explicitly. Ultimately, the defendants obtained footage of the conversations that took place between plaintiffs and defendant defendants. The footage was used as "exclusive backstage footage" on a concert DVD. The DVD was subsequently sold on Amazon.

CONCLUSION

Here, the court held that "no reasonable juror could conclude that plaintiffs had a reasonable expectation of privacy in the recorded conversation" at issue. The following evidence compels this conclusion: (1) the general locale of the meeting was the backstage of the Joe Louis arena during the hectic hours preceding a high-profile concert, where over 400 people, including national and local media, had backstage passes; (2) the concert-promoter defendants were not receptive to the public-official plaintiffs' requests and, by all accounts, the parties' relationship was antagonistic; (3) the room in which plaintiffs chose to converse served as defendants' operational headquarters with security personnel connected to defendants controlling the open doors; (4) there were at least nine identified people in the room, plus unidentified others who were free to come and go from the room, and listen to the conversation, as they pleased; (5) plaintiffs were aware that there were multiple camera crews in the vicinity, including a crew from MTV and a crew specifically hired by defendants to record backstage matters of interest; (6) and video evidence shows one person visibly filming in the room where the conversation took place while plaintiffs were present, thereby establishing that at least one cameraman was openly and obviously filming during the course of what plaintiffs have characterized as a "private conversation." Under these facts and circumstances, plaintiffs could not have reasonably expected that their conversation with defendants would "be free from casual or hostile intrusion or surveillance." *Stone*, 463 Mich at 563.

Boyd v. Review Bd.
Worker's Compensation and Employees' Rights

***Boyd v. Review Bd.*, 13 N.E.3d 950 (Ind. Ct. App. 2014)**

ISSUE

Whether there was sufficient evidence to support the Indiana Department of Workforce Development Board's (the board) determination that Plaintiff, Boyd was ineligible for unemployment compensation benefits because she was discharged for just cause.

RULE

Under the Indiana Compensation Act (Act), "[a]ny decision of the [Board] shall be conclusive and binding as to all questions of fact." Ind. Code § 22-4-17-12(a). When the Board's decision is challenged as contrary to law, [the court] must consider whether there is sufficient evidence to support the Board's factual findings and whether there are sufficient facts to sustain the decision. *S.S. LLC v. Review Bd. of Ind. Dep't of Workforce Dev.*, 953 N.E.2d 597, 602 (Ind. Ct. App. 2011). On review, "(1) findings of basic fact are reviewed for substantial evidence; (2) findings of mixed questions of law and fact—ultimate facts—are reviewed for reasonableness; and (3) legal propositions are reviewed for correctness." *Recker v. Review Bd. of Ind. Dep't of Workforce Dev.*, 958 N.E.2d 1136, 1139 (Ind. 2011). Accordingly, we will affirm the Board's decision if there is substantial evidence to support its findings and if the decision is reasonable in light of those findings. *Coleman v. Review Bd. of Ind. Dep't of Workforce Dev., 905 N.E.2d 1015, 1019 (Ind. Ct. App. 2009).* We do not assess witness credibility or reweigh evidence, and we consider only the evidence most favorable to the Board's decision. *Id.*

CASE DETAILS

Facts

Plaintiff worked at Amazon as a full time warehouse associate beginning in September of 2011. Plaintiff requested and was approved for 5 hours of unpaid personal time to be used on June 23, 2013. The manager who approved her vacation did not know that plaintiff only had 2 hours of vacation time available. Amazon subsequently discharged plaintiff on June 26, 2013.

TimeLine

Plaintiff filed a claim for unemployment compensation with the Indiana Department of Workforce Development (DWD). The DWD found plaintiff was not eligible for unemployment benefits because Amazon had not provided evidence to "establish that the discharge was a result of willful misconduct."

Amazon appealed the decision of the DWD to an Administrative Law Judge (ALJ). The ALJ reversed the DWD's decision, finding that because plaintiff knew she was violating an Amazon work rule and thus was discharged for "just cause." Plaintiff now appeals the decision of the ALJ.

Analysis

The court first notes that in April of 2013, Amazon administered a new attendance policy. The policy gave all employees 40 hours of unpaid personal time. Amazon made clear that any negative balance of unpaid time is grounds for termination. Amazon also sent plaintiff a letter alerting her to the fact that she only had 2 unpaid hours remaining. Therefore, plaintiff knowingly violated Amazon's attendance policy. Thus, when plaintiff returned from vacation she had a negative balance unpaid personal time, which is just cause for termination.

CONCLUSION

For the foregoing reasons, the court held that there was sufficient evidence to support the Board's determination that Amazon terminated plaintiff for just cause, thus disqualifying her from unemployment compensation benefits.

Breuer v. American Express Bank
Financial and Tax Law

***Breuer v. American Express Bank*, FSB, 2014 N.Y. Misc. LEXIS 2931, 2014 NY Slip Op 31698(U) (N.Y. Sup. Ct. June 30, 2014).**

ISSUE

Whether the court should grant summary judgment in favor of plaintiff or defendant where plaintiff is requesting credit card debt to be returned in the form of a check.

RULE

In order to prevail on a motion for summary judgment, the proponent must make a prima facie showing of entitlement to judgment as a matter of law, through admissible evidence, eliminating all material issues of fact (Klein v. City of New York, 89 N.Y.2d 833, 675 N.E.2d 458, 652 N.Y.S.2d 723 [1996]). Once the moving party has satisfied these standards, the burden shifts to the opponent to rebut that prima facie showing, by producing contrary evidence, in admissible form, sufficient to require a trial of material factual issues (*Amatulli v. Delhi Constr. Corp.*, 77 N.Y. 2d 525, 571 N.E.2d 645, 569 N.Y.S. 2d 337 [1999]).

CASE DETAILS

Facts

Plaintiffs initially purchased 2,958 Bluetooth headsets from Amazon.com, totaling $138,996.42. They used an American Express card to make this purchase. Later, they returned all of the headsets and requested a refund. Amazon refunded only a portion of the total price of their original purchase. Plaintiffs sued Amazon for the remainder of the funds from the returned Bluetooth headsets. Amazon issued a refund of $37,307.54, leaving a remainder of $83,410.26 owed to the plaintiffs. The court ordered Amazon to issue a complete refund to the plaintiffs. The funds were requested by the Plaintiff in the form of a check. Instead, Amazon issued the remaining funds back to the American Express credit card that was used for the initial purchase.

The plaintiffs were in a large amount of debt on the credit card account used to make the purchase on Amazon, with a total amount owed of $110,468.39. A settlement between plaintiffs and AMEX was allowed after receiving the refund from Amazon.

After reaching the settlement agreement, Plaintiff asked American Express to send a check for the refund from Amazon. American Express refused and mandated that the funds from the Amazon refund be applied to the plaintiff's debt.

Plaintiff then sued AMEX for the refunded amount that had been applied back to their AMEX Credit Card. Plaintiff moved for summary judgment, claiming breach of contract. AMEX opposes the instant motion and cross motioned for summary judgment.

Analysis

The court found that AMEX showed plaintiffs had no right of ownership to the Amazon refund; therefore, their claims were invalid. Plaintiffs did not provide adequate material requiring a trial of factual issues on either of the causes of action. The Court agreed with American Express and the case was dismissed. Plaintiffs' motion for summary judgment was denied and defendants' cross motion for summary judgment was granted.

CONCLUSION

The court found that AMEX made a prima facie case of entitlement to judgment as a matter of law. The court also found that AMEX was entitled to summary judgment for the conversion claim. Accordingly, the court ordered that plaintiffs' motion for summary judgment was denied, and that defendants' cross motion for summary judgment was granted.

Brickey v. Amazon.com, Inc.
Copyright Infringement; Procedure

***Brickey v. Amazon.com, Inc.*, No. SA-13-CA-961-XR, 2014 U.S. Dist. LEXIS 9297 (W.D. Tex. Jan. 27, 2014)**

ISSUE

The court is determining whether to grant defendants motion to dismiss for failure to state a claim, where plaintiff is seeking punitive damages under the Copyright Act.

RULE

"To survive a motion to dismiss, a complaint must contain sufficient factual matter, accepted as true, to 'state a claim to relief that is plausible on its face.'" *Ashcroft v. Iqbal*, 556 U.S. 662, 678, 129 S. Ct. 1937, 173 L. Ed. 2d 868 (2009) (quoting *Bell Atl. Corp. v. Twombly*, 550 U.S. 544, 570, 127 S. Ct. 1955, 167 L. Ed. 2d 929 (2007)). "A claim has facial plausibility when the plaintiff pleads factual content that allows the court to draw the reasonable inference that the defendant is liable for the misconduct alleged." Id. While detailed factual allegations are not necessary, a plaintiff must provide "more than labels and conclusions, and a formulaic recitation of the elements of a cause of action will not do." *Twombly*, 550 U.S. at 555. However, a complaint can survive a motion to dismiss even if actual proof of the facts alleged is "improbable." *Id.* at 556.

The Copyright Act provides for two kinds of damages. The copyright owner can recover "actual damages and any additional profits of the infringer. . . or. . . statutory damages." 17 U.S.C. § 504(a) (emphasis added); *On Davis v. The Gap, Inc.*, 246 F.3d 152, 172 (2d Cir. 2001).

CASE DETAILS

Facts

This case stems from plaintiff's copyright claim against defendants for the alleged unauthorized sale of plaintiff's CD, "Texas Blues and County Tear Jerkers." Plaintiff claims that although the sale was initially authorized, that the authorization was withdrawn, but defendant continued to sell the CD. Plaintiff seeks statutory damages, punitive damages, and injunctive relief. Here, defendants filed this motion to strike and in the alternative a motion to dismiss because the copyright Act does not authorize punitive damages.

Analysis

The court found that both the Copyright Act and the case law that interprets it do not indicate that congress intended to authorize punitive damages. Even if the court accepted plaintiff's allegations as true, it found that he will be unable to obtain either punitive or mental anguish damages. Therefore, plaintiff's claim was not "plausible on its face" and could be dismissed under Rule 12(b)(6).

CONCLUSION

For the foregoing reasons, the court held that the motion to dismiss plaintiff's claim for punitive and mental anguish damages is granted. Plaintiff was allowed to proceed for any actual damages or, if he can prove willful infringement, for statutory damages.

Brickey v. Amazon.com, Inc.
Procedure – Motion for Summary Judgment

***Brickey v. Amazon.com, Inc.*, No. SA-13-CA-961-XR, 2014 U.S. Dist. LEXIS 22304 (W.D. Tex. Feb. 21, 2014)**

ISSUE

Whether plaintiff provided sufficient evidence of copyright infringement to establish that no genuine issue of material fact exists and that he is entitled to judgment as a matter of law.

RULE

Summary judgment is proper when the evidence shows "that there is no genuine dispute as to any material fact and the movant is entitled to judgment as a matter of law." FED. R. CIV. P. 56(a); *Anderson v. Liberty Lobby, Inc.*, 477 U.S. 242, 250-252, 106 S. Ct. 2505, 91 L. Ed. 2d 202 (1986). Rule 56 "mandates the entry of summary judgment, after adequate time for discovery and upon motion, against a party who fails . . . to establish the existence of an element essential to that party's case, and on which that party will bear the burden of proof at trial." *Curtis v. Anthony*, 710 F.3d 587, 594 (5th Cir. 2013) (quoting *Celotex Corp. v. Catrett*, 477 U.S. 317, 322, 106 S. Ct. 2548, 91 L. Ed. 2d 265 (1986)).

To establish a prima facie case of copyright infringement, a plaintiff must demonstrate: "(1) ownership of a valid copyright, and (2) copying [by the defendant] of constituent elements of the work that are original." *Gen. Universal Sys., Inc. v. Lee*, 379 F.3d 131, 141 (5th Cir. 2004) (citing *Feist Publ'ns, Inc. v. Rural Tel. Serv. Co.*, 499 U.S. 340, 111 S. Ct. 1282, 113 L. Ed. 2d 358 (1991)).

CASE DETAILS

Facts

This case stems from plaintiff's copyright claim against defendants for the alleged unauthorized sale of plaintiff's CD, "Texas Blues and County Tear Jerkers." Plaintiff claims that although the sale was initially authorized, that the authorization was withdrawn, but defendant continued to sell the CD. Plaintiff seeks statutory damages, punitive damages, and injunctive relief. Here, plaintiff seeks grant of his motion for summary judgment.

Analysis

Here, the court finds that a genuine issue of material fact exists of whether any sales of the CD occurred after plaintiff withdrew his authorization. The only evidence of a violation provided by plaintiff are screenshots of the CD for sale. However, these screen shots do not show that the postings were made after plaintiff removed his consent. The court also finds that the fact that the CD's were advertised for sale does not conclusively show that the CDs were actually sold.

CONCLUSION

For the foregoing reasons, the court found that because there is a genuine issue of material fact as to whether any infringement has occurred, that plaintiff is not entitled to summary judgment. The motion is denied.

Brickey v. Amazon.com, Inc.
Copyright Infringement; Procedure

***Brickey v. Amazon.com, Inc.*, No. SA-13-CA-961-XR, 2014 U.S. Dist. LEXIS 97479 (W.D. Tex. July 18, 2014)**

ISSUE

Whether actionable copying occurred here in the form of unauthorized sales of plaintiff's CD, such that a motion for summary judgment is proper.

RULE

Summary judgment is proper when the evidence shows "that there is no genuine dispute as to any material fact and the movant is entitled to judgment as a matter of law." Fed. R Civ. P. 56(a); *Anderson v. Liberty Lobby, Inc.*, 477 U.S. 242, 250-252, 106 S. Ct. 2505, 91 L. Ed. 2d 202 (1986). Rule 56 "mandates the entry of summary judgment, after adequate time for discovery and upon motion, against a party who fails . . . to establish the existence of an element essential to that party's case, and on which that party will bear the burden of proof at trial." *Curtis v. Anthony*, 710 F.3d 587, 594 (5th Cir. 2013) (quoting *Celotex Corp. v. Catrett*, 477 U.S. 317, 322, 106 S. Ct. 2548, 91 L. Ed. 2d 265 (1986)).

To establish a prima facie case of copyright infringement, a plaintiff must demonstrate: "(1) ownership of a valid copyright, and (2) copying [by the defendant] of constituent elements of the work that are original." *Gen. Universal Sys., Inc. v. Lee*, 379 F.3d 131, 141 (5th Cir. 2004) (citing *Feist Publ'ns, Inc. v. Rural Tel. Serv. Co.*, 499 U.S. 340, 111 S. Ct. 1282, 113 L. Ed. 2d 358 (1991)).

CASE DETAILS

Facts

This case stems from plaintiff's copyright claim against defendants for the alleged unauthorized sale of plaintiff's CD, "Texas Blues and County Tear Jerkers." Plaintiff claims that although the sale was initially authorized, that the authorization was withdrawn, but defendant continued to sell the CD. Plaintiff seeks statutory damages, punitive damages, and injunctive relief. Here, defendant seeks grant of its motion for summary judgment.

Analysis

The court finds that plaintiff does not show that any actual sales actually occurred after he withdrew authorization of sale. Plaintiff only provided the court with screen shots of the item listed for sale, but this only proves advertisement of the CD, not an actual sale. Amazon does concede to one sale of a CD after plaintiff withdrew his consent. The court finds, however, that under the "first sale" doctrine no copyright violation occurred because Amazon was the lawful owner of the CD that was sold and therefore it was "entitled without the authority of the copyright owner to sell. 17 U.S.C. § 109(a). Here, plaintiff has no statutory right to recover any additional compensation because the CD was sold by its rightful owner, Amazon. Additionally, plaintiff has failed to create an issue of fact that any other copies of the CD were sold in a way the "first sale doctrine" would not apply.

CONCLUSION

For the foregoing reasons the court grants defendants' motion for summary judgment.

NOTE: This case was appealed by plaintiff. The court however dismissed the appeal for lack of jurisdiction.

Brown Younger v. Lulu.com
Amazon Dismissed from all Claims

***Brown-Younger v. Lulu.com*, 2012 U.S. Dist. LEXIS 91574, 2012 WL 2576214 (N.D. Ill. July 3, 2012).**

ISSUE

Whether plaintiff had a right or reason to include Amazon.com Inc. as a defendant in this action and subsequently file ARDC charges against Amazon attorneys.

RULE

"District courts also can impose both monetary and non-monetary sanctions under Rule 11 for filing or maintaining claims for an improper purpose or without adequate legal or factual support. Fed. R. Civ. P. 11(b).

CASE DETAILS

Facts

This case involves a copyright claim in which plaintiff claims violations due to the unauthorized sale of her self published poetry book. Plaintiff subsequently filed an ARDC charge against the Amazon attorney. Plaintiff claimed the Amazon attorney had previously represented her and so there was a conflict of interest. The court found this to be a straight out lie. Additionally, a prior hearing revealed that Amazon never sold the book, nor was it ever listed on their website

Analysis

The court holds that it would be "totally unfair" to Amazon's counsel for Brown-Younger's ARDC charge to be left uncorrected by her. Although one has a right to file an ARDC charge against an attorney, anyone who exercises a right that harms another must be prepared to pay the price that the law may attach to that exercise.

CONCLUSION

The court concluded that because plaintiff's behavior was so out of line with legal standards she is ordered to file a retraction and withdrawal of the charge against Amazon's attorney with the ARDC by July 12, 2012

Brown-Younger v. Lulu
Procedure

***Brown-Younger v. Lulu.com*, No. 12 C 1979, 2012 U.S. Dist. LEXIS 91574 (N.D. Ill. July 3, 2012).**

ISSUE

The issue here is whether the court should allow an in forma pauperis (IFP) plaintiff to appeal orders resulting from her frivolous claims against Amazon.com Inc., even though they were improperly joined to the suit.

RULE

An applicant seeking IFP status must meet two requirements: (1) inability to pay the filing fee; and (2) the advancement of an apparently non-frivolous claim.

CASE DETAILS

Facts

In this case, a pro se plaintiff made copyright claims against numerous defendants in an attempt to abuse or take advantage of the legal system. Plaintiff fabricated a charge that a lawyer representing Amazon.com Inc. (which she named as a defendant despite total lack of evidence as to Amazon violating her copyright) had previously represented her, but then switched to representing Amazon. Plaintiff further complained of this attorney to the ARDC with false charges of misconduct.

Analysis

The court here found that if it had known at the time of plaintiff's original filing what the events of the case had revealed, that it would have denied plaintiff her IFP status. The court found that any appeal by the plaintiff here would be equally as frivolous as her complaint ultimately proved to be, so that it denies her application for IFP status.

CONCLUSION

The court holds that the court of appeals can deny plaintiff's appeal because they are now aware of the insufficiencies in plaintiffs claim.

Carlin v. Bezos
Copyright Infringement; Procedure

***Carlin v. Bezos*, 2016 U.S. App. LEXIS 9372 (3d Cir. Pa. May 23, 2016).**

ISSUE

Whether the court below erred in granting the Defendant's motion for Summary Judgment?

RULE

To make a valid claim of copyright infringement, the plaintiff must establish: (1) Ownership of a valid copyright, and (2) Unauthorized copying of original elements of plaintiff's work. *Dun & Bradstreet Software Servs., Inc. v. Grace Consulting, Inc.*, 307 F.3d 197, 206 (3d Cir. 2002).

CASE DETAILS

Facts:

Carlin is the author of four self-published books. In 2011, Carlin signed up to use CreateSpace, a subsidiary of Amazon.com and agreed to the terms of the agreement. It granted CreateSpace nonexclusive license to publish, distribute, and sell his books through Amazon.com and other sales channels. CreateSpace agreed to pay Carlin royalties for the sales.

Timeline:

Carlin filed suit in 2014 alleging copyright infringement, alleging that he was not paid the royalties he was entitled to. Carlin appeals the District Court's order granting Summary Judgment to the defendants and denying his cross motion for summary judgment.

Analysis:

The court agrees with the lower court's ruling for granting summary judgment to defendants. The court determined that a reasonable jury could not find that Amazon exceeded the scope of its license. The "evidence" that Carlin suggested to the court merely showed that Amazon offered to sell the books, not completed sales. The court determined that this does not suffice to survive summary judgment.

CONCLUSION

The court affirms the District Court's judgment and denies Carlin's motion.

Celebrate International LLC v. Leapfrog Enterprises Inc.
Patent Infringement

***Celebrate Int'l, LLC v. LeapFrog Enters.*, 2015 U.S. Dist. LEXIS 114407, 2015 WL 5092611 (D. Del. Aug. 28, 2015).**

ISSUE

What are the definitions that the court should apply to the disputed terms in the patents at issue?

RULE

"It is a bedrock principle of patent law that the claims of a patent define the invention to which the patentee is entitled the right to exclude." *Phillips v. AWH Corp.*, 415 F.3d 1303, 1312 (Fed. Cir. 2005) (en banc) (internal quotation marks omitted). [T]he words of a claim are generally given their ordinary and customary meaning... [Which is] the meaning that the term would have to a person of ordinary skill in the art in question at the time of the invention, i.e., as of the effective filing date of the patent application." Id. at 1312-13 (internal quotation marks and citations omitted). "[T]he ordinary meaning of a claim term is its meaning to [an] ordinary artisan after reading the entire patent." Id. at 1321 (internal quotation marks omitted).

CASE DETAILS

Facts

This is a patent infringement case filed by Celebrate International LLC against Leapfrog Enterprises, an Amazon-owned e-reader for kids, regarding the '398 Patent and the '776 Patent.

The '398 and '776 Patents refer to a method for decoding a message embedded in a pattern of pixels. The '776 Patent is an extension of the '398 Patent. Both of these have identical specifications.

This case moves to determine the language necessary for the Plaintiff to submit a proposed order consistent with this memorandum opinion and the terms agreed upon.

Analysis

The following factors are definitive of what delineates the term pixel value according to each party:

a. Plaintiff's proposed construction: Plain and ordinary meaning, or in the alternative, "Values relating to a characteristic of a pixel, including greyscale, brightness, color, size, or dimensions."
b. Defendants' proposed construction: Measurable characteristics of a pixel, such as greyscale, brightness, color, size, or dimensions.
c. Court's construction: Value(s) derived from measurable characteristics of a pixel, including greyscale, brightness, color, size, or dimensions.

The following factors are definitive of what expresses the term binary value according to each party:

a. Plaintiff's proposed construction: Logical value(s) expressed in one or more bits (0s and/or 1s).
b. Defendants' proposed construction: Values that are expressed as either '1' or '0.'
c. Court's construction: Values that are expressed using only 0s and/or 1s.

The following factors are definitive of what constitutes a display according to each party:

a. Plaintiff's proposed construction: Surface, such as a monitor or printed paper, having a visual image.
b. Defendants' proposed construction: An electronic device, such as a cathode ray tube monitor, liquid crystal display or printer, which generates text or images that can be viewed by a human observer.
c. Court's construction: An electronic device, such as a cathode ray tube monitor, liquid crystal display or printer.

CONCLSUSION

Moving forward, the Court states that the parties are to submit a proposed order that is consistent with the terms agreed upon in the court opinion that is suitable for submission to the jury.

Chambers v. Amazon.com Inc. (4th Cir., 2015)
Procedure

Note: This is an appeal to the previous judgment granting motion to dismiss.

***Chambers v. Amazon.com Inc.*, 632 Fed. Appx. 742 (4th Cir. S.C. 2015).**

ISSUE

Whether the motion to dismiss plaintiffs claim for failure to state a reasonable cause of action was proper, where plaintiff fails to meet sufficiency requirements because it does not contain a "short and plain statement of the claim showing that the pleader is entitled to relief," and is conclusory, with no factual support.

RULE

Section 1915(e) of the U.S.C. directs a district court to dismiss a case if the court finds that it is frivolous or malicious, fails to state a claim, or seeks damages from a defendant who is immune from such relief.

"To establish a claim for copyright infringement a plaintiff must prove that [he] possesses a valid copyright and that the defendant copied elements of [the] work that are original and protectable." *Copeland v. Bieber*, 789 F.3d 484, 488 (4th Cir. 2015).

"A copyright owner alleging a violation of [the DMCA] must prove that the circumvention of the technological measure either infringes or facilitates infringing a right protected by the Copyright Act." *Starage Tech. Corp. v. Custom Hardware Engineering & Consulting, Inc.*, 421 F.3d 1307, 1318 (Fed. Cir. 2005).

CASE DETAILS

Facts

Here, plaintiff's complaint he stated that in 2001 he gave 5 CDs to defendant CD Baby, who would act as an "online consignor." By 2014 plaintiff realized that the material was selling beyond the quantity produced and was being redistributed in both digital and physical form. Plaintiff also discovered that other defendants including Amazon.com Inc. and Apple Inc. were selling the copyrighted content in digital and/or physical form. Plaintiff claimed violations of the Copyright Act and the DMCA.

Timeline

The magistrate judge made a recommendation to summarily dismiss the case, finding that plaintiff made conclusory statements of facts showing that only one CD had been sold, and thus he failed to provide support for his claim that any defendant made an unauthorized copy of the material. The district court overruled plaintiff's objections and adopted the recommendation of the magistrate, holding that the complaint and attachments failed to provide sufficient factual support for a cause of action under either the Copyright Act or DMCA.

Analysis

Plaintiff here, did not state sufficient facts to state a plausible claim of copyright infringement. Plaintiff claimed that numerous copies of his CD – more than the five he originally supplied CD Baby – were available from various defendants, but he provided no evidence of this. The court found that plaintiff did not set forth sufficient facts in his complaint to establish either that he possessed a valid copyright or that any of the defendants reproduced copyrighted work.

Plaintiff did not state any facts that could be reasonably inferred to create a DMCA violation. Plaintiff made no claim that he had put into place a technological measure that would have protected a copyright or that any defendant circumvented such a measure.

CONCLUSION

The court here affirms the District Court below and dismisses the case. Oral argument was not needed because the facts and legal arguments were made adequately available in the materials before the court.

Chambers v. Amazon.com Inc. Copyright Infringement; DMCA

***Chambers v. Amazon.com Inc.*, No. 3:14-4890-MGL-PJG, 2015 U.S. Dist. LEXIS 85596 (D.S.C. Feb. 5, 2015).**

ISSUE

Whether the court should summarily dismiss this case.

RULE

The mandated liberal construction afforded to pro se pleadings means that if the court can reasonably read the pleadings to state a valid claim on which the plaintiff could prevail, it should do so; however, a district court may not rewrite a complaint to include claims that were never presented, *Barnett v. Hargett*, 174 F.3d 1128 (10th Cir. 1999), construct the plaintiff's legal arguments for him, *Small v. Endicott*, 998 F.2d 411 (7th Cir. 1993), or "conjure up questions never squarely presented" to the court, *Beaudett v. City of Hampton*, 775 F.2d 1274, 1278 (4th Cir. 1985).

The Copyright Act grants copyright protection to "original works of authorship fixed in any tangible medium of expression." 17 U.S.C. § 102(a). To establish a claim of copyright infringement, a plaintiff must show: (1) ownership of a valid copyright, and (2) that the defendant copied the original elements of the copyrighted work. *Feist Publ'n, Inc. v. Rural Tel. Serv. Co., Inc.*, 499 U.S. 340, 361, 111 S. Ct. 1282, 113 L. Ed. 2d 358 (1991); *Keeler Brass Co. v. Cont'l Brass Co.*, 862 F.2d 1063, 1065 (4th Cir. 1988). The Digital Millennium Copyright Act "was enacted both to preserve copyright enforcement on the Internet and to provide immunity to service providers from copyright infringement liability" for certain actions. *ALS Scan, Inc. v. RemarQ Cmtys., Inc.*, 239 F.3d 619, 625 (4th Cir. 2001).

CASE DETAILS

Facts

Here, the complaint alleges that plaintiff provided defendant, CD baby with 5 CDs in 2001. The CDs each contained eleven songs and one video. Plaintiff claims six of those songs were copyrighted. The plaintiff found out that the CDs were still selling in 2014 beyond the quality ever produced as well as in digital format. Plaintiff has provided screenshots showing the items for sale of both physical and digital listings for the CDs content. Plaintiff seeks statutory and punitive damages and claims that he is "in fear of his life" as well as lives of family members due to the nature of this case.

Analysis

Here, the court found that plaintiff's allegations demonstrated that only one of the CDs have definitively been sold or distributed. Therefore, even if the court concluded that plaintiff controls the copyright to the six songs, the complaint does not provide sufficient allegations to show that any defendant made an unauthorized copy of the material. Although the court must liberally construe a pro se complaint, the plaintiff's allegations were found to be speculative and conclusory. Therefore, the claims are insufficient to show a violation of the Copyright Act or the Digital Millennium Copyright Act.

CONCLUSION

For the foregoing reasons, the court recommended that the complaint be summarily dismissed.

Chambers v. Amazon.com Inc.
Copyright Violation; DMCA

***Chambers v. Amazon.com Inc.*, Civil Action No. 3:14-cv-4890-MGL, 2015 U.S. Dist. LEXIS 85367 (D.S.C. July 1, 2015)**

ISSUE

Whether the district court, here should adopt the decision of the Magistrate judge below and summarily dismiss this case.

RULE

The Magistrate Judge makes only a recommendation to this Court. The recommendation has no presumptive weight. The responsibility for making a final determination remains with this Court. *Mathews v. Weber*, 423 U.S. 261, 270, 96 S.Ct. 549, 46 L.Ed.2d 483 (1976). The Court is charged with making a de novo determination of any portions of the Magistrate Judge's Report to which a specific objection is made. The Court may accept, reject, or modify, in whole or in part, the recommendation made by the Magistrate Judge or may recommit the matter to the Magistrate Judge with instructions. 28 U.S.C. § 636(b)(1).

CASE DETAILS

Facts

Here, plaintiff brought copyright infringement as well as DMCA violation claims against defendants. Plaintiff has alleged that defendants infringed on plaintiff's exclusive right to reproduction of the material.

Timeline

The case was referred to a Magistrate Judge for pretrial management and consideration of pretrial motions. The magistrate recommended that this matter be summarily dismissed. Plaintiff filed objections to the recommendation. Here, the court is deciding whether to adopt the Magistrate's recommendation.

Analysis

The magistrate found that the complaint should be summarily dismissed because it contained insufficient factual allegations to show a violation of the Copyright Act or DMCA. The court here, agreed, and found that plaintiff's arguments failed to cast any doubt on the findings of the Magistrate. Plaintiff's evidence only provides evidence of plaintiff's alleged damages.

CONCLUSION

For the foregoing reasons, the court accepted the report and recommendation of the Magistrate. The case was thus ordered to be summarily dismissed.

Chambers v. Amazon.com Inc., 632 F. App'x 742 (4th Cir. 2015)
Copyright Infringement; DMCA

***Chambers v. Amazon.com Inc.*, 632 F. App'x 742 (4th Cir. 2015)**

ISSUE

Whether the court erred in adopting the Magistrate's recommendation that this case be summarily dismissed because plaintiff did not state any facts in which it could be reasonably inferred that DMCA or Copyright Act violations were present.

RULE

A complaint is subject to dismissal for failure to state a claim if the allegations, taken as true, show the plaintiff is not entitled to relief." *Jones v. Bock*, 549 U.S. 199, 215, 127 S. Ct. 910, 166 L. Ed. 2d 798 (2007). Although "the allegations in pro se complaints should be liberally construed," *De'Lonta v. Angelone*, 330 F.3d 630, 633 (4th Cir. 2003), the complaint must contain factual allegations sufficient "to raise a right to relief above the speculative level" and "to state a claim to relief that is plausible on its face." *Bell Atl. Corp. v. Twombly*, 550 U.S. 544, 555, 570, 127 S. Ct. 1955, 167 L. Ed. 2d 929 (2007).

To establish a claim for copyright infringement under the Copyright Act . . ., a plaintiff must prove that [he] possesses a valid copyright and that the defendant copied elements of [the] work that are original and protectable." *Copeland v. Bieber*, 789 F.3d 484, 488 (4th Cir. 2015). "Absent direct proof of copying, which is hard to come by, a plaintiff may prove copying indirectly, with evidence showing that the defendant had access to the copyrighted work and that the purported copy is 'substantially similar' to the original." *Id.*

Through the DMCA, "Congress sought to mitigate the problems presented by copyright enforcement in the digital age." *MDY Indus., LLC v. Blizzard Entertainment, Inc.*, 629 F.3d 928, 942 (9th Cir. 2010). "A copyright owner alleging a violation of [the DMCA] must prove that the circumvention of the technological measure either infringes or facilitates infringing a right protected by the

Copyright Act." *Storage Tech. Corp. v. Custom Hardware Engineering & Consulting, Inc.*, 421 F.3d 1307, 1318 (Fed. Cir. 2005) (internal quotation marks omitted).

CASE DETAILS

Facts

Here, plaintiff appeals the district court's order granting adopting the magistrate judge's recommendation to summarily dismiss this case. Plaintiff's complaint states that he gave defendant CD Baby five CDs containing 11 songs and 1 video. Plaintiff allegedly owned copyrights on 6 of the 12 pieces of work. Plaintiff discovered that the CDs were selling a a quantity beyond what had been produced in both digital and physical format. Plaintiff claimed violations of the Copyright Act and DMCA.

Timeline

The magistrate issued a recommendation for summary dismissal. The magistrate judge found that plaintiff had not pleaded facts to show that defendant made any unauthorized copies of the material at issue. The district court adopted the magistrate's opinion and issued an order for summary judgment. Plaintiff now appeals the court's decision to adopt the magistrate's recommendation.

Analysis

Copyright Act

The court found that plaintiff did not set forth sufficient facts to state a plausible claim of copyright infringement. Plaintiff alleged that more than the 5 CDs he originally provided were available from various sellers, but provided no evidence to support this contention. Plaintiff did not set for the sufficient facts in his complaint to establish that he held a valid copyright or that any defendant reproduced the copyrighted work.

DMCA

The court also found that plaintiff did not set forth any facts from which it might be inferred that there was a DMCA violation. Plaintiff did not claim to have put a technological measure in place that would have protected a copyright or that any defendant circumvented such a measure.

CONCLUSION

For the foregoing reasons, the court affirms the decision of the district court the adopt the magistrate's recommendation.

Clark v. Amazon.com
Copyright Infringement

Clark v. Amazon.com, 2006 U.S. Dist. LEXIS 69278 (E.D. Cal. Sep. 25, 2006).

ISSUE

Whether the court should grant the plaintiff's motion for injunctive relief that would stop defendant from selling plaintiff's copyrighted book on its website.

RULE

The party seeking a temporary restraining order must provide an affidavit in support of the existence of irreparable injury; an affidavit detailing the notice or efforts to effect notice to the affected parties or counsel; a proposed temporary restraining order with a provision for a bond; and a proposed order for any hearing on a motion for preliminary injunction. L.R. 65-231(c) (4)-(7).

The legal principles applicable to a request for injunctive relief are well established. To prevail, the moving party must show either a likelihood of success on the merits and the possibility of irreparable injury, or that serious questions are raised and the balance of hardships tips sharply in the movant's favor. See *Coalition for Economic Equity v. Wilson*, 122 F.3d 692, 700 (9th Cir. 1997); *Oakland Tribune, Inc. v. Chronicle Publ'q Co.*, 762 F.2d 1374, 1376 (9th Cir. 1985). The two formulations represent two points on a sliding scale with the focal point being the degree of irreparable injury shown. *Oakland Tribune*, 762 F.2d at 1376. "Under any formulation of the test, plaintiff must demonstrate that there exists a significant threat of irreparable injury." Id. In the absence of a significant showing of possible irreparable harm, the court need not reach the issue of likelihood of success on the merits. Id.

CASE DETAILS

Facts

Here, plaintiff initialed a copyright infringement action against defendant in relation to plaintiff's copyrighted book titled "Teenage Street Gangs: Differences,

Membership & Intervention. Plaintiff was seeking an order restraining Amazon from selling the book.

Analysis

The court finds that plaintiff has not demonstrated by affidavit that immediate or irreparable injury, loss, or damage will result if the requested relief is not granted. Further, plaintiff initiated almost one year ago. The court found that the plaintiffs delay in seeking injunctive relief contradicts his allegation of irreparable harm for which emergency relief is required.

CONCLUSION

For the foregoing reasons, the court here recommends that plaintiff's request for a temporary restraining order be denied.

Clark v. Amazon.com
Copyright Infringement

***Clark v. Amazon.com*, No. 2:05-cv-2187-GEB-DAD-PS, 2006 U.S. Dist. LEXIS 78151 (E.D. Cal. Oct. 26, 2006).**

ISSUE

Whether to adopt the magistrate judge's recommendation to deny plaintiff's application for temporary restraining order.

RULE

A court conducts *de novo* review when reviewing a challenge to a magistrate decision. 28 U.S.C. § 636(b)(1)(C).

CASE DETAILS

Facts

Here, plaintiff initialed a copyright infringement action against defendant in relation to plaintiff's copyrighted book titled "Teenage Street Gangs: Differences, Membership & Intervention. Plaintiff was seeking an order restraining Amazon from selling the book. The matter was referred to a magistrate judge. The magistrate judge recommended tat the the plaintiff's application for a temporary restraining order should be denied.

Analysis

The court here reviewed the file and finds that the magistrate judge's recommendation to be supported by both the record and the magistrate's analysis.

CONCLUSION

For the foregoing reasons, the court orders that the magistrate's recommendation be adopted in full and thus that plaintiff's application for a temporary restraining order be denied.

Clark v. Amazon.com
Copyright; Procedure

***Clark v. Amazon.com*, No. 2:05-cv-2187-GEB-DAD-PS, 2007 U.S. Dist. LEXIS 28896 (E.D. Cal. Apr. 19, 2007).**

ISSUE

Whether the court should adopt the magistrate's recommendation denying plaintiff's motion to dismiss.

RULE

A court conducts *de novo* review when reviewing a challenge to a magistrate decision. 28 U.S.C. § 636(b)(1)(C).

CASE DETAILS

Facts

Plaintiff's claim was recommended to a magistrate judge who issued a recommendation to deny plaintiffs motion to dismiss. The magistrate recommendation contained notice that any objections to the recommendation be filed within 10 days. Here, plaintiff has filed objections to the recommendation.

Analysis

The court finds that because the magistrate's recommendation is supported by the record as well as the magistrate's analysis, that the recommendation should be adopted.

CONCLUSION

For the foregoing reasons, the court holds that: (1) the findings and recommendations of the magistrate are adopted in full; and (2) that plaintiffs motion to dismiss is denied.

Clark v. Amazon.com
Copyright Infringement; Procedure

***Clark v. Amazon.com*, No. CIV S-05-2187 GEB DAD PS, 2007 U.S. Dist. LEXIS 19679 (E.D. Cal. Mar. 20, 2007)**

ISSUE

Whether the magistrate recommends granting plaintiffs motion to dismiss.

RULE

Pursuant to 29 USCS § 636(b)(1), "a judge may designate a magistrate [magistrate judge] to hear and determine any pretrial matter pending before the court, except a motion for injunctive relief, for judgment on the pleadings, for summary judgment, to dismiss or quash an indictment or information made by the defendant, to suppress evidence in a criminal case, to dismiss or to permit maintenance of a class action, to dismiss for failure to state a claim upon which relief can be granted, and to involuntarily dismiss an action. A judge of the court may reconsider any pretrial matter under this subparagraph (A) where it has been shown that the magistrate's [magistrate judge's] order is clearly erroneous or contrary to law."

CASE DETAILS

Facts

Plaintiffs filed a document title "Dismissal without Prejudice Pursuant to Federal Rule of Civil Procedure 41(a)(1)." The court construed this document as a motion to dismiss. The magistrate told plaintiffs that the case could not be dismissed under Rule 41(a)(1)(i) because defendants filed an answer to the plaintiff's amended complaint before service of plaintiff's notice. The court thus directed defendants to respond to plaintiffs' notice as a motion to dismiss pursuant to Rule 41(a)(2).

Analysis

The court recommended that because defendants had a pending motion for summary judgment and subsequently plaintiff's filed a counter motion for summary judgment, that plaintiff's motion for dismissal be denied.

CONCLUSION

For the foregoing reasons the court recommended that plaintiffs' notice, that was construed as a motion to dismiss, be denied.

Clark v. Amazon.com
Copyright Infringement

***Clark v. Amazon.com*, No. CIV S-05-2187 GEB DAD PS, 2007 U.S. Dist. LEXIS 34314 (E.D. Cal. May 10, 2007)**

ISSUE

Whether the magistrate should recommend summary judgment where both parties have filed cross motions for summary judgment.

RULE

Summary judgment is appropriate when it is demonstrated that there exists no genuine issue as to any material fact and that the moving party is entitled to judgment as a matter of law. Fed. R. Civ. P. 56(c). See also *Adickes v. S.H. Kress & Co.*, 398 U.S. 144, 157, 90 S. Ct. 1598, 26 L. Ed. 2d 142 (1970); *Owens v. Local No. 169* 971 F.2d 347, 355 (9th Cir. 1992).

CASE DETAILS

Facts

Plaintiffs began this action on October 31, 2005, alleging copyright infringement by six defendants. Plaintiffs alleged that defendants were selling, without permission, copies of plaintiff's book *Teenage Street Gangs: Differences Membership & Intervention.*

Analysis

Defendants Motion

The court finds that defendants statement of 36 undisputed facts is supported by two declarations with exhibits and that defendants motion for summary judgment should be granted. The court finds that the "first sale doctrine" applies and that because defendants sold lawfully obtained copies of the work at issue, plaintiff had no right to interfere with subsequent sales of the book.

Plaintiffs' Motion

The court finds that in plaintiff's cross motion for summary judgment, that plaintiffs fail to address defendants' undisputed facts or defendants' legal arguments. Plaintiff's argue conclusively that defendants are liable for contributory infringement, but plaintiffs cite no evidence that defendants knew of infringement activity by third parties who sold copies of plaintiff's book on the Amazon website.

CONCLUSION

For the foregoing reasons, the court recommends: (1) that defendants' motion for summary judgment be granted; (2) that plaintiffs' cross motion for summary judgment be denied; and (3) that this action be dismissed.

***NOTE ***

This recommendation was adopted by the court in a June 2007 decision. *See; Clark v. Amazon.com*, No. 2:05-cv-2187-GEB-DAD-PS, 2007 U.S. Dist. LEXIS 40392 (E.D. Cal. June 1, 2007). The court there held: (1) The findings and recommendations of the magistrate were adopted in full; (2) that defendants motion for summary judgment be granted; (3) that plaintiffs' cross motion for summary judgment be denied; and (4) that the action is dismissed with prejudice.

Cloud Satchel v. Amazon.com Inc., Barnes & Noble, Inc.
Patent Infringement

***Cloud Satchel, LLC v. Amazon.com, Inc.*, 76 F. Supp. 3d 553, 2014 U.S. Dist. LEXIS 174715 (D. Del. 2014).**

ISSUE

Did Amazon.com Inc., and Barnes & Noble Inc., infringe on Cloud Satchel's Patent?

RULE

There is not an infringement on a patent when the claim at issue is, "directed to one of those patent-ineligible concepts, namely, laws of nature, natural phenomena, and abstract ideas." 134 S. Ct. at 2354-55.

CASE DETAILS

Facts

Cloud Satchel filed suit against Amazon.com and Barnes & Noble, Inc. for patent infringement. Cloud Satchel claimed that the defendants were in violation of patent laws: U.S. Patent No. 5,862,321 ("the '321 patent") and No. 6,144,997 ("the '997 patent") both titled, "System and Method For Accessing And Distributing Electronic Documents". These patents deal specifically with systems and methods of transferring and storing electronic documents. This system "enables mobile users to access all of their electronic documents without being limited by the memory available on a mobile device. (*Id.* at col. 3:36-37). The patented system was said to be a faster method of transferring documents and provided easier storing of documents on portable computers. Amazon and Barnes and Noble filed a motion for summary judgment on the claims due to invalidity. They argue that the claims brought by Satchel are for patent ineligible subject matter.

Plaintiff's Argument

Cloud Satchel argued that Amazon.com Inc. and Barnes and Noble Inc. infringed on their two patents. Plaintiff responds to Amazon's argument that the claims are invalid by stating that Amazon has oversimplified the claims. Cloud Satchel argues that the patent is specific in that it serves to "improve the functioning of the computer and that the claims describe inventive applications of storage and retrieval of electronic documents." (D.I. 86 at 10). They further argue that the claims recite inventive applications of the abstract concept of "storage and retrieval of electronic documents". They conclude that the patents were not directed to an abstract idea.

Amazon's Argument

Amazon.com Inc. and Barnes and Noble Inc. filed a joint motion for summary judgment arguing that Cloud Satchel's claims are invalid. They argue that the claims brought by Cloud Satchel are inpatenable subject matter. They further claim that the patents are "drawn to the abstract principle of cataloguing documents to facilitate their retrieval from storage, a principle that has been in existence for nearly two millennia." (D.I. 83 at 8). Amazon argues that Cloud Satchel's claims "merely recite an abstract principle and instruct the public to apply it with a computer." (D.I. 83 at 11). They conclude that the patents are directed to an abstract idea and therefore are inpatenable subject matter.

CONCLUSION

The United States District Court for the District of Delaware held that the patents were directed to an abstract idea and therefore the claim was invalid. The court granted the motion for summary judgment in favor of Amazon.com and Barnes & Noble.

Clouding IP, LLC v. Amazon.com Inc.
Patent Infringement; Procedure

***Clouding IP, LLC v. amazon.com, Inc.*, 2013 U.S. Dist. LEXIS 73655, 2013 WL 2293452 (D. Del. May 24, 2013).**

ISSUE

The court looked to see if there was Direct Infringement, Induced Infringement, Willful Infringement, and whether they should grant a motion for a more definite statement.

RULE

"To prove induced infringement, the patentee must show direct infringement, and that the alleged infringer knowingly induced infringement and possessed specific intent to encourage another's infringement." *Toshiba Corp. v. Imation Corp.*, 681 F.3d 1358, 1363 (Fed. Cir. 2012)

CASE DETAILS

Facts

Clouding filed for patent infringement against Amazon and Oracle. Clouding IP argues that their claim is limited to post-filing conduct; therefore, pre-filing knowledge is not required to state a claim for inducement. *See, e.g., Walker Digital, LLC v. Facebook, Inc.*, 852 F. Supp. 2d 559, 565 (D. Del. 2012). They further argue that their complaint shows the defendant's intent to infringe by continuing to infringe even after they received the complaint. This shows that they had knowledge of their violation and by continuing, that they intended to violate the patent. The defendants argue that Clouding failed to state a claim for induced infringement and willful infringement. They further argue that the claims do not show the defendants had knowledge of the patents and that the claims fail to show the defendants specifically intended to induce infringement.

Analysis

The court addressed the issue of Direct Infringement, Induced Infringement, Willful Infringement, and a motion for a more definite statement. On the issue of Direct Infringement, the court found that because Clouding provided a description of the accused Oracle products in each count of its FAC and identified one accused product for each count, that their claims for direct infringement meet the sufficiency requirements.

On the issue of Induced Infringement, the court found that Clouding failed to prove intent and therefore dismissed the induced infringement claims.

On the issue of Willful Infringement, the court found that, "there appears to be little practical difference between a pre-complain notice letter informing a defendant about a patentee's allegation of infringement and a subsequently-superseded original complaint formally alleging infringement." The court also finds that the claims brought by Clouding are based on conduct predating the operative amended complaint. Therefore, the court denied the motion to dismiss the willful infringement claims.

On the issue of for a more definite statement, the court found that the claims were not vague or ambiguous and therefore denied Oracle's motion for a more definite statement.

CONCLUSION

The United State District Court held that the Direct Infringement Claims are sufficient; the Induced Infringement claims should be dismissed; the Willful Infringement claims are sufficient, and the motion for a more definite statement should be denied.

Content Guard Holdings, Inc. v. Amazon.Com, Inc.
Procedure

***Content Guard Holdings, Inc. v. Amazon.com, Inc.*, 2015 U.S. Dist. LEXIS 33881 (E.D. Tex. Mar. 19, 2015).**

ISSUE

Should the court grant the defendants' motions to sever?

RULE

Pursuant to Rule 21 of the Federal Rules of Civil Procedure, a district court has the discretion to sever any claim against a party.

CASE DETAILS

Facts

ContentGaurd alleges Defendant's software applications within their apps such as, iTunes, Amazon Kindle, Amazon Instant Video; and hardware and software components are infringing its patent claims. Amazon specifically is accused of infringing on seven of the nine asserted patents.

Defendant, Amazon.com motions to Sever pursuant to Federal Rules of Civil Procedure 20 and 21 and 35 U.S.C. Section 299. Additionally, defendant Motorola motioned to Sever and Supplemental Submission, defendant Apple Inc. motioned to sever and transfer; and defendants HTC, Huawei and Samsung motioned to sever.

Analysis

The court found that after an analysis of the record, there were common questions of fact; there were actual links between those facts; and that the "same transaction, occurrence, or series of transactions or occurrences" was accused. Therefore, the court found that the movants are properly joined as parties under 35 U.S.C. Section 299 and Rule 20 of the Federal Rules of Civil Procedure.

CONCLUSION

The United States District Court denied Amazon's motion to sever finding that they were a properly joined party to the suit. Additionally, the court denied all other named defendants' motion to sever and determined there will be separate trials only for certain claims in this case.

Content Guard Holdings, Inc. v. Amazon.Com, Inc. *Patent Infringement; Procedure; Claim Construction*

***Content Guard Holdings, Inc. v. Amazon.com, Inc.*, 2015 U.S. Dist. LEXIS 34667 (E.D. Tex. Mar. 20, 2015).**

ISSUE

What are the proper definitions that the court should apply to the disputed terms within the patent at issue?

RULE

"It is a bedrock principle of patent law that the claims of a patent define the invention to which the patentee is entitled the right to exclude." *Phillips v. AWH Corp.*, 415 F.3d 1303, 1312 (Fed. Cir. 2005) (en banc) (internal quotation marks omitted). [T]he words of a claim are generally given their ordinary and customary meaning... [Which is] the meaning that the term would have to a person of ordinary skill in the art in question at the time of the invention, i.e., as of the effective filing date of the patent application." Id. at 1312-13 (internal quotation marks and citations omitted). "[T]he ordinary meaning of a claim term is its meaning to [an] ordinary artisan after reading the entire patent." Id. at 1321 (internal quotation marks omitted).

CASE DETAILS

Facts

ContentGuard alleges DRM aspects of certain of Defendant's software applications within their apps such as, iTunes, Amazon Kindle, Amazon Instant Video; and hardware and software components of infringing its patent claims. Amazon specifically is accused of infringing on seven of the nine asserted patents.

Analysis

The United States District Court construed the terms in the Stefik Patents as follows:

A. The court construed "repository" to mean, "a trusted system in that it maintains physical, communications, and behavioral integrity in the support of usage rights" and "trusted" to mean, ""maintains physical, communications, and behavioral integrity in the support of usage rights".

B. The court construed "physical integrity" to mean, "preventing access to information in a repository by a non-trusted system."
C. The court construed "communications integrity" to mean, "only communicates with other devices that are able to present proof that they are trusted systems, for example, by using security measures such as encryption, exchange of digital certificates, and nonces."
D. The court construed "behavioral integrity" to mean, "requiring software to include a digital certificate in order to be installed in the repository."
E. The court construed "content and digital content" to mean, "the digital information (i.e., raw bits) representing a digital work." F. "rights," "usage rights," and "usage rights information".
F. The court construed "rights, usage rights, and usage rights information" to mean, "indications that are attached, or treated as attached, to [a digital work / digital content / content / a digital document] and that indicate the manner in which the [digital work / digital content / content / digital document] may be used or distributed as well as any conditions on which use or distribution is premised."
G. The court construed "usage rights" to mean, "an indication of the manner of use by which a digital work may be used or distributed, as well as any conditions on which manner of use is premised."
H. The court construed "digital works" to have its plain meaning.
I. The court construed "digital document and document" to have its plain meaning.
J. The court construed "requester mode of operation and server mode of operation" to have their plain meaning.
K. The court construed "manner of use" to mean, "a way in which [a digital work / digital content / content / a digital document] may be used, as contrasted with a condition that must be satisfied before such use is allowed."
L. The court construed "render and rendering" to mean, "present[ing] a digital work, such as by playing a digital movie, playing digital music,

playing a video game, running a computer program, displaying a document on a display, or printing on paper."

M. The court construed "authorization object" to mean, "a digital work that can be moved between repositories and that must be possessed in order to exercise a usage right."

N. The court construed "identification certificate and digital certificate" to mean, "a signed digital message that attests to the identity of the possessor."

O. The court construed "nonce and random registration identifier" to mean, "random and variable information unique to a cryptographic session."

P. The court construed "distributed repository" to mean, "a repository adapted for use in a distributed system."

Q. The court construed "document platform" to mean, "a repository for rendering a digital document."

R. The court construed "validating" to mean, "in Claim 5 of the '007 Patent is indefinite.

S. The court construed "determining, by the document platform" to have its plain meaning.

T. The court construed "grammar" to mean, "a manner of defining a valid sequence of symbols for a language."

U. The court construed "description structure" to mean, "a structure which describes the location of content and the usage rights and usage fees, if any such usage fees are required, for a digital work that is comprised of description blocks, each of which corresponds to a digital work or to an interest in a digital work."

V. The court construed "means for communicating with a master repository for obtaining an identification certificate for the repository" the function is "communicating with a master repository for obtaining an identification certificate for the repository," and the corresponding structure is "the external interface means 1206 described in the '859 Patent at 13:52-59; and equivalents thereof."

W. The court construed "means for processing a request from the means for requesting" the function is "processing a request from the means for requesting," and the corresponding structure is "a general-purpose computer; and equivalents thereof."

X. The court construed "means for checking whether the request is for a permitted rendering of the digital content in accordance with rights specified in the apparatus" the function is "checking whether the request is for a permitted rendering of the digital content in accordance with rights specified in the apparatus," and the corresponding structure is "a processor configured to perform the following algorithm and equivalents thereof: first, the requester repository determines whether an authorization certificate or a digital ticket is needed; second, the server repository generates a transaction identifier; third, the server repository determines whether the right is granted and whether time, security, and access based conditions are satisfied; and finally, the server repository determines whether there are sufficient copies of the work to distribute; and equivalents thereof." Y. "means for receiving the authorization ob[j] ect when it is determined that the request should be granted"

Y. The court construed "means for receiving the authorization object when it is determined that the request should be granted" the function is "receiving the authorization object when it is determined that the request should be granted," and the corresponding structure is "a processor configured to perform the following algorithm and equivalents thereof: the server repository transmits a block of data to the requester repository and waits for an acknowledgement, which the requester provides when the block of data has been completely received; unless a communications failure terminates the transaction, that process repeats until there are no more blocks to transmit; finally, the requester repository sends a completion acknowledgement to the server repository; both the server and the requester cancel a transaction if it is interrupted before all of the data blocks are delivered, and commits to it if all of the data blocks have been delivered; and equivalents thereof."

Z. The court construed "means for requesting a transfer of the digital content from an external memory to the storage" the function is "requesting a transfer of the digital content from an external memory to the storage," and the corresponding structure is "user interface 1305, as described in the '576 Patent at 16:20-46; and equivalents thereof."

The United States District Court construed the terms in the Nguyen Patents as follows:

A. The court construed "repository" to mean, "a trusted system in that it maintains physical, communications, and behavioral integrity in the support of usage rights."
B. The court construed "license" to mean, "data embodying a grant of usage rights and/or meta-rights."
C. The court construed "meta-right" to mean, "a right that, when exercised, creates or disposes of usage rights (or other meta-rights) but that is not itself a usage right because exercising a meta-right does not result in action to content."
D. The court construed "usage rights" to mean, "indications that are attached, or treated as attached, to [a digital work / digital content / content / a digital document] and that indicate the manner in which the [digital work / digital content / content / digital document] may be used or distributed as well as any conditions on which use or distribution is premised."
E. The court construed "manner of use" to mean, "a way in which [a digital work / digital content / content / a digital document] may be used, as contrasted with a condition associated with such use.
F. The court construed "state variable" to mean, "a variable having a value, or identifying a location at which a value is stored, that represents status of an item, rights, license, or other potentially dynamic conditions."
G. The court construed "the at least one state variable identifies a location where a state of rights is tracked" to have its plain meaning.
H. The court construed "specifying, in a first license, . . . at least one usage right and at least one meta-right for the item, wherein the usage right and the meta-right include at least one right that is shared among one or more users or devices" to mean, "specifying in a first license, at least

one usage right and at least one meta-right for the item, wherein at least one of the meta-right or the usage right is shared among one or more users or devices."

I. The court construed "means for obtaining a set of rights associated with an item" the function is "obtaining a set of rights associated with an item," and the corresponding structure is "a client environment 30 with a browser capable of connecting to a web server 80 and storing a license 52 that can be interpreted by client component 60, as set forth in the '280 Patent at 4:66-5:21; and equivalents thereof."

J. The court construed "means for determining whether the rights consumer is entitled to the right specified by the meta-right" the function is "determining whether the rights consumer is entitled to the right specified by the meta-right," and the corresponding structure is "authorization manager 508 that authenticates the rights consumer 304 and verifies that the conditions 306 of the license 52 have been satisfied, as described in the '280 Patent at 8:66-9:8, 9:15-18 & 9:63-10:2; and equivalents thereof."

K. The court construed "means for exercising the meta-right to create the right specified by the meta-right" to mean, the function is "exercising the meta-right to create the right specified by the meta-right," and the corresponding structure is "meta-rights manager module 510 that derives new rights from meta- rights 302 in accordance with a set of rules or other logic and updates the state of rights and the current value of the conditions in a state of rights repository, as described in the '280 Patent at 9:9-13 & 9:33-50; and equivalents thereof."

L. The court construed "means for generating a license including the created right, if the rights consumer is entitled to the right specified by the meta-right" to mean, the function is "generating a license including the created right, if the rights consumer is entitled to the right specified by the meta-right," and the corresponding structure is "license server 50 or license manager 803 as described in the '280 Patent at 4:5-14, 5:6-13, 10:35-45, and 10:62-11:16; and equivalents thereof."

The United States District Court construed the terms in the Dunkeld Patent as follows:

A. The court construed "detect[ing] a transfer" to have its plain meaning.
B. The court construed "instance" to mean, ""a file that contains a digital asset, and the file is distinguishable from other files containing the same digital asset."
C. The court construed "other portion" to mean, ""any part of the digital asset, or information prepended or postpended to the digital asset." D. "over said network between user devices"
D. The court construed "over said network between user devices" to mean, "in Claims 8 and 19 of the '556 Patent is indefinite."

CONCLUSION

The United States District Court adopted the constructions as mentioned above.

Content Guard Holdings, Inc. v. Amazon.Com, Inc.
Patent Infringement; Procedure

***Content Guard Holdings, Inc. v. Amazon.com, Inc.*, 2015 U.S. Dist. LEXIS 39807 (E.D. Tex. Mar. 29, 2015).**

ISSUE

Did ContentGaurd plead a case upon which relief can be granted?

RULE

In Re Seagate Tech establishes the rule that willful patent infringement requires proof that, "(1) the infringer acted despite an objectively high likelihood that its actions constituted infringement of a valid patent, (2) this objectively-defined risk was either known or so obvious that is should have been known to the accused infringer."

Under 35 U.S.C. Section 271(b), induced infringement requires proof of "(1) an act of direct infringement by another, and (2) that the defendant knowingly induced the infringement with the specific intent to encourage the other's infringement.

CASE DETAILS

Facts

ContentGaurd alleges DRM aspects of certain of Defendant's software applications within their apps such as, iTunes, Amazon Kindle, Amazon Instant Video; and hardware and software components are infringing its patent claims. Amazon specifically is accused of infringing on seven of the nine asserted patents. Amazon filed a separate Renewed Motion pursuant to 35 U.S.C. Section 101 and addressed the complaint's failure to sufficiently plead induced, contributory, and willful infringement.

Analysis

The court found that ContentGaurd's complaint properly identifies types of products that infringe. Additionally, the court finds that the pleadings are sufficiently plausible to plead a claim of contributory infringement. Finally, the court looked to the pleadings, briefings, and relevant attachments, and when viewing the facts in the light most favorable to plaintiff, found the pleadings are sufficiently plausible to plead a claim of willful infringement.

CONCLUSION

The United States District Court denied the motion to dismiss the amended complaint and the motion to dismiss the second amended complaint. The court ruled in favor of ContentGaurd holding that they had pled a case upon which relief can be granted.

Additionally, on the same filing date (March 29, 2015) with the same title, Content Guard Holdings v. Amazon.com; the District court discussed another named defendant, Apple Inc.'s motion to dismiss pursuant to Rule 12(6)(b) of the Federal Rules of Civil Procedure and Apple Inc.'s renewed motion to dismiss second amended complaint. The court again denied both motions.

Content Guard Holdings, Inc. v. Amazon.Com, Inc.
Patent Infringement; Procedure

ISSUE

Should the court grant the plaintiff's motion to strike evidence that was not produced during the discovery process?

RULE

Pursuant to Federal Rules of Evidence 702, "(1) An expert witness may provide opinion testimony if 'the expert's scientific, technical, or other specialized knowledge will help the trier of fact to understand the evidence or to determine a fact in issue; (2) the testimony is based on sufficient facts or data; (3) the testimony is the product of reliable principles and methods; and (4) the expert has reliably applied the principles and methods to the facts of the case.

CASE DETAILS

Facts

ContentGuard alleges DRM aspects of certain of Defendant's software applications within their apps such as, iTunes, Amazon Kindle, Amazon Instant Video; and hardware and software components are infringing its patent claims. Amazon specifically is accused of infringing on seven of the nine asserted patents.

Plaintiff, ContentGuard Holdings, filed motions to exclude portions of the reports and testimony of Jean Renard Ward, Dr. Brian Noble, Dr. Steve White, Atul Prakash, Dr. Paul Clark, Dr. John P.J. Kelly, and a motion to exclude portions of the noninfringement reports and testimony of Paul Clark, Brian Noble, John Kelly, and Gene Tsudik. Defendants filed a combined motion to strike portions of the expert reports and testimony of Michael T. Goodrich and David Martin.

Analysis

On the issue of Pfleeger references, plaintiff claims that defendants, Apple, Google, HTC, Huawei, Motorola, and Samsung are now attempting to maneuver the court's previous order of excluding the Pfleeger references. Therefore, the court grants the plaintiff's motion as it pertains to the Pfleeger references.

The court previously denied defendant Apple's request to amend its invalidity contentions with any VDE references other than the patent named Ginter. The court granted plaintiff's motion "as it pertains to information about the VDE system that is not disclosed directly from the Ginter patent.

The court granted the plaintiff's motion pertaining to the Wyman patents as invalidity references against he Nguyen patents. Additionally, the court granted the plaintiff's motions (Dkt. No. 679, Dkt. No. 683, Dkt. No. 684, Dkt. No. 685, Dkt. No. 690, Dkt. No. 692 and defendant's motions Dkt. No. 721 pertaining to claim construction positions. All other motions relating to claim construction positions were denied.

Additionally, the court denied the defendant's motion to strike the DOE theories provided in Mr. Goodrich's and Mr. Martin's reports.

The court granted the plaintiff's motion pertaining to the prosecution history estoppel arguments mentioned in Dr. Kelly's report ad denied defendant's motion pertaining to ContentGuard's assertion of the doctrine of equivalents.

Finally, the court granted plaintiff's motion Dkt. No, 688.

CONCLUSION

The United States District court granted plaintiff's motion to exclude portions of the reports and testimony of Jean Ward, Dr. Brian Noble, Dr. Steve White, Atul Prakash, Dr. Paul Clark, Dr. John P.J. Kelly, and the motion to exclude portions of the noninfringement reports and testimony of Paul Clark, Brian Noble, John Kelly, and Gene Tsudik.

The United States District court granted defendants combined motion to strike portions of the expert reports and testimony of Michael R. Goodrich and David Martin.

Content Guard Holdings, Inc. v. Amazon.Com, Inc.
Patent Infringement; Procedure

***ContentGuard Holdings, Inc. v. Amazon.com, Inc.*, 2015 U.S. Dist. LEXIS 53687 (E.D. Tex. Apr. 23, 2015).**

ISSUE

Should the court grant a motion to transfer?

RULE

28 U.S.C. Section 1404(a) provides that "for the convenience of parties and witnesses, in the interest of justice, a district court may transfer any civil action to any other district court division where it might have been brought.

CASE DETAILS

Facts

ContentGuard alleges DRM aspects of certain of Defendant's software applications within their apps such as, iTunes, Amazon Kindle, Amazon Instant Video; and hardware and software components are infringing its patent. Amazon specifically is accused of infringing on seven of the nine asserted patents.

Here, defendant, Apple claims that ContentGuard signed multiple versions of Apple's Developer Program License Agreement, which requires that the suit be transferred. A section of this agreement mentions that if a dispute were to arise between ContentGuard and Apple, that it would be litigated in the Northern District of California. Additionally, Apple argues that because of the language provided in the Confidentiality Agreement (NDA) between the two parties, transfer is appropriate.

Analysis

The court looked to the NDA and found that it was permissive and not mandatory. Therefore, the NDA had "no clear bearing on transfer."

CONCLUSION

The United States District Court denied Apple's opposed motion for leave to supplement the record in support of Apple, Inc.' motion to sever and transfer.

Content Guard Holdings, Inc. v. Amazon.Com, Inc.
Patent Infringement; Procedure

***ContentGuard Holdings, Inc. v. Amazon.com, Inc.*, 142 F. Supp. 3d 510 (E.D. Tex. 2015)**

ISSUE

Should the court grant the motion for continuance of the trial date until after the completion of post-trial briefing.

CASE DETAILS

Facts

ContentGuard alleges DRM aspects of certain of Defendant's software applications within their apps such as, iTunes, Amazon Kindle, Amazon Instant Video; and hardware and software components of infringing its patent claims. Amazon specifically is accused of infringing on seven of the nine asserted patents.

Here, Apple requests a continuance of the trial date until after the completion of post trial briefing.

Analysis

The court finds that the "stipulation in question was not intended to apply to all defendants in the case and does not apply to Apple". Additionally, the court found that the issues within the case between Apple and ContentGuard are "sufficiently disparate such that collateral estoppel does not arise out o the Google verdict of noninfringement."

CONCLUSION

The United States District court denied the motion to continue trial date because the verdict stipulation applies to the OEM defendants and because they found collateral estoppel does not apply.

Corbis Corp. v. Amazon.com, Inc.
Copyright Infringement

***Corbis Corp. v. Amazon.com, Inc.*, 351 F. Supp. 2d 1090, 2004 U.S. Dist. LEXIS 27155, 77 U.S.P.Q.2D (BNA) 1182 (W.D. Wash. 2004).**

ISSUE:

Did Amazon infringe upon Plaintiff's copyrighted images through the use of images by Amazon vendors and Amazon-owned IMDb.com?

CASE DETAILS

Facts

Plaintiff sued Amazon for copyright infringement, unfair competition under the Lanham Act, dilution of Plaintiff's trademarks under the Trademark Act, and tortuously interfering with Plaintiff's business relations. Plaintiff and Amazon both moved for summary judgment.

Plaintiff claimed to have copyright interests in two photographs that Amazon placed on it's website IMDb.com as well as hundreds of photographs that were being sold by vendors on Amazon without Plaintiff's permission.

Analysis

Amazon's policy is to cancel a vendor's listings once someone notifies them of an infringement by an Amazon vendor. Amazon has a Participation Agreement with vendors wherein vendors are forbidden from infringing on intellectual property rights and it is the vendor's responsibility not to do so. Amazon is immune from liability for copyright infringement under Title II of the Digital Millennium Copyright Act ("DMCA")

CONCLUSION:

Amazon is protected from liability for copyright infringement occurring on its third party vendor platform, zShops.com. Amazon qualifies as an Internet Service Provider protected under DCMA, does not have affirmative duty to police possible infringement, but must take reasonable steps if is alerted to infringement.

Court lacks subject matter jurisdiction over infringement claims regarding photographs for which Corbis has not obtained copyright registration. Court dismissed Plaintiff's claim under Lanham Act as it is duplicative of copyright infringement claim.

Cordance Corp. v. Amazon.com, Inc.
Patent Infringement

***Cordance Corp. v. Amazon.com, Inc.*, 730 F. Supp. 2d 333, 2010 U.S. Dist. LEXIS 74368 (D. Del. 2010).**

ISSUE

Whether the court should grant plaintiff's motion for permanent injunction prohibiting Amazon from infringing plaintiff's patent.

RULE

In *eBay Inc. v. MercEchange, LLC.*, the Supreme Court held that "the decision whether to grant or deny injunctive relief rests within the equitable discretion of the district courts, and that such discretion must be exercised consistent with traditional principles of equity, in patent disputes no less than in other cases governed by such standards."

CASE DETAILS

Facts

Plaintiff sued Amazon for patent infringement for its website's "1-click" purchase feature. Plaintiff claimed Amazon's information storage and way of collecting buyer and seller reviews violated Plaintiff's patents.

At trial, a jury found that Amazon had infringed on some of Plaintiff's patents. Plaintiff then filed a motion asking the court to issue a permanent injunction against Amazon from infringing upon its patents, or, in the alternative, an ongoing royalty if Amazon continued to do so. Amazon opposed this motion.

Plaintiff argued that they and Amazon were the only two competitors in the market for digital identity systems enabling one-click shopping and Amazon's infringement has caused Plaintiff's business to suffer.

Amazon argues that they were never direct competitors and its supposed infringement in using the one-click system has nothing to do with Plaintiff's business losses, but rather that has resulted from Plaintiff's poor business decisions, i.e. licensing its software out.

Analysis

The Court found agreed with Amazon and refused to order a permanent injunction as Plaintiff didn't show irreparable harm that couldn't be rectified by monetary payment. The issuance of a royalty was denied because of a pending appeal that would resolve the issue.

CONCLUSION

The court refused to grant a permanent injunction.

Cordance Corporation v. Amazon.com.
Patent Infringement

***Cordance Corp. v. Amazon.com, Inc.*, 855 F. Supp. 2d 244, 2012 U.S. Dist. LEXIS 51268 (D. Del. 2012).**

ISSUE

Should the District Court grant Amazon's request for bill of costs?

CASE DETAILS

Facts

Plaintiff, Cordance Corporation filed suit against defendant, Amazon.com for patent infringement. The case went to trial and the case was adjudicated in favor of Amazon. Amazon filed a bill of costs that amounted to $591,824.69 on November 14, 2011. On November 28, 2011, plaintiff objected to the bill of costs and claimed Amazon was not entitled to the action because, "Amazon engaged in dilatory tactics which increased expenses for both parties." Furthermore, the plaintiff argued that if Amazon should be awarded costs, that the cost should be reduced.

Analysis

The court found that after looking to the evidence presented by Cordance, that they could not, "find that Amazon encumbered the record". Additionally, the court found that there should be a reduction in the amount of costs granted to Amazon. The court held that the appropriate cost should be in the amount of $2,721.53 for ediscovery costs; $1,152.80 for deposition costs; and $34,327.47 for taxation of copying costs.

CONCLUSION

The United States District Court partially granted and partially denied Amazon's request for costs and denied Cordance's request to have the bill of costs denied.

Cox v. Brand 44, LLC
Negligence; Wrongful Death; Procedural

***Cox v. Brand 44, LLC*, 2015 U.S. Dist. LEXIS 143120, 2015 WL 6182469 (D. Mass. Oct. 21, 2015).**

ISSUE

Whether the court should grant defendants' partial motion to dismiss?

RULE

On a motion to dismiss, the court must accept as true the facts alleged in the complaint as well as all reasonable inferences that may be gleaned from those facts. *Amaro v Gani Realty Corp.*, 60 AD3d 491, 876 N.Y.S.2d 1 (1st Dept 2009).

CASE DETAILS

Facts:

Cox filed suit against Brand 44, LLC, Amazon.com Inc., and Playthings Past LLC alleging that their son died after falling off a zip line made by Brand 44 and purchased from Playthings and Amazon. They claim negligent, wrongful death, loss of consortium, breach of warranties, punitive damages, pain and suffering, strict liability, and violation of a Massachusetts law.

Timeline:

Plaintiff filed this action on May 22, 2014 and filed an Amended Complaint on June 1, 2015.

Analysis:

Brand 44 filed a partial motion to dismiss as to the loss of consortium, breach of warranties, punitive damages, pain and suffering and strict liability claims. The court determined that loss of consortium survives but is limited to any loss of consortium suffered by the parents between the time of their son's injury and his death. Additionally, the breach of warranties claim survives as well but the court notes that this is limited to claims for breach of express warranty and the breach of implied warranty of merchantability. Pain and suffering was also allowed to stay as a claim, under Mass. Gen. Laws. Ch. 229 §6. Punitive damages were dismissed, as they could not stand alone as a separate count and should be pursued in connection with the wrongful death claim. Strict liability was also dismissed as Massachusetts law does not recognize strict liability cause of action for a defective product.

CONCLUSION

The court denied the motion as to all claims except for punitive damages and strict liability, as those were granted.

Crowley v. Cybersource Corporation
Copyright; Class Action; Procedural

***Crowley v. Cybersource Corp.,* 166 F. Supp. 2d 1263, 2001 U.S. Dist. LEXIS 17020 (N.D. Cal. 2001).**

ISSUE

Whether Amazon can move to dismiss the amended complaint?

RULE

Pursuant to Rule 12(b)(6) of the Federal Rules of Civil Procedure, the court can dismiss the complaint for failure to state a claim if "it appears beyond doubt that the plaintiff can prove no set of in support of his claim which would entitle him to relief." *Conley v. Gibson*, 355 U.S. 41, 45-46 (1957). The Wiretap Act prohibits the interception of wire, oral, and electronic communications unless prior consent is given to the interception. Additionally, the court can dismiss the claim pursuant to Rule 12(b)(3) for improper venue.

CASE DETAILS

Facts:

Daragh Crowley alleges that he went on Amazon's website and provided them with his name, email, mailing address, credit card number and expiration date, and telephone number. Amazon then transmitted this information to CyberSource to verify the identity and CyberSource stored this information and created a personal profile with it. Crowley alleges that this is in violation of the Wiretap Act and the ECPA.

Analysis:

Amazon and CyberSource filed motions to dismiss by challenging the causes of action in the amended complaint and Amazon filed motion to challenge venue, based on a forum selection clause in their contract. The court found that the forum selection clause does not apply in this case as it only applies to "any action at law or in equity arising out of or relating to these terms and conditions." The claims in this action relate to Privacy and not the Participation Agreement, and therefore the court denies to let it apply in this case. Amazon did not intercept the communication within the meaning of the Wiretap Act because it did not acquire it using a device other than the drive or server on which the email was received. Amazon only received the information transferred to it by Crowley, acting like a second party in the communication. Therefore, there is a failure to state a claim against Amazon under the Wiretap Act. Additionally, Crowley alleges a claim under the ECPA against Amazon. Amazon is an online merchant and not an electronic communication service provider and therefore is not considered under the ECPA and additionally, no unauthorized access occurred.

CONCLUSION

The court grants Amazon's motion to dismiss with leave to amend and their motion to dismiss the second cause of action for violation of ECPA. Amazon's motion to dismiss for improper venue is denied and the court declines to exercise supplemental jurisdiction over the state claims.

Curran v. Amazon.com, Inc.
Privacy Violations

***Curran v. Amazon.com, Inc.*, 2008 U.S. Dist. LEXIS 12479, 86 U.S.P.Q.2D (BNA) 1784, 36 Media L. Rep. 1641 (S.D. W. Va. Feb. 19, 2008).**

ISSUE

Should the court grant Amazon.com's motion to dismiss?

RULE

Pursuant to the Federal Rules of Civil Procedure Rule, 8(a)(2) "requires that a pleaders provide a short and plain statement of the claim showing entitlement to relief."

CASE DETAILS

Facts

Plaintiff, Curran alleged that Amazon.com used a photograph of him that was taken while he was deployed without his consent or compensation. The photograph was used on a book titled, "Killer Elite" authored by Michael Smith. Curran filed suit against multiple defendants, Amazon.com included.

Defendants motioned to dismiss the claim.

Analysis

The court found that the plaintiffs failed to show that the plaintiff was a public figure or a soldier. In order to establish a claim for right of publicity, this must be provided. The court therefore dismissed count I of the complaint for right of publicity. The court additionally dismissed the first prong of count II. The remainder of the motions to dismiss were denied.

CONCLUSION

The court concluded that Amazon's motions to dismiss should be granted for count I and for the first prong of count II with all remainders of the motion to be denied.

Cyberfone Systems, LLC, v. Amazon.com
Patent Infringement

***CyberFone Sys., LLC v. Cellco P'ship*, 885 F. Supp. 2d 710, 2012 U.S. Dist. LEXIS 115740, 2012 WL 3528115 (D. Del. 2012).**

ISSUE

Should the court grant the defendant's motion for summary judgment?

RULE

Pursuant to the Federal Rules of Civil Procedure Rule 56(c), "A court shall grant summary judgment only if the pleadings, depositions, answers to interrogatories, and admissions on file, together with the affidavits, if any, show that there is no genuine issue as to any material fact and that the moving party is entitled to judgment as a matter of law."

CASE DETAILS

Facts

Cyberfone Systems, LLC, assignee of the 060 patent, filed 21 lawsuits involving a total of 175 defendants for patent infringement. This patent is a "system that automatically captures data at a point of transaction and transmitting the data to one or more databases for processing and storage."

On April 30, 2012, the court denied the motions to "(1) sever and/ or dismiss under Federal Rules of Civil Procedure 20, (2) to stay claims; (3) to dismiss direct infringement claims on the merits or based on the sufficiency of the pleadings; (4) to dismiss induced infringement claims based on the lack of pleading pre-suit knowledge." Additionally, the court granted the motions to dismiss claims of contributory infringement.

On May 1, 2012, the court granted defendant's permission to file an early summary judgment motion related to their contention that the 060 patent is invalid under 35 U.S.C. Section 101.

The defendants argue that summary judgment is appropriate because the 060 patent "merely claims the abstract concept of gathering, organizing and forwarding data." Additionally, the claims are not specific to any machine and do not involve the transformation of any article.

Analysis

The court addressed that the issue of claim construction is required before undertaking a section 101 analysis to which they concluded that it may proceed without the benefit of claim construction.

The court looked to see if the patent was an abstract idea and found that the patent recites steps where data is obtained, organized, and stored. The court found that these steps were "nothing more than a disembodied concept of data sorting and storage. Therefore, the court found that this patent was an abstract idea, which is not patentable.

CONCLUSION

The United States District Court found that the 060 patent was an abstract idea and there found the patent to be ineligible under 35 U.S.C. Section 101. The court granted the motion for summary judgment in favor of the defendants.

Cyberfone Systems, LLC, v. Amazon.com
Patent Infringement

***CyberFone Sys., LLC v. Cellco P'ship*, 2012 U.S. Dist. LEXIS 60045, 2012 WL 1509504 (D. Del. Apr. 30, 2012).**

ISSUE

Should the Court grant the motions to sever or dismiss?

RULE

This case involves Federal Rules of Civil Procedure Rule 20 and 21 for misjoinder, where a remedy for misjoinder is severance.

Following the holding in Global Tech, "if a complaint sufficiently identifies, for purposes of Rule 8, the patent at issue and the allegedly infringing conduct, a defendant's receipt of the complaint and decision to continue its conduct despite the knowledge gleaned from the complaint satisfies the requirements".

CASE DETAILS

Facts

Cyberfone Systems, LLC, assignee of the 382 patent and the 060 patent, filed 21 lawsuits involving a total of 175 defendants for patent infringement. A number of defendants moved to sever and to dismiss the claims against them pursuant to Federal Rules of Civil Procedure Rule 20 and 21. Certain defendants claim that they were not properly joined into the suit.

Analysis

The court found that all of the named parties share the same discovery and motion deadlines and therefore denied the motion to sever any parties. On the issue of wireless handset manufacturers and customer's motion to sever, the court denied the motion. Additionally, the court denied the wireless carriers motion to stay.

On the issue of the motion to dismiss infringement claims, the court found that it was not prepared to engage in the claim construction exercise at the current stage of the proceedings and denied Sharp's motion. The court denied that request to dismiss the direct infringement claims.

CONCLUSION

The United States District Court granted in part on the issue of contributory infringement motions and denied in part on the remaining grounds.

CyberFone Sys., LLC v. CNN Interactive Group, Inc
Patent Infringement

***CyberFone Sys., LLC v. CNN Interactive Group, Inc.*, 558 Fed. Appx. 988 (Fed. Cir. 2014)**

ISSUE

Should the court of Appeals affirm the District Court's decision of finding that the patent was invalid under 35 U.S.C. Section 101?

RULE

This court looks to 35 U.S.C. Section 101 to determine whether a patent claim was invalid.

CASE DETAILS

Facts

Cyberfone Systems, LLC, assignee of the U.S. Patent No. 8,019,060 (the 060 patent). This patent pertains to methods and a system for capturing and storing data.

Timeline

In September 2011, Cyberfone sued eighty-one defendants claiming patent infringement.

In May 2012, a number of the named defendants claimed that the 060 patent was unpatenable subject matter.

The District Court held that the patent claims were ineligible matter and were invalid under 35 U.S.C. Section 101.

Analysis

The Court of Appeals found that the categorical data storage mentioned in the patent is an abstract idea that is not patent-eligible. Additionally, the court looked to the exploding data transaction and found that this has no meaningful transformation because " it merely makes the originally-gathered information accessible to different destinations without changing the content or its classification." Therefore, the Court of Appeals agrees with the District court that the 060 patent claims ineligible subject matter- an abstract idea, which is they find to be invalid.

<u>CONCLUSION</u>

The United States Court of Appeals affirmed the District Court's decision.

Del Vecchio v. Amazon.com Inc.
Amazon Dismissed from All Claims

***Del Vecchio v. Amazon.com Inc.*, 2011 U.S. Dist. LEXIS 138314, 2011 WL 6325910 (W.D. Wash. Nov. 30, 2011).**

ISSUE

Should the court grant Amazon's motion to dismiss?

RULE

The court looked to the holding in Friends of the Earth, Inc. v. Laidlaw Envtl. Servs. which stated. "To satisfy Article III's standing requirements, a plaintiff must show (1) it has suffered an "injury in fact" that is (a) concrete and particularized and (b) actual or imminent, not conjectural or hypothetical; (2) the injury is fairly traceable to the challenged action of the defendant; and (3) it is likely, as opposed to merely speculative, that the injury will be redressed by a favorable decision".

CASE DETAILS

Facts

Plaintiff, Del Vecchio filed suit against defendant, Amazon.com for misappropriation of Plaintiffs' and Class Members confidential personal informal and damage to and consumption of their computer assets. Plaintiffs sought relief under the Computer Fraud and Abuse Act.

Defendant argued that the claim should be dismissed because, "(1) they contend that plaintiffs have failed to allege any injury in fact and lack article III standing; and (2) that plaintiffs have failed to allege sufficient facts to support any of their four claimed bases for relief."

Analysis

The court found that Del Vecchio failed to allege any facts to satisfy the amount required to maintain a civil CFAA claim. Additionally, the court found that the plaintiffs failed to plead a necessary element of a claim for relief under the CPA.

CONCLUSION

The court concluded that the defendant's motion to dismiss should be granted because the plaintiffs failed to plead adequate facts to establish any harm.

Del Vecchio v. Amazon.com, Inc.
Procedure; Consumer Protection Law; Unfair Business Practices; Violations of Computer Fraud and Abuse Act.

Vecchio v. Amazon.com, Inc. **No. C11-366RSL, 2012 U.S. Dist. LEXIS 76536 (W.D. Wash. June 1, 2012).**

ISSUE

Whether the plaintiffs have alleged sufficient facts to plead a plausible claim for relief such that the court should not grant defendants motion to dismiss.

RULE

"To survive a motion to dismiss, a complaint must contain sufficient factual matter, accepted as true, to state a claim to relief that is plausible on its face." *Ashcroft v. Iqbal*, 556 U.S. 662, 129 S. Ct. 1937, 1949, 173 L. Ed. 2d 868 (2009).

"Whoever knowingly and with intent to defraud, accesses a protected computer without authorization, or exceeds authorized access, and by means of such conduct furthers the intended fraud and obtains anything of value ... shall be punished." 18 U.S.C. § 1030(a)(4); §1030(e)(2).

To state a claim under Washington's CPA, plaintiffs must allege "(1) an unfair or deceptive act or practice, (2) that occurs in trade or commerce, (3) a public interest, (4) injury to the plaintiff in his or her business or property, and (5) a causal link between the unfair or deceptive act and the injury suffered." *Indoor Billboard/ Wash., Inc. v. Safeco Title Ins. Co.*, 105 Wn.2d 778, 792, 719 P.2d 531 (1986).

"Trespass to chattels is the intentional interference with a party's personal property without justification that deprives the owner of possession or use. *Sexton v. Brown*, 147 Wn. App. 1005, 2008 WL 4616705, at *5 (2008).

"To establish unjust enrichment, the claimant must meet three elements: (1) one party must have conferred a benefit to the other; (2) the party receiving the benefit must have knowledge of that benefit; and (3) the party receiving the benefit must accept or retain the benefit under circumstances that make it inequitable for the receiving party to retain the benefit without paying its value. *Cox v. O'brien*, 150 Wn. App. 24, 37. 206 P.3d 682 (2009).

CASE DETAILS

Facts

This case has to do with "cookies." Not the type of cookies one eats, but cookies that are transferred from a web site to a visitor's hard drive through the visitor's web browser when a web site is visited. *Bose v. Interclick, Inc.*, No. 10-cv-9183, 2011 U.S. Dist. LEXIS 93663, 2011 WL 4343517, at *1 (S.D.N.Y. Aug. 17, 2011). Cookies are transferred automatically; if users do not desire cookies, they must either delete them as they are received or use software to block them.

Plaintiffs allege that Defendant intentionally published a "gibberish" website Compact Policy that fooled their browser into accepting defendant's cookies despite their filter settings. Plaintiff also claims that defendant reprogrammed "flash cookies" to behave as traditional cookies, knowing that plaintiffs' browser software would not recognize them. Last, plaintiff claims that defendant used the information gathered by the cookies for its own benefit and shared that information with third parties despite the terms of its Privacy Notice. Plaintiffs seek relief under the Computer Fraud and Abuse Act (CFAA) and Washington's Consumer Protection Act (CPA). They also assert claims for trespass to chattels and unjust enrichment.

Defendants claim that plaintiff's complaint should be dismissed. Defendants argue that plaintiffs have failed to allege any injury in fact and thus their claim lacks standing.

Analysis

The court grants the defendants motion to dismiss in part. Here, plaintiffs did not plead sufficient facts to establish a $5000 loss or that defendant did anything more than harmlessly intermeddle with their chattel. The court therefore dismissed plaintiffs' CFAA and trespass to chattel claims. The court further finds that because plaintiffs have already had 2 opportunities to amend their complaint that plaintiffs clearly lack the requisite facts to plead a sufficient claim.

As to the CPA and unjust enrichment claims, the court finds that the motion is dependent upon matters outside the pleadings. Therefore, the court analyzed this part of the defendant's motion as a motion for summary judgment. The court then grants plaintiffs' request for a "reasonable opportunity to present all the material that is pertinent to the motion. Fed. R. Civ. P. 12(d).

CONCLUSION

For the foregoing reasons the Court grants the defendants motion to dismiss in part.

Del Vecchio v. Amazon.com, Inc.
Privacy Violation; Procedure

***Vecchio v. Amazon.com, Inc.*, 2012 U.S. Dist. LEXIS 125399 (W.D. Wash. Sep. 4, 2012)**

ISSUE

Whether the court should grant defendants Motion for Protective Order, asking the court to enter an order precluding it form having to comply with Plaintiff's request for production of "all documents concerning Amazon's P3P Compact Policy and any modifications made to the same."

RULE

The Washington Consumer Protection Act requires a specific showing of injury to business or property to state a claim. *Hangman Ridge Training Stables, Inc., v. Safeco Title Ins. Co.,* 105 Wn.2d 778, 792, 719 P.2d 531 (1986).

CASE DETAILS

Facts

Plaintiffs filed their original complaint in March of 2011. The claims against defendants (Amazon) all related to Amazon's use of "cookies" on their computers without their knowledge or consent. Plaintiff's claim that Amazon's deceptive conduct occurred before plaintiffs could ever read Amazons Privacy Notice and Terms of Use. The lower court dismissed two of plaintiffs claims, finding that plaintiffs had not alleged that the suffered any loss to the value of their information or any loss of computer assets. As to the remaining CPA and unjust enrichment claims, the Court found that the Defendant's Conditions of Use and Privacy Notice appear to notify visitors that it will take the very actions which plaintiffs now complain: placing bowser and flash cookies on their computers to monitor and collect information about their shopping habits.

Analysis

The court finds that here, plaintiffs' request falls outside the scope of the time frame allowed by the court to conduct discovery. The court below allowed discovery regarding plaintiffs; objection to defendants notice and conditions, not its Compact Policy. The court states that plaintiffs' claim is dependent on the applicability of defendant's notice and conditions and thus discovery is limited to that issue.

CONCLUSION

For the foregoing reasons, the court grants defendants Motion for Protective Order.

s v. Nicola Angie Siso
Procedure; Attorney's fees

***Deuss v. Siso*, 2014 U.S. Dist. LEXIS 121464 (N.D. Cal. Aug. 29, 2014).**

ISSUE

Whether the court should grant defendant's motion to quash subpoenas and for sanctions?

RULE

Federal Rule of Civil Procedure 45 governs discovery of nonparties by subpoena. It's scope is the same as the scope under Rule 26(b) which allows a party to obtain discovery concerning any nonprivileged matter that is relevant to any party's claim or defense. Fed. R. Civ. P. 45 Advisory Comm.'s Note (1970); Fed. R. Civ. P. 26(b)(1). Under Rule 26, the court on its own or on motion must impost sanctions when an attorney makes a certification that violates the Rule "without substantial justification."

CASE DETAILS

Facts:

Deuss filed an action against Siso to recover money and property he gave Siso during their now terminated marriage engagement. Deuss's attorney violated Federal Rule 45 by issuing subpoenas for Siso's records, including Amazon records, on the same date he filed the complaint. The Plaintiff never withdrew the complaint despite being brought to their attention. Amazon objected the subpoena and the Plaintiff sent a letter stating that "any financial information sought by and within the scope of the subpoena, will be used for solely prosecuting the above-entitled action." Amazon then produced 6 pages of the information.

Timeline:

Mr. Deuss filed this action February 14, 2013 against Ms. Siso. On June 9th, 2014, Ms. Siso filed a Motion to Dismiss. Three days later she also filed a Motion to Quash and for Sanctions. Mr. Deuss also filed a Notice of Voluntary Dismissal Without Prejudice, granted on August 13, 2014.

Analysis:

The court found that the subpoenas violated Rule 26(d)(1) as they were issued the same day the Complaint was filed and served shortly after, before the first conference, pursuant to 26(f). The subpoenas also violated Rule 45(a)(4) that requires service on each party before the service of the subpoena. Therefore, the court decided to quash the motion for subpoenas. Additionally, the court decided to grant the motion for sanctions because counsel made an improper certification and the conduct of the counsel was not substantially justified.

CONCLUSION

Defendant's motion to quash subpoenas and for monetary sanctions is granted.

Device Enhancement LLC v. Amazon.com, Inc
Procedure

Device Enhancement LLC v. Amazon.com, Inc., 2016 U.S. Dist. LEXIS 64600 (D. Del. May 17, 2016)

ISSUE

Whether the court should grant defendants motion to dismiss.

RULE

"A complaint must contain "a short plain statement of the claim showing that the pleader is entitled to relief, in order to give the defendant fair notice of what the ... claim is and the grounds upon which it rests. *Bell Atl. Corp. v. Twombly*, 550 U.S. 544, 555, 127 S. Ct. 1955, 167 L. Ed. 2d 929 (2007).

Section 101 provides that patentable subject matter extends to four broad categories, including: "new and useful process[es], machine[s], manufacture, or composition[s] of matter." 35 U.S.C. § 101; see also *Bilski v. Kappos*, 561 U.S. 593, 601, 130 S. Ct. 3218, 177 L. Ed. 2d 792 (2010) ("*Bilski* II"); *Diamond v. Chakrabarty*, 447 U.S. 303, 308, 100 S. Ct. 2204, 65 L. Ed. 2d 144 (1980).

The Federal Circuit has "never set forth a bright line rule requiring district courts to construe claims before determining subject matter eligibility." *Ultramercial, LLC v. Hulu*, LLC, 657 F.3d 1323, 1325 (Fed. Cir. 2011), vacated sub nom. *WildTangent*, 132 S.Ct. 2431, 182 L. Ed. 2d 1059 (2012). "Although the determination of patent eligibility requires a full understanding of the basic character of the claimed subject matter, claim construction is not an inviolable prerequisite to a validity determination under § 101." Content Extraction, 776 F.3d at 1349 (citing *Ultramercial*, 772 F.3d at 714-15; *Bancorp*, 687 F.3d at 1273-74). However, it may be "desirable—and often necessary—to resolve claim construction disputes prior to a § 101 analysis." *Bancorp*, 687 F.3d at 1273-74.

CASE DETAILS

Facts

In this case plaintiff has filed a complaint alleging patent infringement against defendant Amazon. The patent at issue relates to a "method and system for allowing a user of a terminal device to remotely operate upgraded and / or advanced applications without the need for upgrading the client side application or computational resources."

Analysis

The court first determines whether the claims at issue relate to one of the prescribed patentable subject matters. The court finds that a distinction must be drawn between claims that seek to pre-empt the use of an abstract idea, and claims that seek only to foreclose others from using a particular application of that idea. In this case the court holds that the patent pre-empts all ways of performing the claimed method because the very steps of the method comprise nothing more that the underlying idea itself. Thus the patent governed patent ineligible subject matter.

CONCLUSION

For the foregoing reasons, defendant's motion to dismiss is granted.

Discovery Patent Holdings, LLC v. Amazon.com, Inc.
Patent Infringement; Claim Construction

***Discovery Patent Holdings, LLC v. Amazon.com, Inc.*, 769 F. Supp. 2d 662 (D. Del. 2011).**

ISSUE

What construction of the disputed terms of the patent claim should be adopted by the court?

RULE

A court's analysis of patent infringement is comprised of a well-established two-step process: (1) the meaning of disputed claims are construed; and (2) the allegedly infringing device is compared to the claims as construed. *Markman v. Westview Instruments, Inc.*, 52 F.3d 967, 976 (Fed. Cir. 1995).

CASE DETAILS

Facts

Plaintiff filed this action against defendant Amazon alleging infringement of two of its patents. The court here is examining both parties briefs on claim construction. The court adopts the definitions found in the conclusion below.

CONCLUSION

(1) **Broadcast** – sent to multiple recipients.

(2) **Book** – An electronic version of the textual or graphical information contained in a work such as a novel, encyclopedia, article, magazine, newspaper, catalogue, periodical, manual, speech, law, court decision, or testimony.

(3) **Encrypting the selected electronic book** – decrypting the encrypted data representing text and graphics of an electronic book.

(4) **Information that allows encryption and decryption of the electronic book** – Information that allows encryption and decryption of the electronic book.

(5) **Associate Registration System** – Software and hardware used in registering associates.

(6) **Associate Enrollment System** – Software and hardware used in enrolling associates.

(7) **Compensation System** – Software and hardware used in compensating associates.

(8) **Online Registration System** – Software and hardware used in registering associates.

(9) **Referral Processing System** – Software and hardware used in processing referrals.

(10) **Report Generation System** – Software and hardware used in generating reports.

(11) **Website** – A computer system that serves informational content over a network using the standard protocols of the World Wide Web. A website corresponds to a particular Internet domain, such as Amazon.com, and includes the content associated with a particular organization. AS used herein, the term encompasses both the hardware and software server components that serve the informational content over the network, and the back end hardware and software components, including any non-standard or specialized components, that interact with the server components to perform services for website users.

(12) **Request Message** – Communication requesting a web page corresponding to an item offered for sale.

Dobias-Davis v. Amazon.com.kydc, LLC ***Defamation; Employee's Rights; Procedure***

***Dobias-Davis v. Amazon.com.kydc, LLC*, Civil Action No. 3:15-cv-00393-JAG, 2016 U.S. Dist. LEXIS 3396 (E.D. Va. Jan. 11, 2016).**

ISSUE

Can the claims of defamation and retaliation against Amazon and Hoffman be dismissed?

RULE

Under Title VII and the ADEA, the employers are prohibited from retaliating against employees who oppose discrimination based on gender or age. 29 U.S.C. §623 (d) (ADEA). In bringing a retaliation claim, plaintiff must establish a prima facie case and show that she was engaged in protected activity and the employer took adverse action against them, and the causal relationship between the protected activity and adverse employment action existed. *Causey v. Balog*, 162 F.3d 795, 803 (4th Cir. 1998).

CASE DETAILS

Facts:

Amazon hired Dobias-Davis (Dobias) in 2010. In April of 2012, Dobias was promoted and then transferred to Virginia, a facility with a young workforce and youthful culture. In 2013, Hoffman became Dobias's supervisor. Hoffman displayed discrimination towards Dobias because of her gender and age in violation of the ADEA. Co-workers labeled it a "witch hunt." When Amazon fired Dobias in June 2014, she was the oldest employee in her position employed by Amazon in North America.

Timeline:

Dobias brings a defamation suit against Amazon and Hoffman, as well as two discrimination and two retaliation claims against Amazon. Amazon and Hoffman now move to dismiss the defamation claim and Amazon moves to dismiss the two retaliation claims.

Analysis:

In relation to the defamation claim, the court determined that this case needs more factual development in order for them to determine if there is a failure to state a claim. In relation to the retaliation claim, the court must determine if the plaintiff actually opposed the employment practices made unlawful in Title VII or ADEA, rather than merely objecting to generalized workplace grievances. *Young v. Giant Food Stores, LLC*, No. PWG-14-2006 *33-34 (D. Md. June 8, 2015). The court determined that Dobias failed to participate in the protected activity and therefore the claim is not plausible.

CONCLUSION

The court denies the partial motion to dismiss the defamation claim as this claim need more factual development. The court grants Amazon's partial motion in relation to the retaliation claims because Dobias did not engage in protected activity.

DOLP 1133 Props. II LLC v. Amazon Corporate, LLC
Property and Real Estate Law

***DOLP 1133 Props. II LLC v Amazon Corporate, LLC*, 2015 N.Y. Misc. LEXIS 3019 (N.Y. Sup. Ct. Aug. 17, 2015).**

ISSUE

Whether the court should grant Amazon's motion to dismiss the complaint.

CASE DETAILS

Facts

The claim was filed by Plaintiff following a situation where Amazon wanted to rent commercial space the Plaintiff owned. In contemplation of the complexity of a potential lease, the parties executed a "Letter of Intent" (LOI) wherein they agreed to work to reach a lease between them. The LOI did not bind them to enter a lease, but, it did contain exclusivity language forbidding Amazon from seeking commercial space for the same purpose elsewhere for 60 days. Plaintiff claims they had tenants move out early to begin renovations for Amazon, and that Amazon assured Plaintiff they were not looking for other space and would be moving forward with a lease. Plaintiff claims to have discovered that this assurance was a lie, and Amazon abandoned the lease and rented space for the same purpose elsewhere.

Analysis

The Court ruled that the forum selection in the NDA did not apply, as it was not incorporated in the LOI at issue. The Court dismissed Plaintiff's breach of good faith claim as it was duplicative of the breach of LOI; it found an issue of fact existed as to whether Amazon lied to Plaintiff and therefore did not dismiss the fraud claim. The Court also dismissed Plaintiff's specific performance claim as the LOI specifically stated it did create an obligation to enter a lease.

The court denied Plaintiff punitive damages and attorneys' fees as punitive damages would require "circumstances of aggravation or outrage, or a fraudulent or evil motive on the part of the defendant," and attorneys' fees are not warranted unless prescribed by statute or agreement.

CONCLUSION

For the foregoing reasons, the court granted Amazon's motion to dismiss in part and denied it in part.

Droplets, Inc. v. Amazon.com, Inc.
Patent Infringement; Procedure

***Droplets, Inc. v. Amazon.com, Inc.*, No. 2:11-CV-392, 2012 U.S. Dist. LEXIS 122978 (E.D. Tex. June 27, 2012).**

ISSUE

Whether the court should grant defendants motion to transfer venue where majority of defendants reside in the district of Northern California.

RULE

Title 28, Section 1404(a) of the United States Code provides that "[f]or the convenience of parties and witnesses, in the interest of justice, a district court may transfer any civil action to any other district or division where it might have been brought." A district court has broad discretion in deciding whether to order a transfer. *In re Volkswagen of Am., Inc.*, 545 F.3d 304, 315 (5th Cir. 2008) ("Volkswagen II").

Private Interest Factors

Despite technological advances that reduce the inconvenience of transferring documents across the country, the sources of proof factor must still be considered in determining whether to grant a transfer of venue. *Volkswagen II*, 545 F.3d at 316. The place where the defendant's documents are kept weighs in favor of transfer to that location. *In re Genentech, Inc.*, 556 F.3d 1338, 1345 (Fed. Cir. 2009).

CASE DETAILS

Facts

Plaintiff filed suit against multiple defendants, including Amazon.Com, Inc. (Amazon), alleging patent infringement. Defendants moved to transfer the case to the Northern District of California, asserting it is more convenient for the parties as well as potential witnesses.

Analysis

The court here takes into account private interest factors as well as public interest factors in order to determine whether to grant the motion. As to private interest factors, the court finds that 5 of the 6 defendants are headquartered in the Northern District of California, and that Amazon is headquartered in Seattle, which is much closer to Northern California than is Texas. Further no relevant document or other evidence are physically located in Texas. Thus, sources of proof weighs towards transfer to Northern California. The court next applies the "100-mile rule" a because the Northern District of California is more than 100 miles away from the Eastern district of Texas. The majority of engineers and employees work and or reside in the Northern District of California, and none are located in Texas. The court again finds this factor to weigh in favor of the transfer.

As to public interest factors, the court first looks at court congestion. The court finds this factor to be neutral and does not consider it in determining whether to transfer the case. Next, the court fins that because the majority of documents, potential witnesses, and defendants are closet to the District of Northern California, that the district has a strong local interest in adjudicating this dispute and thus that this factor too weighs heavily in favor of a transfer.

In balancing the factors, the court finds that the location of sources of proof, availability of compulsory process, the convenience for witnesses, and the local interest factors all favor transfer.

CONCLUSION

For the foregoing reasons the court found that defendants have demonstrated that the Northern district of California would be a more convenient venue than the Eastern District of Texas. Thus the motion to transfer venue is granted and the case is transferred to the Northern district of California.

Ekin v. Amazon Servs., LLC
Breach of Contract, Consumer Protection Violations

***Ekin v. Amazon Servs., LLC*, 84 F. Supp. 3d 1172 (W.D. Wash. 2014).**

ISSUE

Whether the court should grant Amazon's motion to compel arbitration.

RULE

Agreements to arbitrate are "valid, irrevocable, and enforceable, save upon such grounds as exist at law or in equity for the revocation of any contract." 9 U.S.C. § 2.

CASE DETAILS

Facts

This case stems from the use of Amazon Prime Services by the Plaintiffs and alleged breach of contract claims directed at Amazon Services LLC. The Plaintiffs disputed the price changes for Amazon Prime Members and claimed that Amazon unlawfully changed the terms and agreements of their Amazon Prime membership. Plaintiffs' main objection to the validity of the arbitration agreement is that Amazon expressly reserves the right to change, without notice, consent, or a refund, its Prime terms and conditions. Plaintiffs claim that under prevailing Ninth Circuit case law, this makes the arbitration agreement, which is incorporated into these COU, unenforceable due to unconscionability.

Analysis

The court found the arbitration agreement to be valid and also that the issue at hand fell within the scope of the agreement.

CONCLUSION

Defendant's Motion to Compel Arbitration is granted. The parties are directed to submit their claims to arbitration. In light of this order, Amazon's Motions to Dismiss are stricken as moot.

Eolas Techs. Inc. v. Adobe Sys. Inc. (E.D. Tex., 2012)
Patent Infringement

***Eolas Techs., Inc. v. Adobe Sys.*, 2012 U.S. Dist. LEXIS 13643 (E.D. Tex. Feb. 3, 2012).**

ISSUE

The issue here is whether the term "browser application" should be limited to web browsers.

RULE

The court here holds that the term "browser application" as "a client program that displays and responds to user interaction with hypermedia documents."

CASE DETAILS

Facts

This opinion examines the meaning of the term "browser application" per its use in U.S. Patent Nos. 5,838,906 and 7,599,985. The court had already construed the disputed terms, but two weeks before trial the parties began to dispute the construction of the term "browser application."

Analysis

The court finds that the plaintiff's definition of "browser application" is too narrow, and that the defendant's definition is too broad. A browser application is for displaying and responding to interaction with hypermedia documents. The first paragraph in the summary of the invention ties the invention to communication in a "distributed hypermedia environment"" and displaying and interacting with "hypermedia documents."

The world wide web is a distributed hypermedia environment, and web browsers are browsers that display and respond to user interaction with hypermedia documents. However, the specification and claims have not limited the browser application to operating only within the internet or world wide web. The specification and claims limit the invention to operating in a slightly broader domain – a distributed hypermedia environment – and limit the browser to processing hypermedia documents. Accordingly, the Court construes the term "browser application" as a "client program that displays and responds to user interaction with hypermedia documents.

CONCLUSION

For the foregoing reasons, the court construes the term "browser application" as "a client program that displays and responds to user interaction with hypermedia documents."

Eolas Techs. Inc. v. Adobe Sys., Inc.
Procedure

***Eolas Techs. Inc. v. Adobe Sys.*, 891 F. Supp. 2d 803 (E.D. Tex. 2012).**

ISSUE

Whether the the costs proposed by defendant are recoverable under 28 U.S.C. § 1920(2).

RULE

Under the Federal Rules of Civil Procedure §54(d) costs are to be awarded to the prevailing party as a matter of course, unless the court directs otherwise. Although the prevailing party is entitled to its costs, the prevailing party must still demonstrate that its costs are recoverable under fifth circuit precedent, and the prevailing party should not burden the Court with costs that are clearly nor recoverable under the law.

CASE DETAILS

Facts

In this case the court is examining the parties' memorandum regarding the defendants' costs in this matter. Here, plaintiffs object to several of defendants proposed costs. Here, plaintiff objects to the costs of: (1) video depositions; (2) electronic discovery costs including document collection, processing, hosting, scanning and conversion; (3) photocopies; (4) CD and DVD copies; (5) graphics professional support at trial; and (6) demonstratives and exhibits for trial.

Analysis

As to video depositions, the court notes that 28 U.S.C. § 1920(2) was amended in 2008 to include "[f]ees for printed or electronically recorded transcripts necessarily obtained for use in the case." The court finds that the printed and electronically recorded transcripts were necessarily obtained for use in this case, and the defendants are entitled to costs of both printed and electronically recorded depositions.

As to document scanning, the court finds the practice to be the equivalent of copying paper documents into electronic form.

As to document collection, processing, and hosting, the court finds that these are not recoverable costs. The amended statute allows for copying of materials as opposed to just papers, but has not been broadened to include general electronic discovery costs that precede copying or scanning of materials.

As to electronic document conversion the court finds that defendants chose to convert their documents which was allowed per the parties' agreement, but was not necessary. Therefore, the costs for conversion were not "necessarily obtained for use in this case, and these costs are not recoverable."

As to photocopies, the court notes that defendants have only identified some of the materials that were copied and why they were necessary to the case. The court allows defendants to recover costs of 50% of the general copying charges, and 100% of the copying charges that were properly detailed.

As to CD and DVD copies, the court holds that they shall be assessed in the same way as photocopy costs: 50% for general entries, and 100% for specific entries.

As to graphics professional support, the court recognizes that professional support for audio and video services during trial expedites the presentation of complex material to jurors, but finds that the defendants' requested $95,000 is excessive and awards them $32,000.

As to demonstratives and exhibits for trial will also be assessed in the same way as photocopy charges: 50% for general entries, and 100% for specific entries.

CONCLUSION

The court orders defendants to resubmit an agreed Bill of Costs to the clerk based on the guidance of this decision. The parties must meet and confer in order to avoid presenting addition costs disputes to the court.

NOTE: Plaintiffs appeal 3 days later and the judgment is affirmed. See *Eolas Techs. Inc. v. Amazon.com Inc.* (Fed. Cir., 2013).

Eon Corp. IP Holdings, LLC v. T-Mobile USA, Inc.
Patent

***EON Corp. IP Holdings, LLC v. T-Mobile United States, Inc.*, 2012 U.S. Dist. LEXIS 76467 (N.D. Cal. June 1, 2012).**

ISSUE

Whether the subpoena requested by plaintiff EON should be granted where the subpoena is for a third party in which the plaintiff has a pending action against that third party.

RULE

Federal Rule 45 provides that any party may serve a subpoena commanding a non-party to attend and give testimony or to produce and permit inspection and copying of documents. Upon a timely motion, the court must quash or modify the subpoena for any one of the reasons set forth in Rule 45(c)(3)(A), such as the subpoena "requires disclosure of privileged or other protected matter and no exception or waiver applies" or it "subjects a person to undue burden.: A rule 45 subpoena is subject to the relevance requirements set forth in Rule 26(b). "Although the party who moves to quash has the burden of persuasion under Rule 45(c)(3), the party using the subpoena mist demonstrate that the information sought is relevant and material to the allegations and claims at issue in the proceedings." *Monge v. Maya Magazines, Inc.*, NO. 2:10-CV-00230-RJC-PA, 2010 WL 2776328, at 4 (D. Nev. Jul. 14, 2010).

CASE DETAILS

Facts

This case involved a patent infringement suit where third party Kineto Wireless, Inc. (Kineto) moved to quash and/or modify a subpoena. The original action was filed on August 4, 2010. ("*Eon v. T-Mobile*"). A separate action was filed in October of 2010 that included defendant Kineto ("*Eon v. Sensus*"). In February 2012, Eon served Kineto with a Rule 45 subpoena for documents and testimony in the *Eon v. T-Mobile* action. In the *Eon v. Sensus* action discovery was prohibited because there had not yet been a Rule 26(f) conference. Kineto claimed the subpoena should be denied because Eon was seeking discovery in this action in order to circumvent the discovery constraint. Eon proposed a modified subpoena limited to information regarding Kineto's Wi-Fi Application sold for use in conjunction with the T-Mobile branded dual-mode devices that are specifically at issue in the above action.

Analysis

The court here does not believe the subpoena should be quashed. The court reasons that because the subpoena has been limited in scope to Kineto's Smart Wi-Fi Application, that Eon's proposed discovery by subpoena is allowable.

CONCLUSION

The court here grants the modified subpoena with two exceptions: Kineto does not need to comply to discovery requests solely related to their internal testing and development or discovery that pre-dates T-Mobiles alleged date of first infringement by use of Kineto's software.

Execware, LLC v. Staples, Inc.
Patent Infringement

***Execware, LLC v. Staples, Inc.*, 2012 U.S. Dist. LEXIS 174885 (D. Del. Dec. 10, 2012).**

ISSUE

Whether the court should dismiss plaintiff's amended complaint against defendant Staples, Inc. ("Staples") for failure to state a clam of both indirect and wilful infringement.

RULE

"To plead a sufficient claim for direct infringement, the complaint must include: (1) an allegation of jurisdiction; (2) a statement that the plaintiff owns the patent; (3) a statement that defendant has been infringing the patent; (4) a statement that the plaintiff has given the defendant notice of its infringement; and (5) a demand for an injunction and damages." *McZeal v. Sprint Nextel Corp.*, 501 F. 3d 1354, 1356057 (Fed. Cir. 2007).

"To prove a cause of action for willful infringement, a patent owner must demonstrate by clear and convincing evidence that the infringer acted despite an objectively high likelihood that its actions constituted infringement: and that this objectively defined risk was ... either known or so obvious that it should have been known to the accused infringer." *In re Seagate Tech., LLC*, 497 F.3d 1360, 1371 (Fed. Cir. 2007).

CASE DETAILS

Facts

The court is examining a patent infringement action in which defendants Amazon.com, Inc. ("Amazon") and Starwood Hotels, are seeking dismissal of plaintiff's amended complaint for failure to state a claim of indirect infringement. Staples, Inc. ("Staples") joined in the motion to dismiss and also sought dismissal for willful infringement. Amazon and Starwood came to a dismissal agreement with plaintiff, which left Staples as the remaining movant.

Analysis

Direct Infringement

The court finds that the amended complaint failed to allege direct infringement of the patent by Staples customers. Claims require a statement that the alleged infringer has been infringing the patent by making, selling, and/or using the allegedly infringing product. The complaint does not allege that Staples' customers actually used the accused software, or that Staples caused its customers to directly infringe the patent.

Willful Infringement

As to indirect infringement, the court finds that plaintiff's failure to plead that Staples had pre-suit knowledge of the patent is fatal to its claim. Plaintiff's amended complaint relies solely on allegations that Staples was made aware of the patent by the filing of the original complaint in the present action. As a result, its claim for willful infringement must fail.

CONCLUSION

The Magistrate recommends that the court grant the motion to dismiss plaintiff's claims in the amended complaint for induced, contributory, and willful infringement of the patent.

Fagerstrom v. Amazon.com, Inc.
Class Action, False and Deceptive Advertising, Unfair Business Practices

---

***Fagerstrom v. Amazon.com, Inc.*, 141 F. Supp. 3d 1051, 2015 U.S. Dist. LEXIS 143295 (S.D. Cal. 2015).**

ISSUE

Whether a party should be compelled to arbitrate a matter if it previously agreed to do so.

RULE

An arbitration agreement may be upheld if the agreement is not unconscionable, the terms are clearly stated and understandable, and each party agrees to the terms freely.

CASE DETAILS

Facts

Consumers claim there is a discrepancy between Amazon's prices and other retailer prices of products. When checking out on Amazon, each customer has to agree to the conditions of use in order to complete their order. Amazon states any dispute will be resolved through binding arbitration.

Analysis

The court concludes that Amazon's arbitration agreement is not deceiving, not unconscionable, the terms are not one-sided, and dismissal is appropriate because the price discrepancy dispute falls within the scope of the agreement.

CONCLUSION

The court grants Amazon's motion to compel arbitration and dismisses this action because the terms of the agreement are fair and benefit both parties.

Fandino v. Amalgam Entm't, LLC
Trademark Infringement

***Fandino v. Amalgam Entm't, LLC*, 2010 U.S. Dist. LEXIS 14684 (S.D.N.Y. Feb. 18, 2010).**

ISSUE

Whether one lawsuit should be litigated over the other according to the first filed rule.

RULE

"[W]here there are two competing lawsuits," courts generally use the first-filed rule and give the first-filed action priority over later filed suits. While deference should be given to the plaintiff's choice of forum, that deference may be overcome by a demonstration of special circumstances. Special circumstances exist where a party files a declaratory judgment action in anticipation of a coercive suit "or where forum shopping alone motivated the choice of forum in the filing of the first suit." Thus, under the proper conditions courts may ignore the timing of a suit to avoid rewarding parties attempting to use the declaratory judgment action in a "race to the courthouse."

CASE DETAILS

Facts

The plaintiff claims she owns the trademark AMALGAM because she was issued a trademark registration number. Amalgam claims they used the mark first. Both parties demanded that the other cease and desist from infringement of the trademark.

Analysis

The court found that defendant's first filed action was not improper and was not filed in response to a threat of the plaintiff's filing a suit. The court noted that there were many opportunities for each party to file suit first. Therefore, the court found that the balance of convenience factor favored the first-filed action here.

CONCLUSION

The court granted the defendants' motion to transfer the case to the District of Massachusetts.

Felix The Cat Prods. v. Cal. Clock Co.
Copyright Infringement/Trademark Infringement

***Felix The Cat Prods. v. Cal. Clock Co.*, 2007 U.S. Dist. LEXIS 25290, 2007 WL 1032267 (S.D.N.Y. Mar. 29, 2007).**

ISSUE

Whether the plaintiff has established a valid copyright and trademark infringement claim.

RULE

To survive a motion to dismiss in a copyright and trademark cause of action, the plaintiff must show the defendant actually copied their work, the copying is illegal because of product similarities and must show harm was suffered from the confusion of the products.

CASE DETAILS

Facts

The plaintiff claims the defendants have infringed on copyright and trademark laws having to do with the plaintiff's interests involving ownership over the character of Felix the Cat. One of the defendants manufactures the Kit-Cat Clock in addition to other related products while the other defendants including Amazon sell those products. Plaintiff claims the Kit-Cat character is a copy of the Felix the Cat character.

Analysis

The plaintiff does not state specific facts about what acts and time the alleged infringement occurred. There has to be factual allegations to give the opposing party fair notice of the claims against them. The court denies defendants motion to dismiss claims against the probability of confusing the two products because the plaintiff may be able to provide facts to support this claim for relief.

CONCLUSION

The court grants the defendant's motion to dismiss based on failure to plead copyright infringement and denies all other claims. The plaintiff has leave to file an amended complaint within 30 days of the date of this order.

Free Kick Master LLC v. Apple Inc
Trademark Infringement

***Free Kick Master LLC v. Apple Inc.*, 140 F. Supp. 3d 975 (N.D. Cal. 2015).**

ISSUE

Whether the court should grant a motion to dismiss if there is no valid claim stated.

RULE

A motion to dismiss may be granted if a party does not state a valid claim of relief and there are not enough facts to show there is a possibility of the other party being liable for harm that may have been caused.

CASE DETAILS

Facts

The plaintiff alleges Amazon offers a mark on their devices for free which infringes on their trademark rights because they were not authorized to do so. Defendants filed a motion for failure to state a claim. A defendant is liable for trademark infringement when they use a mark in a way that would confuse consumers as to its original purpose of the registrant.

Analysis

The plaintiff provided no facts to state Amazon used the mark in a way to confuse consumers. The plaintiff has proven they cannot state a claim of infringement against Amazon. There is also no evidence provided that Amazon continued to encourage third-party distributors to continue the use of the mark after they were aware of the infringement. There is no evidence of the plaintiff giving notice of infringement or that Amazon purposefully intended to interfere with the plaintiff's mark.

CONCLUSION

The court granted the defendant's motion to dismiss because there was no evidence to prove there was a direct trademark infringement and the plaintiff failed to state a claim.

Free Kick Master LLC v. Apple Inc
Trademark Infringement

***Free Kick Master LLC v. Apple Inc.*, 2016 U.S. Dist. LEXIS 25478 (N.D. Cal. Feb. 29, 2016).**

ISSUE

Whether an amended complaint should be dismissed for being raised in an untimely manner when there is no valid claim stated.

RULE

A complaint may be dismissed if there is not a valid statement made claiming the party is eligible for relief that is supported by the facts.

CASE DETAILS

Facts

The court previously dismissed the plaintiff's claim against Amazon and the plaintiff seeks to amend their complaint to recover damages. Amazon seeks to dismiss the claims against them for failure to state a claim. Courts have dismissed claims that are raised in an untimely manner if it was unreasonable and could have been avoided. Defendants have to prove the delay is unfair to them in some way.

Analysis

The previous case was dismissed because the infringement was done by third-party distributors, not Amazon. No facts are stated that Amazon has directly infringed upon the plaintiff's mark. There is no evidence Amazon knowingly used the mark or influenced others to use it.

CONCLUSION

The court granted the motion to dismiss the amended complaint because the plaintiff does not provide any evidence that Amazon has infringed on their mark so there is no valid claim.

FTC v. Amazon.com, Inc.
Consumer Protection Law

***FTC v. Amazon.com, Inc.*, 2016 U.S. Dist. LEXIS 41500, 99 Fed. R. Evid. Serv. (Callaghan) 1443, 2016 WL 1221654 (W.D. Wash. Mar. 29, 2016).**

ISSUE

Whether expert witness testimony should be excluded from evidence.

RULE

Expert witnesses may be excluded if the testimony is not reliable or relevant to the case at hand.

CASE DETAILS

Facts

The FTC alleges Amazon is involved in using unfair practices relating to in-app purchases. FTC seeks to exclude testimony of Amazon's expert witnesses.

Analysis

Amazon's expert witness testimony of Dr. Dhar, Dr. Hoffman, Dr, Craig Rosenberg, and Dr. Andrew L. Sears provide relevant information to the case and will be helpful in providing evidence and the motion to exclude their testimony is denied. The expert witness testimony of Mr. Callahan and Dr. Sabol is not useful to determine the outcome of the case. The motion to exclude the testimony of these two witnesses is granted.

CONCLUSION

The court grants FTC's motion to exclude the expert testimony of the two witnesses that do not provide relevant information to the case and denies the motion to exclude the other expert testimony that provides significant information.

FTC v. Amazon.com, Inc.
Consumer Protection Law

***FTC v. Amazon.com, Inc.*, 2016 U.S. Dist. LEXIS 55569, 2016-1 Trade Reg. Rep. (CCH) P79,600 (W.D. Wash. Apr. 26, 2016).**

ISSUE

Whether Amazon is liable for harm suffered by their customers.

RULE

A court will find a party liable for harm they have caused to consumers when they are involved in unfair or deceptive practices.

CASE DETAILS

Facts

The Amazon platform allows in-app purchases that customers were not familiar with at first. Amazon has received many complaints from adults that were unaware of charges on their account incurred by their children and that they did not consent to the purchases.

Analysis

The court does not find that injunctive relief is warranted, there is not a clear danger of Amazon making the same violation again. FTC has clearly demonstrated that Amazon is liable for unfair consumer practices, FTC's motion for summary judgment as to this aspect is granted. Judgment is granted in FTC's favor.

CONCLUSION

The court granted Amazon's motion for partial summary judgment denying injunctive relief, and granted FTC's motion for summary judgment with respect to liability.

Gerlinger v. Amazon.com, Inc.
Violations of the Sherman Act

***Gerlinger v. Amazon.com, Inc.*, 311 F. Supp. 2d 838 (N.D. Cal. 2004)**

ISSUE

Whether an agreement presents an unfair competitive edge and provides unfair business practices.

RULE

Section 1 of the Sherman Act forbids contracts, combinations, or conspiracies in restraint of trade, including price-fixing agreements between competitors. See 15 U.S.C. § 1. The Mirror Site Hosting Agreement is without question, an "agreement." The question is whether the Agreement is "unreasonable" under section 1. *Am. Ad.Mgmt. v. GTE Corp.*, 92 F.3d 781, 788. See also *N'west Wholesale Stationers, Inc. v. Pac. Stationery and Printing Co.*, 472 U.S. 284, 289, 86 L. Ed. 2d 202, 105 S. Ct. 2613 (1985). To determine whether the agreement is unreasonable, the court must decide at the threshold whether it is per se illegal or whether it must be analyzed under the "rule of reason." *Paladin Assocs., Inc. v. Montana Power Co.*, 328 F.3d 1145, 1155 (9th Cir. 2003).

CASE DETAILS

Facts

A product listed for sale on Amazon's website may also be listed by other companies. Amazon also has entered into agreements with other retailers to sell different products. Amazon entered into a service agreement with Borders and must maintain certain service levels or Borders may terminate the agreement. The plaintiff alleges the agreement between Amazon and Borders eliminates competition between former rivals in the market for online sales of books and consumers are denied a competitive choice for online book purchases.

Analysis

The court finds that the agreement does not affect the price that Borders can list their books at on their own website. There is not enough evidence to determine if the agreement presents an anticompetitive effect. The defendant's motion for summary judgment also cannot be ruled on for lack of evidentiary support.

CONCLUSION

The court denies the defendant's motion for summary judgment and the plaintiff's motion for judgment on the pleadings is denied because intent to monopolize is not proven. The court also dismissed the plaintiff's state law unjust enrichment claim because there was never a contract between the plaintiff and the defendants. The parties are requested to further address the antitrust injury issue at a later time since the injury is not clear from the record.

Gerlinger v. Amazon.com, Inc.
Consumer Protection Law / Antitrust Violations

***Gerlinger v. Amazon.com, Inc.*, 2005 U.S. Dist. LEXIS 26019 (N.D. Cal. Oct. 31, 2005)**

ISSUE

Whether the plaintiff alleges a valid claim for antitrust violations.

RULE

A court may dismiss an antitrust claim if the moving party does not provide evidence of violations or evidence of suffering and injury as a result.

CASE DETAILS

Facts

Plaintiff filed an action against defendants for allegedly violating state and federal antitrust laws through their store agreement because of higher prices. The previous court granted the defendants judgment on the pleadings. The plaintiff purchases books online and purchased books directly from at least one of the defendants. The defendants sell books online and entered into an agreement that Amazon determines the selection of products offered along with terms of sale and the prices except for those available for in-store pickup.

Analysis

The plaintiff did not state any ways in which the defendants violated antitrust laws or show any harm suffered. There was no actual evidence of injury provided by the plaintiff for the antitrust claim or the unfair competition claim so they will not survive a motion to dismiss.

CONCLUSION

The court granted the motion to dismiss the antitrust claims and the unfair competition claim because there is no evidence the defendants caused any harm.

Gerlinger v. Amazon.com, Inc.
Consumer Protection Law / Antitrust Violations

***Gerlinger v. Amazon.com, Inc.*, 526 F.3d 1253 (9th Cir. Cal. 2008).**

ISSUE

Whether a claim was properly dismissed for failure to stste a valid claim for antitrust violations.

RULE

A claim may have been properly dismissed if there is no evidence of harm or injury having a causal relationship to the antitrust violation provided by the alleged injured party.

CASE DETAILS

Facts

The appellant's antitrust claim was dismissed by the lower court. The appellant originally claimed the defendants violated antitrust laws because he had to purchase an item for a higher price because of a marketing agreement.

Analysis

The district court's judgment dismissing the plaintiff's action for lack of standing is affirmed. Antitrust standing is a requirement for a party to recover damages which the plaintiff failed to establish.

CONCLUSION

The court affirmed the judgment of the district court dismissing plaintiff's claims for lack of standing for antitrust violations.

Gibson v. Amazon.com
Copyright Infringement

***Gibson v. Amazon.com*, 2011 U.S. Dist. LEXIS 102065, 2011 WL 4020187 (C.D. Cal. Sept. 8, 2011).**

ISSUE

Whether the court should grant summary judgment for a case that does not involve copyright infringement.

RULE

A court may grant summary judgment for a party where there is no evidence provided by the opposing party for copyright infringement.

CASE DETAILS

Facts

The defendants move for summary judgment alleging they are not liable for copyright infringement. The plaintiff claims the defendants are liable for copyright infringement of her book.

Analysis

Amazon has neither published nor sold the book in question, their only involvement is through third-party sellers which is legal. The plaintiff does not show any support for her claim. The plaintiff seems to misunderstand the facts, the internet, and the law.

CONCLUSION

The court grants the defendants' motion for summary judgment and denies the plaintiffs' motion for summary judgment because there are no violations of copyright infringement.

Gibson v. Amazon.com
Procedure

Gibson v. Amazon.com **Case No. 3-13-1136. United States District Court, M.D. Tennessee, Nashville Division, October 29, 2013.**

ISSUE

Whether the court should reschedule the initial case management conference date.

RULE

A court may reschedule an initial case management conference so both parties can meet and confer to exchange information before the conference occurs so everything goes smoothly.

CASE DETAILS

Facts

The plaintiff filed a motion for admission of information for this occasion only which the court granted. The court ordered a meet and confer case management conference to discuss matters of the case.

Analysis

The court ordered the parties to meet and confer to discuss the different theories of the case, resolve issues if possible, and exchange initial disclosures prior to the initial case management conference.

CONCLUSION

The court orders the counsel to e-file the proposed order prior to an initial case management conference and bring their calendars and take into account everyone's schedule in determining a date for the case.

Gillette v. Amazon.com
Workers' Compensation and Employee Rights

***Gillette v. Amazon.com*, 2016 Del. Super. LEXIS 168 (Del. Super. Ct. Jan. 22, 2016).**

ISSUE

Should the District Court affirm the Industrial Accident Board's decision?

RULE

To be eligible for benefits under the Delaware Workers' Compensation Act, a claimant must prove that she sustained a personal injury by accident arising out of and in the course of employment. Del. Code Ann. tit. 19, § 2304. The claimant has the burden of proving her claim by a preponderance of the evidence. Del. Code Ann. tit. 29, § 10125(c). The determination of whether an injury arises out of and in the course of employment is highly factual, and is resolved under a totality of the circumstances analysis.

CASE DETAILS

Facts

Amazon hired Lucky Gillette in August of 2013 as a warehouse associate. A year later, Gillette began to experience pain and spasms in her mid-back while packing items at work. She visited a physician on August 5, 2014. On August 22, 2014, she filed a petition to determine compensation with the board.

Lucky Gillette appealed a January 30, 2015 decision of the Industrial Accident Board. This decision denied Gillette's Petition to determine compensation due for a back injury that occurred while working for Amazon.com. Additionally, the Industrial Accident Board discredited Lucky Gillette's testimony of witnesses. The board concluded that there was no enough evidence to support a claim that the injury was a work-related incident.

Gillette argued on appeal that the board abused its discretion by not looking to the medical evidence. Specifically, appellant argued that the board failed to address, "whether her mid-back injury was an aggravation of a preexisting condition that would not have occurred but for the alleged work incident.

Analysis

The court found that the plaintiff failed to show that the board acted unreasonably or capriciously in crediting the employer's witnesses over her own. Additionally, the court found that the Board was free to reject plaintiff's witness, Dr. Swaminathan's opinion because it was based on information that the plaintiff had provided. Finally, the court held that, "because the Board found that appellant did not meet her burden of proving that she sustained a mid-back injury in a specific work incident on August 4, 2014, the Board was not required to address whether her alleged injury was an aggravation of a preexisting condition that would not have occurred but for the alleged incident".

CONCLUSION

The District Court affirmed the Boards decision to deny the petition to determine compensation due. The court found there was no legal error on behalf of the board.

Girafa.com, Inc. v. Amazon.com, Inc.
Patent Infringement

***Girafa.com, Inc. v. Amazon.com, Inc.*, 2008 U.S. Dist. LEXIS 99196 (D. Del. Dec. 9, 2008).**

ISSUE

Should the court grant the motion for preliminary injunction?

RULE

Pursuant to 35 U.S.C. Section 283 and the holding in eBay, Inc. v. MercExchange, "Injunctions may issue in accordance with the principles of equity. The decision to grant or deny injunctive relief is an act of equitable discretion by the district court".

CASE DETAILS

Facts

Girafa was formed in 1999 and marked the technology of the 904 patent. This patent involved an improvement to "user interfaces for search engine technology." Girafa alleged that Snap, Smartdevil, and Amazon/Alexa/AWS were using the patented technology. Girafa moved for preliminary injunction.

Analysis

The court found that the two novel elements of the patent were, "(a) using thumbnail visual images of a homepage of a linked-to website, instead of a thumbnail visual images of the linked-to webpage; and (b) providing the thumbnail visual images via an image server that is separate from a web server."

Additionally, the court declined to adopt Girafa's claim construction.

CONCLUSION

The court concluded that there were substantial questions concerning the infringement claims and their validity and denied Girafa's motion for preliminary injunction.

Golden Bridge Technology, Inc. v. Apple, Inc.
Patent Infringement; Procedural

***Golden Bridge Tech., Inc. v. Apple Inc.*, 2012 U.S. Dist. LEXIS 130286 (C.D. Cal. Sept. 11, 2012).**

ISSUE

Whether the defendants were properly joined and whether the Central District of California is a proper venue?

RULE

Patent infringement joinder is ruled by 35 U.S.C. § 299, which is a higher standard for joinder. It prohibits joinder unless the relief arises out of the same transactions relating to infringement of the patent in suit by the same accused product. 35 U.S.C. §299. 28 U.S.C. §1404 (a) for *forum non conveniens* governs motions to transfer. It states that court have the broad discretion to transfer based on a subjective, "case-by—case consideration of convenience and fairness." *Jones v. GNC Franchising Inc.*, 211 F.3d 495, 498 (9th Cir. 2000).

CASE DETAILS

Facts:

Golden Bridge Technology (GBT) is alleging patent infringement against numerous defendants, including Amazon.com. Amazon.com, along with a few other defendants is alleging that the defendants were improperly joined and therefore the court should sever the suit. Additionally, if the court grants severance the defendants would like a motion to transfer to be granted as well, as the Central District of California is an inconvenient forum.

Analysis:

The court found no evidence that the defendants had any relationship relating to the products or infringement. It determined that defendants were unrelated competitors that design, manufacture, and sell smartphones and other data communication devices and that although they may be similar, there is no evidence that they collaborated together to infringe the patent.

Additionally, the court found that the motion to transfer for Amazon was not valid as all of the Defendants had sufficient contacts in the district and the court had personal jurisdiction. The court also recognized that this was the forum that GBT has chosen. The court also is not convinced that there will be savings of judicial resources. The court finds procedural issues with granting both the motion to sever and the motion to transfer.

CONCLUSION

The court grants the Defendants' motion to sever and denied the motion to transfer as to Amazon, as they had enough contact with the forum.

Golden Bridge Technology, Inc. v. Apple, Inc.
Patent Infringement; Procedure

***Golden Bridge Tech., Inc. v. Apple Inc.*, 937 F. Supp. 2d 490 (D. Del. 2013).**

ISSUE

Whether collateral estoppel is applicable?

RULE

Collateral estoppel requires the issues to be identical, the issue to be actually litigated and necessary to the decision, and the party needed to be filly represented in the prior action.

CASE DETAILS

Facts:

Golden Bridge Technology (GBT) is alleging patent infringement against numerous defendants, including Amazon.com. The patent infringement is related to wireless cellular networks and a method to establish a communication link between a mobile station and a base station.

Timeline:

GBT filed suit in 2005 in Texas alleging infringement of the patent against Nokia and Lucent. In January 2007, the Texas court found that the patent infringement claims are invalid under 35 U.S.C. §102 (b). The Federal Circuit affirmed in May 2008.

Analysis:

The court found that it cannot apply collateral estoppel because the issue decided by the Texas court is not identical to that being litigated in the present case. The patents were examined after the conclusion of the Texas litigation and therefore, the court is not bound by the Texas decision. However, the court finds that the definition of "access preamble" and "preamble" from the Texas legislation are applicable, as long as they include spreading prior to transmission.

CONCLUSION

The court sets forth a standard of interpretation for the claim language in the patents and denied application of collateral estoppel.

Gribbins v. Amazon.com
Worker's Compensation and Employees' Rights

***Gribbins v. Amazon.com*, Case No. 2003-CA-002208-WC. Court of Appeals of Kentucky, March 2004.**

ISSUE

Should the court of appeals affirm the Workers' Compensation Board judgment?

RULE

Following the holding in *Snawder v. Stice*, "In a workers' compensation claim, the burden of proof and risk of persuasion rests with the claimant."

CASE DETAILS

Facts

Ina Barnett Gribbins, plaintiff, was employed by Amazon.com where she injured her lower back. She was found to have 5% impairment to use of her body and she appealed to the board. Gribbins alleged that in addition to the back injury she had a urinary tract infection, acid reflux disease and that the judge was biased against her. The board affirmed the decision and Gribbins again appealed.

Again, she alleged the cervical spine injury and that the Administrative Law judge was biased against her. She further alleged her injuries caused a 28% impairment, not a 5% impairment.

Analysis

The court found that the evidence did not show a finding in Gribbins' favor.

CONCLUSION

The court, finding that the evidence did not fall in favor of Gribbins, affirmed the order of the Workers' Compensation Board.

Gribbins v. Amazon.com
Workers' Compensation and Employees' Rights

***Gribbins v. Amazon.Com*, 2005 Ky. Unpub. LEXIS 67 (Ky. Apr. 21, 2005).**

ISSUE

Should the Supreme Court of Kentucky affirm the lower court's decision?

RULE

Following the holding in Snawder v. Stice, "In a workers' compensation claim, the burden of proof and risk of persuasion rests with the claimant."

CASE DETAILS

Facts

Ina Barnett Gribbins, plaintiff, was employed by Amazon.com where she injured her lower back. She was found to have 5% impairment to her body and she appealed to the board. Gribbins alleged that in addition to the back injury she had a urinary tract infection, acid reflux disease and that the judge was biased against her. The board affirmed the decision and Gribbins again appealed. The court of Appeals of Kentucky affirmed the workers' compensation board opinion.

The case was then taken to the Supreme Court of Kentucky where Gribbins appealed the court of appeals judgment of affirming the worker's compensation boards affirming of the Administrative Law Judge's award.

Analysis

The Supreme Court of Kentucky found that, "there was substantial evidence upon which the ALJ could rely and, consequently, the Board and the Court of Appeals were correct in their decisions".

CONCLUSION

The Supreme Court of Kentucky affirmed the opinion of the Court of Appeals.

Guardian Media Techs., Ltd. v. Amazon.com, Inc.
Patent Infringement; Procedure

***Guardian Media Techs., Ltd. v. Amazon.com, Inc.*, 2013 U.S. Dist. LEXIS 171254 (C.D. Cal. Dec. 3, 2013).**

ISSUE

Whether defendants were improperly joined where it is alleged that defendants conduct was part of the same transaction or occurrence.

RULE

Persons . . . may be joined in one action as defendants if: (A) any right to relief is asserted against them jointly, severally, or in the alternative with respect to or arising out of the same transaction, occurrence, or series of transactions or occurrences; and (B) any question of law or fact common to all defendants will arise in the action. Fed. R. Civ. P. 20(a)(2).

If the court determines that parties are mis-joined, the court may, at any time, add or drop a party, or sever any claim against a party. Fed. R. Civ. P. 21.

CASE DETAILS

Facts

Plaintiff brought this action against defendants Amazon.com, Inc.; Best Buy Co., Inc.; Costco Wholesale Corp.; Overstock.Com, Inc.; RadioShack Corp.; Sears, Roebuck and Co.; Target Corp.; and Wal-Mart Stores, Inc. Defendants are alleged to have "made, had made, installed, used, imported, provided, supplied, distributed, sold, and/or offered for sale products and/or systems . . . that infringed, or when used, infringed one more claims of plaintiff's patents.

Analysis

The court found that there is no indication that the defendants acted in concert, or that their conduct was connected in any way.

CONCLUSION

The court ultimately ordered plaintiff to show cause in writing, why the court should not dismiss without prejudice all defendants except Amazon.Com, Inv. on the grounds of improper joinder. Failure to respond will result in dismissal of the action.

Gusler v. Amazon.com Inc.
Copyright Infringement; Unjust Enrichment

***Gusler v. Fischer*, 580 F. Supp. 2d 309, 2008 U.S. Dist. LEXIS 75454 (S.D.N.Y. 2008).**

ISSUE

Should the court grant the defendant's motion to dismiss, or in the alternative, summary judgment?

RULE

This case looks to the Federal Rules of Civil Procedure 12(b)(6) for a dismissal of the case. Additionally, the court looks to the Federal Rules of Civil Procedure Rule 56 for summary judgment.

To establish copyright infringement on a summary judgment motions, a plaintiff must demonstrate: "(1) ownership of a valid copyright, and (2) unauthorized copying of the copyrighted work." *Eliya, Inc. v. Kohl's Department Stores.*

CASE DETAILS

Facts

Gusler claims that in 1997 he designed an electric vacuum device to extract fluid from the nose of an infant. This device was registered with the United States Copyright Office. In 2006, Gusler was notified that there was a product similar to his designs that were being sold at Toys "R" Us, Inc., Target Corporation, Amazon.com Inc., Chelsea & Scott, Ltd., and Wal-Mart Stores, Inc.

Gusler asserts copyright claims copyright infringement claims under the Copyright Act, 17 U.S.C. Section 501, 504 against defendants. Additionally, he claims unjust enrichment against all defendants.

Amazon.com, along with other defendants, Listro Associates, Unisar Inc., Target Corporation, Toys "R" Us, Inc., Chelsea & Scott, Ltd., and Wal-Mart Stores, Inc. moved for a dismissal of the claims against them pursuant to the Federal Rules of Civil Procedure 12(b)(6). In the alternative, the defendants have moved for summary judgment pursuant to the Federal Rules of Civil Procedure.

Analysis

The court found that Gusler has only made allegations that his product incorporated protectable original design elements. Gusler fails to identify any of these elements "which have been copied and which he believes are either physically or conceptually separable from the utilitarian aspects of the product. Therefore, the court finds that he fails to prove that this product is subject to a copyright protection.

As for the unjust enrichment claims, the court finds that this claim against Fischer should be dismissed.

CONCLUSION

The United States District Court granted the corporate defendant's motion for summary judgment. The unjust enrichment claim against Fischer was dismissed and the breach of contract and misrepresentation of trade secrets claims against Fischer will proceed.

Hamilton v. Amazon.com, Inc.
Procedure

***Hamilton v. Amazon.com, Inc.*, 2002-Ohio-7377 (Ohio Ct. App., Montgomery County Dec. 31, 2002).**

ISSUE

Whether the court can recognize plaintiff's claim on appeal where he has failed to comply with Civ. R. 53(E)(3)(b).

RULE

"A party shall not assign as error on appeal the court's adoption of a finding of fact of conclusion of law unless the party has objected to that finding or conclusion under this rule." Civ. R. 53(E)(3)(b).

CASE DETAILS

Facts

Plaintiff is appealing from the trial court's holding, adopting a magistrate's decision, that plaintiff brought this claim against defendant Amazon.com, Inc. (Amazon) in the wrong venue. A provision of the on-line terms that Amazon has set up for any customer using its site to order products included a forum selection clause requiring users to seek redress for any legal claims in the state of Washington where Amazon is headquartered. The magistrate and the court below ruled that plaintiff could not file an action in the Dayton Municipal Court because he was bound by the forum selection clause.

Plaintiff appealed this decision, but he did not file any objections to the magistrate's decision as required by Civ. R. 53(E)(3)(b).

Analysis

The court holds that because plaintiff failed to comply with the Federal rules of civil procedure by objecting to the magistrate's report, that the errors he assigned on appeal are not cognizable by the court.

CONCLUSION

For the foregoing reasons the plaintiff's two assignments of error are overruled and the judgment below is affirmed.

Hammer v. Amazon.com Inc.
Defamation, Copyright Infringement; Breach of Contract

***Hammer v. Amazon.com*, 392 F. Supp. 2d 423, 2005 U.S. Dist. LEXIS 33398 (E.D.N.Y. 2005).**

ISSUE

Should the District Court grant Amazon's motion to dismiss?

RULE

A District Court should grant a motion to dismiss only if "it is clear that no relief could be granted under any set of facts that could be provided consistent with allegation" *H.J. Inc. v. Northwestern Bell Tel. Co.*

CASE DETAILS

Facts

Jeffrey Hammer and Amazon.com entered into an agreement where Hammer sold his books on the website. Plaintiff alleged that he published five books between the years 1999- 2002. Plaintiff further alleged that Amazon was aware of negative reviews made by Trendl and should have removed them from the system. Amazon, after receiving many complaints and having been made aware of the civil action between plaintiff and Trendl, removed the book from the website. Jeffrey Hammer therefore alleged that there was a breach of contract.

Additionally, Amazon provided counsel to Trendl to defend Trendl in the action. Plaintiff filed suit against Amazon claiming (1) defamation; (2) violation of the copyright laws; (3) breach of contract; (4) violation of his First Amendment Rights; (5) discriminatory business practices/ violation of the antitrust laws; (6) conversion. The plaintiff requested injunctive relief and over $100 million in damages.

Plaintiff filed motions for recusal, partial remand of this matter to state court, and leave to amend the complaint. Amazon filed motions to dismiss the complaint, for permanent injunction, for enjoining plaintiff from commencing any subsequent actions in federal court relating to or arising out of review of his books on Amazon.com and requiring plaintiff to append a copy of the courts injunction to any further complaint, and civil contempt sanctions.

Analysis

The court denied the plaintiff's recusal motion because the motion does not have proper grounds for recusal. The court denied the plaintiff's partial remand motion because there are two adequate and independent grounds for removal of the instant action. Additionally, the court denied the plaintiff's motion for leave to amend the complaint to add a claim for conspiracy.

The court found that because the defamation claims were predicated upon statements that were mere opinions, they dismissed the defamation claim. Additionally, there was no allegation that anyone copied plaintiff's work and therefore dismissed the copyright claim. Plaintiff furthermore failed to allege any state action, thus his First Amendment claims are dismissed. Additionally, the plaintiff's claims for discriminatory business practices and conversion were dismissed.

CONCLUSION

The United States District Court denied the plaintiff's motions for recusal, partial remand, and for leave to amend the complaint. The court grants Amazon's motion for a permanent injunction and denied the motion for civil contempt sanctions.

Hard 2 Find Accessories, Inc. v. Amazon.com, Inc.
Antitrust Law Violations

***Hard 2 Find Accessories, Inc. v. Amazon.com, Inc.*, 58 F. Supp. 3d 1166 (W.D. Wash. 2014).**

ISSUE

Whether Amazon may terminate or suspend an agreement if a seller does not abide by the agreed upon terms.

RULE

A court may allow an agreement to stand and dismiss claims that are not supported by facts.

CASE DETAILS

Facts

The plaintiff was a former seller on Amazon and entered into an agreement to abide by Amazon's Business Solutions Agreement. The agreement states Amazon or the sellers may terminate or suspend the agreement by notice to the seller for any reason at any time. Amazon notified the plaintiff that two of their listings had been removed because of notification that the products were counterfeit. Amazon removed the plaintiff's selling privileges, cancelled its listings, and placed a temporary hold on any funds in its account because all items for sale on Amazon must be authentic.

Analysis

Plaintiff fails to provide any information that Amazon breached the agreed upon contract and that cause of action must be dismissed. There is no evidence to support any of the plaintiff's claims. The plaintiff did not allege any facts to support their claim, breach of contract was not proven, there were no facts to support trademark conspiracy, and the unjust enrichment claim failed.

CONCLUSION

The court granted the defendants motion to dismiss. All claims against Amazon are dismissed.

Hard 2 Find Accessories, Inc. v. Amazon.com, Inc.
Antitrust Law Violations/Amazon Dismissed From All Claims

***Hard 2 Find Accessories, Inc. v. Amazon.com, Inc.*, 2014 U.S. Dist. LEXIS 160980, 2014-2 Trade Cas. (CCH) P78,968 (W.D. Wash. Nov. 17, 2014).**

ISSUE

Whether there is a valid case against Apple when the suit stems from a demand to stop selling infringing products.

RULE

A party may have immunity from a lawsuit if the claims arise from cease-and-desist letter demanding to stop the use and sale of products that are infringing on trademarks.

CASE DETAILS

Facts

The plaintiff was a former seller on Amazon and entered into an agreement to abide by Amazon's Business Solutions Agreement. The agreement states Amazon or the sellers may terminate or suspend the agreement by notice to the seller for any reason at any time. Amazon notified the plaintiff that two of their listings had been removed because Apple made a notification that the products were counterfeit. Amazon removed the plaintiff's selling privileges, cancelled its listings, and placed a temporary hold on any funds in its account because all items for sale on Amazon must be authentic.

Analysis

Apple has immunity from suit in this matter. The plaintiff fails to show evidence that Apple's letter to stop using infringing items was unfounded. The plaintiff does not provide any facts to support their claims.

CONCLUSION

The court granted the defendant's motion to dismiss and closed the case.

Hart v. Amazon.com, Inc.
Copyright Infringement

***Hart v. Amazon.com, Inc.*, 2015 U.S. Dist. LEXIS 164627, 117 U.S.P.Q.2D (BNA) 1584, 44 Media L. Rep. 1250 (N.D. Ill. Dec. 8, 2015).**

ISSUE

Whether a party has a valid claim for copyright infringement.

RULE

To state a claim for copyright infringement, a party must prove ownership of a valid copyright, and copying of specific original pieces of the work.

CASE DETAILS

Facts

Plaintiff authored three books and chose not to publish them to the public. Plaintiff discovered one of the books was for sale on Amazon. Plaintiff sent a letter to Amazon asking for the books to be removed from the website.

Analysis

The plaintiff does not prove Amazon's posting of titles directly copies any of their work and dismisses the claim. The plaintiff fails to make a claim that third-party sellers are liable for copyright infringement. The plaintiff fails to provide facts to support any of their claims.

CONCLUSION

The court grants the defendant's motion for judgment on the pleadings as to direct infringement. The plaintiff has an opportunity to try and fix the problem and state a proper claim and file an amended complaint.

Hendrickson v. Amazon.com, Inc.
Copyright Infringement

***Hendrickson v. Amazon.com, Inc.*, 298 F. Supp. 2d 914 (C.D. Cal. 2003).**

ISSUE

Whether Amazon has infringed on an owner's copyright by allowing the sale of a DVD.

RULE

A party is not liable for copyright infringement if they are an internet service provider and meet the criteria to be protected under the safe harbor provision requiring knowledge of infringing activity, does not benefit financially from the infringement, and removes all material after notice of infringement.

CASE DETAILS

Facts

The plaintiff owns the copyright to the movie *Manson*, and has not released it in DVD format yet. The plaintiff claims the defendants are liable for copyright infringement because they sold the *Manson* DVD. The copyright owner must monitor for potential infringing sales of their products and an internet service provider must have knowledge of product infringement. A service provider may be protected under the safe harbor provision if there is no actual knowledge of infringing activity, does not receive and financial benefit directly from the infringing activity, and removes all material after notice of infringement.

Analysis

Amazon is not considered the direct seller of the DVD because they meet the criteria for an internet service provider and are protected by the safe harbor provision. Amazon had no knowledge of the infringing material, there is no evidence to show they had the ability to know about or control the infringing sale, and could not have responded to the notice of claimed infringement. Summary judgment for Amazon is appropriate since there is no direct infringement.

CONCLUSION

The court grants Amazon's motion for summary judgment because they qualify for the safe harbor affirmative defense and each party is ordered to pay for their own costs.

Hendrickson v. Amazon.com, Inc.
Copyright Infringement

***Hendrickson v. Amazon.com, Inc.*, 181 Fed. Appx. 692, 2006 U.S. App. LEXIS 12720, Copy. L. Rep. (CCH) P29,180 (9th Cir. Cal. 2006).**

ISSUE

Whether a lower court judgment granting attorney fees should be upheld.

RULE

A court may remove a lower court judgment granting attorney's fees if it is found to be an abuse of discretion and there is no clear explanation for awarding the fees.

CASE DETAILS

Facts

Attorney's fees should be compensated when the services are reasonable and contribute to winning a lawsuit.

Analysis

The attorney's fees award is vacated and remanded in favor of the defendants to determine if their services attribute to the success of the case.

CONCLUSION

The court vacated and remanded the award of attorney's fees for the lower court to analyze and determine if the attorney services helped the case prevail.

Hickman v. Amazon Fulfillment
Employee's Rights; Procedure

***Hickman v. Amazon Fullfilment,* 2015 U.S. Dist. LEXIS 168782 (W.D. Pa. Dec. 17, 2015).**

ISSUE

Whether the court should grant defendant's Motion to Dismiss?

RULE

The court must liberally construe factual allegations in pro se pleadings. *Erickson v. Pardus*, 551 U.S. 89, 94 (2007).

CASE DETAILS

Facts:

Plaintiffs filed suit alleging that they were injured at work due to them working hard and having feet problems, that they were discriminated against at work because Gregory was helping Parry who is handicapped and was told to get away from her, and that some of the problems with other employees at work have a lot to do with being biased towards them and others at work.

Analysis:

Defendants have filed a Motion to Dismiss the complaint. The court determined that the complaint fails to contain sufficient facts to demonstrate that the exhaustion requirements have been met. Therefore, the court determined that the proper disposition is to dismiss the complaint without prejudice and grant leave to amend to cure the deficiencies.

CONCLUSION

The court granted the defendant's Motion to Dismiss.

Hickman v. Amazon Fulfillment
Employee's Rights; Procedure

***Hickman v. Amazon Fullfilment*, 2016 U.S. Dist. LEXIS 45937 (W.D. Pa. Apr. 5, 2016).**

ISSUE

Whether the court should grant defendant's Motion to Dismiss?

RULE

The court must liberally construe factual allegations in pro se pleadings. *Erickson v. Pardus*, 551 U.S. 89, 94 (2007).

CASE DETAILS

Facts:

Plaintiffs filed suit alleging that they were injured at work due to them working hard and having feet problems, that they were discriminated against at work because Gregory was helping Parry who is handicapped and was told to get away from her, and that some of the problems with other employees at work have a lot to do with being biased towards them and others at work. Plaintiff filed a complaint that was dismissed in December 2015, and now files an amended complaint that defendant challenge as well.

Analysis:

Defendants have filed a Motion to Dismiss the amended complaint. The court determined that plaintiff has neither pled nor proved that he filed charges of discrimination with the E.E.O.C. or P.H.R.C. before initiating this federal lawsuit and therefore the Amended Complaint must be dismissed, without prejudice, as his employment discrimination claims are premature. The court additionally determined that leave to amend will be denied as the Plaintiff had been afforded multiple opportunities to cure the deficiencies in the pleadings.

CONCLUSION

The court granted the defendant's Motion to Dismiss the amended complaint.

Hinton v. Dick's Sporting Goods, Inc.
Negligence; Procedural

ISSUE

Whether the court should grant plaintiff's motion for additional time within which to respond the the motion for summary judgment.

RULE

The Motion for Time must be filed in a timely manner and the party requesting more time must support the requested relief with good cause. Fed. R. Civ. P. 6(b)(1)(A).

CASE DETAILS

Facts:

Marsha Hinton filed suit on September 25, 2013 against defendants alleging that they sold her hunting equipment that had been recalled by the Consumer Product Safety Commission (CPSC). She decided to buy the hunting equipment subject to recall. Her son subsequently had died in a hunting accident in November of 2012. On October 2013, Amazon removed the proceeding to this court. She now sues for injunction, negligence, intentional non recall conduct, gross negligence, breach of implied warranty of merchantability, failure to warn and breach of duty of good faith and fair dealings. She requests punitive damages. On January 7, 2014, Defendants filed their Motion for Summary Judgment and Sanctions. Plaintiff's response to the motion was due on January 24, 2014, and she filed her Motion for Time on January 23. Plaintiff requests her time to respond to be extended until 10 days after Defendant Bass Pro responds to her written discovery requests.

Analysis:

Plaintiff filed a Motion for Time in a timely matter and with good cause.

CONCLUSION

The court granted the Motion for Additional Time to Respond to the Motion for Sanctions and Motion for Summary Judgment.

Hinton v. Dick's Sporting Goods, Inc.
Negligence; Procedural

***Hinton v. Dick's Sporting Goods, Inc.*, 2014 U.S. Dist. LEXIS 24426 (S.D. Miss. Feb. 26, 2014).**

ISSUE

Whether the Motion to Stay Proceedings and the Motion to Sever should be granted?

RULE

The court has broad discretion to stay proceedings "as an incident to its power to control its own docket." *Clinton v. Jones*, 520 U.S. 681, 706 (1997) (citing *Landis v. N. Am. Co.*, 299 U.S. 248 (1936)). The party seeking a stay bears the burden of demonstrating necessity. *Id.* at 708.

CASE DETAILS

Facts:

Marsha Hinton filed suit on September 25, 2013 against defendants alleging that they sold her hunting equipment that had been recalled by the Consumer Product Safety Commission (CPSC). She decided to buy the hunting equipment subject to recall. Her son subsequently had died in a hunting accident in November of 2012. On October 2013, Amazon removed the proceeding to this court. She now sues for injunction, negligence, intentional non recall conduct, gross negligence, breach of implied warranty of merchantability, failure to warn and breach of duty of good faith and fair dealings. She requests punitive damages. On January 7, 2014, Defendants filed their Motion for Summary Judgment and Sanctions. Plaintiff's response to the motion was due on January 24, 2014, and she filed her Motion for Time on January 23. She was granted a Motion for Time on February 7, 2014. On the same day, she filed her Motion to Stay.

Analysis:

The court rejects Plaintiffs request to stay of proceedings. There is no indication of when Plaintiff is expected to receive the CPSC's response. The court decided that it is unwilling to delay the case for an indefinite amount of time until the Plaintiff receives the information. Additionally, the Plaintiff does not offer anything in support of her presumption that the CPSC file will contain information that will be determinative of whether the climbing stick is subject to recall. The court also denies the motion to depose L. J. Smith prior to responding to the motion of summary judgment as she failed to show what information Smith possess that bears on the request for summary judgment.

CONCLUSION

The court granted the Motion to Stay is denied and Plaintiff shall file her responses to the Motion to Sever and Summary Judgment within 7 days of the order.

Hinton v. Dick's Sporting Goods, Inc.
Negligence

Hinton v. Dick's Sporting Goods, Inc., 2013 U.S. Dist. LEXIS 172245 (S.D. Miss. Dec. 6, 2013)

ISSUE

Whether the Motion for Immediate Hearing on Permanent Injunction should be granted?

RULE

In order for the court to grant a Motion for Immediate Hearing on Permanent Injunction the Plaintiff must prove an actual success based on the merits. A permanent injunction is granted only where a full trial on the merits has occurred. *ITT Educ. Servs., Inc. v. Arce,* 533 F.3d 342, 347 (5th Cir. 2008) (citing *Univ. of Tex. v. Camenisch,* 451 U.S. 390, 296 (1981)).

CASE DETAILS

Facts:

Marsha Hinton filed suit on September 25, 2013 against defendants alleging that they sold her hunting equipment that had been recalled by the Consumer Product Safety Commission (CPSC). She decided to buy the hunting equipment subject to recall. Her son had died in a hunting accident in November of 2012. On October 2013, Amazon removed the proceeding to this court. She now sues for injunction, negligence, intentional non recall conduct, gross negligence, breach of implied warranty of merchantability, failure to warn and breach of duty of good faith and fair dealings. She requests punitive damages. Currently there is a Motion for Immediate Hearing on Plaintiff's Request for Permanent Injunction and a Counter-Motion for Pre-Conference Examination of Evidence.

Analysis:

The court states that the plea for an immediate hearing for permanent injunction is premature as the plaintiff must show actual success on the merits and has not done so here. She has merely shown a likelihood of success. Her request fails to give rise to any threat of irreparable injury. She purchased the items believing they were recalled and she did not hesitate to buy the product when she believed it was recalled. Therefore, the likelihood of her obtaining an injury due to the items during this lawsuit is nonexistent.

CONCLUSION

The court denied the Plaintiff's Motion for Immediate Hearing and denied the Counter Motion as well.

Hinton v. Dick's Sporting Goods, Inc.
Negligence; Procedure

***Hinton v. Dick's Sporting Goods, Inc.*, 2014 U.S. Dist. LEXIS 137243 (S.D. Miss. Sept. 29, 2014).**

ISSUE

Whether the Motion to Strike, Motion in Limine and Motion for Permission to File a Surrebuttal Birief should be granted?

CASE DETAILS

Facts:

Marsha Hinton filed suit on September 25, 2013 against defendants alleging that they sold her hunting equipment that had been recalled by the Consumer Product Safety Commission (CPSC). She decided to buy the hunting equipment subject to recall. Her son subsequently had died in a hunting accident in November of 2012. On October 2013, Amazon removed the proceeding to this court. She now sues for injunction, negligence, intentional non recall conduct, gross negligence, breach of implied warranty of merchantability, failure to warn and breach of duty of good faith and fair dealings. She requests punitive damages. On January 7, 2014, Defendants filed their Motion for Summary Judgment and Sanctions. Plaintiff's response to the motion was due on January 24, 2014, and she filed her Motion for Time on January 23. She was granted a Motion for Time on February 7, 2014. On the same day, she filed her Motion to Stay, which was also granted.

Analysis:

The court rejects the Motion to Strike as there is no need to strike the Report from the Record. The court will simply disregard it when reaching the decision for Summary Judgment. Additionally, the Motion in Limine is premature and therefore will not be granted either, as there is no need for it yet, and was filed prematurely. Additionally, the court grants the Motion to File a Surrebuttal Brief, as the court can use these arguments in ruling for Summary Judgment.

CONCLUSION

The court granted the Motion for Permission to File a Surrebuttal Brief and denied the Motion to Strike and Motion in Limine. It granted other defendant's Motions for Summary Judgment.

Hinton v. Amazon.com
Procedure

***Hinton v. Amazon.com.DEDC, LLC*, 72 F. Supp. 3d 685 (S.D. Miss. 2014).**

ISSUE

Should the court grant eBay's motion to dismiss?

RULE

The court looks to broad immunity pursuant to 47 U.S.C. Section 230, which bars a plaintiff's claim against a defendant.

CASE DETAILS

Facts

Plaintiff Marsha Hinton, purchased hunting equipment which was subject to recalls issued by the United States Consumer Product Safety Commission. Hinton purchased the equipment through eBay's website for her son, Timothy Hinton. Timothy Hinton died in connection with a hunting accident.

On October 25, 2013, Amazon filed a notice of removal asserting that the court possessed jurisdiction over this cause for federal question, diversity of citizenship, and supplemental jurisdiction.

Analysis

The court looked to 47 U.S.C. Section 230, which bars a plaintiff's claim against a defendant and found that this did bar plaintiff's claim against EBay.

CONCLUSION

The United States District Court found granted the motion to dismiss in favor of defendant, eBay.

Hobbs v. Rui Zhao
Procedure; Negligence

***Hobbs v. Rui Zhao*, 2014 U.S. Dist. LEXIS 161533 (N.D. Okla. Nov. 17, 2014).**

ISSUE

Whether the Plaintiff's Motion to Leave to Amend will be granted?

RULE

Rule 15 of the Federal Rules of Civil Procedure states that the courts should "freely grant leaves to amend when justice so requires." Fed. R. Civ. P. 15(a)(2). The court can deny the motion if it believes that it is filed in bad faith to cause undue delay or a dilatory motive. The local rule requires motions to add parties to "be accompanied by a proposed order." LcvR 7.2(I).

CASE DETAILS

Facts

Zhao was a commercial driver in the U.S. for four weeks when he drove to an Amazon distribution center in Kentucky to pick up cargo. Amazon sent a bid for the cargo to all transportation companies that Amazon had approved. Zhao picked up the cargo and began transporting it to Arizona. On December 8, 2012, he got into an accident and the plaintiff suffered serious injuries. Hobbs filed in Oklahoma naming Zhao and his insurer as defendants. This was removed to the present court on the basis of jurisdiction. Four months later, Plaintiff amended his complaint to add Amazon and Grand as defendants.

Analysis

Plaintiff seeks to amend his complaint to add two new defendants. The court has found three reasons to deny the motion to amend: (1) The deadline for motions for joinder had passed four months ago; (2) Plaintiff did not comply with the Local Civil Rule; and (3) Plaintiff has a motive for undue delay. Plaintiff has given the court no reason to believe that he could not have added the defendants at an earlier point and therefore the court denies his application.

CONCLUSION

The motion to amend the complaint to add two more defendants is denied.

Hobbs v. Rui Zhao
Procedure; Negligence

***Hobbs v. Rui Zhao*, 2015 U.S. Dist. LEXIS 11762 (N.D. Okla. Feb. 2, 2015).**

ISSUE

Whether defendant, Amazon's Motion for Summary Judgment should be granted.

RULE

Rule 56 of the Federal Rules of Civil Procedure states that summary judgment is appropriate when there is no genuine dispute of a material fact and the moving party is entitled to a judgment as a matter of law. *Celotex Corp. v. Catrett*, 477 U.S. 317, 322-23 (1986). The party must show a lack of sufficient evidence to establish an existence of an element essential to a party's case. *Id.* at 317.

CASE DETAILS

Facts:

Zhao was a commercial driver in the U.S. for four weeks when he drove to an Amazon distribution center in Kentucky to pick up cargo. Amazon sent a bid for the cargo to all transportation companies that Amazon had approved. Zhao picked up the cargo and began transporting it to Arizona. On December 8, 2012, he got into an accident and the plaintiff, Hobbs suffered serious injuries. Hobbs filed in Oklahoma naming Zhao and his insurer as defendants. This was removed to the present court on the basis of jurisdiction. Four months later, Plaintiff amended his complaint to add Amazon and Grand as defendants.

Analysis:

Defendant, Amazon, seeks to have the Motion for Summary Judgment granted on the claims of negligent entrustment and negligent hiring. Plaintiff failed to show that Amazon owed them a duty of care under the applicable Oklahoma statute for negligent entrustment and there is no evidence that the cargo became dangerous after being loaded. Therefore the court granted summary judgment to the negligent entrustment claim. Additionally, the court found no evidence for the negligent hiring claim, as Amazon did not specifically hire Zhao for the task and therefore was not an employer.

CONCLUSION

The court granted summary judgment to the negligent entrustment and negligent hiring claims. Amazon was dismissed from the case.

Huong Hoang v. Amazon.com, Inc.
Breach of Contract

***Huong Hoang v. Amazon.com, Inc.*, 2012 U.S. Dist. LEXIS 45498, 2012 WL 1088165 (W.D. Wash. Mar. 28, 2012).**

ISSUE

Whether a claim is stated for a breach of contract and violation of consumer protection statutes.

RULE

When a claim is stated in a short and plain statement and is credible on the surface it may survive a motion to dismiss.

CASE DETAILS

Facts

Plaintiff paid a fee to sign up for the IMBDPro service to connect with casting directors and obtain roles. Plaintiff claims the service took her personal information and added it to her profile without her authorization and has harmed her career.

Analysis

The plaintiff's breach of contract claim will survive the motion to dismiss because there is a valid contract, there may be a breach of duty and she has proven she suffered damage. Defendants did not show the plaintiff gave permission to use her information. Plaintiff's fraud claim fails because there is no specific evidence provided to support it. The plaintiff meets the requirements to state a breach of contract claim and damage suffered. The plaintiff states a valid claim under the Washington Consumer Protection Act because she plead an unfair or deceptive practice in trade or commerce that affects public interest and there is a causal link between the plaintiff's harm and the deceptive act.

CONCLUSION

The court denies defendants' motion to dismiss because the plaintiff sufficiently states a claim for breach of contract and violation of the Washington Consumer Protection Act. The court also grants the defendants' motion to dismiss the plaintiff's claim for fraud. The case will proceed to further litigation.

Huong Hoang v. Amazon.com, Inc.
Procedure – Motion to Dismiss

***Huong Hoang v. Amazon.com, Inc.*, 2012 U.S. Dist. LEXIS 191386 (W.D. Wash. July 2, 2012).**

ISSUE

Whether the court should grant defendants motion to dismiss plaintiff's fraud claims.

RULE

Rule 12(b)(6) requires a court to dismiss a claim when there is no cognizable legal theory or an absence of sufficient facts alleged to support a cognizable legal theory. *Navarro v. Block*, 250 F.3d 729, 732 (9th Cir. 2004). Rule 9(b) requires that when fraud is alleged, a party must state with particularity the circumstances constituting the fraud. Fed. R. Civ. P. 9(b).

CASE DETAILS

Facts

In an earlier proceeding, the court dismissed two of plaintiffs four original causes of actions, but allowed plaintiff's claims for breach of contract and consumer protection to stay. The court allowed plaintiff leave to amend their complaint in order to satisfy the particularity requirements. The second amended complaint contains privacy policies from defendants Amazon.com Inc. and Imdb. Com, that plaintiff claims were in effect at the time plaintiff used defendant's services. Defendants assert that plaintiff still fails to meet the pleading requirements with their amended complaint and that plaintiff fails to distinguish between defendants Amazon and IMDB.

Analysis

The court finds that plaintiff's fraud claim still fails to meet the federal requirements with regard to Amazon.com. Plaintiff has only alleged one misstatement by Amazon.com. The court finds that this misstatement is not alleged with the necessary particularity because plaintiff does not allege when the misconduct occurred. The court finds that plaintiff fails to state a claim for fraud under Washington Law because plaintiff fails to describe how Amazon.com's statement was false.

CONCLUSION

Plaintiff fails to allege the circumstances of fraud with particularity as required by the federal rules and also does not state the elements of a fraud claim under Washington law. Thus the court dismisses plaintiff's fraud claim.

In Re: Amazon.com, Inc.
Procedure

***In re Amazon.com, Inc.*, 2014 U.S. Dist. LEXIS 100716 (W.D. Ky. July 23, 2014)**

ISSUE

Can plaintiffs justify a blanket grant of equitable tolling for punitive and current opt-in plaintiffs given the circumstances of this case?

RULE

Following the holding in Smith v. T-Mobile and 29 U.S.C. Section 216(b), "no employee other than the plaintiff "shall be a party plaintiff to action unless he gives his consent in writing to become such a party and such consent is filed in the court in which such action is brought".

CASE DETAILS

Facts

This was a multidistrict class action that consolidated several proceedings brought by Amazon.com fulfillment center employees.

In October of 2010, plaintiff Busk, filed a nationwide collective and class action alleging that defendants violated the Fair Labor Standards Act for failure to pay hourly employees minimum wage and overtime premium pay, where applicable. The District of Nevada dismissed the case. Plaintiffs appealed to the Ninth Circuit, which was reversed. Defendants unsuccessfully petitioned for a rehearing.

Analysis

The court found that "a blanket equitable tolling of all current and prospective opt-in plaintiffs was unjustified and premature".

CONCLUSION

The court denied the plaintiff's motion for an equitable tolling.

Vance v. Amazon.com, Inc.
Procedure

Vance v. Amazon.com, Inc. **(In re Amazon.com, Inc.), 2016 U.S. Dist. LEXIS 48650 (W.D. Ky. Mar. 30, 2016).**

ISSUE

Whether the Supreme Court's ruling in *Integrity Staffing Solutions, Inc. v. Busk* also resolved the parties state law claims here.

RULE

Following the holding in *Commercial Money v. Ill. Union Ins.*, "to avoid a judgment on the pleadings, a complaint must contain direct or inferential allegations respecting all the material elements under some viable legal theory."

CASE DETAILS

Facts

This case deals specifically with the court deciding whether the Supreme Court's ruling in *Integrity Staffing Solutions, Inc. v. Busk*, also resolved their state law claims. Defendants claimed that it did and requested judgment on the pleadings.

Plaintiffs, Aaron and Tina, were among a group of individuals in the suit who claimed that their job required at length screening before exiting the worksite. They were not paid for the ten to thirty minutes it took to screen. The Supreme Court decision in dusk "did away" with the plaintiff's federal claims.

Analysis

The court held that, "the Portal-to Portal Act was an amendment to and not wholly distinct from the FLSA, and Kentucky law instructs that federal law should be applied in the absence of state law.

CONCLUSION

The court granted defendant's motion for judgment on the pleadings.

In re Amazon.com Inc.
Patent Infringement

***In re Amazon.com, Inc.*, 476 Fed. Appx. 738 (Fed. Cir. 2012).**

ISSUE

Whether the court will allow the transfer of this case to another venue.

RULE

A court may allow transfer of venue upon receiving a response from the parties involved.

CASE DETAILS

Facts

Amazon has submitted a writ of mandamus directing the United States District Court for the Eastern District of Texas to vacate an order denying a motion to transfer a case and directing to transfer to the United States District Court for the Western District of Texas.

Analysis

The court ordered Global Sessions LP et al. and any other parties involved to respond no later than February 8, 2012.

CONCLUSION

The court ordered Global Sessions LP et al. to respond no later than February 8, 2012.

In re Amazon.com Inc.
Patent Infringement

***In re Amazon.com Inc.*, 478 Fed. Appx. 669 (Fed. Cir. 2012)**

ISSUE

Whether the transfer of venue would be more convenient for witnesses in case.

RULE

A court may deny a venue transfer if it is not more convenient for all parties and non-parties involved.

CASE DETAILS

Facts

Global Sessions filed a patent infringement suit against Amazon. The defendants are headquartered in the Western District of Texas and important documents are located near the Eastern District of Texas. The lower court determined Amazon had not met its burden to prove the transfer of venue would be more convenient.

Analysis

No defendant is headquartered in the place they are requesting to transfer. Transfer does not make any sources of proof more easily accessible. Amazon has not provided clear evidence that the transfer of venue would be more convenient.

CONCLUSION

The court denies Amazon's petition for writ of mandamus. The lower court did not abuse its discretion denying the transfer of venue.

In re Grand Jury Subpoena to Amazon.Com dated Aug. 7, 2006
Procedure

***In re Grand Jury Subpoena to Amazon.com* dated Aug. 7, 2006, 246 F.R.D. 570 (W.D. Wis. 2007).**

ISSUE

Whether the grand jury's withdrawal of the subpoena was proper.

CASE DETAILS

Facts

After a June trial the court granted a motion to quash the subpoena requiring Amazon.Com to supply information regarding customer identities related to books sales of a seller accused of tax and wire/phone fraud. On July 9, 2007, the government moved to withdraw the grand jury's subpoena to Amazon.Com.

Analysis

The court finds that a grand jury does not need court permission to withdraw a subpoena. Amazon clearly does not oppose this result, but the court believes Amazon must be "irritated" by the timing. (In a previous action Amazon was granted motion to quash the subpoena's requirements). The magistrate judge here, finds that despite the timing of the withdrawal, that it is logical and prudent under the circumstances.

CONCLUSION

The court finds holds that all documents relating to the Amazon subpoena shall remain sealed until the grand jury returns an indictment against the alleged criminal seller, or closes its investigation, whichever occurs first.

In re Grand Jury Subpoena (Amazon.com), 246 F.R.D. 570 (W.D. Wis. 2007)
Procedure – Motion to Quash Grand Jury Subpoena

In re Grand Jury Subpoena (Amazon.com), 246 F.R.D. 570 (W.D. Wis. 2007)

ISSUE

Whether the court should grant defendant Amazon.com's motion to quash part of a subpoena requesting information regarding the identity of the customers who purchased books from a certain seller under criminal investigation.

RULE

"Although a grand jury subpoena is presumed valid and enforceable, if the witness demonstrates a legitimate First Amendment concern raised by the subpoena, then the government must make an additional showing that the grand jury actually needs the disputed information. The reviewing court should use its discretion to fashion a solution that accommodates the legitimate needs of both the grand jury and the protesting witness."

CASE DETAILS

Facts

In August, 2006, a federal grand jury issued a subpoena to Amazon.com (Amazon) seeking information about a seller of used books. The grand jury is investigating whether this seller evaded taxes or engaged in a mail fraud/wire fraud scheme involving the sale of about 24,000 books over four years on Amazon's website. The subpoena required Amazon to provide all records relating to the seller, including the thousands of customers who had bought books from the seller. The government limited the scope of the subpoena to 120 book buyers, 30 for each of the four years of the seller's activity on Amazon's website. Amazon has provided the information requested except for the identities of the customers.

Analysis

The court finds that the main issue with the subpoena is that it allows the government to examine the reading habits of specific individuals without their prior knowledge or permission. However, the court also finds that the government has a "bona fide" need to contact and interview at least some of the people who bought books from the alleged criminal seller on Amazon.Com. The court finds that the government is not entitled to unrestricted access to the identities of even a small sample of this group without each book buyer's permission.

CONCLUSION

The court ultimately holds that finding volunteer witnesses from the pool of customers who bought books from the seller will be the best way to satisfy the governments needs without violating first amendment rights of the customers. Amazon will send letters that will allow any used book buyer who chooses to cooperate with the investigation to contact the government and arrange an interview.

In re Grand Jury Subpoena to Amazon.com, Inc.
Procedure

***In re Grand Jury Subpoena to Amazon.com, Inc.*, 246 F.R.D. 570 (W.D. Wis. 2007)**

ISSUE

Whether the court should grant defendants motion to unseal the record of the subpoena dispute between Amazon and the Grand Jury where there has been an indictment against the criminal seller of used books on Amazon.Com.

RULE

F.R. Crim. P. 6(e)(2) states that "No obligation of secrecy may be imposed on any person except in accordance with Rule 6(e)(2)(B)," which does not list grand jury witnesses. Rule 6(e)(6) states that "Records, orders and subpoenas relating to grand jury proceedings must be kept under seal to the extent and as long as necessary to prevent the unauthorized disclosure of a matter occurring before the grand jury."

CASE DETAILS

Facts

The grand jury returned an indictment against a bookseller accused of tax evasion and wire fraud. Amazon.Com Inc. (Amazon) sent the court a letter asking this court to keep its promise to unseal the record of the subpoena dispute between Amazon and the grand jury. The U.S. attorney's office responded and said that all documents related to this dispute will remain sealed. Amazon subsequently filed a reply brief where it limited its request to its own submissions and the court's orders.

Analysis

The court finds that there is no longer a reason to maintain the secrecy of the courts orders mediating the subpoena dispute because Amazon has already provided documents pursuant to the uncontested part of the subpoena, and an indictment has already been issued. Further the court finds that since the grand jury removed the challenged sections of its subpoena, that the court's sealed orders did not result in the production of any evidence to the grand jury. Thus, unsealing the orders would not disclose any information obtained and used as part of the investigation.

CONCLUSION

The court ordered that Amazon's motion to unseal its own motions and briefs and this court's orders is granted.

In Re Zappos.com Inc.
Procedure

***In re Zappos, Inc.*, 893 F. Supp. 2d 1058 (D. Nev. 2012).**

ISSUE

Should the court grant defendant, Zappos' motion to compel arbitration and stay action?

RULE

The Federal Arbitration Act (FAA) states that, "contractual arbitration agreements shall be valid, irrevocable, and enforceable, save upon such grounds as exist at law or in equity for the revocation of any contract."

CASE DETAILS

Facts

This case was commenced following a security breach of servers belonging to defendant, Amazon.com who was in business with Zappos.com. Plaintiffs are Zappos customers whose personal information was on the Zappos page while they were purchasing goods. This particular motion discussed Zappos' motion to compel arbitration and stay action.

While Amazon.com is a named defendant, they claim that Amazon does not do business with Zappos and is incorrectly named as a party to this suit.

CONCLUSION

Zappos' motion to compel arbitration and stay action was denied because the party had not previously agreed to arbitrate. Additionally, the court found "there is no contract and even if there was, it would be illusory and therefore unenforceable.

*This is based on two separate opinions, the information in this case can also be found in *In Re Zappos.com Inc., Customer Data Security Breach Litigation.* 893 F. Supp.2d 1058. No. 3:12-CV-00325-RCV-VCP. September 27, 2012. In both of the documents, the notes indicate that Amazon was a named defendant, however contend that Amazon does not do business with Zappos.com and is therefore incorrectly named.

In re Zappos.Com, Inc.
Breach of Contract

***In re Zappos.com, Inc.*, 2013 U.S. Dist. LEXIS 128155, 2013 WL 4830497 (D. Nev. Sept. 9, 2013).**

ISSUE

Should the court grant the motion to dismiss?

RULE

This court follows the rule provided in the Federal Rules of Civil Procedure Rule 8(a)(2) which requires "only a short and plain statement of the claim showing that the pleader is entitled to relief." Additionally, the court looks to Rule 12(b)(6) which "mandates that a court dismiss a cause of action that fails to state a claim upon which relief can be granted."

CASE DETAILS

Facts

The case was commenced following a security breach of servers belonging to defendant, Zappos.com. Plaintiffs are Zappos customers whose personal information was on the Zappos page while they were purchasing goods. This is a motion to dismiss.

On June 14, 2012, the defendant's motion to transfer six extra-district actions to the current district was granted. Among those cases were Richards v. Amazon.com, Stevens v. Amazon.com, Penson v. Amazon.com, Elliott v. Amazon.com, and Habashy v. Amazon.com.

Analysis

The court found that the Plaintiffs have "sufficiently alleged that they have had to pay money to monitor their credit scores and secure their financial information due to the increased risk of criminal fraud against them occasioned by defendant's negligent loss of their personal information.

The court dismissed the claims for public disclosure of private facts and violation of the FCRA because Zappos was not alleged to have intentionally disclosed the plaintiff's personal information during the security breach.

The court additionally, dismissed the contractual claims because there was no evidence of an express or implied contract between the customers and Zappos.com.

The court treated the negligence claims as negligent misrepresentation claims and found that the claim against Zappos for negligently misstating the safety was not barred by the economic loss doctrine.

For the unjust enrichment claims, the court found that the plaintiff did not allege having bestowed any gratuitous benefit upon defendant and dismissed the claim.

The court dismissed the claim for declaratory relief finding that "as it is on its face duplicative of the causes of action elsewhere directly asserted."

When looking to the statutory claims, the court did find that the plaintiffs successfully stated a claim for the violation of California Business Professional Code Section 172000 and for California Civil Code Section 1798.80.

For the claim under FLA.STAT. Section 501.201. the court dismissed the claim finding that the plaintiffs needed to make a more definite statement.

For the claim under the Massachusetts statute, the court dismissed. Additionally, the court dismissed the claims under the Nevada Deceptive Trade Practices Act.

The court did not dismiss the claim under the New York Deceptive Trade Practices Act.

For the claim under the TEX. BUS. & COM.CODE Section 17.41, the court dismissed. Yet, the court did not dismiss the claim alleging that defendant was in violation of 17.50(a)(3).

For the claim under the Virginia Consumer Protection Act, the court dismissed.

The court found that the plaintiffs have sufficiently alleged a violation of section 19.225.010.

CONCLUSION

The United States District Court denied in part and granted in part the motions to dismiss brought by defendant Zappos.com and Amazon.com.

In re Zappos.Com, Inc.
Procedure

***In re Zappos.com, Inc.*, 108 F. Supp. 3d 949 (D. Nev. 2015)**

ISSUE

Should the court grant the defendant's motion to dismiss, motion to strike, and motion for leave?

RULE

Pursuant to the Federal Rule of Civil Procedure, Rule 12(b)(1), "Lack of standing is a defect in subject-matter jurisdiction and may properly be challenged."

CASE DETAILS

Facts

The case was commenced following a security breach of servers belonging to defendant, Zappos.com. On June 14, 2012, the defendant's motion to transfer six extra-district actions to the current district was granted.

Here, defendant Amazon.com filed a motion to dismiss, defendant Zappos.com filed a motion to strike Prayers for Punitive Damages and Restitution, and a motion for leave to file excess pages.

Analysis

Zappos argued that the plaintiffs have a lack of standing because they have not alleged any actual damages. The court found that for the issue of decreased value in plaintiff's personal information, the plaintiff's did not allege any facts supporting this claim and therefore do not have standing. The court additionally found that the plaintiffs did not allege any facts to support a claim for threat of future harm against Zappos.

The court granted Zappos' motion to dismiss; yet they also granted the plaintiff's leave to amend their complaints.

CONCLUSION

The District Court granted the motion to dismiss, denied the motion to strike, and granted the motion for leave.

Infinite Data LLC v. Amazon.com Inc. (D. Del., 2014)
Patent Infringement

***Infinite Data LLC v. Amazon.com Inc.*, 2014 U.S. Dist. LEXIS 8849 (D. Del. Jan. 23, 2014).**

ISSUE

The issue here is whether the court should grant a motion to stay (motion to temporarily delay judicial proceedings) in order to simplify the issues for trial by litigating against Mellanox Technologies (the creator of the technology at issue) first in order to help determine the issues of infringement and invalidity.

RULE

"The standard for granting a stay is: (1) whether granting the stay will simplify the issues for trial; (2) whether discovery is complete and a trial date is set; and (3) whether granting a stay would cause the non-moving party to suffer undue prejudice from any delay, or a clear tactical disadvantage. *Vehicle IP LLC v. Wal-Mart Stores, Inc.*, 2010 WL 4823393, *1 (D.Del. 2010).

CASE DETAILS

Facts

In this case the judge was assigned twenty-one cases in which plaintiff Infinite Data has sued for patent infringement. In another case, Mellanox Technologies has sued plaintiff, seeking a declaratory judgment that its technology does not infringe plaintiff's patent, and that the patent is invalid. Plaintiff counterclaims that Mellanox's technology does infringe its patent. Mellanox has alleged that "many" of the defendants in this action have sent Mellanox indemnification requests; most of them are users / customers of Mellanox technology.

All twenty-one defendants have filed motions to stay. Defendants claim that they do use Mellanox technology and that the Mellanox case should thus be decided first.

Analysis

The court first notes that the second prong of the rule favors a stay. The motions have been filed at the beginning of the case. At this stage, a trial date had not been set.

As to the first prong, the court holds that Mellanox knows its technology better than the defendants do and is in the best position to litigate the issues of infringement and invalidity. Thus it is likely that the issues will be simplified if Mellanox litigation takes place first.

As to the third prong, the court states that there is always prejudice in delay, but that here, the delay can be compensated by monetary damages.

CONCLUSION

The court finds that a stay would likely help simplify the issues, but that fairness to the plaintiff must be considered as well. Plaintiff did not sue Mellanox and the court believes defendants should have only one shot at invalidity. Thus, the court holds that defendants who want Mellanox to take that "shot" for them will be bound to that decision and granted a stay, and those defendants who want to be able to litigate invalidity will be denied a stay and will litigate on the same schedule as Mellanox.

Innovative Office Prods. v. Amazon.com, Inc.
Patent Infringement; Procedure

***Innovative Office Prods. v. Amazon.com, Inc.*, 2012 U.S. Dist. LEXIS 59090 (E.D. Pa. Apr. 26, 2012).**

ISSUE

Whether the court should enter default judgment in favor of plaintiff, Innovative Office Products.

RULE

The United States Court of Appeals for the Third Circuit established that three factors govern a district court's determination as to whether a default judgment should be entered: "(1) prejudice to the plaintiff if default is denied; (2) whether the defendant appeals to have a litigable defense, and (3) whether defendant's delay is due to culpable conduct."

CASE DETAILS

Facts

This was a patent infringement case brought by Innovative Office Productions against Amazon.com, eBay Inc., Alibaba.com, S. Link, Zeetron, GainGame, Lapworks, Neoteric Solution, iGear USA LLC, and Bafbiz. Plaintiff alleged that their 293 and 719 patents were infringed. Amazon.com was voluntarily dismissed from the action.

Innovative Office moved for an entry of default judgment and a permanent injunction.

Analysis

The court found that Innovative Office would suffer prejudice if the request for default judgment were denied. Additionally, the court found the elements weighed in favor of a permanent injunction.

CONCLUSION

The court granted the plaintiffs motion.

International Game Tech. v. Dist. Court
Procedure

Int'l Game Tech., Inc. v. Second Judicial Dist. Court, 122 Nev. 132 (Nev. 2006).

ISSUE

Whether the District Court (lower court) abused its discretion by improperly refusing to dismiss defendants action.

RULE

Nevada's False Claim Act, codified at Nev. Rev. Stat. ch. 357, permits persons to become "private attorneys general," which grants them the right and financial incentive to sue on behalf of the State and its political subdivisions if money, property or services provided by the State, or its political subdivisions, are involved.

A writ of mandamus is available to compel the performance of an act that the law requires as a duty resulting from an office, trust or station, or to control an arbitrary or capricious exercise of discretion, and is appropriate when a district court manifestly abuses its discretion by improperly refusing to dismiss an action. A writ of prohibition is the counterpart to a writ of mandamus and is available when a district court acts without or in excess of its jurisdiction. *State of Nevada v. Dist. Ct. (Anzalone)*, 118 Nev. 140, 146-47, 42 P.3d 233, 237 (2002).

CASE DETAILS

Facts

In this case, petitioners challenge the decisions of respondents, district courts and district court judges, who refused to dismiss actions brought under Nevada's False Claims Act (FCA). The real party in interest, retailer Amazon.com Inc., et al joined the petition.

Plaintiffs, who were private citizens in the underlying suit, brought false claims actions based on alleged tax deficiencies against the retailers. In his motion, the Attorney General argued, inter alia, that good cause existed for dismissal. Petitioners, in their request for relief, asserted that the district courts wrongfully applied the good cause standard by which the Attorney General could move to dismiss false claims actions. Similarly, in the second case, the Attorney General articulated a legitimate government purpose for dismissing the actions.

Analysis

The supreme court concluded that the Attorney General's assertion that these FCA actions implicated issues that were better left to the tax department's expertise constituted a basis for good cause dismissal; however, the supreme court did not preclude the possibility that some tax matters could be brought under the FCA. In the instant cases, though, no party demonstrated that the Attorney General acted improperly in moving to dismiss the underlying actions; therefore, the district courts manifestly abused their discretion when they refused to dismiss the underlying tax-based false claims actions for good cause.

CONCLUSION

The court granted the writs of mandamus. The supreme court directed the district courts to grant the motions to dismiss the underlying false claims actions.

IPXL Holdings, L.L.C. v. Amazon.com, Inc.
Patent Infringement

***IPXL Holdings, L.L.C. v. Amazon.com, Inc.*, 333 F. Supp. 2d 513 (E.D. Va. 2004).**

ISSUE

Whether there is a claim for patent infringement with use of a similar product system.

RULE

A court may determine there is no claim for infringement when the products in dispute have different features and do not exceed the patent limitations.

CASE DETAILS

Facts

Plaintiff alleges the defendant's "1-Click" ordering feature infringes on their patent. Amazon has a "1-Click" ordering feature for customers to place orders quickly, the plaintiff claims they are the rightful owner of that patent.

Analysis

Here, the court finds that defendant's system features do not exceed the limitations of the plaintiff's patent and therefor do not qualify as a patent infringement. IPXL's argument produces no genuine issue of material fact to support a valid claim. The claim is invalid and indefinite because the plaintiff's make an effort to claim both a system and a method for using that system.

CONCLUSION

The court grants Amazon's motion for summary judgment on the issue of the claim being invalid because the plaintiff cannot claim infringement on a system and method for using it. The court denies the plaintiff's summary judgment the patent is obvious.

IPXL Holdings, L.L.C. v. Amazon.com, Inc.
Patent Infringement

***IPXL Holdings, L.L.C. v. Amazon.com, Inc.*, 430 F.3d 1377 (Fed. Cir. 2005).**

ISSUE

Whether Amazon's system infringed the appellant's patent to make a valid claim to survive summary judgment.

RULE

A party that makes a claim stating they own a patent for a device and the method steps for using it is invalid because a seller of the device would not know a user of the device would later perform the claimed method.

CASE DETAILS

Facts

Appellant patent owner sued defendant alleging the seller's system for business transactions with customers infringed on the owner's patent. The patent owner appealed the orders of the lower court which granted summary judgment to the defendant and awarded attorney fees as well.

Analysis

The district court erred in granting Amazon attorney fees, Amazon did not file a timely request. The district court properly granted Amazon summary judgment for the infringement claim.

CONCLUSION

The court affirmed summary judgment for the patent infringement claim and reversed the order awarding attorney fees to Amazon because the award was improper.

Joseph v. Amazon.com, Inc., et al.
Antitrust Law Violations

***Joseph v. Amazon.com, Inc.*, 46 F. Supp. 3d 1095, 2014 U.S. Dist. LEXIS 121050, 42 Media L. Rep. 2496 (W.D. Wash. 2014).**

ISSUE

Whether Amazon should be granted summary judgment for alleged antitrust violations?

RULE

A court may grant summary judgment when the opposing party does not provide any facts to show there is a genuine issue of material fact to proceed to trial.

CASE DETAILS

Facts

The plaintiff here is bringing a federal antitrust claim against defendant, Amazon, alleging an unlawful "tying" arrangement, libel, malice, personal injury, and breach of contract.

Analysis

The plaintiff failed to allege Amazon has made continuing violations or that Amazon coerced a business arrangement to support their action. Amazon's standard Conditions of Use clearly state that customer's posting reviews own the content and give Amazon permission to use it, Amazon does not publish any of the reviews and has not willingly harmed the plaintiff in anyway. Amazon is allowed immunity from the plaintiff's claims of libel. Amazon is entitled to summary judgment for the plaintiff's claim involving breach of contract. Amazon is also entitled to judgment on the pleadings for the malice and personal injury claims.

CONCLUSION

The court grants Amazon's motion for summary judgment and/or judgment on the pleadings. Plaintiff's motion for summary judgment is denied because the plaintiff did not provide evidence to show Amazon harmed him.

JVW Enters. v. Amazon.com, Inc.
Patent Infringement

***JVW Enters. v. Amazon.com, Inc.*, 175 Fed. Appx. 344 (Fed. Cir. 2006).**

ISSUE

Whether a prior court decision that was reversed and remanded should be vacated and remanded for further proceedings.

RULE

A court may vacate and remand a case if a ruling in a case has been reversed in part.

CASE DETAILS

Facts

JVW previously sued a wholesaler for patent infringement and no infringement was found so JVW appealed. The district court's decision was reversed in part and remanded in part.

Analysis

Since the district court reversed the previous case in part and remanded in part, the court should vacate and remand this case.

CONCLUSION

The court grants the appellant's motion to vacate judgment and grants remand to hear the case with a prior defendant that has come out of bankruptcy and is now a valid party. All sides will pay for their own costs.

Kabbaj v. Google, Inc.
Procedure

***Kabbaj v. Google, Inc.*, 2014 U.S. Dist. LEXIS 47425 (D. Del. Apr. 7, 2014).**

ISSUE

Whether the court should grant defendants motion to dismiss where they are merely the hosts of defamatory content created by a third party.

RULE

Under Federal Rule 12(b)(6), a motion to dismiss may be granted only if, accepting the well-pleaded allegations in the complaint as true and viewing them in the light most favorable to the plaintiff a court concludes that those allegations "could not raise a claim of entitlement to relief." *Bell Atl. Corp. v. Twombly*, 550 U.S. 544, 558 (2007).

§ 230 of the Communications Decency Act provides, "immunity requires three elements: (1) defendant must be a provider or user of an interactive computer service; (2) the asserted claims must treat defendant as a publisher or speaker of information and (3) the challenged communication must be "information provided by another information content provider."

CASE DETAILS

Facts

In this case, plaintiff's amended complaint alleged that unknown third parties authored and posted online content that defamed plaintiff. Plaintiff further alleges that defendants are liable because this content was allegedly hosted on services operated by defendants Google, Inc., Amazon.com Inc., and Yahoo! Inc. Plaintiff has claims against defendants for: (1) declatory and injunctive relief; (2) tortious interference with a contract; (3) negligent and intentional infliction of emotional distress; and (4) libel per se. The complaint particularly alleges that Amazon created several accounts wherein it published / sold novels authored by third-parties and published user comments that defamed plaintiffs.

Analysis

The court first notes that each defendant is an interactive computer service provider. Under § 230r an interactive computer service is "any information service, system, or access software provider that provides or enables computer access by multiple users to a computer server." 47 U.S.C. § 230 (f)(2). Amazon's services (including its online bookstore) fall into this category of interactive computer service provider.

Next, the court holds that if a defendant did not create or author the statement in controversy but rather is provided that statement by a third-party information content provider, then that defendant cannot be held liable under the act. Here, the amended complaint does not allege that ant defendant created or authored the defamatory statements. Since plaintiff is seeking to impose liability for information provided by "another information content provider," § 230 applies to the claims.

Finally, the court finds that Plaintiff's claims are attempting to tread defendants as the publisher of a third party's statements. The court holds that defendants are immune under the Act against Plaintiff's allegations because they cannot be held liable for opting to publish a third party's statements.

Ultimately the court finds the amended complaint does not state, nor will it be able to state, any viable claims against defendants with respect to their decision to publish third party statements. The defendants motion to dismiss is granted.

CONCLUSION

For the foregoing reasons the court will: (1) Grant defendants' motions to dismiss; (2) deny plaintiffs motions for leave to amend; (3) and dismiss as moot the remaining motions.

Kelley v. Amazon.com, Inc.
Employee's Rights

Kabbaj v. Google, Inc., 2014 U.S. Dist. LEXIS 47425 (D. Del. Apr. 7, 2014).

ISSUE

Whether a court should grant summary judgment for a defendant who terminated an employee.

RULE

A court may grant summary judgment to a party that demonstrates there is no genuine dispute of material fact that would affect the outcome of the case and the employee was rightfully terminated.

Case Details

Facts

This is a wrongful termination and employee's rights case. Plaintiff Jodie Kelley alleges that her former employer, a subsidiary of Amazon.com, Inc., violated state and federal law by failing to accommodate her disabilities and relying upon her requests for medical leave as a reason for terminating her employment. Throughout her employment at Amazon, Plaintiff experienced frequent migraine headaches and struggled with pain and other symptoms caused by endometriosis.

Jodie Kelley began working for Defendant Amazon in 2006 as a Customer Service Associate in Amazon's call center in Kennewick, Washington. Her primary responsibility in this position was to assist Amazon.com customers with problems or questions related to their online purchases over the telephone. Like all Amazon CSAs, Plaintiff's job performance was measured in terms of Expressed Dissatisfaction Rate or EDR. This metric captured the percentage of a particular CSA's customers whose problems the CSA was unable to resolve.

In February 2008, Plaintiff was promoted to a Customer Service Lead position. In this role, Plaintiff was responsible for coaching and assisting other CSAs in meeting Amazon's performance expectations, monitoring call volumes, assisting with team meetings, helping customers who asked to speak with a manager, and filing escalation requests. In August 2009, Plaintiff voluntarily stepped down from this position for medical reasons and in anticipation of attending cosmetology school. Plaintiff continued to work for Amazon on a part-time basis as a CSA assigned to the "Search and Rescue Team." In that role, Plaintiff's primary responsibility was to handle customer problems and complaints that had not been resolved during the customer's initial contact with a customer service representative.

In October 2009, Plaintiff resumed full-time employment as a CSA on the Search and Rescue Team. Shortly thereafter, Plaintiff's job performance began to decline. In November 2009, Plaintiff was placed on a performance improvement plan after her EDR slightly exceeded the Search and Rescue Team's assigned goal. Plaintiff successfully completed this plan.

In July 2010, however, Plaintiff again exceeded her assigned EDR goal and was placed on another performance plan but failed to meet the requirements of this plan. As a result, Plaintiff was issued a verbal warning and placed on another performance plan in August 2010, yet failed to meet these conditions as well. In the weeks that followed, Plaintiff's EDR scores continued to exceed her team's assigned goals.

In November 2010, Plaintiff was issued a written warning and placed on a third consecutive performance plan. She was also provided additional training and coaching in an effort to improve her performance. During the course of this training, Plaintiff's supervisor and others noted that Plaintiff "had a problem with her tone while dealing with customers and was not taking enough time with each customer. She came across as unapologetic, distracted, short, uninterested, uncaring and rushed."

Despite receiving this additional coaching, Plaintiff failed to meet the requirements of the November Plan. She was placed on a final performance improvement plan in February 2011. Plaintiff was also issued a Final Written Warning advising her that failure to comply with the Final Plan could result in termination. Ultimately, Plaintiff's performance did not improve. When she failed to meet the expectations outlined in the Final Plan, Amazon terminated her employment.

Analysis

Plaintiff acknowledges that she did not specifically inform Amazon that her performance issues were related to her disabilities. Nevertheless, she insists that

Amazon, upon discovering a connection between her performance issues and medical issues, Kelley states that Amazon would have been required to grant her a performance-related accommodation.

Kelley's argument is ineffective. As a threshold matter, the evidence of a causal relationship between Plaintiff's deficient performance and her disabilities is entirely speculative. Aside from Plaintiff's self-serving "belief" that the two were connected, the only evidence to potentially support such a finding is the conclusory opinion of Plaintiff's gynecologist that the two might be related: "The symptoms caused by Plaintiff's migraines and endometriosis] have an effect on Ms. Kelley's interaction with others, whether in person or over the telephone. When experiencing these symptoms, one would experience different inflections in their voice, and come across with a different "tone." Ms. Kelley would experience at times a frustration which might come across in how she was dealing with customers."

CONCLUSION

The court grants the defendant's motion for Summary Judgment and denies the plaintiff's cross-motion for Summary Judgment, there is no evidence to support the plaintiff's claims.

Kousnsky v. Amazon.Com, Inc.
Copyright Infringement

***Kousnsky v. Amazon.com, Inc.*, 2014 U.S. Dist. LEXIS 185880 (S.D.N.Y. May 13, 2014).**

ISSUE

Whether a copyright claim should be dismissed if a party bringing suit does not sufficiently state the components of copyright infringement.

RULE

A case may be dismissed if a plaintiff fails to state factual evidence showing the other party should be liable for copyright infringement.

CASE DETAILS

Facts

The plaintiff alleges the defendants infringed his copyright by publishing, selling, and distributing works of art created by the plaintiff. The plaintiff had an agreement with a publisher to allow the reproduction of his images for customers and does not limit any sales.

Analysis

The use of the image was authorized by the copyright owner so there is no evidence to show the defendants are liable for any misconduct.

CONCLUSION

The court grants the motion to dismiss the case, the plaintiff did not provide evidence to survive a motion for judgment.

Kounsky v. Amazon.com, Inc.
Copyright Infringement

***Kousnsky v. Amazon.Com, Inc.*, 631 Fed. Appx. 22, 2015 U.S. App. LEXIS 20380, Copy. L. Rep. (CCH) P30,849 (2d Cir. N.Y. 2015).**

ISSUE

Whether a court should allow amendment to a complaint to include specific details not previously heard.

RULE

A court may allow a complaint to be amended if the additional information will help satisfy the elements to state a claim.

Case Details

Facts

Plaintiff Isack Kousnsky signed an agreement with third-party company Pyramid, allowing them to "publish, promote, sell and distribute photography provided by [Kousnsky] in all size posters and print format . . . by any means [Pyramid] reasonably uses now or in the future."

Later, Kousnsky sued Amazon for copyright infringement for failing to take corrective action when he notified them that a third party was infringing his rights by selling his artwork on Amazon's website.

Analysis

The Agreement between the two parties gave Pyramid the exclusive rights to the artwork; therefore, Kousnsky could not bring a copyright infringement claim against Pyramid for selling his work pursuant to the terms of the Agreement.

CONCLUSION

The Court dismissed the case because not only did the Plaintiff fail to make out a cause of action against the third party who allegedly infringed, Plaintiff also failed to show any duty on the part of Amazon to take corrective action or any alleged infringing conduct by Amazon.

Lasoff v. Amazon.com, Inc.
Trademark Infringement, Antitrust Violations, Unfair Business Practices

---

***Lasoff v. Amazon.com, Inc.*, 2016 U.S. Dist. LEXIS 9878, 2016 WL 355076 (D.N.J. Jan. 28, 2016).**

ISSUE

Whether a venue transfer should be granted when an agreement signed by both parties states the proper venue.

RULE

A court may allow venue transfer when private and public interest factors are not harmed in doing so and it is convenient for all parties and the venue agreement signed is reasonable.

CASE DETAILS

Facts

Plaintiff is an Amazon seller suing Amazon in New Jersey for trademark infringement, anti-trust violations and unfair practices claims after Amazon allegedly allowed other sellers to sell similar products under Plaintiff's trademark.

Pursuant to the forum selection clause of the agreement seller entered into with Amazon prior to selling its products on Amazon's site, Amazon asked the court to transfer this case to Washington. The Court agreed with Amazon and granted its request to transfer the case to Washington.

Analysis

The agreement between both parties contains a choice of law provision requiring a Washington court to apply that law. There are no public or local interests that strongly go against having the case heard in Washington.

CONCLUSION

The court grants the defendant's motion to transfer venue to the United States District Court for the Western District of Washington because it was agreed upon in a signed contract.

Lexington Luminance LLC v. Amazon.com
Procedure; Patent Infringement

***Lexington Luminance LLC v. Amazon.com, Inc.*, 6 F. Supp. 3d 179 (D. Mass. 2014).**

ISSUE

Should the court grant Amazon's motion for judgment on the pleadings?

RULE

According to 35 U.S.C. Section 282(a), "Patents are presumed valid by finding claims indefinite only if reasonable efforts claim construction prove futile, courts have accord respect to the statutory presumption of validity and we do protect the inventive contribution of patentees, even when the drafting of their patents has been less than ideal".

Pursuant to Rule 12(c) of the Federal Rules of Civil Procedure, a party may move for judgment on the pleadings.

CASE DETAILS

Facts

The 851 patent relates to the "fabrication of semiconductor devices such as light-emitting devices in misfit systems". The patent describes, "trenches having a sloped etching profile with a smooth rotation of micro-facets without a prescribed angle of inclination". In 2012, Lexington sued Amazon.com and Amazon Digital Services alleging that the Kindle e-readers created by amazon were in violation of patent infringement of the 851 patent.

Amazon moved for judgment on the pleadings. The parties also have argued their proposed claim constructions. The proposed constructions are to define the terms, "trenches", "having", "micro-facets", "sloped etching profile with a smooth rotation of microfacets", "a sloped etching profile without a prescribed angle of inclination", "so as to guide the extended lattice defects away from propagating into the active layer", and "said substrate is selected rom the group comprising"

Analysis

The court found that the claim failed to narrow the composition of the substrate to any degree of substantial certainty. Ultimately, the court found claim 1 of the 851 patent to be indefinite.

CONCLUSION

The District Court allowed Amazon's motion for judgment on the pleadings. Judgment was entered on Amazon's counterclaim for a declaration of invalidity in its favor and Lexington's complaint was dismissed.

Lexington Luminance LLC v. Amazon.com.
Procedure; Patent Infringement

***Lexington Luminance LLC v. Amazon.com Inc.*, 601 Fed. Appx. 963 (Fed. Cir. 2015).**

ISSUE

Whether the court of appeals should revers the district court's holding that plaintiff's patent claims patent ineligible subject matter.

RULE

Following the holding in *Nautilus, INC., v. Biosig Instruments*, "A patent claim is invalid for indefiniteness if its language, when read in light of the specification and the prosecution history, fails to inform, with reasonable certainty, those skilled in the art about the scope of the invention".

CASE DETAILS

Facts

Lexington Luminance, plaintiff, appealed from a District Court construing claim of U.S. Patent 6,936,851 (the 851 patent) and granting judgment on the pleadings that the claim was indefinite.

The 851 patent relates to the "fabrication of semiconductor devices such as light-emitting devices in misfit systems". The patent describes, "trenches having a sloped etching profile with a smooth rotation of micro-facets without a prescribed angle of inclination". In 2012, Lexington sued Amazon.com and Amazon Digital Services alleging that the Kindle e-readers created by amazon were in violation of patent infringement of the 851 patent. Both partied filed claim construction briefs and the district court granted amazon's motion. The court rejected Lexington's proposed construction of "Trenches" based on the 851 patent's disclosure that the "substrate surface features can be mesas." Additionally, the court rejected Lexington's proposed constructions of "having" and "sloped etching profile with a smoother rotation of micro-facts without a prescribed angle of inclination".

Amazon motioned for judgment on the pleadings alleging that claim 1 was indefinite on two grounds. First that the expression "as as to guide the extended lattice defects away from propagating into the active layer" which would render the claim indefinite. Additionally, Amazon argued that the claim was indefinite because of its use of the phrase "said substrate is selected from the group compromising group III-V, group IV, group II-VI elements and alloys, ZnO, spinel and sapphire". The district court granted Amazon's motion on this ground.

In March of 2014, the district court entered a final judgment of invalidity.

<u>Analysis</u>

The court first found that the district court erred in holding the claim indefinite in reciting an open Markush group. When analyzing what definiteness involves, the court found that it involve more than "an examination of the technical correctness of the use of a Markush expression that may have slipped past the examining process." They add that it involves evaluation of the claim in light of the written description. The court concluded that the meaning of the contested claim language is that "the substrate must contain one or more of the enumerated members of the claimed group." The court of appeals found that the district court erred in finding the claim to be indefinite because of the imperfect usage of Markush terminology.

Additionally, the court found that Amazon's argument that the district court erred in not invalidating the claim for indefiniteness based on the expression "so as to guide the extended lattice defects away from propagating into the active layer" to be unpersuasive. The court concluded that claim 1 of the 851 patent is not invalid for indefiniteness and vacate the judgment of invalidity.

The court of appeals held that the district court erred in construing "trenches" and adopted Lexington's proposed meaning to be "areas in the surface of the substrate from which some amount of material is removed in order to create a pattern on the surface of the substrate.

Finally, the court vacated the district court's constructions of "sloped etching profile with a smooth rotation of micro-facets and sloped etching profile without a prescribed angle of inclination and remanded for the district court to construe those limitations in a manner that does not exclude figures 2b and 4b."

CONCLUSION

The United States Court of Appeals found that the district court erred in construing the claim and in holding the claim indefinite. The court remands.

eLexington Luminance LLC v. Amazon Digital Servs. *Patent Infringement; Procedure*

***Lexington Luminance LLC v. Amazon Digital Servs.*, 2016 U.S. Dist. LEXIS 46023 (D. Mass. Apr. 4, 2016).**

ISSUE

Whether the court should construe the disputed claim terms?

RULE

Claim construction is a question of law for the court. *Markman v. Westview Instruments, Inc.*, 517 U.S. 370, 388-389 (1996). The construction that stays true to the claim language and most naturaly aligns with the patent's description of the invention will be, in the end, the correct construction. *Phillips v. AWH Corp.*, 415 F.3d 1303, 1316 (Fed. Cir. 2005).

CASE DETAILS

Facts:

Plaintiff filed a lawsuit for patent infringement against Amazon.com and Amazon Digital Services Inc. The suit is on remand from the Federal Circuit for claim construction of the alleged patents-in-suit.

Timeline:

Lexington filed this lawsuit on November 29, 2012. Amazon filed its answer and counterclaims, asserting an invalidity defense and a counterclaim for a declaratory judgment that the patent is invalid. Amazon then moved for judgment on the pleadings on the defense.

Analysis:

The court construed the terms in the patents in suit as follows:

- "whereby said plurality of inclined lower portions are configured to guide extended lattice defects away from propagating into the active layer" constitutes a limitation and does not require any construction

- "a sloped etching profile . . . without a prescribed angle of inclination" means "sloped etched sides without a specified angle of inclination and the term "etching" is three-dimensional
- "a sloped smooth etching profile . . . without a prescribed angle of inclination" means "a sloped [*39] smooth etched side without a specified angle of inclination;"
- "the sides of said etched trenches are without a prescribed angle of inclination" means" the sides of said etched trenches are without specified angle of inclination;"
- "a sloped etching profile with a smooth rotation of micro-facets" means "sloped etched sides without sharp corners."

CONCLUSION

The court set forth claim construction of the disputed terms, and defined them as found above.

Masck v. Sports Illustrated
Copyright Infringement; Procedural- Motion to Dismiss

***Masck v. Sports Illustrated*, 2013 U.S. Dist. LEXIS 81677 (E.D. Mich. June 11, 2013).**

ISSUE

Whether the court should grant the Defendants' Motion to Dismiss?

RULE

Federal Rule of Civil Procedure12(b)(6) allows the court to make an assessment as to whether the plaintiff has stated a claim upon which relief may be granted. See Fed. R. Civ. P. 12(b)(6). "Federal Rule of Civil Procedure 8(a)(2) requires only 'a short and plain statement of the claim showing that the pleader is entitled to relief,' in order to 'give the defendant fair notice of what the ... claim is and the grounds upon which it rests.'" *Bell Atlantic Corp. v. Twombly*, 550 U.S. 544, 555, 127 S. Ct. 1955, 167 L. Ed. 2d 929 (2007) (citing *Conley v. Gibson*, 355 U.S. 41, 47, 78 S. Ct. 99, 2 L. Ed. 2d 80 (1957). Even though the complaint need not contain "detailed" factual allegations, its "factual allegations must be enough to raise a right to relief above the speculative level on the assumption that all of the allegations in the complaint are true." *Ass'n of Cleveland Fire Fighters v. City of Cleveland*, 502 F.3d 545, 548 (6th Cir. 2007) (quoting *Bell Atlantic*, 550 U.S. at 555).

CASE DETAILS

Facts:

Plaintiff took an iconic photo of Defendant Desmond Howard on November 23, 1991 at Michigan Stadium. The photo was taken of Howard after running back a punt for a touchdown during a football game. Plaintiff alleged he was the only photographer who got a sharp shot of this now iconic pose. Plaintiff made a copy of the photo and sent it to Sports Illustrated for publication in a planned issue. Plaintiff did not register the photo with the Copyright Office until August 31, 2011. Plaintiff found out Getty had the image, and filed a lawsuit against multiple defendants alleging copyright infringement.

Analysis:

Copyright infringement lends itself readily to abusive litigation. Therefore, greater particularity in pleading through showing 'plausible grounds' is required. *Nat'l Bus. Dev. Servs. Inc.*, 299 F. App'x at 512. Plaintiff only states that Amazon has the right and ability to supervise the content of its website Amazon.com. This does not meet the pleading requirement as there are no factual allegations from which it may determine that Amazon had the ability to supervise the infringing conduct. The product in question is not Amazon's website but the merchandise sold on its website. However, Amazon was well aware of the potential infringement because plaintiff requested the products be removed from Amazon's website.

CONCLUSION

The court determined that the contributory infringement claim survives, while the vicarious infringement motion must be dismissed.

Masck v. Sports Illustrated
Procedure; Copyright Infringement

***Masck v. Sports Illustrated*, 5 F.Supp.3d 881 (E.D. Mich., 2014)**

ISSUE

The issue here is whether the court should grant defendants motion for summary judgment where plaintiff has waited to register the copyright until after several violations of the copyright occurred.

RULE

"Under the Copyright Act, a plaintiff can only recover "an award of statutory damages ... with respect to any one work, for which any one infringer is liable individually, or for which any two or more infringers are liable jointly and severally, in a sum of not less that $750 or more than $30,000 as the court considers just." 17 U.S.C § 504(c)(1). The infringement starts when the first infringing act occurs. *Johnson v. Jones*, 149 F.3d 494, 504 (6th Cir. 1998).

CASE DETAILS

Facts

This case is a copyright infringement action based on the photo of college football player Desmond Howard ("Howard") taken by plaintiff on November 23, 1991. This photo became iconic because it depicted Howard in what is now known as the "Heisman Pose" which is performed by lifting a leg and stretching out one's left arm. Plaintiff claims he was the only photographer to get a clear image of the pose. Plaintiff wrote "Photo ©" on the cardboard surrounding the original slide he sent to Sports Illustrated ("SI") and was told by his lawyers that this mark was sufficient as a copyright. Thus plaintiff did not register the copyright until August 31, 2011. Over time plaintiff observed many instances of infringing uses of his photograph. The photo was sold on Amazon.com and plaintiff requested with no success that the photo be removed from Amazon.

Analysis

Defendants claim that plaintiff should have filed a copyright earlier, however the court here disagrees and notes that plaintiff acted under the advice of his lawyer not to register the copyright. The court holds that plaintiff provides reasonable explanations for why delays in filing for the copyright may have happened. This leaves a question of fact and makes issuance of summary judgment on the matter relating to Amazon improper.

CONCLUSION

The court holds that because there is a question of fact as to what the actual dates of infringement are as well as whether the facts alleged are sufficient for a damages award, that summary judgment is not proper and a jury must hear this case.

McGee v. Amazon.com
Employee's Rights; Procedural

***McGee v. Amazon.com*, 2013 Del. Super. LEXIS 33 (Del. Super. Ct. Jan. 31, 2013).**

ISSUE

Whether the court should reverse the opinion of the Unemployment Appeals Board to deny McGee compensation benefits?

RULE

On appeal, the Court's review of the UIAB's decision is limited to determining whether the UIAB's findings and conclusions are supported by substantial evidence and free of legal error. Substantial evidence is defined as "such relevant evidence as a reasonable mind might accept as adequate to support a conclusion." Stated alternatively, substantial evidence is "that evidence from which an agency fairly and reasonably could reach the conclusion it did Specifically, "[i]t is more than a scintilla of evidence, but less than a preponderance."

CASE DETAILS

Facts:

McGee was employed by Amazon.com as a warehouse associate from April 2007 to June 2011. He was terminated from his employment on June 17, 2011 due to excessive absenteeism and tardiness. He challenges the UIAB's finding that he was ineligible to receive benefits because he was discharged from work for just cause.

Timeline:

McGee filed a claim for unemployment benefits effective June 19, 2011. The Claims Deputy denied it July 15, as did the Appeals Referee on August 22, 2011. The Unemployment Insurance Appeal Board decided on March 18, 2012 to deny McGee unemployment compensation benefits.

Analysis:

The court determined that there was substantial evidence on the record to support the UIAB's finding that Amazon had just cause to discharge McGee and that this decision was free of legal error.

CONCLUSION

The court affirms the decision of the UIAB.

M-Edge Accessories LLC v. Amazon.Com Inc.
Patent Infringement

***M-Edge Accessories LLC v. Amazon.Com Inc.*, 2013 U.S. Dist. LEXIS 311 (D. Md. Jan. 2, 2013).**

ISSUE

Whether the court should grant summary judgment for patent infringement.

RULE

If after looking at evidence in favor of the non-moving party the court can determine that the sale of a product does not damage the party claiming infringement and is producing fair business competition, there is no infringement.

CASE DETAILS

Facts

M-Edge alleged Amazon infringed on their patent. Amazon moves for summary judgment on all claims and M-Edge moves to strike the testimony of two Amazon expert witnesses. Amazon launched its Kindle Device and M-Edge began to sell Kindle accessories in which M-Edge claims Amazon has infringed on their patent by selling similar accessories.

Analysis

There is a genuine issue of material fact for a "Shasta" pocket cover of the product M-Edge is claiming infringement; summary judgment is denied in relation to that. Amazon is entitled to summary judgment for another cover on the product because it is not substantially the same as M-edge's product. M-Edge has failed to produce evidence to show Amazon was involved in unfair business competition or that Amazon has damaged M-Edge's business in anyway. The court will not exclude one of Amazon's expert testimony because the information may be relevant to provide evidence in trial. The court strikes testimony of one of Amazon's expert witnesses because it is not related to the patent damages and is irrelevant.

CONCLUSION

The court grants summary judgment to Amazon for all claims except the patent infringement claim against the Shasta pocket cover. The court grants M-Edge's motion to strike an expert testimony that is immaterial and denies the motion to strike an expert testimony that is material to the infringement claims.

M-Edge Accessories LLC v. Amazon.com Inc.
Patent Infringement; Procedural; Unfair Competition; Violation of the Lanham Act

---

M-Edge Accessories LLC v. Amazon, Inc., 2013 U.S. Dist. LEXIS 165422 (D. Md. Nov. 21, 2013).

ISSUE

What are the definitions that the court should apply to the disputed terms in the patent at issue.

RULE

It is the bedrock principle of patent law that the claims of the patent define the invention to which the patentee is entitled the right to exclude. *Innova/Pure Water, Inc. v. Safari Water Filtration Sys., Inc.*, 381 F.3d 1111, 1115 (Fed. Cir. 2004).

CASE DETAILS

Facts:

Plaintiff creates accessories for mobile electronic devices. Defendant, Amazon.com, offers online shopping for a variety of goods, most of which are produced by others, through its highly successful Internet website. M-Edge became a special partner with Amazon and created cases and protective covers for the Kindle. Plaintiff obtained a patent covering certain features of the device but it was not the only supplier of Kindle accessories sold on Amazon. Amazon did not give enough notice when it launched a new version of the Kindle and sold knockoffs. M-Edge alleges patent infringement, unfair competition, Lanham Act Violations and Intentional Interference with Contracts.

Analysis:

The court determines the following:

1. In Claims 1, 4, 5, 6, 7, 8, 11, 14, 15, 16, and 17, the term "pocket" means "a receptacle in which is received the portion of the base that is referred

to as the 'substantially flat portion' in Claims 1 and 6 and as the 'planar base' in Claims 8 and 17."

2. In Claims 1, 6, 8, 11, 14, and 17, the term "formed between" means "located between."
3. Base Coupling:
   a. The term in Claim 1 "capable of moving relative to the substantially flat portion" means "capable of moving in any manner relative to the substantially flat portion."
   b. The term in Claims 6, 8, and 17 "movably coupled to [or with] the substantially flat portion [planar base, elongated planar base]" means "attached to [*30] the substantially flat portion [planar base, elongated planar base] so as to enable relative movement of any type."
4. In Claims 1, 2, 6, 8, and 17, the term "neck" means "a structure that connects the light housing to the base that is manipulatable so as to be capable of changing the position of the light housing."
5. The term "flexible neck" in Claim 2 means "not rigid."
6. In Claims 5, 7, and 16, the term "coupled to" means "attached to."
7. The term "has an opening formed at an edge of one of the interior surfaces" [Claim 1] and "having an opening formed at an edge of the interior surface" [Claim 8] means that the pocket opening must be formed at an edge of an interior surface – but not necessarily adjacent to the spine.
8. The term "extends away from the spine" in Claim 1 means that "the direction of extension, starting from the open end of the pocket into which the planar base is inserted, is away from the spine."
9. The term "elongated planar base" in Claim 17 means "a planar base of a shape that has a substantial difference between its width and length, such as does a rectangle compared to a square and an oval compared to a circle."
10. In Claims 1, 6, 8, and 17, the term "disposed [*31] within" means "contained within."
11. The term "sized to be received" in Claim 17 means "of a size that will enable it to fit."

CONCLUSION

The court determines that the claim construction is as above stated.

M-Edge Accessories LLC v. Amazon.com Inc.
Patent Infringement

***M-Edge Accessories LLC v. Amazon.com Inc.*, 2015 U.S. Dist. LEXIS 10095 (D. Md. Jan. 29, 2015).**

ISSUE

Whether Amazon should be granted its motion its summary judgment.

RULE

A motion for summary judgment shall be granted if the pleadings and supporting documents "show that there is no genuine issue as to any material fact and that the movant is entitled to judgment as a matter of law." Fed. R. Civ. P. 56(c)(2).

CASE DETAILS

Facts

Plaintiff owns a patent for a book cover for e-readers with a book light. Amazon made two book covers for e-readers, one with a slot for a book light. Plaintiff sued Amazon for patent infringement, unfair competition, tortious interference with business practices and false advertising under the Lanham Act. Amazon moved for summary judgment on all claims, and Plaintiff opposed this request and further asked the court to exclude the testimony of two of Amazon's witnesses.

Analysis

The Court found there was a question of fact for the jury regarding whether Amazon's book cover with the slot for a book light infringed upon the Plaintiff's patent. However, for the book cover without a slot for a book light, the Court found in favor of Amazon and dismissed that claim.

Conclusion

Amazon was granted summary judgment on all claims other than the patent infringement claim against the book cover that provided a slot for a book light.

Plaintiff was able to bar the testimony of one witness as to Amazon's good corporate character, Amazon's liability for unfair competition, and M-Edge's alleged bad acts or non-patent damage claims.

Milo & Gabby LLC v. Amazon.com
Lanham Act; Copyright Infringement; Patent Infringement;

***Milo & Gabby, LLC v. Amazon.com, Inc.*, 12 F. Supp. 3d 1341 (W.D. Wash. 2014).**

ISSUE

Should the court grant defendant, Amazon's motions to dismiss?

RULE

Pursuant to Rule 12(b)(6) of the Federal Rules of Civil Procedure, when looking to see if the court should grant a motion to dismiss, the court must determine whether the plaintiff has alleged sufficient facts to state a claim for relief which is plausible on its face".

Sony Music Entertainment establishes a two-part test to determine whether a state law claim is preempted by the copyright act. "(1) the court must determine whether the subject matter of the state law claim falls within the subject matter of copyright as described in 17 U.S.C. section 102 and 103. (2) if the subject matter prong has been met, the court must determine whether the rights asserted under state law are equivalent to the rights contained in 17 U.S.C. Section 106."

CASE DETAILS

Facts

Milo & Gabby, LLC designs and sells animal-shaped pillow cases in addition to bedding products. Karen Keller and her husband are the founders and product designers of the company. On September 11, 2007, the Milo & Gabby design mark was registered with the U.S. Patent and Trademark Office. The company's website marketing images were protected by the U.S. Copyrights.

Plaintiffs allege that Amazon.com began selling inauthentic copies of their products. As a result, on October 24, 2013, plaintiffs filed suit against Amazon.com alleging Amazon was using Plaintiff's intellectual property to wrongfully market, sell, and distribute inferior-quality knockoffs of the plaintiff's animal-shaped pillow cases on Amazon's website.

Defendant Amazon.com, Inc. asked the court to dismiss Plaintiff's claims for unfair competition, right of publicity, trademark counterfeiting, and indirect patent and copyright infringement. Amazon.com motions to dismiss because, they argued, that the plaintiff's complaint failed to state a claim.

Analysis

Amazon argued that the unfair competition claim was insufficient under the federal pleading requirements arguing first that "paragraph 33 of the unfair competition claim amount to nothing more than a formulaic and impermissible recitation of the elements of the CPA claim." Additionally, Amazon argues that the plaintiff's use of the term infringing refers to plaintiff's two preceding causes of action for patent and copyright infringement.

The court found that the CPA claim asserts rights indistinguishable from those rights expressly granted, and thus preempted, by the Copyright Act. The court dismissed count III without prejudice.

In regards to count V, the right of publicity, Amazon argues first, "that plaintiffs have not pled facts establishing standing to assert the claim and second, that under the Supremacy Clause of the U.S. Constitution, they Copyright Act expressly preempts plaintiffs state law claim because it is based solely on the alleged infringement of copyrighted works." The court found that the publicity claim was insufficient on its face and preempted by the Copyright Act and therefore dismissed the claim.

Amazon argued that in regards to Count VII, Trademark counterfeiting, that claim fails because plaintiffs have not plausibly alleged either "(1) that Amazon reproduced Plaintiff's registered trademark, and (2) that Amazon intentionally used the mark knowing that it was counterfeit." The court found that the plaintiffs offered no factual basis to support this claim and therefore dismissed the trademark-counterfeiting claim.

The court also allowed portions of plaintiff's prayer for relief. "Paragraph C of the complaint is stricken in part as to the words and increased or enhanced damages; paragraph D of the complaint is stricken; and paragraph L of the complaint is stricken in part as to the words 'inducement and contributory infringement'".

CONCLUSION

Amazon's motion to dismiss claims III, V, VII of the complaint were granted. Plaintiff's request for relief seeking redress for inducement, willful, or contributory infringement is stricken, and plaintiffs were ordered to show cause as to why the FAC system LLC should not be joined as a necessary party.

Milo & Gabby LLC v. Amazon.com
Lanham Act; Copyright Infringement; Patent Infringement; Trademark Infringement

---

***Milo & Gabby, LLC v. Amazon.com, Inc.*, 2015 U.S. Dist. LEXIS 117213 (W.D. Wash. Sept. 1, 2015).**

ISSUE

Should the court grant defendant, Amazon's motion for attorney's fees and costs?

RULE

The court, under *Fogerty c. Fantasy, Inc.*, has the discretion to grant attorney's fees and costs to the prevailing party on a copyright claim, and must follow that "prevailing plaintiffs and prevailing defendants are to be treated alike by the courts".

CASE DETAILS

Facts

Milo & Gabby, LLC designs and sells animal-shaped pillow cases in addition to bedding products. Karen Keller and her husband are the founders and product designers of the company. On September 11, 2007, the Milo & Gabby design mark was registered with the U.S. Patent and Trademark Office. The company's website marketing images were protected by the U.S. Copyrights.

Plaintiffs allege that Amazon.com began selling knockoff copies of their products. As a result, on October 24, 2013, plaintiffs filed suit against Amazon.com alleging Amazon was using Plaintiff's intellectual property to wrongfully market, sell, and distribute inferior-quality knockoffs of the plaintiff's animal-shaped pillow cases on Amazon's website.

The defendants were previous granted several motions to dismiss and they then brought a motion for attorney's fees and costs based on those dismissed claims. Amazon argued that they were entitled to fees and costs because they were the prevailing party under both the Copyright Act and the Lanham Act.

Analysis

The court found that the plaintiffs were not frivolous; they did not find that the arguments made by the plaintiffs were unreasonable, and they did not find that "an award of costs is necessary to advance considerations of deterrence. The court denied the motion for fees and costs under the Copyright Act.

The claims by plaintiff under the Lanham Act were found to be unreasonable and groundless by the court. Previously, the court had dismissed these claims on summary judgment for failure to show evidence of a valid enforceable mark entitled to protection. Additionally, the plaintiffs were found to be "willfully ignorant" of the courts previous dismissal of the claims under the Lanham Act. As a result, the court awarded defendant, Amazon.com attorney's fees and costs under the Lanham Act claims.

CONCLUSION

The United States District court denied the motion for fees under the Copyright Act claims, but granted attorney's fees and costs under the Lanham Act claims.

Milo & Gabby LLC v. Amazon.com
Lanham Act; Copyright Infringement; Patent Infringement; Trademark Infringement

---

***Milo & Gabby, LLC v. Amazon.com, Inc.*, 2015 U.S. Dist. LEXIS 143252 (W.D. Wash. Oct. 21, 2015).**

ISSUE

Should the court grant the defendant's motions for the exclusion of evidence or discussion relation to or supporting plaintiff's dismissed claims.

CASE DETAILS

Facts

Milo & Gabby, LLC designs and sells animal-shaped pillow cases in addition to bedding products. Karen Keller and her husband are the founders and product designers of the company. On September 11, 2007, the Milo & Gabby design mark was registered with the U.S. Patent and Trademark Office. The company's website marketing images were protected by the U.S. Copyrights.

Plaintiffs allege that Amazon.com began selling knockoff copies of their products. As a result, on October 24, 2013, plaintiffs filed suit against Amazon.com alleging Amazon was using Plaintiff's intellectual property to wrongfully market, sell, and distribute inferior-quality knockoffs of the plaintiff's animal-shaped pillow cases on Amazon's website.

Defendants motion in Limine asking the court to exclude any mention of the Keller children or that "their images have been depicted in the third-party seller's marketing materials and product packaging on the basis that it is irrelevant to the only remaining claim in the case." Additionally, defendants claim that this is highly prejudicial because the information was likely to inflame emotions that could improperly influence the jury.

Defendants moved to exclude any evidence or discussion relating to or supporting plaintiffs dismissed claims.

Analysis

The court denied the motion to exclude any mention of the Keller children and found that "giving the broad range of potential evidence that plaintiffs could seek to introduce and the nature of the remaining claim, the court will rule upon specific evidentiary objections during the course of the trial.

For the motion to remove evidence of dismissed claims, the court denied the motion in part. While the plaintiffs were precluded from specifically discussing their dismissed claims, the court will rule upon specific evidentiary objections during the course of trial.

The court denied the defendant's motion to seek an order from the court to preclude the plaintiffs from offering any evidence or argument in support of damages.

The court granted the defendant's motion to preclude any evidence of the parties' respective financial positions as prejudicial.

The court granted the defendant's motion to preclude plaintiffs from drawing any comparison between any of its own commercial products and the accused products in support of their patent infringement.

The court denied the defendant's motion that plaintiffs remove certain statements from their website.

CONCLUSION

The district court granted in part and denied in part the motions brought by Amazon.com, defendant.

Milo & Gabby LLC v. Amazon.com
Lanham Act; Copyright Infringement; Patent Infringement; Trademark Infringement.

***Milo & Gabby, LLC v. Amazon.com*, 2015 U.S. Dist. LEXIS 149939 (W.D. Wash. Nov. 3, 2015).**

ISSUE

Should the court grant Amazon's motion to dismiss?

RULE

The Federal Circuit defines Section 271(a) "offer to sell" liability according to the norms of traditional contractual analysis.

CASE DETAILS

Facts

Plaintiffs Milo & Gabby, LLC, and Karen Keller sought money damages from Amazon.com, defendant, for offering to sell products that allegedly infringed some of plaintiff's designs. Additionally, plaintiffs sought an order that would prevent Amazon from importing, offering to sell, or selling the products in the future.

The court previously had determined that third parties, De Fang Sun, Chongqin World First Electronic commerce Co, T Liu, FAC System, Dinding Zou, Qiumei Zhang, Charlotte Xia, Nimble Joy, Amanialarashi2165, and Monaqo, were the parties responsible for providing products that were infringed. Additionally, the court found that Amazon had not sold any of the infringed products.

After a jury hearing, the jury found that amazon did not, "communicate description of the allegedly infringed products, communicate the price at which the allegedly infringed products could be purchased, provide the descriptions of the allegedly infringed products, set the price at which the allegedly infringed products could be sold, set quantities of the allegedly infringed products for sale, or communicate that it was willing to enter into a bargain to sell the allegedly infringed products."

Analysis

The court having looked at the evidence and testimony found that Amazon did not offer to sell the alleged infringed products. There was no manifestation of the willingness of Amazon to enter into a bargain.

CONCLUSION

The District Court found adopted the verdict of the jury and found that Amazon.com was not liable for "offering to sell" the alleged infringing products at issue in this matter. A judgment was placed in favor of Amazon.com and all claims against Amazon.com were dismissed.

Mobile Telecommunications Technologies v. Amazon.com, Inc.
Patent Infringement; Procedure

***Mobile Telcoms. Techs., LLC v. Amazon.com, Inc.*, 2014 U.S. Dist. LEXIS 138786 (E.D. Tex. Aug. 26, 2014).**

ISSUE

Should the district court grant defendant, Amazon.com's motion to dismiss?

RULE

Under 35 U.S.C. "A claim for induced infringement requires, "proof of (1) an act of direct infringement by another, and (2) that the defendant knowingly induced the infringement with specific intent to encourage the other's infringement."

CASE DETAILS

Facts

Plaintiff, Mobile Telecommunications alleged patent infringement against Amazon.com for their 946 patent, their 748 patent, and their 428 patent. These patents relate to wireless messaging systems. The 946 Patent is named "Nationwide Communication System" and the 428 Patent is titled "Method and Device for Processing Undelivered Data Messages in a Two-Way Wireless Communications System".

Amazon.com motioned to dismiss the claim of induced infringement. Additionally, Amazon challenged MTEL's contributory infringement pleading. Finally, Amazon challenged the willful infringement pleading.

Analysis

The court found the Mobile Telecommunications pleading for induced infringement to be sufficient. Additionally, the court found the Mobile Telecommunications pleading for contributory infringement claim to be sufficient. Finally, the court found the dismissal of the willful infringement claim would be inappropriate.

CONCLUSION

The United States District Court denied the defendant's motion to dismiss because they found the claims brought by plaintiff, Mobile Telecommunications were sufficient.

Mobile Telecommunications Technologies v. Amazon.com, Inc. *Patent Infringement; Claim Construction*

***Mobile Telcoms. Techs., LLC v. Amazon.com, Inc.*, 2014 U.S. Dist. LEXIS 156454 (E.D. Tex. Nov. 5, 2014).**

ISSUE

What definitions should the court apply to the disputed terms in the patent at issue here?

RULE

The Supreme Court of the United States read, "35 U.S.C. Section 112 too require that a patent's claims, viewed in light of the specification and prosecution history, inform those skilled in the art about the scope of the invention with reasonable certainty."

CASE DETAILS

Facts

Plaintiff, Mobile Telecommunications alleged patent infringement against Amazon.com for their 946 patent, their 748 patent, and their 428 patent. These patents relate to wireless messaging systems. The 946 Patent is named "Nationwide Communication System" and the 428 Patent is titled "Method and Device for Processing Undelivered Data Messages in a Two-Way Wireless Communications System". The court adopted the definitions of the disputed terms as outlined below.

Analysis

The court concluded that, "probe message," meant, "a message that is generated by the network operations center to locate a mobile unit can be reached."

The court concluded that, "a portion of the displayed message" was to have its plain and ordinary meaning.

The court found that for claim 8 of the 428 patent no construction was necessary and to follow the plain and ordinary meaning.

The court found that," means for extracting a corrected message from the radio frequency signal" had the function to be, "extracting a corrected message from the radio frequency signal" and the corresponding structure was, "display and storage logic section 1508 or 1708, and an error correcting code; and equivalents thereof."

The court found that, "means for generating upon receiving" was indefinite.

The court found that, "means for generating, upon power restoration to the transmitter, a registration message if a probe message has been received while the transmitter was powered off" the function was, "generating, upon power restoration to the transmitter a registration message if a probe message has been received while the transmitter was powered off" and the corresponding structure was, "registration message generation (RMG) module 404, and memory 212, configured to perform the algorithm set forth in the 428 patent at 6:41-47; and equivalents thereof."

The court found that, "means for making" was indefinite.

The court found that, "means for automatically transmitting undelivered data messages to the mobile unit upon receiving a registration message from the mobile unit" the function was, "automatically transmitting undelivered data messages to the mobile unit upon receiving a registration message from the mobile unit" and the corresponding structure was, "registration message processing (RMP) module 306, memory storage unit 110, and message transmitting unit 108, configured to perform the algorithm set forth in the 428 Patent at 8:28-42; and equivalents thereof."

CONCLUSION

The court adopted the meanings of the disputed terms as stated above.

Multi Time Machine, Inc. v. Amazon.com, Inc.
Trademark Infringement

***Multi Time Mach., Inc. v. Amazon.com, Inc.*, 792 F.3d 1070 (9th Cir. 2015).**

ISSUE

Whether an issue of fact existed as to whether Amazon created a likelihood of confusion and thus infringed on manufacturers trademarks because Amazon's website search response displayed aesthetically similar watches manufactured by competitors and did not state that Amazon did not carry the manufacturer's products.

RULE

Under the Lanham Act, a defendant infringes a trademark when the defendant uses the mark in commerce in a manner likely to cause confusion as to a good's source. Trademark infringement also occurs when the trademark's use in commerce is likely to cause confusion as to the affiliation, association, or approval of the trademark holder with the trademark user. A defendant who infringes another's trademark is liable for damages and subject to injunction. 15 U.S.C.S. §§ 1114(1)(a),1125(a)(1).

CASE DETAILS

Facts

This is a trademark infringement case involving Plaintiff Multi Time Machine Inc. and Amazon.com's use of its trademark. Plaintiff did not sell items on Amazon, but when customers searched for it, Amazon returned results with Plaintiff's trademark and listings from other sellers. Plaintiff argued that Amazon could have confused customers with these search results.

Plaintiff sued Amazon for violation of Lanham Act and Trademark Infringement. Amazon moved for summary judgment which the lower court granted. Plaintiff appealed.

Analysis

The court considers eight non-exhaustive factors to determine whether a trademark use causes likelihood of confusion: (1) strength of the mark(s); (2) proximity or relatedness of the goods; (3) similarity of the marks; (4) evidence of actual confusion; (5) marketing channels; (6) degree of consumer care (7) the defendants' intent; and (8) likelihood of expansion.

The court found that Amazon clearly labeled the products it carried, by brand name and model, as well as a photograph of the item. The court further held that no rational trier of fact could possibly find that a reasonably prudent consumer accustomed to online shopping would likely be confused by the Amazon search results.

CONCLUSION

The court held that the district court correctly granted summary judgment in favor of Amazon.

Nazomi Communicaitons v. Nokia
Patent Infringement; Procedure

***Nazomi Communs., Inc. v. Nokia Corp.*, 2011 U.S. Dist. LEXIS 76057, 2011 WL 2837401 (N.D. Cal. July 14, 2011).**

ISSUE

Whether the court should grant Nokia's motion to move for judgment on the pleadings?

RULE

Pursuant to Federal Rule of Civil Procedure 12(c), a party can move for judgment on the pleadings after the pleadings are closed but within such time as to not delay trial. The court will take plaintiff's allegations as true and "liberally construe the complaint in favor of the plaintiff." *Jenkins v. McKeithen*, 395 U.S. 411, 421 (1969).

CASE DETAILS

Facts

Nazomi is a corporation that deals with enhancing the performance of applications that run on Java and other platforms. Phone manufacturers have adopted their technology and products. On June 18, 2006, Nazomi was awarded the patent for a "Java virtual machine hardware for RIDC and CISC processors." On May 29, 2007, they were awarded a separate patent for "Java hardware accelerator using a microcode engine." Nazomi alleges that Nokia infringed on their patent.

Analysis

Nazomi alleges that the date in the complaint is not when the manual was written but rather when Nazomi notified Nokia of the existence of the patents-in-suit and the infringement harm. Nazomi alleges that Nokia knowingly infringed, but had failed to state specific facts that support this conclusion.

CONCLUSION

The court granted the motion for judgment on the pleadings with leave to amend.

Nicosia v. Amazon.com.
Class Action Lawsuits; Amazon dismissed from all claims

***Nicosia v. Amazon.com, Inc.*, 84 F. Supp. 3d 142 (E.D.N.Y. 2015).**

ISSUE

Should the court grant defendant's motion to dismiss?

RULE

Pursuant to Rule 12(b)(6) for a motion to dismiss, "a number of other courts have construed motions to dismiss based on the existence of mandatory arbitration clauses as motions to compel arbitration.

CASE DETAILS

Facts

Plaintiff brought a punitive class action against Amazon.com alleging that Amazon had sold and continued to sell weight loss supplements containing sibutramine. Sibutramine is a "controlled substance that has never been permitted for sale without a prescription from a licensed physician, that is associated with a serious risk of cardiovascular events and strokes, which is in violation of various federal and state consumer protection laws and in breach of various implied warranties."

Amazon.com motioned to dismiss claiming that the claims were governed by a mandatory arbitration clause and class action waiver. Nicosia motioned for a preliminary injunction.

Analysis

The court looked to the arbitration clause signed by both parties and found that the plaintiff was bound to the terms of the conditions of use and therefore was bound to mandatory arbitration.

CONCLUSION

The court concluded that the arbitration clause was enforceable and granted Amazon's motion to dismiss pursuant to the clause. The court denied plaintiff's motion for preliminary injunction.

Nomura v. Amazon.com, Inc.
Patent Infringement; Procedure

***Nomura v. YouTube, LLC*, 2012 U.S. Dist. LEXIS 174332 (N.D. Cal. Dec. 7, 2012).**

ISSUE

Whether the court should grant Nomura's action to strike defendants claim construction briefs.

RULE

The Patent Local Rules are designed to encourage an expeditious resolution of patent infringement disputes, by requiring parties to disclose certain information upfront. Further, the rules require the parties to, inter alia, exchange proposed terms for claim constructions, exchange preliminary claim constructions and extrinsic evidence, and file a joint claim construction and prehearing statement. Patent L.R. 4.

CASE DETAILS

Facts

On August 7, 2007, plaintiff, Nomura was awarded a patent for a "video-on-demand system." The patent is directed for a three-tiered architecture for inputting, converting and storing video data files that are accessed, downloaded and viewed by customers. Nomura alleges YouTube and Amazon infringed on this patent.

Timeline

On August 31, 2012, the parties filed a Joint Claim Construction Statement ("JCCS") identifying ten terms in the patent as most significant to the claim. Since the JCCS, the parties have agreed upon the meaning of two terms. On October 15, 2012, Nomura filed his opening claim construction brief in support of his purposed claims. On October 29, 2012, defendants filed responsive claim construction briefs. On November 12, 2012, Nomura moved in both actions to strike defendants introduction of new evidence and to preclude defendants from asserting new claim construction positions.

Analysis

The court found that defendant's modifications appear too narrow and clarify the disputed issues before the court. The court decided that it will consider the new evidence only to the extent that it helps the court construe the disputed terms. The court finds that the modifications and new evidence do not unfairly prejudice Nomura.

CONCLUSION

The court denies the Plaintiff's Motion to Strike.

Nomura v. Amazon.com, Inc.
Patent Infringement; Procedure

***Nomura v. YouTube, LLC*, 2013 U.S. Dist. LEXIS 18292 (N.D. Cal. Feb. 8, 2013).**

ISSUE

What definitions should the court apply to the disputed terms of the patent at issue here?

CASE DETAILS

Facts

On August 7, 2007, Nomura was awarded a patent for a "video-on-demand system." The patent is directed for a three-tiered architecture for inputting, converting and storing video data files that are accessed, downloaded and viewed by customers. Nomura alleges YouTube and Amazon infringed on this patent.

Timeline

On December 14, 2012, the court held a claim construction hearing to construe the disputed terms of the patent. On August 31, 2012, the parties filed a Joint Claim Construction Statement ("JCCS") identifying ten terms in the patent as most significant to the claim. Since the JCCS, the parties have agreed upon the meaning of two terms. On December 7, 2012, the court denied Nomura's motion to strike modifications.

Analysis

The court determines that "configured to not be remotely accessible device" shall mean, "configured to prevent or deny access by a customer's remote," "sorted by category and classified in indexed master files," shall mean "organized by category and indexed in master files," "a backup video storage unit" shall mean "an additional video data storage," "for storing back-up video data files" shall mean "unit for storing copies of the video data files," "a first data input station configured for uploading" shall mean "a hardware device configured to receive" and "customers" shall mean "system users."

CONCLUSION

The court determined the meaning of the disputed terms in the patent as defined above.

Nomura v. Amazon.com, Inc.
Patent Infringement; Procedure

***Nomura v. Amazon.Com, Inc.*, 2013 U.S. Dist. LEXIS 122895 (N.D. Cal. Aug. 28, 2013).**

ISSUE

Whether the court should grant Amazon's Motion to File Under Seal?

RULE

In order to be sealable, a document must be "privileged or protectable as to a trade secret or otherwise entitled to protection under the law." Civ. L.R. 79-5(a). Under local rules, "a stipulation, or a blanker protective order that allows a party to designate documents as sealable, will not suffice to allow the filing of documents used in dispositive motions." *Kamakana v. City & Cnty. of Honolulu*, 447 F.3d 1172, 1179 (9th Cir. 2006).

CASE DETAILS

Facts

On August 7, 2007, Nomura was awarded a patent for a "video-on-demand system." The patent is directed for a three-tiered architecture for inputting, converting and storing video data files that are accessed, downloaded and viewed by customers. Nomura alleges YouTube and Amazon infringed on this patent.

Timeline

On August 31, 2012, the parties filed a Joint Claim Construction Statement ("JCCS") identifying ten terms in the patent as most significant to the claim. Since the JCCS, the parties have agreed upon the meaning of two terms. On October 15, 2012, Nomura filed his opening claim construction brief in support of his purposed claims. On October 29, 2012, defendants filed responsive claim construction briefs. On November 12, 2012, Nomura moved in both actions to strike defendants introduction of new evidence and to preclude defendants from asserting new claim construction positions. On December 7, 2012, the court denied

Nomura's motion to strike modifications. On December 14, 2012, the court held a claim construction hearing to construe the disputed terms of the patent. On February 8, 2013, the court determined the patent language.

Analysis

Amazon requests a court order to seal exhibits to the declaration of Sara N. Kerrane in support of its motion to dismiss for failure to prosecute. Amazon also requests that the court seal portions of its motion for summary judgment of non-infringement and declarations. The court determined that these documents are not privileged information and do not contain trade secrets and therefore cannot be entitled to protection under the law.

CONCLUSION

The court denies Amazon's motion to seal documents.

OIP Techs., v. Amazon.com, Inc.
Patent Infringement

***OIP Techs., Inc. v. Amazon.com, Inc.*, 788 F.3d 1359 (Fed. Cir. 2015).**

ISSUE

The court is deciding on appeal whether plaintiffs patent infringement claim against Amazon.com Inc. ("Amazon") should be dismissed because the patent does not claim patentable subject matter.

RULE

"A patent may be obtained for any new and useful process, machine, manufacture, or composition of matter, or any new and useful improvement thereof." 35 U.S.C. § 101. "The Supreme Court has long held that this provision contains an important implicit exception: Laws of nature, natural phenomena, and abstract ideas are not patentable.: *Ass'n for Molecular Pathology v. Myriad Genetics, Inc.*, 133 S. Ct. 2107, 2116 (2013) (quoting *Mayo Collaborative Servs. V. Prometheus Labs., Inc.*, 132 S. Ct. 1289, 1293 (2012).

CASE DETAILS

Facts

In March 2012, plaintiff filed patent infringement claims against Amazon, alleging an infringement of "Patent '713" which claims computer implemented methods for "pricing a product for sale." The '713 patent teaches a price optimization method that helps vendors automatically reach better pricing decisions through automatic estimation and measurement of actual demand to select prices. Amazon filed a motion to dismiss plaintiffs complaint, arguing the patent claims ineligible subject matter.

Timeline

The lower court granted Amazon's motion, finding that the claims merely used a computer to implement the abstract idea of price optimization and therefore is ineligible for patent protection under 35 U.S.C. § 101.

Analysis

The court held that here, the claims are directed to the concept of "offer based price optimization," and that this concept is similar to other fundamental economic concepts found to be "abstract ideas" by both the Supreme Court and this court. The court ultimately finds that relying on a computer to perform routine tasks more quickly or more accurately is insufficient to render a claim patent eligible.

CONCLUSION

Because the '713 patent claims the abstract idea of "offer based price optimization" and lacks an "inventive concept" sufficient to "transform" the claimed subject matter into a patent-eligible application of that idea, this court affirms the District Court, and denies plaintiff's claim against Amazon.

Okocha v. Amazon.com
Copyright Infringement; Procedure

***Okocha v. Amazon.com*, 153 Fed. Appx. 849, 2005 U.S. App. LEXIS 23788 (3d Cir. N.J. 2005).**

ISSUE

Whether the court of appeals should affirm the lower court's grant of summary judgment in favor of Amazon.

RULE

Pursuant to 17 U.S.C.S. Section 109, "Reselling a copy of a previously purchased book does not infringe upon the right of distribution."

CASE DETAILS

Facts

Plaintiff, Okocha, was an author who appealed the order of the lower court that granted summary judgment in favor of Amazon.com in suit for copyright infringement, conspiracy, fraud, negligent/intentional infliction of emotional harm, and loss of future wages claims.

Analysis

The court of appeals found that the author failed to show he owned a valid copyright of his book. Additionally, the plaintiff failed to show the bookseller copied the material. The court additionally found that the author failed to provide admissible evidence to show that Amazon and third party sellers had conspired to violate his copyrights.

CONCLUSION

The court of appeals affirmed the district court's order and denied the plaintiff's motion to expedite. Additionally, the court granted the plaintiff's motion to file supplementary proof and a supplemental appendix.

Olympic Devs. AG, LLC v. Barnesandnoble.com LLC
Patent Infringement; Procedure

***Olympic Devs. AG, LLC v. Barnesandnoble.com LLC* (N.D. Cal., 2011).**

ISSUE

The court here is ruling on the parties' stipulation to stay (temporarily postpone) the proceedings pending re-examination of the patent at issue in this claim.

CASE DETAILS

Facts

Plaintiff originally filed patent infringement claims against multiple defendants, including Amazon.com, Inc. ("Amazon").

The parties by and through use of their counsel stipulate the following:

(1) The litigation proceedings shall be stayed pending the reexamination of the patent at issue.

(2) All case management dates shall be vacated except for the following:

  a. The parties shall submit an updated joint case management statement.

  b. An interim case management conference shall be held as currently scheduled.

CONCLUSION

This action is stayed in its entirety pending completion of the reexamination of the patent at issue.

On Demand Machine Corp. v. Amazon.com.
Patent Infringement

***On Demand Mach. Corp. v. Ingram Indus.*, 442 F.3d 1331 (Fed. Cir. 2006).**

ISSUE

Should the court reverse the United States District Court's jury verdict of infringement?

RULE

Pursuant to *Richardson v. Suzuki Motor Co., Ltd.*, "The reviewing court determines whether a reasonable jury, on correct instruction of law, could reasonably have reached the verdict reached by this jury; that is, was there substantial evidence in support of the verdict, when disputed questions of fact and factual inferences are resolved in favor of the party that received the verdict."

CASE DETAILS

Facts

Amazon.com, along with Ingram Industries, Inc. and Lightening Source, Inc. were defendants in a suit filed by On Demand Machine Corp. for Patent infringement. On Demand argued that patent number 5,465,213 (the Ross patent) was infringed. This patent was for "a system and method of manufacturing a single book copy".

Ingram created a subsidiary company, other named defendant, Lightning Source. Amazon.com is connected to the other defendants because Amazon.com has the ability to order single or multiple copies from Lightening Source. Ingram was informed that Lighting Source was infringing on the Ross patent, yet after both parties sought the advice of council, they declined the offer of a license by Ross.

The United States District Court for the Eastern district of Missouri found Amazon along with other named defendants to be liable. The jury awarded plaintiff $15,000,000 in damages.

The defendants appealed the verdict and the District Court holding that claimed if the claim construction were correct, there would not have been a guilty verdict of infringement. Additionally, Amazon argues that the damages award was excessive.

Analysis

The court looked to defendant's argument that the district court construed and instructed the jury on "sales information" too broadly and agreed with defendants. The court held that "the prosecution history requires this claim construction, for the inclusion of promotional information was a material distinction from the prior art." The court concluded that "sales information" was an incorrect term given to the jury. Additionally, the court found that if there were a correct construction of the claim, causes 3 and 4 would not have been met by Lightning Source's activities.

The term "customer" was also argued to be incorrect because the district court's adaptation of the term meant, anyone who "buys goods or services" as opposed to a more limited interpretation. The court found that "the district court's definition of 'customer' cannot eliminate these constraints in order to embrace the remote large-scale production of books for publishers and retailers."

On the issue of "printing on paper pages", the court of appeals found that the district court erred in construction of this clause. Additionally, they found that if this were correct, a reasonable jury would not find that it "reads on a process of printing on large sheets or webs of paper that require the further processing step of cutting into pages after printing.

On the issue of the "preamble", the court of appeals found that the district court's instruction that the preamble does not limit the claim was incorrect.

CONCLUSION

The United States Court of Appeals of the Federal Circuit found that the jury verdict of infringement was based on a partially incorrect claim construction. Additionally, the Court of Appeals believed that if the claim construction was correct, that a reasonable jury would not find the patent to be infringed. The Court reversed the lower court's judgment, and ruled in favor of Amazon.com and other named defendants here.

Overstock.com, Inc. v. New York State Dept. of Taxation & Fin
Financial and Tax Law

***Overstock.com, Inc. v New York State Dept. of Taxation & Fin.*, 20 N.Y.3d 586 (N.Y. 2013).**

ISSUE

Should the court of appeals affirm the lower court's decision in finding the law to be constitutional?

RULE

Tax Law Section 1101 (b) (8) (vi) " ... subjects online vendors, without a physical presence in New York, to state sales and compensating use taxes if the vendors use in-state residents to solicit business in New York through the residents' websites.

CASE DETAILS

Facts

Amazon.com, plaintiff, offered an "Associates Program" where third parties could place their links on their own websites that would direct the users to the Amazon website. Plaintiff, Overstock.com also sells merchandise through the Internet. In April of 2008, the legislature amended the Tax Law. Amazon commenced action on April 25, 2008 claiming that the statute was unconstitutional. Overstock commenced action on May 30, 2008 making similar arguments.

The Appellate Division affirmed the portions of the orders that "dismissed the facial challenged under the Commerce and Due Process Clauses and declared the statute constitutional." The plaintiffs then appealed.

Analysis

The court found that the plaintiffs failed to demonstrate that the statute was facially unconstitutional under either the Commerce or the Due Process Clause.

CONCLUSION

The court of appeals affirmed the lower court's judgment.

Parallel Iron LLC v. Acknowledge Inc.
Procedure

Parallel Iron LLC v. Acknowledge Inc. **(D. Del., 2012).**

ISSUE

The court here is deciding whether to grant defendant EMC Corporation's motion for attorney's fees.

RULE

The relevant standard for a motion for attorney's fees is that the defendant's motion "should only be granted if the defendant shows that (1) the litigation is brought in subjective bad faith, and (2) the litigation is objectively baseless." *Old Reliable Wholesale Inc. v. Cornell Corp.*, 635 F.3d 539, 543-44 (Fed. Cir. 2011).

CASE DETAILS

Facts

Plaintiff owns the '565 patent and sued 15 companies including Amazon.com Inc. ("Amazon") alleging infringement of that patent. The patent was subject to a terminal disclaimer requiring that it have common ownership with another patent, the '526 patent, in order to be enforceable. Ring technology owned both patents at one point, but assigned the '565 patent to one of its subsidiaries about 18 months before litigation of this case.

Amazon sent an email to plaintiff explaining the terminal disclaimer issue and advised plaintiff that if they continued the suit they would be subject to sanctions. The same day, plaintiff advised all defendants that plaintiff would be dismissing the case.

Defendant EMC, is seeking to recover over $200,000 in attorneys' fees by having the case declared exceptional.

Analysis

The court finds that defendant EMC has not proved that the litigation was brought, or continued in subjective bad faith. The court first holds that plaintiff must have made a costly mistake. Second, the court notes that there was nothing to be gained by plaintiff in splitting ownership of the patents, but a lot to lose in doing so. Finally, the court states that the reaction to Amazon's email was a "prompt fold" that can be interpreted as a sign of good faith.

CONCLUSION

For the foregoing reasons the court denied the motion to recover attorney's fees. Defendant EMC has not shown "subjective bad faith" on behalf of the plaintiff.

Parallel Networks, LLC v. Abercrombie & Fitch Co.
Patent Infringement

***Parallel Networks, LLC v. Abercrombie & Fitch Co.*, 704 F.3d 958 (Fed. Cir. 2013).**

ISSUE

The court is determining on appeal whether the District court erred in granting summary judgment for defendants.

CASE DETAILS

Facts

Plaintiff filed four cases against 120 defendants, including Amazon.Com, Inc. All defendants have in common that their websites provided "applets" in response to user requests in a manner that, according to plaintiff, infringed its patent.

Timeline

The district court ordered a Markman hearing to construe three terms in two claims and then granted summary judgment of non-infringement for most defendants based on its constructions. It denied plaintiff's Rule 59(e) motion to amend its contentions to assert infringement against 45 defendants based on the claim constructions.

Analysis

Here, the court denied plaintiff's challenges to the claim constructions. The court agreed with the district court that plaintiff was seeking to amend its infringement contentions in order to make arguments that could have been made before the entry of summary judgment. The district court's claim construction was not an intervening change in the law.

CONCLUSION

The court affirms the decision of the district court and holds that plaintiff has "no good explanation for its failure to bring its new infringement contentions earlier and thus has brought any perceived prejudice on itself."

Parisi v. Sinclair
Tortious Interference

***Parisi v. Sinclair*, 774 F. Supp. 2d 310 (D.D.C. 2011).**

ISSUE

Should the court grant defendant, Amazon.com's motion for summary judgment?

RULE

Pursuant to the Federal Rules of Civil Procedure Rule 56 (a) "Summary judgment is proper where the moving party shows that there is no genuine dispute as to any material fact and the movant is entitled to judgment as a matter of law."

CASE DETAILS

Facts

Plaintiffs, Daniel Parisi, Whitehouse.com, Inc., Whitehouse Network LLC, and White House Communications Inc. brought a diversity action against defendants, Books-A-Million (BAM), Barnes & Noble, Barnesandnoble.com (B&N), and Amazon.com, Inc. Plaintiffs sought to recover for libel per se, false light invasion, misappropriation of privacy, business disparagement, tortious inference with economic advantage, and civil conspiracy. These claims arose after the internet listing and sales of the book, *Barack Obama & Larry Sinclair: Cocaine, Sex, Lies & Murder?* written by Larry Sinclair.

The statements found in the book caused the website Whitehouse.com to shut down in 2008. Additionally, Parisi had planned to sell the site to a mainstream political news entity and alleged that due to Sinclair's defamation, he was unable to do so. Plaintiff alleged damages of $30,000,000. Amazon.com along with BAM and B&N offered the book for sale. Amazon.com specifically offered the book in hard copy and on Kindle. Amazon.com did not review the substance of the book; the product description, the product details, or the customer reviews. The plaintiffs allege that there was a promotional statement on the bookseller's website stating, "You'll read how the Obama campaign used internet porn king

Dan Parisi and Ph.D. fraud Edward I. Gelb to conduct a rigged polygraph exam in an attempt to make the Sinclair story go away".

Amazon.com motioned for summary judgment, BAM motioned to dismiss and B&N motioned for summary judgment.

Analysis

The court found that the plaintiffs have failed to provide evidence that supports their claim that B&N and Amazon.com did play a role in the creation or development of the promotional statements for the book. As a result, the court found that the defendants, B&N and Amazon.com were entitled to summary judgment for the claims of defamatory promotional statements appearing on their websites.

Additionally, the court found that plaintiffs had failed to carry their burden on the issue of Amazon's actual malice.

CONCLUSION

The District Court granted BAM's motion to dismiss, Amazon's motion for summary judgment, and B&N's motion for summary judgment.

*** There is a similar, almost identical copy of this opinion, seen in "Daniel Parisi v. Lawrence Sinclair, Civil Case No. 10-897 (RJL) Date: March 31, 2011.**

Perfect 10, Inc. v. Amazon.com, Inc.
Copyright Infringement

***Perfect 10, Inc. v. Amazon.com, Inc.*, 508 F.3d 1146 (9th Cir. Cal. 2007).**

ISSUE

Should the court of appeals affirm the lower court's decision?

RULE

Pursuant to 17 U.S.C.A. Section 501(a), "Plaintiffs must satisfy two requirements to present a prima facie case of direct infringement: (1) they must show ownership of the allegedly infringed material and (2) they must demonstrate that the alleged infringers violate at least one exclusive right granted to copyright holders.

CASE DETAILS

Facts

Perfect 10, Inc. filed suit against Google Inc. for copyright infringement. The District Court preliminarily enjoined defendant from creating and publicly displaying thumbnail versions of plaintiff copyright holder's images, but did not enjoin the engine operator from linking to third-party websites that displayed infringing full-size versions of the images. Perfect 10 additionally brought suit against Amazon.com. Amazon.com was not preliminarily enjoined from giving users access to information provided by Google. Both Perfect 10 and Google appealed.

Analysis

The court of appeals looked to the district courts analysis of whether a claim against Amazon.com was likely to succeed and agreed that Perfect 10 did not show likelihood that it would prevail on the merits on its claim that Amazon.com directly infringed its images. Additionally, the court agreed that Amazon.com did not have the "right and ability to supervise the infringing activity of Google or third parties".

However, the court acknowledged the district court's failure to consider whether Amazon.com had actual knowledge of the infringing material within its system, and therefore instructed, on remand, for the district court to decide on this issue.

The court found that Google's fair use defense would likely succeed and reversed the lower courts decision that Google's thumbnail version of the images constituted a direct infringement. The court additionally erred in "its secondary liability analysis because it failed to consider whether Google and Amazon knew of their infringing activities.

Finally, the court found that the district court failed to consider whether Google and Amazon were entitled to the limitations on liability.

CONCLUSION

The court of appeals reversed the district court's ruling and vacated the preliminary injunction regarding Google's use of the thumbnail images. Additionally, the court reversed the district court's rejection of the claims that Google and Amazon were secondarily liable. All other rulings were affirmed.

Personal Webb Technologies, LLC v. Amazon.Com
Patent Infringement; Procedure

ISSUE

Whether the court should interpret the claim language in this case?

RULE

In claim construction, the court is able to examine the patent's intrinsic evidence to define the patented invention's scope. *Phillips v. AWH Corp.*, 415 F.3d 1303, 1312 (Fed. Cir. 2005)(en banc)(quoting *Innova/Pure Water Inc. v. Safari Water Filtration Sys., Inc.*, 381 F.3d 1111,1115. (Fed. Cir. 2004)). Claims are invalid if they fail to point out and distinctively claim the subject matter that the applicant regards as the invention. 35 U.S.C. §112(b). If a party seeks to invalidate a claim, they must show clear and convincing evidence that one skilled in the art would not understand the scope of the claim when read in light of the specification. *Intellectual Prop. Dev., Inc. v. UA- Columbia Cablevision of Westchester, Inc.*, 336 F.3d 1308, 1319 (Fed. Cir. 2003).

CASE DETAILS

Facts:

PersonalWeb Technologies sued the multiple defendants for infringement of their patent. The oral argument was held in court on July 18, 2013. There are nine asserted patents, all claiming to a common application.

Analysis:

The court determined many terms in the applicable patents. "A data system" would mean a "sequence of bits," "data files" is to mean "a named data item," "substantially unique identifier/ data identifier/ True Name/digital identifier" are "an identity for a data item generated by processing all of the data in the data item and only the data in the data item, through an algorithm that makes the identifier substantially unique." "Access means for accessing a particular data item using the identifier of the data item" has a function of "accessing a particular data item using the identifier of the data item." "Existence means for determining whether a particular data item is present in the system, by examining the identifiers of the plurality of data items" has a function of determining whether a particular data item is present in the system, by examining the identifiers of the plurality of data items. "Local existence means for determining whether an instance of a particular data item is present at a particular location in the system, based on the identifier of the data item" has a function of "determining whether an instance of a particular data item is present in the system, by examining the identifiers of the plurality of data items." "A file system," "identifier," "sufficient number of copies," "licensed/ unlicensed," "distributing a set of data files across network of servers" require no construction.

CONCLUSION

The court interprets the claim language in the case in the manner set above.

Personalized Media Communications, LLC v. Amazon.Com, Inc.
Patent Infringement; Procedure

***Personalized Media Communs., LLC v. Amazon.com, Inc.*, 2015 U.S. Dist. LEXIS 104369 (D. Del. Aug. 10, 2015).**

ISSUE

Whether the court should grant the Defendant's Motion for Judgment on the Pleadings?

RULE

Rule 12(c) governs motions for judgment on the pleadings and states that it is to be reviewed under the same standard as a Rule 12(b)(6) motion to dismiss. *Turbe v. Gov't of the Virgin Islands*, 938 F.2d 427, 428 (3d Cir. 1991). The court must accept the factual allegations in the complaint and take them in the light most favorable to the non-moving party.

CASE DETAILS

Facts:

Personalized Media Company (Personalized) filed its patent infringement action on September 23, 2013. Personalized alleges that Amazon infringed nine of their patents. On July 21, 2014, the parties stipulated on the dismissal of the claims in regards to the two of the patent infringement claims. The patents are directed to "the use of control and information signals embedded in electronic media content to generate output for display that is personalized and relevant to a user."

Analysis:

The court found that claim 13 of the '243 patent is directed to the abstract idea of combining information from multiple sources and using personal information to create a customized presentation. Therefore, it found the patent ineligible. Additionally, the court determined that claim 1 of the '252 patent claims a very specific method of updating operating instructions and seems quite generic.

It is also abstract and lacks an incentive concept. It is ineligible. Claim 1 of the '304 patent recites an abstract idea of decryption. There is additionally no inventive concept to render the abstract idea patent eligible. Claim 9 of the '587 patent is also not personalized content and claims an abstract idea. It is not patent eligible. Claim 2 of the '749 patent claims that abstract idea of promoting programming and lacks an inventive concept and therefore is ineligible. Claim 18 of '791 patent and claim 6 of the '956 patent are also abstract and are therefore ineligible.

CONCLUSION

The court grants the defendant's Motion for Judgment on the Pleadings.

Peters v. Amazon Services LLC
Breach of Contract; Unjust Enrichment

***Peters v. Amazon Servs., LLC*, 2 F. Supp. 3d 1165, 2013 U.S. Dist. LEXIS 185964 (W.D. Wash. 2013).**

ISSUE

Was Amazon.com liable for breach of contract, breach of fiduciary duty, in violation of Washington's Consumer Protection Act and unjust enrichment?

RULE

Under the Federal Arbitration Act, a court's role is "limited to determining (1) whether a valid agreement to arbitrate exists and, if it does, (2) whether the agreement encompasses the dispute at issue".

CASE DETAILS

Facts

Plaintiff, Jo Ellen Peters, was a third party Amazon.com seller who sued Amazon for breach of contract, breach of fiduciary duty, violations of Washington's Consumer Protection Act, and unjust enrichment. These claims are brought on behalf of a class of people who "opened a seller account with Amazon and for whom Amazon has received Payment Transaction funds for at least one buyer on the Amazon.com website since March 15, 2009". There additionally is a punitive subclass of "All persons or entities in the U.S. (1) who were provided written notice from Amazon that their account had been suspended; (2) who, at the time of such notice, had funds on account with Amazon; and (3) Amazon did not transmit such funds to the seller by the shorter of a (a) 90 days following the initial date the account was suspended by Amazon, or (b) the date on which the seller was provided written notification that Amazon's review was complete and the decision to close the account was final."

Another plaintiff in the case, Ken Lane, was an amazon.com seller who agreed to the participation agreement. After Amazon.com received multiple complaints, they permanently suspended his account, while still being in possession of money from pending sales. Five days later, Lane created a second account and agreed to the Business Solutions Agreement. This account was then blocked because Amazon.com had suspended Lane's selling privileges. Lane then proceeded to create a third account and again agreed to the Business Solution Agreement, which allowed for any disputes to be resolved through arbitration. The third account was then blocked. He then created a fourth account, which was then blocked.

Ms. Peters opened a seller's account to sell "hard to find DVDs". A month later, Amazon.com, suspended the account claiming she failed to complete the seller review process. Plaintiff claimed that during her suspension, Amazon was in possession of funds from her sales. The account was later closed and Peters demanded Amazon forward the money from her sales.

Defendant, Amazon Service LLC motioned to compel arbitration.

Analysis

The court found that the Business Solution Agreement (BSA), contained a forum selection clause mandating arbitration. Additionally, the court found that the plaintiffs agreed to the BSA. The court found plaintiff's argument that the participation agreement to be a program policy to be incorrect. The court argues that first, "what matters for the present motion is the agreement plaintiffs intended, as manifested by the contract language; second, plaintiff's theory that any information on the amazon.com website is a program policy is out of step with basic contract interpretation principles to avoid absurd results; and third, Amazon's reply neutralizes plaintiffs' factual representations."

As a result, the court found that there was a valid agreement to arbitrate. Additionally, the court found that the plaintiffs claim fell within the scope of the arbitration clause.

CONCLUSION

The District Court granted the motion to compel arbitration.

Phila. Contributionship Ins. Co. v. Neoteric Solutions Inc. *Procedure*

***Phila. Contributionship Ins. Co. v. Neoteric Solutions,* Inc., 2016 U.S. Dist. LEXIS 23673 (D.N.J. Feb. 24, 2016).**

ISSUE

Whether the court should grant defendants motion to dismiss because the court lacks the appropriate personal jurisdiction.

RULE

"When a defendant challenges a court's exercise of personal jurisdiction, the plaintiff bears the burden to prove, by a preponderance of the evidence, facts sufficient to establish personal jurisdiction." *Carteret Sav. Bank, FA v. Shushan*, 954 F.2d 141, 146 (3d Cir. 1992). "These facts must demonstrate that the defendant purposefully availed itself of the privilege of conducting activities within the forum State, thus invoking the benefits and protections of its laws." *Toys "R" Us, Inc. v. Step Two, S.A.*, 318 F.3d 446, 451 (3d Cir. 2003) (quoting *Asahi Metal Indus. Co., Ltd. v. Superior Court of California*, 480 U.S. 102, 109 (1987)). "The plaintiff must also show the defendant reasonably should anticipate being brought into Court in the subject forum. *See Toys "R" Us, Inc.*, 318 F.3d at 451.

CASE DETAILS

Facts

Plaintiff brought this claim, alleging that a replacement battery purchased from defendant caused a fire a property owned by plaintiffs insured. Plaintiffs now seek to recover monetary damages for the amount paid to its insured. Plaintiff argues that the battery was defectively designed and manufactured. Defendant filed a third party complaint against Dongguan Hosowell Technology Co. Ltd. and Hosowell Technology Co., Ltd. Both companies have a distribution center in California called Bay Valley, which is also a named defendant.

Defendant claims that Hosowell caused any of the alleged defects in the replacement battery. Hosowell moves to dismiss the third party claims.

Analysis

The court is satisfied that defendant has established a *prima facie* case of personal jurisdiction and is entitled to limited discovery on the issue of jurisdiction. Defendant provided an exhibit that clearly shows Hosowell is selling products through a company located in New Jersey, which would establish jurisdiction. The court also finds that in the interest of fairness plaintiff should be permitted to conduct jurisdictional discovery of the other third party defendants.

CONCLUSION

The court recommends that third party defendants' motion to dismiss be denied, and that third-party plaintiffs be permitted to take jurisdictional discovery of hosowell limited to service of a maximum of ten interrogatories directed specifically to the issue of personal jurisdiction.

Piao Shang Indus. Co. v. Acco Brands Corp.
Patent Infringement; Procedure

***Piao Shang Indus. Co. v. Acco Brands Corp.*, 2011 U.S. Dist. LEXIS 67417 (C.D. Cal. June 23, 2011).**

ISSUE

Whether the court can allow plaintiff's claim to continue where it does not appear that plaintiff's claim against defendants arise out of the same transaction or occurrence.

RULE

"Persons ... may be joined in one action as defendants if: (A) any right to relief is asserted against them jointly, severally or in the alternative with respect to or arising out of the same transaction, occurrence or series of transactions or occurrences; and (B) any questions of law or fact common to all defendants will arise in the action." *League to Save Lake Tahoe v. Tahoe Regional planning Agency*, 558 F.2d 914, 917 (9th Cir. 1997).

CASE DETAILS

Facts

Plaintiff's complaint alleges a single claim against defendants Acco Brands, Amazon.com, Best Buy, and Bracketron for patent infringement. Plaintiff alleges that each of the defendants "makes, uses, provides, offers to sell, and sells various devices that embody plaintiff's patented invention for a telephone cradle.

Analysis

The court finds that it is not clear that plaintiff's claims against defendants arise out of the same transaction or occurrence because each defendant sells a different device allegedly infringing on the patented invention.

CONCLUSION

The court orders plaintiff to show cause in writing why one or more parties should not be dropped from this case for improper joinder. The plaintiff, alternatively, may file separate actions against each of the defendants.

Power Play Mktg. Group v. Treasure Transp., Inc. *Procedure*

***Power Play Mktg. Group v. Treasure Transp., Inc.*, 2014 U.S. Dist. LEXIS 93597 (D.S.D. July 10, 2014).**

ISSUE

Whether a default judgment should be entered against a defendant for not appearing.

RULE

A person who may be jointly liable in a case may not have judgment entered against them until all other joint matters have been decided, one party defaulting does not lead to final judgment for all.

CASE DETAILS

Facts

US Truck and Treasure Transportation did not respond to Power Play's motion for default judgment. A default was filed against US Truck by the clerk of the court.

Analysis

The court decides to keep US Truck in default and not enter judgment until the matter against the other defendants has been heard.

CONCLUSION

The court denies the plaintiff's motion for default judgment. Judgment will not be entered against US Truck until the other defendants have been heard.

Pragmatus Mobile, LLC v. Amazon.Com, Inc.
Patent Infringement; Procedure

***Pragmatus Mobile, LLC v. Amazon.Com, Inc.*, 2015 U.S. Dist. LEXIS 82256 (D. Del. June 17, 2015).**

ISSUE

Whether the court should grant Amazon's motion to stay litigation pending *inter parties* review (IPR)?

RULE

The court considers three factors when deciding whether to stay on litigation pending IPR: "whether a court would unduly prejudice or present a clear tactical disadvantage to the non-moving party, whether a stay will simplify the issues in question and trial of the case, whether discovery is complete and whether a trial date has been set." *Neste Oul OYJ v. Dynamic Fuels, LLC*, 2003 WL 3353984, at *1 (D. Del. July 2, 2013).

CASE DETAILS

Facts:

Pragmatus Mobile has filed suit against Amazon.Com and other defendants alleging patent infringement claims. Amazon has in turn, filed a motion to stay litigation.

Analysis:

The court found that the Defendants" delay in petitioning for IPR could create at least some tactical disadvantage for the plaintiff and a stay may unduly prejudice plaintiff. The timing of the filing by the Defendants suggests that they are requesting this motion as a tactical advantage and therefore, the court looks down upon this request. Weighing the factors, the court stated that they did not favor granting the stay.

CONCLUSION

The court denied Amazon's motion to stay litigation.

Premium Products, Inc. v. Pro Performance Sports, LLC, et al.
Patent Infringement; Procedure

***Premium Prods. v. Pro Performance Sports, LLC*, 997 F. Supp. 2d 433 (E.D. Va. 2014).**

ISSUE

Whether disqualifying Spiegel was clearly erroneous or contrary to law where the magistrate found that Spiegel was likely to be a necessary witness, was not a pro se litigant and Premium did not qualify for the substantial- hardship exception?

RULE

Under 28 U.S.C. §636 (b)(1)(A), a party can object to the disqualification of counsel and a district judge may reconsider a pretrial matter decided by a magistrate judge" where it has been shown that the magistrate judge's order is clearly erroneous or contrary to law." 28 U.S.C. §636 (b)(1)(A). The Virginia Rule of Professional Conduct (VRPC) 3.7, the witness- advocate rule, states that a necessary witness in a trial cannot be the counsel for the trial unless they fall under the substantial-hardship exceptions.

CASE DETAILS

Facts

Premium alleges that Pro Performance design of the Universal Kicking Tee infringed a patent and trade dress held by Premium by the Triplex Stealth kicking tee. Premium brings claims of unfair competition and false advertising in addition to the infringement claims. On December 20, 2013, the defendants filed a Motion to Disqualify Spiegel from representing Premium in its infringement case. The Judge in the District Court granted the motion, because Spiegel, as sole inventor of the device at issue and sole prosecuting attorney of the patent and trade dress at issue, was likely to be a necessary witness in the action. Premium now appeals.

Analysis

The witness-advocate rule is mandatory and not subject to waiver by either party. The court must have everyone's interest in mind and must act in a way to protect the integrity of the legal system as a whole. Additionally, the court must determine whether the person would be a necessary witness in the case. As Spiegel is the sole inventor and the sole prosecuting attorney of the patent and trade dress infringement, he will be a necessary witness at trial. Siegel's dual roles as a lawyer and witness would create the appearance of impropriety. The court affirms the magistrate's ruling that Spiegel is disqualified from representing Premium as the magistrate did not err or rule contrary to law.

CONCLUSION

The court affirms the magistrate's ruling that Spiegel is disqualified from representing Premium.

Pullins v. Amazon.Com.INDC, Inc.
Employee's rights; Procedural

***Pullins v. Amazon.com.indc*, LLC, 2015 U.S. Dist. LEXIS 137272 (S.D. Ind. Oct. 8, 2015).**

ISSUE

Whether the court should grant the plaintiff's Motion for Leave to File Surreply and Defendant's Motion for Summary Judgment?

RULE

In a Motion for Summary Judgment, the facts should be looked at in the most favorable light to the non moving party. Summary Judgment is appropriate when there is no genuine issue of material fact and the moving party in entitled to judgment as a matter of law. *Celotex Corp. v. Catrett*, 477 U.S. 317, 322-323 (1986).

CASE DETAILS

Facts:

Pullins sued Amazon under the Civil Rights Act of 1964, alleging that Amazon retaliated against him for engaging in protected activity. Amazon operates an order fulfillment center in Plainfield, Indiana and Indianapolis, Indiana. Amazon has a Productivity Policy that sets forth minimum productivity expectations. Pullins was hired in June 2011 as a warehouse associate in Plainfield. In April 2013, Pullins transferred to Indianapolis where he trained and worked. Once he received tenure, he failed to meet the productivity expectations of 100%. On June 7, he was given a written warning indicating that for 6 weeks he failed to meet performance expectations for his position. Pullins disputed the warning stating that the work assignments were unfair and that the expected productivity was unreasonable during the night shift, as there was too much down time.

On June 12, Pullins filed a Charge of Discrimination with Equal Employment Opportunity Commission alleging age discrimination. He received a second written warning on June 18. On June 19, Pullins filed a second Charge of Discrimination with the EEOC alleging age, race, and gender discrimination as well as retaliation.

He was offered the opportunity of retraining and on July 5 was retrained in pack. His productivity trended upward, but still failed to meet the productivity expectations. He was then given his final warning and that if he did not meet and maintain the expectations, he would be terminated. In September, Pullins productivity began to decrease and Amazon terminated Pullins on September 26. A hearing was held in front of the Amazon panel and they affirmed Pullins' termination and Pullins filed suit in this court. Defendant moved for summary judgment and Plaintiff moved for leave to file a surreply.

Analysis:

Plaintiff's motion for leave to file a surreply is untimely and does not respond or object to any new evidence cited in the Defendant's reply, and is therefore denied. Defendant's Summary Judgment Motion shall be looked at in a light most favorable to Pullins. Defendant's request that the Court strike Pullins' appendix is untimely and denied.

The court finds that Pullins cannot show that he met Amazon's legitimate performance expectations. The undisputed evidence is that Pullins failed to meet the productivity standards repeatedly and was coached and counseled and even retrained and yet his performance did not end up improving enough to meet standards. He was given three warnings and did not meet expectations. Additionally, Pullins cannot identify an employee that was treated more favorably. He also fails to establish a case of retaliation, and even if he could do so, Amazon has been able to prove a legitimate, nondiscriminatory reason for termination of his employment. Pullins fails to identify any Amazon policy or any evidence to suggest that further warnings were required. Pullins also makes several different allegations, however, offers no evidence as to support those allegations.

CONCLUSION

The court denies the Plaintiff's Motion to Leave to File a Surreply and grants the Defendant's Motion for Summary Judgment.

Raya v. Amazon.Com
Procedure; Employee Rights

***Raya v. Amazon.com, LLC*, 2015 U.S. Dist. LEXIS 86006 (N.D. Cal. June 30, 2015).**

ISSUE

Whether the court should grant plaintiff, Raya's Motion to Remand?

RULE

Removal is proper under 28 U.S.C. § 1441 where an action is one in which federal district courts have original jurisdiction. 28 U.S.C. §1441(a). The Class Action Fairness Act "CAFA" gave district courts original jurisdiction of any civil action in which the matter in controversy exceeds the sum or value of $5,000,000, exclusive of interests and costs, and is a class action in which the parties satisfy among other requirements, minimal diversity. *Abrego Abrego v. The Dow Chemical Co.*, 443 F.3d 676, 680 (9th Cir. 2006) (quoting 28 U.S.C. § 1332(d).).

CASE DETAILS

Facts

On March 18, 2015, plaintiff, Raya filed suit alleging Amazon's California hourly non-exempt employees in its warehouse operations were "not provided Second Unpaid 30-minute Meal Periods for qualifying shifts exceeding 12 hours in length nor paid one hour of compensation at the employees' regular shift rate in lieu thereof; not provided third paid 10 minute rest periods for qualifying shifts exceeding 10 hours in length nor paid one hour of compensation at the employees' regular rate in lieu thereof; not provided with complaint wage statements showing the start and end dates of each pay period, nor the address of the employers as required by Cal. Labor Code section 226."

Analysis

The court agrees with Amazon's argument that irrespective of any sums it has attributed to the other causes of action or claims, the amount attributable to the fourth cause of action alone exceeds the jurisdictional threshold. The court found that the amount in controversy is reasonable under the fourth cause of action and therefore Amazon met its burden of demonstrating that the amount in controversy is greater than $5 million.

CONCLUSION

The court denied Raya's motion to remand.

Raya v. Amazon.Com
Procedure; Employee Rights

***Raya v. Amazon.com, LLC*, 2015 U.S. Dist. LEXIS 85997 (N.D. Cal. July 1, 2015).**

ISSUE

Whether the court should grant Amazon's Motion to Dismiss or Stay?

RULE

The first-to-file rule gives the district court power to decline jurisdiction over an action when a complaint involving the same parties and issues has already been filed in another district. It is intended for promoting efficiency of the courts. Three factors are analyzed in regards to the first to file rule: "chronology of lawsuits, similarity of the parties, and similarity of the issues."

CASE DETAILS

Facts

On March 18, 2015, plaintiff, Raya filed suit alleging Amazon's California hourly non-exempt employees in its warehouse operations were "not provided Second Unpaid 30-minute Meal Periods for qualifying shifts exceeding 12 hours in length nor paid one hour of compensation at the employees' regular shift rate in lieu thereof; not provided third paid 10 minute rest periods for qualifying shifts exceeding 10 hours in length nor paid one hour of compensation at the employees' regular rate in lieu thereof; not provided with complaint wage statements showing the start and end dates of each pay period, nor the address of the employers as required by Cal. Labor Code section 226."

Analysis

Amazon brings a motion to dismiss or stay on the ground that a case currently pending in Kentucky that was filed 15 months prior to this action meets the rule's similarity requirements. The court disagrees. It acknowledges that there are similarities between the cases but it is not enough to meet the first-to-file requirements and for that purpose, they are substantially dissimilar.

CONCLUSION

The court denied Amazon's motion to dismiss or stay.

Red Pine Point LLC v. Amazon.Com, Inc.
Patent Infringement; Procedure

Red Pine Point LLC v. Amazon.Com, Inc. **Case No. 14C 00274; 14C 00290. United States District Court Northern District of Illinois Eastern Division, July 2014.**

ISSUE

Should the court grant defendant Amazon's motion to transfer venue to the Northern District of California?

RULE

Pursuant to 28 U.S.C. § 1404(a), the court can transfer venue of a case to another district or division where it might have been brought for the convenience of parties and witnesses, in the interests of justice.

CASE DETAILS

Facts

Red Pine Point LLC has filed multiple lawsuits alleging patent infringement against multiple defendants.

Analysis

The court recognized that the companies are in the Northern District of California and it would be more convenient for them. The bulk of witnesses that have knowledge of design and manufacture of the accused products are in or near the Northern District of California. The bulk of documents are in California and Washington. The court determined that the related and consolidated cases are to be transferred to the Northern District of California.

CONCLUSION

The court granted the motion to transfer venue to the Northern District of California.

Research Frontiers, Inc. v. E Ink Corp.
Patent; Claim Construction

***Research Frontiers, Inc. v. E Ink Corp.*, 2016 U.S. Dist. LEXIS 38441 (D. Del. Mar. 24, 2016).**

ISSUE

Here, the court is determining what definition to apply to disputed terms of the patent at issue.

RULE

"A claim in a patent provides the metes and bounds of the right which the patent confers on the patentee to exclude others from making, using, or selling the protected invention." *Corning Glass Works v. Sumitomo Elec. USA., Inc.*, 868 F.2d 1251, 1257 (Fed. Cir. 1989).

CASE DETAILS

Facts

Plaintiff is a developer of suspended particle technology that is used in display and light control applications. Plaintiff owns the patents at issue in this case. Defendant, E Ink Corp. supplies electronic paper displays that are incorporated into eBooks, eReaders, and other display products. The parties submitted 10 disputed terms to the court in order to reconcile their meaning.

CONCLUSION

The court defines the terms as follows:

491 Patent

(1) Light Modulating Unit – Means a unit which controls light transmission using a suspension of particles.
(2) Light Valve – Means a cell formed of two walls that are spaced apart by a a small distance, at lease one wall being transparent, the walls

having electrodes thereon usually in the form of transparent conductive coatings.

(3) Liquid light valve suspension – Means a liquid suspension of particles opening through particle alignment and closing through Brownian movement.

(4) In direct contract with the cross linked polymer matrix – Should be given its plain and ordinary meaning.

185 Patent

(1) Light modulating unit comprising a suspension – Means a unit which controls light transmission using a suspension of particles opening through particle alignment and closing thorough Brownian movement.

(2) Light Valve – Means a cell formed of two walls that are spaced apart by a small distance, at lease one wall being transparent, the walls having electrodes thereon usually in the form of transparent conductive coatings.

(3) Light Valve Suspension – Means a liquid suspension of particles opening through particle alignment and closing through Brownian movement.

(4) Heat Reflective – Means capable of reflecting heat (infrared radiation).

(5) Said Particles – Means the group of anisometrically shaped particles.

956 Patent

(1) SPD Film – Means a film comprising a suspension of particles to control light transmission through the film, opening through particle alignment and closing through Brownian movement.

(2) "The walls are formed of a substrate and the film and the substrate are adhered to one another by coating either the film or the substrate or both the film and the substrate with an adhesive, placing the film and the substrate into contact and adhering the film and the substrate" – Means the walls are each formed of a substrate and the film and either or both of the substrates are adhered to one another by coating either the film, or either or both of the substrates, or both the film and either

or both of the substrates with an adhesive, placing the film and either or both of the substrates into contact and adhering the film and either or both of the substrates.

(3) The walls are formed of a substrate and the film and the substrate are adhered to one another by the method of – Means the walls are each formed of a substrate and the film and one or both of the substrates are adhered to one another by the method of.

NOTE – In a separate opinion, filed 6 days after this opinion the court denied defendants motion for partial summary judgment that the asserted claims are invalid despite the plaintiffs written admissions.

Ricchio v. Amazon.Com, Inc.
Copyright Infringement

***Ricchio v. Amazon.Com, Inc.*, 2012 U.S. Dist. LEXIS 52088 (E.D. Wis. Apr. 13, 2012).**

ISSUE

Whether plaintiff meets the poverty requirements such that his motion to proceed in forma pauperis should be granted.

RULE

"Section 1915 is meant to ensure indigent litigants meaningful access to federal courts, and applies to both non - prisoner plaintiffs as well as those who are incarcerated." *Floyd. V. United States Postal Ser.*, 105 F.3d 274, 275-77 (6th Cir. 1997).

CASE DETAILS

Facts

Plaintiff filed a copyright infringement action against Amazon.com, Inc. (Amazon). Plaintiff asserts that defendant unlawfully displayed the cover art for and sold his book on defendant's website. Normally there is a $350 filing fee for cases in federal court. 28 U.S.C. § 1914(a). However, plaintiff has requested to proceed in forma pauperis, pursuant to 28 U.S.C. § 1915.

Analysis

The court found that here, plaintiff meets the poverty requirements found in 28 U.S.C. § 1915. Plaintiff here has an income of $778 per month of which $754.16 goes to fixed expenses.

CONCLUSION

The court held that plaintiff's request to proceed in forma pauperis is granted.

Ricchio v. Amazon.com, Inc.
Copyright Infringement

***Ricchio v. Amazon.com, Inc.*, 2012 U.S. Dist. LEXIS 147193, 40 Media L. Rep. 2481, 2012 WL 4865016 (E.D. Wis. Oct. 12, 2012).**

ISSUE

Whether the court should grant plaintiffs motion to appoint counsel and defendants motion to dismiss.

RULE

Although civil litigants do not have a constitutional or statutory right to counsel, this court has the discretion to request attorneys to represent indigents in appropriate cases pursuant to 28 U.S.C. § 1915. *Luttrell v. Nickel*, 129 F.3d 933, 936 (7th Cir. 1997). "As a threshold matter, litigants must make a reasonable attempt to secure private counsel." *Zarnes v. Rhodes*, F.3e 285, 288 (7th Cir. 1995). "Once this threshold requirement has been met, the court must address the following question: given the difficulty of the case, does this plaintiff appear to be competent to try the case him or herself and, if not would the presence of counsel likely make a difference in the outcome of the case." *Id.*

CASE DETAILS

Facts

Plaintiff brings this action for copyright infringement against defendant Amazon.Com, Inc. (Amazon). In 1999 plaintiff sold 365 copies of his book to defendant so that defendant could sell the book on its website. Plaintiff alleges that in 2000, defendant began permitting third parties to use its website to sell copies of plaintiff's book and that plaintiff received no money from these sales. Defendant allowed images of the cover of the book to be posted in connection with these sales.

Defendant brings a motion to dismiss on the grounds that plaintiff's claims are barred by the doctrine of claim preclusion and because the claim failed to state a cause of action.

Analysis

The court finds that here, even though plaintiff has failed to find counsel on his own, that the issues of the case are straightforward and uncomplicated. Therefore, the court does not believe that the presence of counsel is likely to make a difference in this case. Further the court finds that the claims asserted by plaintiff are barred because the lower court dismissed those claims with prejudice. The court finds that plaintiff failed to state a claim for copyright infringement. Plaintiff alleges that defendant is allowing third parties to sell copies of the book without authorization, but he does not claim that any of the books being sold on defendant's website are counterfeit copies.

CONCLUSION

For the foregoing reasons the court denies plaintiff's motion to appoint counsel and defendant's motion to dismiss is granted.

RMail LTD v. Amazon.com, Inc.
Patent Infringement; Procedural

***RMail Ltd. v. Amazon.com, Inc.*, 2013 U.S. Dist. LEXIS 34912 (E.D. Tex. Mar. 11, 2013).**

ISSUE

Whether the court should construe the patents in suit in favor of the plaintiff or defendant?

RULE

Claim construction is an issue of law for the court to decide. *Markman v. Westview Instruments, Inc.*, 52 F.3d 967, 970-971 (Fed. Cir. 1995). To decided what the meaning of the claims are, the courts look to the claims, the specification and the prosecution history.

CASE DETAILS

Facts:

Plaintiff brings suit alleging infringement of patents which relate to technologies for providing proof of message transmission, delivery and content. They are called "Feldbau Patents" and one is asserted against all the defendants in the suit. The Tomkow Patents are also alleged in this suit.

Analysis:

The court construes the patents in suit by interpreting the language and content and determines that the claim construction is set and shall be followed accordingly.

CONCLUSION

The court determined claim construction for the two patents in suit.

Robbins v. Unemployment Insurance Appeals Board
Patent Infringement; Procedure

***Robbins v. Unemployment Ins. Appeals Bd.*, 2016 Del. Super. LEXIS 31 (Del. Super. Ct. Jan. 25, 2016).**

ISSUE

Whether the decision of the Board should be affirmed?

RULE

Pursuant to 19 Del. C. § 3323(a), the Superior Court's jurisdiction is limited to review for errors of law, together with a limited factual review. Review is limited to "whether there is substantial evidence in the record to support the Board's findings and whether such findings are free from legal error. The court does not weigh the evidence, determine questions of credibility, or make its own factual findings." *Murphy & Landon, Pa. v. Pernio*, 121 A.3d 1215, 1222 (Del. 2015).

CASE DETAILS

Facts:

Robbins sought unemployment compensation from Amazon after termination of his employment on December 16, 2014. Robbins was in an accident on November 11, 2014 and was injured. He returned to work December 16, as he was restricted to work by a doctor's note through December 11, 2014. On December 16, he determined he was not able to perform his work tasks so he left. He did not provide a doctor's note excusing him after the first note he provided through December 11, 2014. The Claims Deputy and Appeals Referee both separately decided that Robbins was not entitled to benefits as he voluntarily quit. The Unemployment Insurance Appeals Board determined that Robbins was not entitled to unemployment compensation benefits as he voluntarily quit without good cause. Robbins appealed.

Analysis:

The court found substantial evidence on the record that Robbins voluntarily quit his employment. Burden below was on Robbins to establish his good cause for leaving Amazon. The Board's decision was that Robbins did not meet his burden of proof by substantial evidence and this decision is affirmed.

CONCLUSION

The court affirmed the Board's decision.

Roe v. Amazon.com
Privacy Violation; Unlawful Use of Images

***Roe v. Amazon.com*, 2016 U.S. Dist. LEXIS 33297 (S.D. Ohio Mar. 15, 2016).**

ISSUE

Whether the court should grant the defendant's motion for judgment on the pleadings.

RULE

Following the holding in Commercial Money Ctr., Inc. v. Illinois Union Ins, "To withstand a Rule 12(c) motion for judgment on the pleadings, a complaint must contain direct or inferential allegations respecting all the material elements under some viable legal theory.

CASE DETAILS

Facts

Plaintiffs, John and Jane Roe, filed suit after the publication of their engagement photograph was placed on the cover of an erotic book, titled *A Gronking to Remember* written by Jane Doe. Amazon.com, Inc. Barnes & Noble, Inc., Apple Inc., and Smashwords published the book. The cover of the book, plaintiffs allege was appropriated by the defendants for commercial gain. Plaintiffs never gave permission for the use of this photograph. Following the publicity. Plaintiffs claim their image was held up to ridicule and embarrassment. The book was used in jokes on the Tonight Show and Jimmy Kimmel Live and additionally was read before the press at media day for the XLIX Super Bowl.

Plaintiffs allege wrongful appropriation of their persona for commercial purposes as made actionable under Ohio Revised Core Section 2741, "invasion of privacy as that tort is recognized in the State of Ohio," and "tort liability for violation of Restatement Second of Torts 652."

Defendant Amazon.com, Barnes & Noble Inc., and Smashwords Inc., sought out summary judgment. Defendant, Jane Doe added a motion for judgment on the pleadings.

Analysis

The court found that defendant, Jane Doe was not entitled to judgment on the pleadings against plaintiffs on Count I. Additionally, defendant Jane Doe was denied her motion for judgment on the pleadings.

The corporate defendants, Amazon.com included, sought summary judgment asserting that they are not publishers of the book and that any use on their part was incidental. Additionally, they argue they did not know or had any reason to know of the alleged wrongdoing. The court found that the plaintiffs failed to show any facts to support the accusation that the corporate defendants were publishers. The court therefore concluded that the corporate defendants were not publishers.

CONCLUSION

The United States District Court denied defendant, Jane Doe's motion for judgment on the pleadings, and granted corporate defendant's motions for summary judgment.

Rosner v. Amazon.com
Defamation; Procedural

***Rosner v Amazon.com*, 132 A.D.3d 835 (N.Y. App. Div. 2d Dep't 2015).**

ISSUE

Whether the court should affirm the decision of the lower court to dismiss the claims?

RULE

In a motion to dismiss a complaint pursuant to CPLR 3211(a)(7) for failure to state a cause of action, a court must accept the facts alleged in the complaint as true and accord the plaintiff the benefit of every possible favorable inference and determine only whether the factual allegations fit within any cognizable legal theory.

CASE DETAILS

Facts:

Plaintiff is the author of a book that is sold on Amazon.com. On November 13, 2012, an anonymous review of the plaintiff's book was posted on Amazon stating that plaintiff sent emails peddling his book. Amazon refused to remove the comment at plaintiff's request and plaintiff filed action to recover for defamation.

Timeline:

The plaintiff appeals from an order of the Supreme Court, Kings County, which granted the defendant's motion pursuant to CPLR 3211 (a)(7) to dismiss the amended complaint and a judgment of the same court in favor of the defendant and against him dismissing the amended complaint. Amazon moved to dismiss the amended complaint for failure to state a cause of action. October 24, 2013, the Supreme Court granted the motion.

Analysis:

For a defamation claim, the plaintiff must allege that defendant published a false statement to a third party without authorization and it caused special harm or constituted defamation per se. Here, the plaintiff failed to state a cause of action to recover damages for defamation, since he acknowledged that he sent the emails. The court affirmed the lower court's dismissal of the amended complaint.

CONCLUSION

The court affirmed the lower court's dismissal of the amended complaint.

Routt v. Amazon.com Inc.

Copyright Infringement; Procedural; Violation of the Lanham Act

---

***Routt v. Amazon.com, Inc.*, 2012 U.S. Dist. LEXIS 170602, 105 U.S.P.Q.2D (BNA) 1089, Copy. L. Rep. (CCH) P30,334 (W.D. Wash. Nov. 30, 2012).**

ISSUE

Should the court grant the defendant's Motion to Dismiss?

RULE

A complaint must contain a "short and plain statement of the claim showing that the pleader is entitled to relief." Fed. R. Civ. Pro. 8 (a)(2). The purpose of this rule is to "give the defendant fair notice of what the claim is and the grounds upon which it rests." *Bell Atlantic v. Twombly*, 550 U.S. 544, at 555.

CASE DETAILS

Facts:

The plaintiff filed suit against defendant for copyright infringement. Ms. Routt holds various copyrights, which she alleges Amazon affiliates infringed through Amazon's Associates Program. Ms. Routt is a mixed-media artist and designer of jewelry, apparel and collectables. She created, owns and operates SandysBeachGifts.com, and has filed multiple applications for copyright protection with the United States Copyright Office directed to various photographs she has created. Routt alleges that these Associate websites displayed her photographs without her permission.

Analysis:

Ms. Routt has not alleged sufficient facts for the court to infer that Amazon had control over the infringing actions of its Associates. Ms. Routt does not allege sufficient non-conclusory factual matter to state a plausible claim that the relationship between Amazon and its associates is anything other than the relationship described in the agreement. She does not make any specific allegations that would allow the court to reasonably infer that Amazon had control over its Associates or their infringing activities.

CONCLUSION

The court grants the motion to dismiss the complaint with leave to amend within 15 days.

Routt v. Amazon.com
Copyright Infringement

***Routt v. Amazon.com, Inc.*, 2013 U.S. Dist. LEXIS 26265, Copy. L. Rep. (CCH) P30,388, 2013 WL 695922 (W.D. Wash. Feb. 26, 2013).**

ISSUE

Should the court grant Amazon.com's motion to dismiss?

RULE

A complaint must contain "a short and plain statement of the claim showing that the pleader is entitled to relief . . . " Fed. R. Civ. Pro. 8(a)(2). The purpose of this rule is to "'give the defendant fair notice of what . . . the claim is and the grounds upon which it rests.'" *Bell Atlantic v. Twombly*, 550 U.S. 544 at 555, 127 S. Ct. 1955, 167 L. Ed. 2d 929 (quoting *Conley v. Gibson*, 355 U.S. 41, 47, 78 S. Ct. 99, 2 L. Ed. 2d 80 (1957)).

CASE DETAILS

Facts

Plaintiff, Sandy Routt, alleged that Amazon.com's associates had used her copyrighted photographs on their website without her permission. Routt filed suit alleging copyright infringement and false designation of origin under the Lanham Act, 15 U.S.C. Section 1125(a).

Defendant, Amazon.com motioned to dismiss the first amended complaint.

Analysis

The court found that Ms. Routt's original complaint failed to state a claim. The FAC was found to be different in three ways, none which the court deemed to justify a different result on the second motion to dismiss.

The court first found that "it makes no difference to the court's analysis that the FAC summarizes the terms of Amazon's Associates Agreement." Second that "it does not change the court's analysis that the FAC contains several documents elaborating on the Amazon Associate Agreement, including 'Associates Program

Operating Agreement' and a list of 'Associates Program Excluded Products." Third, the court found that the "two paragraphs of new factual information do not contain sufficient factual matter such that they state a plausible claim for relief when added to the allegations in the original complaint." The amendments were found to not change the court's analysis.

CONCLUSION

The United States District Court granted Amazon.com's motion to dismiss.

Sandybeachgifts.com v. Amazon.com, Inc.
Lanham Act; Copyright Infringement

***Sandybeachgifts.com v. Amazon.com, Inc.*, 584 Fed. Appx. 713 (9th Cir. Wash. 2014)**

ISSUE

Should the court of appeals affirm the United States District Court's dismissal of plaintiff's claims?

RULE

Following the holding in *Perfect 10, Inc. v. Visa Int'l Serv.*, "To state a claim for vicarious copyright infringement, a plaintiff must allege that the defendant has (1) the right and ability to supervise the infringing conduct and (2) a direct financial interest in the infringing activity."

Following the holding in *Hard Rock Café Licensing Corp. v. Concession*, "Vicarious liability under the Lanham Act requires a finding that the defendant and the infringer have an apparent or actual partnership, have authority to bind one another in transactions with third parties, or exercise joint ownership or control over the infringing product"."

CASE DETAILS

Facts

Plaintiff, Sandy Routt, alleged that Amazon.com's associates had used her copyrighted photographs on their website without her permission. Routt filed suit alleging copyright infringement and false designation of origin under the Lanham Act, 15 U.S.C. Section 1125(a).

The United States District court dismissed the action for failure to allege sufficient facts to establish that Amazon should be liable for its associates' conduct.

Analysis

The court found that Routt did not adequately allege that Amazon exercises any direct control over their associates' activities and therefore cannot be found liable for its associates' conduct.

CONCLUSION

The Court of Appeals found that Routt failed to state a claim for vicarious liability and affirmed the order of the lower court in favor of Amazon.com

Sanmedica Int'l, LLC v. Amazon.com, Inc.
Trademark Infringement

***Sanmedica Int'l, LLC v. Amazon.com, Inc.*, 2015 U.S. Dist. LEXIS 50470 (D. Utah Mar. 27, 2015).**

ISSUE

Whether the court should grant Amazon's motion for summary judgment because use of the mark here did not cause confusion among consumers.

RULE

"The court shall grant summary judgment if the movant shows that there is no genuine dispute as to any material fact and the movant is entitled to judgment as a matter of law." When analyzing a motion for summary judgment, the court must "view the evidence and draw all reasonable inferences therefrom in the light most favorable to the party opposing summary judgment." However, "the non-moving party must present more than a scintilla of evidence in favor of his position." A dispute is genuine only "if the evidence is such that a reasonable jury could return a verdict for the nonmoving party." "The fact that the parties have filed cross-motions for summary judgment does not affect the applicable standard."

CASE DETAILS

Facts

Plaintiff Western Holdings owns the trademark for SeroVital, a dietary supplement. Plaintiff SanMedica has a license to use the SeroVital trademark. SanMedica offered SeroVital for sale on the Amazon platform, and it was ultimately removed for a policy violation. However, Amazon's system still generated and published ads on search engines such as Google and Bing when consumers searched for SeroVital.

Plaintiff Sanmedica LLC sued Amazon for (1) trademark infringement under the Lanham Act; (2) unfair competition based on false representation in violation of Lanham Act; (3) unjust enrichment; (4) injunctive relief; (5) declaratory relief; and (6) violation of the Utah Truth in Advertising Act. Amazon moved for summary judgment and Plaintiff cross motioned for summary judgment. Amazon moved for summary judgment on Plaintiffs' trademark infringement, unfair competition, unjust enrichment and URAA claims.

Analysis

The court found that Amazon did engage in unauthorized use of trademark since it continued to use the image after the item had been removed, but consumers could not purchase the goods once they clicked on the trademark. Therefore, under the Lanham Act there is no likelihood of confusion since unauthorized use did not influence any sales.

The court further held that initial interest confusion based on false representation under Lanham Act is a question for jury.

CONCLUSION

The court granted Amazon's motion for summary judgment in part and denied the motion in part. Plaintiff's motion for partial summary judgment was denied.

Schnall v. AT&T Wireless Services
Procedure

***Schnall v. AT&T Wireless Servs., Inc.*, 2010 Wash. LEXIS 61 (Wash. 2010).**

ISSUE

Whether Washington will believe the trial court did not abuse its discretion by declining to certify such a class.

CASE DETAILS

Facts

AT&T customers filed a nationwide class action alleging the company misled consumers when it billed them for a charge that was not included in advertised monthly rates and was not described clearly in billing statements. The trial court denied the class action. The court of appeals reversed.

CONCLUSION

The Court found that the action should not be certified as a nation wide class action, holding "a nationwide class action would be unmanageable and unduly burdensome on the trial court and he state judicial system and serve no real benefit to plaintiffs who are free to bring statewide class actions in their home state."

Schnall v. AT&T Wireless Services
Procedure

***Schnall v. AT&T Wireless Servs., Inc.*, 171 Wn.2d 260 (Wash. 2011).**

CASE DETAILS

Facts

AT&T customers filed a nationwide class action alleging the company misled consumers when it billed them for a charge that was not included in advertised monthly rates and was not described clearly in billing statements.

The trial court denied the class action and the court of appeals reversed.

CONCLUSION

The Court found that the action should not be certified as a nation wide class action, holding "a nationwide class action would be unmanageable and unduly burdensome on the trial court and he state judicial system and serve no real benefit to plaintiffs who are free to bring statewide class actions in their home state. They court reversed in part and affirmed in part.

Schneider v. Amazon.com, Inc.
Procedure

***Schneider v. Amazon.com, Inc.*, 108 Wn. App. 454 (Wash. Ct. App. 2001).**

ISSUE

Whether the lower court erred in dismissing plaintiffs claim against Amazon where Amazon was the provider or user of interactive computer services, plaintiff treats Amazon as a publisher, and Amazon is not the information content provider.

RULE

Under § 230 of the Communications Decency Act of 1996 (CDA), interactive computer service providers are immune from publisher liability. Three elements are required for § 230 immunity: The defendant must be a provider or user of an "interactive computer service"; the asserted claims must treat the defendant as a publisher or speaker of information and the information must be provided by another "information content provider."

CASE DETAILS

Facts

Plaintiff Schneider wrote several books about taxation and asset protection. The books are available at the website of Amazon.com, Inc. (Amazon). In addition to enabling purchases, the web site provides a forum for users to air their opinions about books. Amazon posted visitor's comments about plaintiff and his books. The comments were negative and one alleged plaintiff was a felon. Plaintiff's employee complained. Amazon's representative promised to remove the postings within one to two business days. Two days later, the posting had not been removed.

Analysis

Amazon is a Provider or User of Interactive Computer Services

The court holds that Amazon is a provider or user of interactive computer services because the statutory definition provides that access providers are only a subclass of the broader definition of interactive service providers entitled to immunity. According to the complaint, Amazon allows users of its site to comment about authors and their work thus providing an information service that enables access by multiple users. This brings Amazon perfectly within the statutory definition of a provider or user of interactive computer services.

Plaintiff's Claims Treat Amazon as a Publisher

The court states that publication includes the failure to remove content when first communicated by another party. In the complaint plaintiff alleged that Amazon exercises discretion over the posting of comments at its site. Thus plaintiff's complaint treats Amazon as a publisher.

Amazon is Not the Information Content Provider

The court notes that immunity is only available when the content is not provided by the service entity. The court defines an information content provider as "any person or entity that is responsible, in whole or in part, for the creation or development of information provided through the Internet of any other interactive computer service. The court rejects plaintiff's arguments that because Amazon had the right to edit the posting, and because Amazon claims licensing rights in the posted material, Amazon in effect became the content provider.

CONCLUSION

For the foregoing reasons, because all three elements for § 230 immunity are satisfied. The trial court properly concluded § 230 of the CDA bars plaintiff's claims against Amazon.

Scott v. Cingular Wireless
Class Action

***Scott v. Cingular Wireless*, 161 P.3d 1000, 160 Wn.2d 843 (Wash., 2007).**

ISSUE

Whether the class action waiver signed by plaintiffs is unconscionable because it undermines Washington's CPA to the extent that it is "injurious to the public."

RULE

An agreement that has a tendency "'to be against the public good, or to be injurious to the public'" violates public policy. *King v. Riveland*, 125 Wn.2d 500, 511, 886 P.2d 160 (1994) (quoting *Marshall v. Higginson*, 62 Wn. App. 212, 216, 813 P.2d 1275 (1991)). An agreement that violates public policy may be void and unenforceable. Restatement (Second) of Contracts § 178 (1981). Washington's CR 23 authorizes class actions and demonstrates a state policy favoring aggregation of small claims for purposes of efficiency, deterrence, and access to justice. *See, e.g., Darling* [852] *v. Champion Home Builders Co.*, 96 Wn.2d 701, 706, 638 P.2d 1249 (1982)

CASE DETAILS

Facts

The plaintiffs filed a class action suit against Cingular Wireless (Cingular) alleging that Cingular had overcharged its customers between $1 and $40 per month by illegally adding roaming and hidden charges.

Timeline

The trial court entered an order mandating individual arbitration because of an arbitration clause found in Cingular's standard subscriber contracts. That arbitration clause prohibited class action litigation and arbitration.

Analysis

The court holds that the class action waiver is unconscionable because it effectively denies many consumers to protection of Washington's Consumer

Protection Act (CPA) and because it effectively exculpates Cingular from liability for a whole class of wrongful conduct. It is, therefore unenforceable.

CONCLUSION

The court holds that because the arbitration clause itself provides that if any part is found unenforceable, the entire clause shall be void. Thus, there is no basis to compel arbitration. The court therefore vacates the order of the trial court compelling arbitration and remands for further proceedings in line with this opinion.

Script Sec. Sols. L.L.C. v. Amazon.com, Inc. Procedure

***Script Sec. Solutions L.L.C. v. Amazon.com, Inc.*, 2016 U.S. Dist. LEXIS 34259 (E.D. Tex. Mar. 16, 2016).**

ISSUE

The court is determining whether to grant defendants motion to dismiss the complaints against it.

RULE

"Whoever actively induces infringement of a patent shall be liable as an infringer." 35 U.S.C. § 271(b). "[L]iability for inducing infringement attaches only if the defendant knew of the patent and that 'the induced acts constitute patent infringement.'" *Commil USA, LLC v. Cisco Systems, Inc.*, 135 S. Ct. 1920, 1926, 191 L. Ed. 2d 883 (2015) (quoting *Global-Tech Appliances, Inc.* v. SEB S.A., 563 U.S. 754, 131 S. Ct. 2060, 2068, 179 L. Ed. 2d 1167 (2011)).

A complaint properly pleads a claim of contributory infringement if it contains sufficient facts from which the court may conclude that the claim is plausible. *In re Bill of Lading Transmission & Processing System Patent Lit.*, 681 F.3d 1323, 1337 (Fed. Cir. 2012).

A claim for willful patent infringement requires proof that (1) "the infringer acted despite an objectively high likelihood that its actions constituted infringement of a valid patent," and (2) "this objectively-defined risk (determined by the record developed in the infringement proceeding) was either known or so obvious that it should have been known to the accused infringer." *In re Seagate Tech.*, LLC, 497 F.3d 1360, 1371 (Fed. Cir. 2007).

CASE DETAILS

Facts

Plaintiff is a Texas corporation with its principal place of business in Austin, Texas. Plaintiff has filed claims alleging that defendants directly, indirectly, and willfully infringed their patents. Defendant Amazon has filed a motion to dismiss for improper venue, as well as arguing that plaintiff failed to plead indirect and willful infringement. The complaints were amended, but defendants re-filed their motions to dismiss.

Analysis

Motion to Dismiss for Improper Venue

Here, the 2011 revision to section 1391 (venue rule) containing the words "except as otherwise provided by law" does not undermine that section 1391(c) provides a definition of residency not only for the general venue statute, section 1391, but also for certain specific venue statutes. Thus Amazon's statutory interpretation of the venue statute fails and and the section 1391(c) definition of residency applies to section 1400(b).

Induced Infringement

The court finds that here plaintiff has plead that the specific products alleged to infringe; the functionality of the products that infringe; that Amazon had knowledge of the patents before the filing of the initial complaint and at the time that the first complaint was filed; that the defendants arranged to remain willfully blind to plaintiff's patents by adopting a policy of not reviewing the patents of others; and that the defendants induced customers to infringe the patents by instructing them in advertising and promotion to use the accused products in an infringing way.

Contributory Infringement

The court finds that accused is selling software products with an activation component that performs the patented method steps. The complaint is found to contain facts to infer that the activation component at issue has no use other than to perform the method steps. The allegations are thus sufficient to plead contributory infringement against Amazon.

Willfulness

The court finds that because plaintiff has pleaded knowledge of the patent, that defendants' customers are infringing, and the defendants encourage this infringement, that plaintiff has pleaded sufficiently that defendants were aware of the patents before the filing of this action.

CONCLUSION

For the foregoing reasons, the motions to dismiss the complaints are denied.

Segal Co. (Eastern States), Inc. v. Amazon.Com
Procedure

***Segal Co. (Eastern States), Inc. v. Amazon.Com*, 280 F. Supp2d (W.D. Wash., 2003).**

ISSUE

Whether to grant defendants motions to dismiss because plaintiff's claims fail to plead facts sufficient to raise a cause of action.

RULE

"Federal Rule 9(b) requires plaintiffs to state the time, place, and specific content of the false representations as well as the identities of the parties to the misrepresentation." *Teamsters Local # 427 v. Philco-Ford Corp.*, 661 F.2d 776, 782 (9th Cir. 1981). "The complaint must detail what is false or misleading about a statement, and why it is false." *In re Glen Fed, Inc. Secs. Litig.* 42 F.3d 1541, 1548 (9th Cir. 1994) (en banc).

In order to state a claim for relief under the CPA, plaintiffs must allege that acts by defendant were unfair or deceptive, occurred in the course of trade or commerce, affected the public interest, and caused injury to plaintiff's' business. *Hangman Ridge Training Stables, Inc. v. Safeco Title Ins, Co.*, 105 Wash.2d 778, 780, 719 P.2d 531 (1986).

CASE DETAILS

Facts

In June 2002, defendant engaged plaintiff to prepare stock – option valuation and employee compensation proposals for defendant. Plaintiff began work in July 2002 and provided defendant with updates for accruing fees and costs for the work in progress. On August 12, 2002, defendant informed plaintiff that it would no longer need its services. Plaintiff requested payment of over $390,000 and defendant refused payment. Plaintiff filed this action alleging breach of contract, unjust enrichment, fraud, and violations of the Washington State Consumer Protection Act (CPA).

Analysis

Motion to Dismiss

The court finds that in this case, plaintiff fails to specify the identities of the alleged fraud perpetrators, the time and place the fraudulent statements were made, and exactly what statements were fraudulent. Therefore, the complaint does not state the circumstances of fraud with sufficient particularity to satisfy the requirements of Rule 9(b).

Motion for Partial Summary Judgment

Defendant moves for partial summary judgment on plaintiffs' CPA claim, arguing that the facts presented do not constitute a CPA violation as a matter of law. The court finds that this motion is more appropriately construed as a motion to dismiss for failure to state a claim upon which relief can be granted under Federal rule 12(b)(6). The court finds that plaintiffs fail to plead sufficient facts showing that defendant's conduct was unfair or deceptive, or that defendant's conduct affected the public interest. Plaintiffs never assert that defendant contacted members of the general public, nor do plaintiffs claim that defendant execute contracts with any other parties. Plaintiffs have not pleaded sufficient facts to link defendant's alleged contractual breach to a public interest impact.

CONCLUSION

Plaintiffs fail to state a CPA claim upon which relief can be granted. The court grants the motion to dismiss.

Segal v. Amazon.com, Inc.
Procedure

***Segal v. Amazon.com, Inc.*, 2011 U.S. Dist. LEXIS 29183 (W.D. Wash. Mar. 7, 2011).**

ISSUE

The court is deciding three issues in this case:

(1) Whether to grant defendant's motion to compel plaintiffs to appear for their depositions, which would compel plaintiffs to provide contact information for their disclosed witnesses, and to continue the deadlines for completing discovery and filing dispositive motions;
(2) Whether to grant Plaintiffs' motion to compel the deposition of defendants' Rule 30(b)(6) witness; and
(3) Whether to grant Plaintiffs' motion to compel defendant to augment its responses to plaintiff's discovery requests.

RULE

The parties must conduct discovery simultaneously. One party cannot withhold discovery pending receipt of its own requested discovery. Fed. R. Civ. P. 26(d)(2)(B). "Discovery by one party does not require any other party to delay its discovery." Id.

CASE DETAILS

Facts

This case arises from plaintiffs' use of defendant's Amazon marketplace to sell textbooks and other merchandise on the internet. Plaintiffs allege that Amazon improperly withheld $1300 of plaintiffs' funds in their "Seller Account" for a period of time pending Amazon investigation of plaintiff's sales practices.

Analysis

As to defendant's motion to compel plaintiff's depositions and witness contact information and for a continuance, the court finds that plaintiffs must provide contact information for all of the fact witnesses they have disclosed within ten days of the date of this order. If plaintiffs do not oblige, the Court will order that those witnesses are precluded form testifying or offering declarations in support of plaintiffs' case.

As to plaintiffs' motion to compel a rule 30(b)(6) deposition, the court finds that plaintiffs' request is overbroad and seeks information not reasonably calculated to lead to the discovery of admissible evidence. The court further finds that plaintiffs have failed to serve a proper deposition notice or to identify with reasonably particularity the topics to be covered. The court however, because plaintiffs are self represented will offer guidance. Defendant has offered to provide a witness to testify about matters related to plaintiffs' account and their experience on Amazon Marketplace. If plaintiffs serve a proper deposition notice, they will be allowed to depose a witness on those topics.

As to plaintiff's motion to compel supplemental discovery responses, the court finds that it too is overbroad because they are not prosecuting a class action.

CONCLUSION

The court ultimately grants defendants motion to compel. The discovery deadline is extended 45 days from the date of this order. Plaintiffs' motion to compel is granted in part and denied in part. Plaintiffs' motion to compel the production of addition documents is denied.

Sen v. Amazon.com, Inc.
Settlement Agreement; Trademark Infringement; Unfair Competition; False Advertising

---

***Sen v. Amazon.com, Inc.*, 2013 U.S. Dist. LEXIS 178447, 2013 WL 6730180 (S.D. Cal. Dec. 19, 2013).**

ISSUE

The issue here is whether the court should grant defendant Amazon.Com, Inc.'s Motion to Enforce the Settlement where both defendant and plaintiff, Sen have signed the settlement, but plaintiff is attempting to add additional terms to the agreement.

RULE

"It is well settled that a district court has the equitable power to enforce summarily an agreement to settle a case pending before it. However, the district court may enforce only complete settlement agreements. *Callie v. Near*, 829 F.2d 888, 890 (9th Cir. 1987). "To be enforced a settlement agreement must meet to requirements. First, it must be a complete agreement. Second, both parties must have either agreed to the terms of the settlement or authorized their respective counsel to settle the dispute." *Harrop v. Western Airlines, Inc.* 550 F.2d 1143, 1144-45 (9th Cir. 1977).

CASE DETAILS

Facts

This case stems from plaintiffs claim of infringement of its trademark, "Baiden," used in connection with Plaintiff's product, the Baiden Mitten. Plaintiff claims that defendant used plaintiff's mark in online promotions on various search engines without plaintiff's consent. These promotions diverted internet traffic to Amazon's website with competitor products. Plaintiff alleged that this cost online traffic and sales of its product. The parties reached a settlement. However, later, plaintiff sent an email attempting to add terms to the settlement agreement. The settlement terms include a "release of all claims," and the last line of the agreement states the the undersigned "acknowledge and agree that this settlement was made before the Court and is binding and judicially enforceable." Both parties signed the agreement.

Analysis

The court first finds that the agreement is a complete and unambiguous agreement that the parties intentionally entered into. The court finds that a reasonable person would understand that "a release of all claims ... and a dismissal of the above entitled action" to mean that the person is agreeing to just that, releasing their claims and dismissing the action. The court states that this language is neither vague nor ambiguous. Further, the court holds that the last line of the agreement, would be interpreted by a reasonable person to mean that the agreement is fully binding and enforceable by a court of law.

Next, the court finds that the agreement contains all the necessary material terms and that plaintiff's additional concerns are unfounded. First, Plaintiff is not prohibited from using the Amazon platform, and is allowed to continue her use of the platform to market and sell her product. Second, Amazon has agreed to stop using plaintiff's mark and the agreement gave plaintiff modes of enforcing the agreement.

Finally, the court finds that the agreement contains consideration. In this case plaintiff gave up her claims in exchange for an undertaking by defendant that it was not legally obligated to do. Defendant agreed to provide plaintiff an alternative method of resolving issues in regard to her mark. This is not ordinarily provided by the Amazon platform. Thus there is valid consideration.

CONCLUSION

For the foregoing reasons, the court granted defendant's Motion to Enforce the Settlement Agreement as embodied by the original agreement, and judgment for the defendant was ordered according to the terms of the agreement.

SFA Systems, LLC v. Amazon.com
Patent Infringement; Claim Construction

***SFA Sys., LLC v. Amazon.com, Inc.*, 2013 U.S. Dist. LEXIS 189807 (E.D. Tex. Apr. 11, 2013).**

ISSUE

Should the court grant the defendant's motion for summary judgment?

RULE

Pursuant to the holding in *Phillips v. AWH Corp*, "It is a bedrock principle that the claims of a patent define the invention to which the patentee is entitled the right to exclude.

CASE DETAILS

Facts

Plaintiff, SFA Systems, has filed many suits for violation of the 525 Patent previous to this case. In addition to the 525 Patent, the plaintiffs also allege violation of the 341 Patent. The 341 Patent is directed to systems that "detect changes in information relating to events in a sales system, automatically initiate an operation based on the event, determine whether the event has occurred previously and update other events if the operation I automatically initiated."

Defendants Amazon.com motioned for summary judgment claiming invalidity based on "(1) apparatus claims reciting method steps; (2) insoluble ambiguity of the preamble term 'intelligently integrating' and (3) insoluble ambiguity of the wherein clause."

Analysis

The court looked to define the term "sales process" where the parties disputed on whether or not "sales process" should include defendants' proposed real world process and salesperson elements. The court construes "sales process" to mean "a process of selling goods or services, including two or more phases such as lead generation, time with customer, order management, and customer retention."

For the term, "facilitate/facilitating/ facilitate a sales process" the court found that they had previously clarified that "sales process" is a real-life activity but that it does not exclude computer involvement."

For the term, "facilitate a new action" the court found that there was no need to further construct "new action".

The court found that "a computer implemented sales system" did not require construction.

The court construed "event manager" to mean, "hardware and or software that is within a computer implemented sales system."

The court construed "event occurring within/ in the system" to mean "an operation of the software or hardware making up the sales system."

The court construed "context" to mean "information already existing within the system that becomes relevant upon the occurrence of an event".

When looking to the defendant's motion for summary judgment, the court denied the motion. The court found that defendants failed to show by clear and convincing evidence hat these claims are insoluble due to an impermissible mix of apparatus limitations and method steps. Additionally, the court found that the defendants "did not provide a meritorious basis for either finding the preamble language a limitation or finding such language insolubly ambiguous." Finally, the court denied the defendant's motion for summary judgment of indefiniteness of the 341 Patent independent claims 1, 13, 27,31, 31, and 33.

CONCLUSION

The United States District Court denied the defendant Newegg's motion for partial summary judgment and defendant Amazon.com's motion for partial summery judgment.

Shulman v. Amazon.com, Inc.
Workers' Compensation and Employees' Rights

***Shulman v. Amazon.com, Inc.*, 2013 U.S. Dist. LEXIS 20984 (E.D. Wis. Feb. 15, 2013).**

ISSUE

Whether a plaintiff should be sanctioned for their behavior where they have wasted the time and resources of the judicial system by filing frivolous actions.

RULE

"When dealing with a frivolous litigator who, despite due warning or the imposition of sanctions, continues to waste judicial resources, we impose a filing bar preventing the litigant from filing in this court or any federal court in this circuit." *McCready v. eBay, Inc.*, 453 F.3d 882, 892 (7th Cir. 2006).

CASE DETAILS

Facts

The court previously dismissed this matter for lack of personal jurisdiction. The plaintiff has inherently increased the costs of litigation with their meaningless filings.

Analysis

The court fund the plaintiff should be sanctioned because he filed frivolous complaints that ultimately wasted judicial resources and unnecessarily increased the cost of litigation.

CONCLUSION

The court denies the plaintiff's motion for relief from the sanctions judgment and orders the plaintiff to pay the defendant's attorney fees that resulted from this motion.

Shulman v. Amazon.com, Inc.
Workers' Compensation and Employees' Rights

***Shulman v. Amazon.com, Inc.*, 2013 U.S. Dist. LEXIS 58029 (E.D. Wis. Apr. 22, 2013)**

ISSUE

Whether a party should be relieved from an award of sanctions.

RULE

A party will not be relieved from sanctions awarded by the court when they file irrelevant motions to a court ruling.

CASE DETAILS

Facts

The court previously ordered the plaintiff to pay the defendant's attorney's fees that came from a motion. The court warned the plaintiff if he filed another baseless motion he may be subject to a filing bar. The court denied the plaintiff's motion to access the Electronic Court Filing System and Shulman moves to reconsider the sanctions.

Analysis

Procedural deadlines are put in place for a reason and may not be ignored for frivolous reasons. The plaintiff's arguments are irrelevant to the court's ruling.

CONCLUSION

The court denies the plaintiff's motion for relief from the award of sanctions and orders the plaintiff to pay Amazon's attorney fees because of previous motions filed that were unrelated to court rulings.

Shulman v. Amazon.com, Inc.
Workers' Compensation and Employees' Rights

***Shulman v. Amazon.com, Inc.*, 2013 U.S. Dist. LEXIS 76975 (W.D. Wash. May 30, 2013).**

ISSUE

Whether a complaint should be dismissed for failure to state a claim or because it is barred by the statute of limitations.

RULE

A claim may be dismissed if there is no clear and convincing evidence that a party may have caused harm and specific relief is not requested.

CASE DETAILS

Facts

The plaintiff's federal claim was filed outside the two-year statute of limitations so it is time barred. Plaintiff filed another similar complaint in state court the last day before the two-year statute of limitations expired and was removed to federal court. The plaintiff must allege the family medical leave act violation was deliberately made by the defendant in order to be able to bring an action within three years of the last event of the case. The plaintiff failed to show the defendant willfully and recklessly did not allow him to visit his terminally ill mother so the extended three-year statute of limitations is not applicable.

Analysis

The facts provided by the plaintiff do not show a willful violation of the family medical leave act and there is no claim for relief. An employer does not have to grant leave for the purpose of researching care options.

CONCLUSION

The court grants the defendant's motion to dismiss because the complaint was filed outside the two-year statute of limitations, making it time barred, and the plaintiff fails to state an actual claim under the family medical leave act.

Shive v. Amazon.com Inc.
Procedure

***Shive v. Amazon.Com, Inc.* Cv 15-406 Jb/Wpl, United States District Court for The District of New Mexico.**

ISSUE

Whether an entire case should be dismissed based on the failure to respond to an order to show cause for a separate party.

RULE

A case will not be dismissed for a failure to respond to a court order if the response has nothing to do with the party in question.

CASE DETAILS

Facts

Sears filed a motion to dismiss the claims against it for plaintiff's failure to comply with a court order to show cause of some of the defendants to move the case forward. Those defendants were dismissed because the plaintiff did not respond. Sears wants all of the cases dismissed because of this failure to comply.

Analysis

The plaintiff's failure to comply has no relation to the claims against Sears. The plaintiff did not act unreasonable towards Sears.

CONCLUSION

The court denies Sear's motion to dismiss all claims because the defendant's failure to respond is irrelevant to the claims against Sears. The case will proceed with litigation.

Shulman v. Amazon.com.kydc LLC
Employee's Rights; Procedural- Sanctions

***Shulman v. Amazon*, 2014 U.S. Dist. LEXIS 113506 (E.D. Ky. Aug. 15, 2014).**

ISSUE

Whether the court should grant Defendants' Motion for Sanctions?

RULE

The Sixth Circuit generally views the resolution of a motion for sanctions, costs and fees as a dispositive matter. The magistrate judge must conduct the necessary proceedings and enter a recommended disposition in a timely manner. Fed. R. Civ. P. 72(b).

CASE DETAILS

Facts

Shulman filed this action in December 2012 against his former employer, Amazon alleging violations of the Americans with Disabilities Act, Kentucky Civil Rights Act and Employee Retirement Income Securities Act. Plaintiff also alleges that Defendants breached their implied contract of continued employment.

Timeline

In August of 2013, the district court entered its Scheduling Order, setting forth general deadlines for the parties and referring all discovery issues to another judge.

Analysis

The court considers four factors when determining whether sanctions are appropriate: (1) Whether the party's failure to cooperate in discovery is due to willfulness, bad faith or fault; (2) Whether the adversary was prejudiced by the dismissed party's failure to cooperate in discovery; (3) Whether the dismissed party was warned that failure to cooperate could lead to dismissal; and (4) Whether less drastic sanctions were imposed or considered before dismissal. *Harmon v. CSX Transp., Inc.*, 110 F.3d 364, 366-67 (6th Cir. 1997). The court determined there was no evidence of plaintiff's intent to thwart judicial proceedings or reckless disregard for the effect of his conduct on the proceedings.

CONCLUSION

The Defendants' Motion for Sanctions is denied.

Shulman v. Amazon.com.kydc LLC
Employee's Rights; Procedure

***Shulman v. Amazon.com.kydc, LLC*, 2015 U.S. Dist. LEXIS 51291 (E.D. Ky. Apr. 20, 2015).**

ISSUE

Should the court grant Defendants' Motion for Summary Judgment?

RULE

Summary judgment is appropriate when there is no genuine dispute as to any material fact and the movant is entitled to judgment as a matter of law. Fed. R. Civ. P. 56(a).

CASE DETAILS

Facts:

Amazon offered Shulman employment as a Warehouse Associate and included in the offer letter that he will be an at-will employee. Shulman accepted the offer. The physical demands of the position included standing, walking, lifting up to sixty pounds, bending, reaching, kneeling and crouching for eight to twelve hour shifts. Amazon has productivity standards and has escalating consequences if employees fail to meet these standards. Records show Shulman struggled with meeting production standards and was warned on multiple occasions. He alleged he needed special accommodations and provided doctors documentation for this. He failed to meet standards and was fired. Shulman filed this action in December 2012 against his former employer, Amazon alleging violations of the Americans with Disabilities Act, Kentucky Civil Rights Act and Employee Retirement Income Securities Act. Plaintiff also alleges that Defendants breached their implied contract of continued employment. Defendants now move for Summary Judgment.

Timeline:

On March 29, 2012 Shulman filed a Notice of Charge of Discrimination with the Equal Employment Opportunity Commission and this was dismissed. He then filed a lawsuit in Fayette Circuit Court, which was removed to federal court. August of 2013, the district court entered its Scheduling Order, setting forth general deadlines for the parties and referring all discovery issues to another judge.

Analysis:

The prima facie case for disability discrimination has 5 elements: (1) the plaintiff is disabled; (2) the plaintiff is otherwise qualified to perform the essential functions of the position, with or without reasonable accommodation; (3) the plaintiff suffered an adverse employment action because of his or her disability; (4) the employer knew or had reason to know of the plaintiff's disability; (5) the position remained open while the employer sought other applicants or the disabled individual was replaced. *Whitfield v. Tennessee*, 639 F.3d 253, 259 (6th Cir. 2011). The court will presume that Shulman has successfully stated a prima facie case of disability and burden shifts to Amazon to articulate legitimate non-discriminatory reason for his termination. Amazon articulates a legitimate non-discriminatory reason for terminating Shulman: not meeting Amazon standards. Therefore, there is a failure to state a claim and the court dismisses the claims.

CONCLUSION

The court granted the Defendants' Motion to Dismiss

Singleton v. Amazon.com.
Breach of Contract

***Singleton v. Amazon.com*, 2015 Cal. App. Unpub. LEXIS 1962 (Cal. App. 4th Dist. Mar. 20, 2015).**

ISSUE

Whether the court here should reverse the trial court's order denying plaintiff his petition to vacate the arbitration award.

RULE

On review of the trial court's judgment confirming the arbitration award, we apply the standards of section 1286, requiring "'the court shall confirm the award as made... unless in accordance with this chapter it corrects the award and confirms it as corrected, vacates the award or dismisses the proceeding.'" (*Ikerd v. Warren T. Merrill & Sons* (1992) 9 Cal.App.4th 1833, 1841, 12 Cal. Rptr. 2d 398.) "Our review of an arbitration award requires us to extend to it every intendment of validity and the party claiming error has the burden of supporting his contention." (Ibid., citing *Cobler v. Stanley, Barber, Southard, Brown & Associates* (1990) 217 Cal.App.3d 518, 526, 265 Cal. Rptr. 868; *Evans v. Centerstone Development Co.* (2005) 134 Cal.App.4th 151, 157, 35 Cal. Rptr. 3d 745 (*Evans*).)

CASE DETAILS

Facts

Plaintiff, Stanley Singleton sued defendants, Amazon.com and Evan James, for breach of contract and fraudulent misrepresentation, over their disputes over Amazon Services Business Solutions Agreement that Singleton has signed to enable him to sell merchandise on Amazon's website.

The action was stayed while arbitration proceeded under the parties' arbitration agreement, which eventually ruled in Amazon's favor. Singleton appealed, "denying his petition to vacate the arbitration award and granting Amazon's cross-petition to confirm it, and the judgment of dismissal." Singleton argued that the award should be vacated because, "the underlying agreement was void due to a fraudulent provision, and thus the award was procured through corruption".

Analysis

The court looked to Singleton's argument of fraud and found that the arbitrator did not erroneously deny his fraud claim. The court then looked to the adequacy of hearing and found that the trial court correctly determined that the statutory requirements or vacating the award were not met. Therefore, the court found that the trial court did not err in confirming the arbitration award.

CONCLUSION

The Court of Appeals affirmed the trial court's decision finding that the trial court did not err in their ruling.

SIPCO v. Amazon.com
Patent Infringement

***Sipco, LLC v. Amazon.com, Inc.*, 2012 U.S. Dist. LEXIS 150940 (E.D. Tex. Oct. 19, 2012).**

ISSUE

What definitions should the court apply to the disputed terms in the patent at issue here?

RULE

Pursuant to the holding in *Burke, Inc., v. Bruno Indep. Living Aids, Inc.*, "A claim in a patent provides the metes and bounds of the right which the patent confers on the patentee to exclude others from making, using or selling the protected invention".

CASE DETAILS

Facts

Plaintiff, SIPCO LLC asserted U.S. Patents 551, 838, and 492. These patents relate to "mesh networking, where devices can communicate through any of the multiple paths created by overlap between the wireless ranges of devices in a network". The 551 patent was titled, "Wireless Communication Networks for Providing Remote Monitoring of Devices". The 838 patent is titled, "Method for Monitoring and Controlling Residential Devices". The 492 patent is titled, "Systems and Methods for Monitoring and Controlling Remote Devices".

The court discussed the construction of disputed terms.

Analysis

The court construed "plurality of remote devices" to mean, "two or more devices, at least one of which includes a sensor".

The court construed "host computer" to mean, "computer, connected to a wide area network, that monitors and controls a plurality of remote devices."

The court construed "wide area network" to have its plain and ordinary meaning".

The court construed "sensor" to mean, "device that monitors or measures the state or status of a condition and provides information concerning the condition".

The court construed "repeaters" to mean, "wireless devices that can receive original data messages and resend repeated data messages but that do not send original data messages".

The court construed "distinct residential automation applications" to mean, "plurality of applications, each of which serves a different automation purpose for a residence".

The court construed "gateway" to mean "device that is capable of converting and further communicating information and that includes: (1) a look-up table to assist in identifying various devices transmitting data to the gateway; (2) program code for evaluating incoming data and determining action to be taken; and (3) a look-up table associating function codes with the interpretation thereof."

The court construed "function code" to mean, "code corresponding to a function or condition".

The court construed "function code mapped from the received first sensor data signal" to mean, "function code associated with a sensor data signal".

The court construed "generic set of function codes configured for distinct applications" to mean, "one or more first function codes assigned to a first application and one or more second function codes, distinct from the first function codes, assigned to a second application distinct from the first application".

The court construed "first sensor data signal from the first local control system is mapped to a corresponding function code of the generic set of function codes" to mean, "the selected function code is chosen based on the first sensor data signal".

The court construed "means for receiving each of the original data messages and repeated data messages" to be a means-plus-function term, the function being "receiving each of the original data messages and the repeated data messages". Additionally the corresponding structure is "a site controller 150 including an antenna 400, an RF transceiver 402, a central processing unit 404, and power supply 410, and equivalents thereof."

The court construed "means for identifying, for each message, the remote device associated with the corresponding sensor data signal" to be a means-plus-function term, the function being "identifying, for each received message, the remote device associated with the corresponding sensor data signal." Additionally, the structure is "a site controller 150, including the following and equivalents thereof; (1) a central processing unit 404; (2) a power supply 410; and (3) a memory 406 with look up table(s) 414 for identifying a remote transceiver and/or memory sectors 416 for identifying a remote transceiver".

The court construed "scalable address" to mean "an address that has a variable size based on the size and complexity of the system."

The court construed "remote device" to mean, "one or more devices, at least one of which include a sensor".

The court construed "command indicator" to mean, "an indicator that: (1) specifies a command; and (2) comprises a code".

The court construed "scalable message" to mean, "message in which the size of the message is varied".

The court construed "scalable data value comprising a scalable message" to mean, "a data value comprising a message in which the size of the message is varied."

The court construed "configured to" to have its "plain and ordinary meaning".

CONCLUSION

The court discussed the construction of disputed terms and defined the terms in dispute.

Site Update Solutions, LLC v. Accor N, Am., Inc. *Procedure*

***Site Update Solutions, LLC v. Accor North America, Inc.*, 2013 U.S. Dist. LEXIS 72765 (N.D. Cal. May 21, 2013).**

ISSUE

The court here is determining whether to grant defendant Newegg's motion to declare case exceptional and for an award of attorney's fees.

RULE

"The Federal Circuit has established two instances in which a party's behavior may transform an ordinary case into an "exceptional" one, specifically when a party either engages in litigation misconduct or pursues a "frivolous claim." If the court determines that the case is "exceptional" under one of the two criteria, it must then ascertain whether an award of attorneys' fees is appropriate and, if so, the amount of the award.

CASE DETAILS

The court conducted a "meta-analysis" of the parties' claim construction positions, as well as their other positions in this case and finds that the case is not exceptional and so does not warrant an award of attorneys' fees to Newegg. Plaintiff may have been on the losing side of several arguments, but losing is not sufficient for a finding of objective baselessness and subjective bad faith.

CONCLUSION

Newegg's motion to declare this case exceptional and for an award of attorney's fees is denied.

Smartdata, S.A. v. Amazon.Com, Inc.
Procedure

***SmartData, S.A. v. Amazon.com, Inc.*, 2015 U.S. Dist. LEXIS 152606 (N.D. Cal. Nov. 10, 2015).**

ISSUE

The court here is determining whether to grant defendant Amazon.Com, Inc.'s (Amazon) motion for attorney's fees where Amazon claims that plaintiff acted in bad faith coupled with the improper purpose of manipulating the proceedings.

RULE

"In order to impose sanctions under the court's inherent power, a district court must make a specific finding of bad faith (or conduct tantamount to bad faith) or reckless misstatements of law and fact ... coupled with an improper purpose such as an attempt to influence or manipulate proceedings on one case in order to gain tactical advantage in another case." *Fink v. Gomez*, 239 F.3d 989, 994 (9th Cir, 2001).

CASE DETAILS

Facts

Plaintiff filed the underlying complaint alleging that defendant Amazon infringed its patent entitled "Modular Computer" (the '757 patent). Defendant filed a motion to dismiss and argued that the patent was invalid. Plaintiff ultimately dismissed its complaint voluntarily. Defendant subsequently filed this motion to recover attorney's fees.

Analysis

Here, plaintiffs claim they had difficulty filing its dismissal prior to the hearing, while plaintiff should have notified the court of its difficulties in filing its dismissal prior to the hearing, the poorly timed dismissal was not held as a finding of bad faith. The court further holds that an inference can not be drawn from the fact that plaintiff delayed dismissal of the case in order to extort a settlement fee from defendant. The court states that there are many reasons parties choose to resolve their disputes in out-of-court settlement proceedings.

CONCLUSION

The court finds that plaintiff's conduct in the present suit does not rise to the level of bad faith and declines to impose sanctions under its inherent authority.

Smartflash LLC v. Apple Inc.
Procedure

***Smartflash LLC v. Apple, Inc.*, 2015 U.S. Dist. LEXIS 70259, 2015 WL 3453343 (E.D. Tex. May 29, 2015).**

ISSUE

Whether Amazon.com. Inc.'s (Amazon) motion to stay will be granted pending review of the asserted patents at issue.

RULE

Under § 18(b) of the Leahy-Smith America Invents Act, Pub. L. No. 112-29, 125 Stat. 284 (September 16, 2011), the request for a stay for such transactional proceedings of covered business method patents is codified. § 18(b) states:

(1) IN GENERAL, – If a party seeks a stay of a civil action alleging infringement of a patent under Section 281 of title 35 of, United States Code, relating to a transitional proceeding for that patent, the court shall decide whether to enter a stay based on –
   a. Whether a stay, or the denial thereof, will simplify the issues in question and streamline the trial;
   b. Whether discovery is complete and whether a trial date has been set;
   c. Whether a stay, or the denial thereof, would unduly prejudice the nonmoving party or present a clear tactical advantage for the moving party and
   d. Whether a stay, or the denial thereof, will reduce the burden of litigation on the parties and on the court.

(2) REVIEW. – A party may take an immediate interlocutory appeal from a district court's decision under paragraph (1). The United States Court of Appeals for the Federal Circuit shall review the district court's decision to ensure consistent application of established precedent, and such review may be de novo.

CASE DETAILS

Facts

Plaintiff Smartflash filed a lawsuit against Amazon asserting patent infringement. In separate litigation, Apple and Samsung submitted motions to stay to the court and upon receiving them the court order briefing on the issue of a stay in the Amazon action.

Analysis

The court grants Amazon's motion to stay. The court here finds that the Amazon case is in its very early stages. Substantial opportunities are still available for cost saving and issue simplification. Plaintiff will not be unduly prejudiced by a sty. There is no evidence that Amazon knew of its alleged infringement for more than a few months.

CONCLUSION

The court holds that a stay in warranted in the Amazon litigation. Accordingly, the motion is granted.

Soverain Software LLC. v. Amazon.com
Patent Infringement

***Soverain Software LLC v. Gap, Inc.*, 340 F. Supp. 2d 760 (E.D. Tex. 2004).**

ISSUE

Should the court grant Amazon.com's motion to compel production of non-privileged documents?

RULE

Following the holding in *Hodges Grant & Kaufmann v. United States*, "The attorney-client privilege protects communications made in confidence by a client to his lawyer for the purpose of obtaining legal advice. The privilege also protect communications from the lawyer to his client, at least if they would tend to disclose the client's confidential communication."

CASE DETAILS

Facts

The dispute arose over whether Soverain could claim attorney-client privilege with regard to documents that contain communications between Open Market, Inc. and Divine, Inc., who were the former owners of the patents asserted in the case. Amazon.com argued that Soverain could not assert the privilege because Soverain was not the corporate successor of the companies; rather they purchased a portion of the assets.

Defendant, Amazon.com Inc. motioned to compel production of non-privileged documents. Amazon argued that the privilege was waived when "less than all of the Divine's assets were transferred first to Saratoga before the transfer to Soverain.

Analysis

The court held that "the desire of the purchaser of a bankrupt's assets to not acquire the bankrupt's liabilities should not lead, by that fact, to the waiver of all privileges attendant to the assets". Ultimately, the court disagreed with Amazon's argument and denied the motion.

CONCLUSION

The United States District Court denied Amazon.com's motion to compel production of non-privileged documents.

Soverain Software LLC v. Amazon.com
Patent Infringement

***Soverain Software L.L.C. v. Amazon.com, Inc.*, 383 F. Supp. 2d 904 (E.D. Tex. 2005).**

ISSUE

Should the court grant the defendant's motion for summary judgment?

RULE

Pursuant to the Federal Rules of Civil Procedure Rule 56(c) "Summary judgment shall be rendered when the pleadings, depositions, answers to interrogatories, and admissions on file, together with the affidavits, if any, show that there is no genuine issue as to any material fact and that the moving party is entitled to judgment as a matter of law."

CASE DETAILS

Facts

Plaintiff, Soverain Software brought an action against Amazon.com alleging "the vendor infringed on the three patents acquired by the patentee relating to methods for controlling and monitoring access to network servers through a session identifier." Specifically, the plaintiffs allege that their 780 patent, their 492 patent and their 314 patent were infringed. Additionally, the defendant filed a motion for partial summary judgment for lack of notice of alleged infringement. The defendants claim that the plaintiff failed to ensure that their licensees comply with the marketing statute.

Analysis

The court found that Soverain had failed to raise a material fact issue as to "whether Raptor and Intershop marketed their products." Additionally, Soverain failed to raise a fact issue that would defeat summary judgment.

CONCLUSION

The court concluded that because Soverain had presented evidence to raise a fact issue as to whether it personally complied with the marketing statute by, "marking its Transact software, but has not come forward with any evidence of its licensees' compliance or that Amazon had actual notice of its alleged infringement", Amazon's motion was denied in relation to Soverain's personal compliance. The court granted the motion in all other aspects.

Soverain Software LLC v. Amazon.com
Patent Infringement; Procedure

***Soverain Software LLC v. Amazon.com, Inc.*, 356 F. Supp. 2d 660 (E.D. Tex. 2005).**

ISSUE

Should the court grant the defendant's motion to stay?

RULE

When deciding whether to stay, the court must consider, "(1) whether a stay will unduly prejudice or present a clear tactical disadvantage to the nonmoving party, (2) whether a stay will simplify the issues in question and trial of the case, and (3) whether discovery is complete and whether a trial date has been set."

CASE DETAILS

Facts

Plaintiff, Soverain Software brought an action against Amazon.com alleging "the vendor infringed on the three patents acquired by the patentee relating to methods for controlling and monitoring access to network servers through a session identifier." Specifically, the plaintiffs allege that their 780 patent, their 492 patent and their 314 patent were infringed.

Defendant, Amazon filed a motion to stay proceedings pending completion of a reexamination of patents in connection with plaintiff patentee's claims for patent infringement.

Analysis

When looking to whether a stay would unduly prejudice or present a tactical disadvantage to Soverain, the court found that this supported a stay. For the issue of whether a stay would simplify the issues in the case, the court found that the simplification was not persuasive. Finally, when looking at whether discovery is complete and whether a trial date had been set, the court found that this weighed heavily in favor of denying a stay.

CONCLUSION

After looking to the three determining factors, the court found that they did not weight in favor of a stay and denied the motion.

Spears v. Amazon.com
Negligence; Breach of Contract

***Spears v. Amazon*, 2013 U.S. Dist. LEXIS 18384, 34 I.E.R. Cas. (BNA) 1783, 27 Am. Disabilities Cas. (BNA) 1430 (E.D. Ky. Feb. 12, 2013).**

ISSUE

Should the court grant defendant, Amazon.com's motion for summary judgment?

RULE

Following the holding in, Bear, Inc., v. Smith, "To establish a claim for fraud in the inducement under Kentucky law, a party must prove the following six elements by clear and convincing evidence: (1) material representation (2) which is false (3) known to be false or made recklessly (4) made with inducement to be acted upon (5) acted in reliance thereon and (6) causing injury".

CASE DETAILS

Facts

Plaintiff, Joseph F. Spears applied at Amazon and interacted with recruiting coordinator, Kathy Bush, for a position as a service technician. Spears also applied for a similar position at Intelligrated. Bush, made Spears a second offer for employment with a higher salary. The offer made by Amazon included a $22.00 per hour wage; in addition to 504 shares of Amazon.com in common stock and Spears accepted the position.

After hiring Spears, Amazon became aware of a problem with the compensation package, which Spears was later notified. The letter offered a $500 cash bonus, yet the shares were 464 shares lower than the amount he had been offered. Despite this, he continued employment for a year. During the year, he was recorded three times where Amazon needed to counsel Spears as to his job performance. Among these records was Spears being warned for improperly leaving work early. Additionally, Spears performance review was rated as "needs improvement".

Spears filed suit against Amazon on November 4, 2010 for breach of contract and promise, negligent misrepresentation, and fraud. Plaintiff, Joseph F. Spears alleged that defendant, Amazon.com "fraudulently induced him to accept a position of employment in the company, or in the least negligently misrepresented the nature of compensation of the employment; that Amazon inappropriately terminated him on the basis of his disability in retaliation for a worker's compensation claim, and in transgression of public policy."

Amazon.com motioned for summary judgment alleging that the claims were without merit. Amazon argued that summary judgment should be granted in their favor on the fraud claim.

Analysis

The court found that Spears had created a genuine issue of material fact as to whether or not Amazon made the offer to Spears in reckless disregard of its falsity. Additionally, the court found that Spears produced evidence to suggest that the error might have been larger and more institutional than Amazon represented. The court also found that Spears established a genuine issue of material fact as to whether the worker's compensation claim was a motivating factor in his termination.

However, the court did find that Spears could not "make a showing sufficient to establish an essential element of his claim for wrongful discharge on the basis of disability" and entered judgment in favor of Amazon.com Additionally, the court found that KRS Section 337.060 was not applicable and therefore there was no genuine issue of material fact as to his claim for wrongful discharge in violation of public policy, and therefore entered judgment in favor of Amazon.com

CONCLUSION

The United States District Court denied Amazon's motion for summary judgment for the fraud claims in the inducement, negligent misrepresentation, and workers' compensation. The court granted Amazon's motion for summary judgment for the claims of wrongful discharge on the basis of disability and in violation of public policy.

Spears v. Amazon.com.kydc, LLC
Workers Rights; Procedure

***Spears v. Amazon.com.kydc, LLC* Case No. C12-1922 RAJ. United States District Court Western District of Washington at Seattle, June 2013.**

ISSUE

Whether the court should grant the defendants' Motion to Dismiss?

RULE

Pursuant to Federal Rule of Civil Procedure 12 (b)(6), the court can grant a motion to dismiss if the complaint fails to state a claim upon relief can be granted. The court construes all the allegations as true and draws inferences in favor of the plaintiff.

CASE DETAILS

Facts

In his First Amended Complaint, Spears states that Amazon.com hired him as a service technician on July 7, 2008. Prior to Spears beginning work, he received a letter dated June 19, 2008, from Amazon asking him to "clarify and confirm" the terms of Spears' upcoming employment with Amazon. The letter stated that Spears' compensation benefits will include shares of Amazon.com common stock. He signed the letter on June 27, 2008 accepting the terms. After working with Amazon for 5 months, received another letter informing him that the number shares referenced was not accurate and would not be approved by the Board. Instead they stated they would give him 120 shares and will provide him with a one-time $500 bonus.

Timeline

The case was removed from Pulaski Circuit Court under 28 U.S.C. §1441, as the parties were diverse and the amount in controversy was satisfied.

Analysis

Spears alleges that Amazon breached its employment contract with him when they failed to provide him with the amount of stock promised him originally. The court determined this was an at-will employment, which creates little or no obligation to perform on either party. Either party is free to terminate the relationship at any time without fear of breaching a contract. The court additionally studied the language that granted Spears the ability to receive the 504 shares, an illusory promise and not a stock grant. Additionally, the court examined the fraud and negligent misrepresentation claims. These were considered plausible as each of the elements for fraud in the inducement may be present and the negligent misrepresentation claim was properly pled.

CONCLUSION

The court dismisses the condition stock grant and promissory estoppel claims. The court allows the fraud and negligent misrepresentation claims to continue.

State ex rel. Beeler, Schad & Diamond, P.C. v. Ritz Camera Ctrs., Inc.
Unfair Business Practices

***State ex rel. Beeler, Schad & Diamond, P.C. v. Ritz Camera Ctrs., Inc.*, 377 Ill. App. 3d 990, 316 Ill. Dec. 128, 878 N.E.2d 1152 (2007)**

ISSUE

The court here is answering six certified questions from the Illinois Supreme Court:

(1) "As a matter of law, if a remote retailer does not collect and remit use tax on sales to Illinois customers, can it make a 'knowingly' false record or statement, as required to create liability under the Illinois Whistleblower Reward and Protection Act, 740 ILCS 175/1?"

(2) (a) As a matter of law, does the Whistleblower Act require the existence of an actual record or statement to support a claim or can the failure to keep a record be actionable?

(b) As a matter of law, can documents memorializing a purchase (i.e. invoices or packing receipts) that show in the line item for tax '$ 0.0' or in some other way that tax is not being collected be considered 'false' under the Whistleblower Act where the retailer that created those documents does not collect tax?

c) Under the Whistleblower Act, as a matter of law, is it necessary that a false statement be submitted to or actually relied upon by the State?"

(3) "Does the application of the general provisions of the Whistleblower Reward and Protection Act, 740 ILCS 175/1, to enforce the sales and use tax laws improperly deprive taxpayers of the specific rights and privileges afforded them under the Protest Monies Act (30 ILCS 230/1), the Taxpayer's Bill of Rights, 20 ILCS 2502/1, and/or the statutory administrative procedures offered by the Illinois Department of Revenue, 35 ILCS 105/1; 35 ILCS 120/1, such that the Whistleblower Reward and Protection Act cannot be used to enforce the collection of taxes due the State?"

(4) "Is the Illinois Department of Revenue the sole entity authorized by the Illinois General Assembly to assess and collect use tax?"

(5) "Does the Illinois Whistleblower Reward and Protection Act, 740 ILCS 175/1, apply to alleged tax liabilities under the Use Tax Act?"

(6) (a) Does the Illinois Whistleblower Reward and Protection Act, 740 ILCS 175/1, violate the Attorney General clause of the Illinois Constitution, Article V, Section 15, by improperly usurping the exclusive authority of the Attorney General to initiate and conduct litigation on behalf of the State?

(b) Does the Illinois Whistleblower Reward and Protection Act, 740 ILCS 175/1, as applied to tax matters, violate either the Attorney General clause or the Executive Compensation clause of the Illinois Constitution, Article V, Sections 15 and 21?"

CASE DETAILS

Facts

Plaintiff law firm, acting on behalf of the State of Illinois, filed a complaint alleging that defendant retailers had violated the Illinois Whistleblower Reward and Protection Act as to use tax. The defendants filed a joint motion to dismiss, but it was denied. The court here on interlocutory appeal is answering six certified questions directed to this court by the Illinois Supreme Court.

Analysis

The court here found that a remote retailer could not make a knowingly false record or statement to create liability under the Act if it disclosed that no use tax was due or collected based on its reasonable interpretation of the law. The court next found that the act required an actual record or statement. Documents that contained purchase information that disclosed that no use tax was being collected could not be considered fault so to create liability under the act. Further, under the act, a false record or statement did not have to be submitted to or relied upon by the state. A claim brought under the act did not deprive taxpayers of their rights so that the act could not be used to enforce collection of taxes because litigants were given all the protections provided in civil proceedings. The

Illinois Department of Revenue was not the sole entity authorized to assess and collect use tax when fraudulent records and statements were created. The Act applied to alleged tax liabilities under the Use Tax Act when fraudulent records and statements existed. Finally, the Act did not violate Ill. Const. art. V, §§ 15 and 21, relating to the attorney general and to executive compensation. *State ex rel. Beeler, Schad & Diamond, P.C. v. Ritz Camera Ctrs., Inc.*, 377 Ill. App. 3d 990, 993, 316 Ill. Dec. 128, 131, 878 N.E.2d 1152, 1155 (2007)

CONCLUSION

The court here responded to the six questions, and the case was then remanded.

Stevenson v. Amazon.com, Inc.
Workers' Compensation and Employees' Rights

***Stevenson v. Amazon.Com, Inc.*, 2016 U.S. Dist. LEXIS 21172 (D. Mass. Feb. 22, 2016).**

ISSUE

Whether a claim should be dismissed for not providing enough evidence.

RULE

A court may dismiss a claim if a party is improperly added to a complaint or there is no factual evidence to support the claim.

CASE DETAILS

Facts

Plaintiff was cited for insubordination and failure to perform work duties and alleges these charges are false and claims she was denied access to her personal files where false information was added. Plaintiff also alleges her employer violated her due process and equal protection rights.

Analysis

The claims against Amazon are subject to dismissal because the plaintiff does not state any facts proving Amazon caused her harm. The request for Amazon's surveillance videos is not adequate to include them as a party. The plaintiff's constitutional claims against her employer will not prevail because no governmental action is alleged.

CONCLUSION

The court dismissed the claims against Amazon because they were not directly involved and were improperly named in the suit. The claim against Security Industry Specialists, Inc., was also dismissed because no governmental action was stated.

Stout v. Hartford Life & Accident Ins. Co.
Workers' Compensation and Employees' Rights

***Stout v. Hartford Life & Accident Ins. Co.*, 2012 U.S. Dist. LEXIS 172088 (N.D. Cal. Dec. 4, 2012).**

ISSUE

Whether documents should be sealed from access by the public.

RULE

A court may seal confidential documents if the production of the record to the public would harm the parties involved.

CASE DETAILS

Facts

The parties seek to seal a policy and procedure manual that consists of confidential material and if published would cause harm to the defendants.

Analysis

The court finds the defendants' reasons for sealing the documents are sufficient except for one document that can be redacted and published without causing any harm.

CONCLUSION

The court grants the plaintiff's leave to file documents under seal because publishing them would cause sufficient harm and the court orders one of the documents to be redacted and filed in the public record.

Supnick v. Amazon.com, Inc.
Privacy Violation; Class Action Lawsuits; Procedure

***Supnick v. Amazon.com, Inc.*, 2000 U.S. Dist. LEXIS 7073, 2000 WL 1603820 (W.D. Wash. May 18, 2000).**

ISSUE

Whether the court should grant the plaintiff's motion for a federal class certification.

RULE

Pursuant to Federal rule 23(a), for a class certification state that "one or more members of a class may sue or be sued as representative parties on behalf of all members only if: (1) the class is so numerous that joinder of all members is impracticable; (2) there are questions of law or fact common to the class; (3) the claims or defenses of the representative parties are typical of the claims or defenses of the class; and (4) the representative parties will fairly and adequately protect the interests of the class."

CASE DETAILS

Facts

Plaintiff, Supnick, moved for class certification in a suit where it was alleged that defendants violated the Electronic Communications Privacy Act and violated plaintiff's and others' common law rights through their collection of personal information on the internet. Defendant, Amazon.com claimed that the plaintiffs failed to meet the requirements for federal class certification.

Analysis

The court looked to Numerosity and found that defendants did not dispute Numerosity. For the issue of commonality, the court found that "the interpretation of the relevant party policies presents a common question of law or fact that can be resolved by this court". For the issue of typicality, the court found that defendants failed to show why the manner in which the plaintiff's obtained the software was relevant and why the issue should have any bearing on the question of typicality. For the issue of fair and adequate protection of class interests, the court found that Supnick would fairly and adequately protect the interests of the class. Overall, the court found that the class action was the superior method of resolving the controversy.

CONCLUSION

The court concluded that because the class was maintainable under Rule 23, and that the class action was the best method for litigating the dispute, the plaintiff's motion was granted.

itzer v. Litex Indus.
Patent Infringement; Amazon Dismissed from All Claims

***Switzer v. Litex Indus.* Case No. 11-cv-01174-REB. D. Colo., May 3, 2011.**

ISSUE

Whether the court should determine a briefing schedule to resolve matters of this case.

RULE

A court may order and establish a briefing schedule to organize claims before a case can proceed to resolution.

CASE DETAILS

Analysis

The court ordered the parties to file a joint claim construction statement of all the terms and claims the parties agree and disagree on which shall be limited to fifteen pages. The plaintiff's brief on claim construction shall be filed thirty days after the joint claim construction statement is filed. The parties shall follow the deadlines for a response and reply brief. The plaintiff brief on claim construction and defendant's response brief shall be limited to twenty pages. The parties shall convene a telephone motions hearing within ten days after the reply brief is filed.

CONCLUSION

The court orders that the parties shall file a joint claim construction statement of the patents at issue, limited to fifteen pages, shall be filed thirty days after the statement is filed, deadlines for filing a response brief and reply shall be followed, a response brief shall be limited to twenty pages, and the parties shall convene a telephone motions hearing within ten days after the reply brief is filed to set a time for a hearing. The court will determine further action in its discretion.

Switzer v. Litex Indus.
Amazon Dismissed from All Claims

***Switzer v. Litex Indus.* Case No. 11-cv-01174-REB. D. Colo., August 23, 2011.**

ISSUE

Whether the court should dismiss a defendant named as a party to a case.

RULE

A court may approve dismissal of a party to a case as they see fit.

CASE DETAILS

Facts

A stipulation for dismissal of the defendant, Amazon.com, Inc. was filed.

Analysis

The plaintiff's claims against Amazon are dismissed and the parties are ordered to pay their own attorney fees and costs, and Amazon is dropped as a named party to this action.

CONCLUSION

The court grants the stipulation dismissing Amazon as a defendant, the parties have to pay their own attorney's fees, and the case is amended to drop Amazon as a named party to this case.

TainoApp, Inc. v. Amazon.com.
Patent Infringement; Procedure

***TainoApp, Inc. v. Amazon.com, Inc.*, 2014 U.S. Dist. LEXIS 177361 (D.P.R. Dec. 24, 2014).**

ISSUE

Should the court grant defendant, Amazon.com's motion for transfer?

RULE

28 U.S.C. Section 1404(a), allows a district court to "transfer any civil action to any other district where it may have been brought for the convenience of parties and witnesses, in the interest of justice."

CASE DETAILS

Facts

Plaintiff, TainoApp, Inc. filed suit against, defendant, Amazon.com for patent infringement. Amazon.com denied liability and motioned to transfer venue to the Northern District of California.

Analysis

The court looked to the convenience of the parties and witnesses and found that a trial in Puerto Rico would substantially disrupt the business routine of "Amazon, Lab 126 witnesses, and relevant E Ink and Freescale witnesses that are more familiar with the design and operation of relevant components of the accused device."

Additionally, the court looked to the availability of documents. The court found the availability of documents weights against transfer.

The court looked to the possibility of consolidation and found that this was in favor of the transfer.

The court found that the order in which the district court obtained jurisdiction did not have any particular significance.

CONCLUSION

The court concluded that the interest of justice favored transfer, and granted the motion to transfer.

TainoApp, Inc, v. Amazon.com, Inc. *Procedure*

***TainoApp, Inc. v. Amazon.Com Inc.*, 2015 U.S. Dist. LEXIS 153490 (N.D. Cal. Nov. 12, 2015).**

ISSUE

Should the court award Amazon.com a bill of costs?

RULE

Pursuant to The Federal Rules of Civil Procedure Rule 54 "Unless a federal statute, these rules, or a court order provides otherwise, costs, other than attorney's fees, should be allowed to the prevailing party.

CASE DETAILS

Facts

On May 11, 2015, the court issued an order granting TainoApp's motion for voluntary dismissal with prejudice. On September 22, 2015, the court denied Amazon's motion for sanctions. On October 6, 2015, Amazon.com filed a bill of costs and TainoApp filed objections.

Analysis

The court looked to see who was the prevailing party. The court found that Amazon.com had met its burden to show that it was the prevailing party. Additionally, the court looked to the award of costs. The court found that TainoApp had not met its burden to overcome the presumption that costs should be awarded and found Amazon.com's costs to be reasonable.

CONCLUSION

The District Court overruled TainoApp's objections and awarded costs in the amount of $1,005.00.

Technology Innovations, LLC. v. Amazon.com
Procedure; Patent Infringement

***Tech. Innovations, LLC v. Amazon.com, Inc.*, 2013 U.S. Dist. LEXIS 115352 (D. Del. Aug. 15, 2013).**

ISSUE

Did plaintiff, Technology Innovations show cause for the assertion of the 407 patent in thier original complaint?

RULE

Pursuant to 35 U.S.C. Section 285, "a court in exceptional cases ay award reasonable attorney fees to the prevailing party."

CASE DETAILS

Facts

On August 8, 2011, Technology Innovations, (TI) filed suit against Amazon.com for patent infringement. TI claimed that Amazon infringed on the 407 patent. Amazon.com motioned to dismiss and filed a motion for sanctions. On April 25, 2012, the court denied Amazon's motions but stated that the court, "would consider a renewed motion if it is later determined, after discovery and a full claim construction record, that TI's assertion of the 407 patent against Amazon's products was so lacking in merit that the imposition of sanctions warranted."

TI sought dismissal of Amazon's counterclaim for attorney fees with respect to the 407 patent claiming "35 U.S.C. Section 285 does not provide a basis for an independent counterclaim, fees are not an appropriate issue to raise before trial, and the issue is not ripe because Amazon is not the prevailing party within the statute's meaning."

Analysis

The court found that under section 285, sanctions for attorney's fees against TI for the assertion of the 407 would be proper. Additionally, the court found that the 285 counterclaim failed to state a claim and therefore the court granted TI's motion to dismiss counterclaim III.

CONCLUSION

The United States District Court ordered that TI must show cause on or before September 12, 2013 for why the assertion of the 407 patent was proper under the requirements of Rule 11.

Technology Innovations, LLC. v. Amazon.com
Procedure; Patent Infringement

***Tech. Innovations, LLC v. Amazon.com, Inc.*, 35 F. Supp. 3d 613 (D. Del. 2014).**

ISSUE

Should the court grant Amazon.com's motions for summary judgment and motion to exclude?

RULE

Pursuant to the Federal Rules of Civil Procedure rule 56 (a), "The court shall grant summary judgment if the movant shows that there is no genuine dispute as to any material fact and the movant is entitled to judgment as a matter of law."

CASE DETAILS

Facts

On August 8, 2011, Technology Innovations, (TI) filed suit against Amazon.com for patent infringement. TI claimed that Amazon infringed on the 407 patent and the 965 patent. Amazon.com motioned to dismiss and argued that the Kindle e-reader could not be found to infringe the 407 patent under any possible claim construction. Additionally, Amazon.com filed motions for sanctions for inclusion of the 407 patent. The motion to dismiss was denied and the Rule 11 sanctions were denied with an option to entertain a renewed motion.

Amazon.com motioned for summary judgment of invalidity and non-infringement of the 965 patent, and a motion to exclude the testimony and evidence of Dr. Conte and Mr. McCourt.

Analysis

Amazon.com argued that if one uses the term letter to refer to the combination, "one can not longer say that the letter is enclosed within the envelope. The court agreed with Amazon's reasoning and found that claim 1 was not amendable to construction. The court found the claim was invalid and granted Amazon's motion for summary judgment of invalidity of the 965 patent. Additionally, the court denied TI's cross-motion for partial summary judgment of no invalidity.

The court construed the meaning of "book" and adopted TI's construction, but agreed with Amazon.com that "the invention refers only to printed materials and does not suggest that the patentee invented an electronic book.

Finally, the court found that "TI was not objectively reasonable under the circumstances" and found that sanctions were warranted.

CONCLUSION

The District Court granted Amazon.com's motion for summary judgment of invalidity and died TI's motion for partial summary judgment of no invalidity. Amazon's motions for summary judgment of non-infringement and to exclude testimony and evidence was denied as moot.

Technology Innovations, LLC. v. Amazon.com
Procedure; Patent Infringement

***Tech. Innovations, LLC v. Amazon.Com, Inc.*, 2014 U.S. Dist. LEXIS 100061 (D. Del. July 23, 2014).**

ISSUE

Should the court grant Amazon.com's motion for attorney fees?

RULE

The court applied the "lodestar" approach which results from "multiplying the amount of time reasonably expended by reasonable hourly rates".

CASE DETAILS

Facts

On August 8, 2011, Technology Innovations, (TI) filed suit against Amazon.com for patent infringement. TI claimed that Amazon infringed on the 407 patent. Amazon.com motioned to dismiss and argued that the Kindle e-reader could not be found to infringe the 407 patent under any possible claim construction. Additionally, Amazon.com filed motions for sanctions for inclusion of the 407 patent. The motion to dismiss was denied and the Rule 11 sanctions were denied with an option to entertain a renewed motion.

Amazon.com was directed to submit an accounting of reasonable attorney fees.

Analysis

The court found that attorney fees should be awarded to Amazon for the claims against them relating to the 407 patent. The court denied Amazons request that TI and its counsel be held jointly liable for any fees awarded.

CONCLUSION

The court concluded that the award should be the attorney fees denoted by Amazon as 407 specific to be $103,714.37 and for the 407 claim construction exercise of $26,332.46.

Technology Innovations, LLC. v. Amazon.com
Procedure; Patent Infringement

***Tech. Innovations, LLC v. Amazon.com, Inc.*, 2015 U.S. Dist. LEXIS 51415 (D. Del. Apr. 20, 2015).**

ISSUE

What is the appropriate amount in which Amazon.com should be awarded in attorney fees?

RULE

The court applied the "lodestar" approach which results from "multiplying the amount of time reasonably expended by reasonable hourly rates".

CASE DETAILS

Facts

On August 8, 2011, Technology Innovations, (TI) filed suit against Amazon.com for patent infringement. TI claimed that Amazon infringed on the 407 patent. The court awarded summary judgment to Amazon.com and directed Amazon.com to submit an accounting of reasonable attorney fees.

Analysis

The court now looked to seven categories: (1) For Amazon's motion to dismiss the 407 patent and for sanctions. The court awarded an amount of $22,771.00. (2) For the invalidity contentions, the court awarded $7,275. (3) For Amazon's opposition to TI's attempt to file an amended complaint to withdraw the 407 patent, the court awarded no fees. (4) For Amazon's counterclaim, the court awarded no attorney fees. (5) For Amazon's reply to show cause order, the court awarded $21,000.00. (6) For the Markman process, the court awarded no attorney fees. (7) For the expenses, the court awarded no expenses to Amazon.

CONCLUSION

The court awarded a total of $51,046.00 in attorney fees to be awarded to Amazon.com.

Telebuyer, LLC v. Amazon.com.
Patent Infringement; Procedure

***Telebuyer, LLC v. Amazon.com, Inc.*, 2014 U.S. Dist. LEXIS 147794 (W.D. Wash. Oct. 16, 2014).**

ISSUE

Should the court grant the defendant's motion to limit the number of patent claims?

RULE

Following the holding in, *In Re Phenylpropanolamine*, "the district court has broad discretion to administer the proceedings."

CASE DETAILS

Facts

Telebuyer, plaintiff filed suit against Amazon.com for patent infringement. Telebuyer alleged that Amazon "by offering goods and services to customers through its websites, uses systems and/or methods that directly infringe one or more claims of seven related U.S. Patents."

Amazon.com brought a motion to "limit the number of patent claims asserted by Plaintiff Telebuyer, LLC in the litigation, and to appoint a technical advisor." This was because there were nearly 800 patent claims.

Analysis

The court held that Telebuyer should limit the number of asserted claims to "not more than ten claims to limit each patent and not more than a total of 32 claims within ten days of the date of the order." Additionally, the court found that the appointment of a technical advisor was appropriate in the case.

CONCLUSION

The court concluded that Amazon's motion should be granted.

Telebuyer, LLC v. Amazon.Com, Inc.
Procedure

***Telebuyer, LLC v. Amazon.com, Inc.*, 2015 U.S. Dist. LEXIS 18200 (W.D. Wash. Feb. 13, 2015).**

ISSUE

Whether to grant defendant Amazon.Com, Inc.'s, motion to redact portions of the transcript from a technology tutorial held in December of 2014.

RULE

"Compelling reasons sufficient to outweigh the public's interest in disclosure and justify sealing court records exist when such court files might have become a vehicle for improper purposes, such as the use of records to ... to release trade secrets. *Kamakana v. City and County of Honolulu,* 447 F.3d 1172, 1178 (9th Cir. 2006). "The right to inspect and copy judicial records is not absolute, and the common law right of inspection has bowed before the power of a court to insure that its records are not used ... as sources of business information that might harm a litigant's competitive standing." *Nixon v. Warner Commc'ns, Inc.,* 435 U.S. 589, 598 (1978).

"A trade secret may consist of any formula, pattern device, or compilation of information which is used on one's business, and which gives him an opportunity to obtain an advantage over competitors who do not know or use it." Restatement of Torts § 757. Cmt. B.

CASE DETAILS

Facts

On December 17, 2014, the parties presented to the court, a presentation describing the technology at issue in this lawsuit. Amazon has moved to redact portions of the transcript from that presentation that it alleges contain "highly confidential information," the disclosure of which "would lead to competitive harm" from third parties.

Analysis

The court finds that Amazon seeks to redact portions of the transcript that "discuss confidential technical information, including internal processes and algorithms." This is information that falls squarely within the definition of "trade secrets." The court holds that the excerpts are limited to only that information which may reasonably constitute a trade secret. Therefore, Amazon has demonstrated sufficient justification for redacting the transcript.

CONCLUSION

For the foregoing reason the court grants Amazon's motion and orders that the transcript from the December 17, 2014 hearing be redacted.

Telebuyer, LLC v. Amazon.com, Inc.
Patent Infringement; Procedure

***Telebuyer, LLC v. Amazon.com, Inc.*, 2015 U.S. Dist. LEXIS 96391 (W.D. Wash. July 23, 2015).**

ISSUE

Should the court grant defendant, Amazon.com's motion for summary judgment?

RULE

Pursuant to the Federal Rules of Civil Procedure, Rule 56 (a), "Summary judgment is proper if the movant shows there is no genuine dispute as to any material fact and the movant is entitled to judgment as a matter of law."

CASE DETAILS

Facts

Telebuyer, plaintiff filed suit against Amazon.com for patent infringement. Telebuyer alleged that Amazon "by offering goods and services to customers through its websites, uses systems and/or methods that directly infringe one or more claims of seven related U.S. Patents."

Amazon.com brought a motion to "limit the number of patent claims asserted by Plaintiff Telebuyer, LLC in the litigation, and to appoint a technical advisor." This was because there were nearly 800 patent claims. This motion was granted.

In February of 2015, Amazon filed a motion for summary judgment alleging that the Asserted patents were invalid.

On June 11, 2015, Telebuyer identified four representative claims for the court to review. The four claims were, claim 185, 74, 24, and 55. The purpose of these patents was for "commercial transactions conducted electronically on the Internet."

Amazon argued that the claims were invalid because they were drawn to patent-ineligible subject matter- "the abstract idea of connection buyers and sellers through the use of generic computers and they contain no inventive concept."

Analysis

In determining if the representative claims were direct to an abstract idea, the court found looked to the two-step Alice framework. First the court when determining whether Telebuyer's representative claims were directed to patent-ineligible subject matter, found that the claims were direct to the abstract idea of connection buyers and sellers. When the court looked to see if the patents were innovative concepts, the court found that Telebuyer failed to disclose anything new. The claims were well-known technologies.

CONCLUSION

The court, after applying the Alice framework, found that each of the representative claims were directed to patent-ineligible subject matter. Therefore, the court granted the defendant's motion for summary judgment.

The Author's Guide v. Google Inc.
Copyright Infringement; Violations of the Sherman Act

***Authors Guild v. Google Inc.*, 770 F. Supp. 2d 666, 2011 U.S. Dist. LEXIS 29126, 98 U.S.P.Q.2D (BNA) 1229, 79 Fed. R. Serv. 3d (Callaghan) 114, Copy. L. Rep. (CCH) P30,057, 2011-1 Trade Cas. (CCH) P77,387 (S.D.N.Y. 2011).**

ISSUE

Should the court grant the plaintiff's motion for final approval of the proposed settlement of this class action?

RULE

This case follows Rule 23 (e) of the Federal Rules of Civil Procedure which requires a settlement of a class action to be approved by the court.

CASE DETAILS

Facts

In 2004, Google created a digital book library, scanning more than 12 million titles through their agreements with other research libraries. The class action arose when many claimed that Google's digital library was in violation of the copyright laws. While this digital library is beneficial to many, millions of the scanned books were still under copyright and Google did not obtain copyright permission to scan the books.

In 2005, the class action against Google for copyright infringement was brought.

In October of 2008, the parties filed a proposed settlement agreement, which received multiple objections.

In November of 2009, the parties executed the Amended Settlement Agreement (ASA) and filed a motion for final approval.

In February of 2010, the court conducted a fairness hearing.

The ASA authorized Google to (1) continue to digitalize Books and Inserts, (2) sell subscriptions to an electronic Books database, (3) sell online access to individual Books, (4) sell advertising on pages from Books, and (5) make certain other prescribed uses. The major objections to this agreement were (1) the adequacy of class notice, (2) Adequacy of Class Representation, (3) Scope of Relief Under Rule 23, (4) Copyright Concerns, (5) Antitrust Concerns, (6) Privacy Concerns, (7) International Law Concerns.

Among the named concerns, Amazon.com specifically raised antitrust concerns, claiming that the ASA would give Google a de facto monopoly over unclaimed works. This meant that Google would have control over the search market.

Analysis

The court addressed all of the raised concerns in regards to the settlement and found that the concerns were valid. The court believed that the ASA should be revised due to the fact that it was not fair, adequate, or reasonable.

CONCLUSION

The United States District Court concludes that ASA is not fair, adequate, or reasonable. The court holds that while the digitalization of books would benefit many, the Amended Settlement Agreement (ASA) would be going too far. The motion for final approval of the ASA is denied.

Tompkins v. Able Planet Inc.
Patent Violations; Procedure

***Tompkins v. Able Planet Inc.*, No. 6:10-cv-58, 2011 U.S. Dist. LEXIS 153068 (E.D. Tex. Feb. 17, 2011)**

ISSUE

Whether the claims here were distinguishable, such that the court could exercise its discretion to sever the claims.

RULE

Federal Rule of Civil Procedure 21 establishes that "[o]n motion or on its own, the court may at any time, on just terms, add or drop a party." Because Rule 21 does not provide a standard for determining if parties are improperly joined, courts apply Rule 20 to analyze misjoinder. *Acevedo v. Allsup's Convenience Stores, Inc.*, 600 F.3d 516, 521 (5th Cir. 2010) (per curium). Rule 20 allows joinder of defendants when: (1) their claims arise out of the same transaction, occurrence, or series of transactions or occurrences and (2) there is at least one common question of law or fact linking all the claims.

CASE DETAILS

Facts

This case is an action for patent violations. Plaintiff claims that defendants advertised products as patented when the defendants had actual knowledge that the products were in fact unpatented. The court notes that there are two distinct groups of defendants, those who manufactured the products, and those who advertised the products.

Analysis

The court finds that here, each of plaintiff's claims focuses on a single unrelated product. The allegedly unpatented products include headphones, punching bags, flashlights, tents, espresso machines, and baby bottles. The court finds that in order to ensure fairness to the parties and to support judicial economy that they should exercise their discretion and sever the claims. The court finds that severance according to product manufacturer is the most appropriate means of partitioning the case.

CONCLUSION

The court orders that the claims in plaintiff's amended complaint be severed based on its product manufacturer.

Toysrus.com, LLC v. Amazon.Com Kids
Breach of Contract

***Toysrus.com, LLC v. Amazon.Com Kids*, No. A-0292-04T5, 2005 N.J. Super. Unpub. LEXIS 811 (Super. Ct. App. Div. Apr. 12, 2005)**

ISSUE

The court here, on appeal is deciding whether to reverse the trial court's order granting a preliminary injunction against defendants from using new "one to one" technology because defendants breached their contract with plaintiff.

RULE

This contract contains a choice of law provision that requires application of Delaware law. "Delaware courts look first to the language of the contract." *Rhone-Poulenc Basic Chems. Co. V. Am. Motorists Ins. Co.*, 616 A.2d 1192, 1195 (Del. 1992). "Recognizing that there may be occasions when it is appropriate to consider undisputed background acts to place a provision in its historical setting, Delaware courts consider extrinsic evidence to ascertain the parties' intention only when the provisions of the contract are ambiguous." *Eagle Indus., Inc. v. DeVilbiss Health Care, Inc.*, 702 A.2d 1228, 1232 (Del. 1997).

One who seeks the extraordinary remedy of a preliminary injunction "must establish a threat of substantial, immediate, irreparable harm a reasonable probability of ultimate success on the merits, and relative hardships that favor a grant of an injunction prior to a full hearing. *Ispahani v. Allie Domecq Retailing USA*, 320 N.J. Super. 494, 498, 727 A. 2d 1023 (App. Div. 1999).

CASE DETAILS

Facts

Plaintiff Toys R Us (Plaintiff) and defendant Amazon.com Inc. (Amazon) entered an agreement in which plaintiff sells toys through two virtual stores located on Amazon's website. Amazon provides support for plaintiff's sales and is paid a fee by plaintiff of $50,000,000. Plaintiff brought this action to prevent Amazon from using new "one to one" technology that permits third parties to sell toys, games and baby products on its website. Plaintiff alleges that the proposed use of one to one violates its exclusive right to sell under the parties' agreement. The trial court granted a preliminary injunction and it is now on appeal by Amazon.

<u>Analysis</u>

The court found that the trial judge failed to consider the contractual language when evaluating plaintiff's likely success and the threat of irreparable harm. The court finds that the construction of the contract shows that the language limited to "one to one" program to certain products. The court further finds that the trial judge did not make findings or explain reasons for concluding that plaintiff was likely to succeed in establishing a violation of its exclusive rights, nor that there would be irreparable harm.

<u>CONCLUSION</u>

For the foregoing reasons the court reverses the trial courts decision. The provisions granting and modifying a preliminary injunction are reversed and the restraints are vacated.

TRE Milano, LLC v. Amazon.com, Inc.
Trademark Infringement; Sale of Counterfeit Goods

***Milano v. Amazon*, 2012 Cal. App. Unpub. LEXIS 6163 (Cal. App. 2d Dist. Aug. 22, 2012).**

ISSUE

Whether Amazon can be held responsible for the infringement of a third-party seller when Amazon took immediate action once Amazon was informed of the their-party's infringement and thus whether the trial court abused its discretion in denying the preliminary injunction.

RULE

When considering whether or not to issue a preliminary injunction, the trial court considers two factors: (1) the likelihood plaintiff will prevail on the merits of its case at trial and (2) the interim harm plaintiff is likely to suffer if the injunction is denied weighed against the interim harm defendant is likely to suffer if the injunction is granted. *ReadyLink Healthcare v. Cotton* (2005) 126 Cal.App.4th 1006, 1016; *14859 Moorpark Homeowner's Assn. v. VRT Corp.* (1998) 63 Cal.App.4th 1396, 1402.

CASE DETAILS

Facts

Tre Milano owns and markets the InStyler® Rotating Hot Iron Hair Straightener (InStyler). Amazon offers InStylers for sale on its website. Some of these are sold by third parties through Amazon and are counterfeit.

Tre Milano brought this action against Amazon and the third party sellers for damages and an injunction. Tre Milano seeks both compensatory and punitive damages for trademark infringement. It also seeks a permanent injunction barring Amazon and the third party sellers "from selling, offering for sale, or advertising any purported 'InStyler' products in California, or in the alternative, an injunction precluding [Amazon and the third party sellers] from selling, offering for sale, or advertising any counterfeit 'InStyler' products in California."

Analysis

The court affirmed denial of Plaintiff's request for preliminary injunction. The court found that Amazon itself was not guilty of direct trademark infringement, it was the service provider, not the seller. Further, Amazon was not responsible for infringement by third-parties and could not be held contributorily liable since it took immediate action once notified of third-party's infringement. Finally, Amazon was not guilty of contributory infringement, in that, when it was presented with evidence of infringement, it took action to remove the infringing listings, and it was not willfully blind to third party infringement.

CONCLUSION

The court held that the trial court did not abuse its discretion in denying the preliminary injunction because plaintiff did not show that the harm it would suffer would have been so great that it outweighed plaintiff's failure to show a likelihood of prevailing on the merits of its case.

Tuxis Techs., LLC v. Amazon.Com, Inc.
Procedure; Patent Infringement

***Tuxis Techs., LLC v. Amazon.com, Inc.*, 2014 U.S. Dist. LEXIS 122457 (D. Del. Sept. 3, 2014).**

ISSUE

The court is determining whether to grant defendant Amazon.Com, Inc.'s, Motion to Dismiss for Failure to State a Claim.

RULE

At the motion to dismiss stage a patent claim can be found directed towards patent ineligible subject matter if the only plausible reading of the patent must be that there is clear and convincing evidence of ineligibility. *Ultramercial, Inc., v. Hulu, LLC,* 772 F.3d 1335, 1339 (Fed. Cir. 2013). "The Supreme Court has recognized three narrow categories of subject matter outside the eligibility bounds of § 101 – laws of nature, physical phenomena, and abstract ideas." *Ultramercial,* 772 F.3d at 1341.

CASE DETAILS

Facts

The court here is examining a patent infringement case filed by Plaintiff Tuxis Technologies, LLC (plaintiff) against defendant Amazon.Com, Inc. The patent relates to a method of "upselling;" a common marketing technique.

Analysis

The court finds that the concept of "upselling" in the field of marketing is "as old as the field itself," and thus that the claim involves patent ineligible subject matter. The court notes that the limitations set out in the claim do narrow its scope, but not enough to save the claim from invalidity.

CONCLUSION

For the foregoing reasons the court grants Amazon's motion to dismiss for failure to state a claim.

Tuxis Techs., LLC v. Amazon.Com, Inc.
Procedure; Patent Infringement

***Tuxis Techs., LLC v. Amazon.com, Inc.*, 2015 U.S. Dist. LEXIS 37128 (D. Del. Mar. 25, 2015).**

ISSUE

Whether the court should grant defendant Amazon.Com, Inc.'s, (Amazon) motion to dismiss for failure to state a claim where Amazon claims the patent is for ineligible subject matter.

RULE

"The Supreme Court has recognized an implicit exception for three categories of subject matter not eligible for patentability – laws of nature, natural phenomena, and abstract ideas. *Alice Corp. Pty. V. CLS Bank Int'l*, 134 S. Ct. 2347, 2354 (2014). "The purpose of these carve outs is to protect the basic tools of scientific and technological work." *Mayo Collaborative Servs. V. Prometheus Labs., Inc.*, 132 S. Ct. 1289, 1293 (2012).

"First the court must determine whether the claims are drawn to a patent-ineligible concept. *Alice Corp. Pty. V. CLS Bank Int'l*, 134 S. Ct. 2347, 2354 (2014). If the answer is yes, the court must look to the elements of the claim both individually and as an ordered combination to see if there is an inventive concept. *Id.* A claim that recites an abstract idea must include additional features to ensure that the claim is more than a drafting effort designed to monopolize the [abstract idea]. *Id.*

CASE DETAILS

Facts

The court here is examining a patent infringement case filed by Plaintiff Tuxis Technologies, LLC (plaintiff) against defendant Amazon.Com, Inc. The patent relates to a method of "upselling;" a common marketing technique.

Analysis

The court finds that in applying the rule from the *Alice* case, that the patent claims clearly are drawn to patent ineligible subject matter. The court holds that the concept of "upselling" is a longstanding commercial practice. Even though limitations narrow the scope of the claims, these limitations do not amount to an "inventive concept." Thus all of the claims of the patent are invalid.

CONCLUSION

The court holds that for the foregoing reasons, Amazon's motion to dismiss will be granted with respect to all claims of the patent.

Unicolors, Inc. v. Shoreline Wear, Inc.
Procedural - Protective Order

***Unicolors, Inc. v. Shoreline Wear, Inc.*, 2016 U.S. Dist. LEXIS 72508 (C.D. Cal. May 24, 2016).**

ISSUE

Whether the court should grant the Protective Order to "govern the handling and disclosure of documents, things, and information produced in this action ... "

RULE

When discovery is likely to involve production of confidential, proprietary or private information for which special protection from public disclosure and from use for any purpose other than prosecuting this litigation, a protective order may be granted.

CASE DETAILS

Facts

The action is likely to include trade secrets, customer and pricing lists and other valuable research development, commercial, financial, technical and/or proprietary information for which special protection for public disclosure during discovery and from use for any purpose other than prosecution of this action may be warranted.

Analysis:

The parties understand and acknowledged that this protective order does not govern the use of materials at trial. The court granted the protective order as it would include privileged information that should be protected by the law from the public.

CONCLUSION

The court granted the protective order.

United Pet Grp., Inc. v. Doe
Trademark Violation; Procedure

***United Pet Grp., Inc. v. Doe* (E.D. Mo., 2013)**

ISSUE

Whether the court should grant Plaintiff's motion for expedited discovery which would force Amazon.Com, Inc. (Amazon) to release the identity of sellers accused of trademark violations.

RULE

"Expedited discovery can be granted when the party seeking discovery establishes good cause, i.e., that the need for expedited discovery, in consideration of the administration of justice, outweighs prejudice to a responding party. *Semitool, Inc. v. Tokyo Electron Am., Inc.*, 209 F.R.D. 273, 276 (N.D. Cal. 2002).

CASE DETAILS

Facts

In this case, plaintiff claims that a number of John Doe defendants unlawfully distributed and sold counterfeit products and/or packaging using plaintiff's FURminator trademarks and logos (FURminator Marks) on various websites including Amazon.Com. Plaintiff has requested, but Amazon refused to provide information that would allow plaintiff to identify defendants. Plaintiff is seeking an order for expedited discovery in order to identify the sellers.

Analysis

The court finds that plaintiff has demonstrated good cause because it has shown potential irreparable harm from infringement, no prejudice to defendants, and limited availability of information sought and thus grants the motion for expedited discovery.

CONCLUSION

For the foregoing reasons the court grants plaintiff's motion for expedited discovery and orders that plaintiff may serve subpoenas on Amazon.com to obtain information necessary to identify the John Doe defendants.

United States v. Apple Inc. ***Violations of the Sherman Act***

United States v. Apple Inc., 952 F. Supp. 2d 638 (S.D.N.Y. 2013).

ISSUE

Whether defendants Apple Inc. (Apple), and five book publishing companies conspired to raise, fix, and stabilize the retail price for newly released and bestselling trade e-books in violation of the Sherman Anti-Trust Act.

RULE

"Section 1 of the Sherman Anti-Trust Act outlaws every contract, combination ..., or conspiracy, in restraint of trade or commerce among the several states." 15 U.S.C. § 1. To establish a conspiracy in violation of § 1, "plaintiffs must show (1) a combination or some form of concerted action between at least two legally distinct economic entities that (2) constituted an unreasonable restraint of trade either per se or under the rule of reason." *Primetime 24 Joint Venture v. Nat'l Broad. Co.*, 219 F.3d 92, 1103 (2d Cir. 2000).

CASE DETAILS

Facts

Apple was aware that the "Big Six" United States publishing companies wanted to raise e-book prices above the $9.99 price point charged by Amazon for many e-book versions of NY Times best selling books. Apple also knew that the publishers were acting collectively to pressure Amazon to abandon its pricing strategy. At their first meetings in December of 2009, the publishers made Apple aware of their dislike of Amazon's pricing. Apple assured the publishers it was willing to work with them to raise those pries.

Apple and the publisher defendants both want to eliminate competition at the retail level. Apple did not want to compete with Amazon, and and the publisher defendants wanted to raise the price point for e-books.

Analysis

Apple decided to offer the defendants the opportunity to move from a wholesale model -- where a publisher receives its wholesale price for each e-book and the retailer sets the retail price – to an agency model, where a publisher sets the retail price and the retailer sells the e-book as its agent. The agreements also included a price parity provision, which protected Apple by allowing it to match the lowest retail price listed on any competitor's e-book store, and also imposed severe financial penalties on the publisher defendants if they did not force Amazon to change their business models to an agency model. The court finds that apple violated Section 1 of the Sherman Anti-Trust act and ordered scheduling of a trial for injunctive relief and damages.

CONCLUSION

For the foregoing reasons, based on the trial record, the court finds that Apple conspired to restrain trade in violation of Section 1 of the Sherman Act.

United Video Props. v. Amazon.com, Inc.
Patent Infringement; Procedure; Claim Construction

***United Video Props. v. Amazon.com, Inc.*, 2012 U.S. Dist. LEXIS 86914 (D. Del. June 22, 2012).**

ISSUE

What definitions should the court apply to the disputed terms in the patent at issue here?

RULE

Claim construction is an issue of law reviewed de novo. *Lighting Ballast Control LLC v. Philips Elecs. N.A. Corp.*, No. 2012-2014, 2014 WL 667499, at *10 (Fed. Cir. Feb. 21, 2014). When the court construes asserted claims, the terms are given "their ordinary and accustomed meaning as understood by one of ordinary skill in the art. *Dow Chem. Co. v. Sumitomo Chem. Co.*, 257 F.3d 1364, 1372 (Fed. Cir. 2001).

CASE DETAILS

Facts:

Rovi offers program guide products to cable providers and other distributors. Rovi owns patents for: (1) an electronic schedule system with access to both stored television schedule information and status information for live programs and (2) a system that allows a user to select and immediately purchase a pay program from an interactive program guide. Rovi sued Amazon alleging infringement of 5 patents including the two named above.

Analysis:

The court determines the construction of the following terms:

- "viewing location" = residence or other building where a television signal is received from a programming source
- "modern" = hardware that translates audio signals transmitted over a telephone line into digital information for a computer and vice versa

- "displaying.. with electronic television program guide"= using the electronic television program guide to visually overlay on a screen
- "program listings" = entries that provide information about particular television programs
- "electronic television program guide" = an electronic application that provides television program schedule and channel information
- "standardized product" = a category of product
- "time and date stamping an order placed by the user with the electronic television program guide"= the order placed by the user with the electronic television program guide is time and date stamped"
- "multimedia informational system"= a system for providing multimedia information
- "data feed" = an updatable transmission of data sent by a television programming provider over television signals
- "a receiver" = a device which can receive television signals, including data transmitted over those signals
- "video-on-demand program listing"= an entry that provides information about a particular video-on-demand program
- "interactive program guide"= an application that produces interactive display screens that include television program schedules and channel information
- "package"= a set of two or more programs available for sale as a single unit

CONCLUSION

The court determined claim construction for the disputed terms in the patents.

United Video Properties, Inc. v. Amazon.com, Inc.
Patent Infringement; Procedural

***United Video Props., Inc. v. Amazon.com,* Inc., 561 Fed. Appx. 914 (Fed. Cir. 2014).**

ISSUE

Whether the court below erred in the claim construction it adopted and thus in the application of the meaning of the patent to the lower court's holding of no infringement.

RULE

Claim construction is an issue of law reviewed de novo. *Lighting Ballast Control LLC v. Philips Elecs. N.A. Corp.*, No. 2012-2014, 2014 WL 667499, at *10 (Fed. Cir. Feb. 21, 2014). When the court construes asserted claims, the terms are given "their ordinary and accustomed meaning as understood by one of ordinary skill in the art. *Dow Chem. Co. v. Sumitomo Chem. Co.*, 257 F.3d 1364, 1372 (Fed. Cir. 2001).

CASE DETAILS

Facts

Rovi offers program guide products to cable providers and other distributors. Rovi owns patents for: (1) an electronic schedule system with access to both stored television schedule information and status information for live programs and (2) a system that allows a user to select and immediately purchase a pay program from an interactive program guide. Rovi sued Amazon alleging infringement of 5 patents including the two named above. The district court determined claim construction for the patents and determined that there was no valid claim, and therefore dismissed the case. Plaintiff now appeals.

Analysis

The court stated that intrinsic evidence includes the claims, the written description and the prosecution history. They do not rely on the prosecution history to construe the meaning of the claim to be narrower than it would otherwise be unless a patentee limited or surrendered claim scope through clear and unmistakable disavowal. The court determines that under the asserted claims, Amazon did not infringe and the lower court's claim construction was affirmed.

CONCLUSION

The court determined claim construction by the lower court was affirmed as well as the judgment of non-infringement.

Univ. Press v. Amazon.com
Patent Infringement; Procedural

***Univ. Press v. Amazon.com*, 2001 U.S. Dist. LEXIS 26987 (N.D. Cal. Nov. 29, 2001).**

ISSUE

Whether the court should grant defendants' Motion to Dismiss?

RULE

For a motion to dismiss based on forum selection clause, the plaintiff's pleading are not accepted as true. Instead, a Rule 12 (b)(3) permits the district court to consider facts outside of the pleadings, and the party challenging the clause must present evidence to justify its non-enforcement.

CASE DETAILS

Facts:

Plaintiff is the owner of University Press and the publisher of the scientific book *Astrobiology*. Amazon is a well-known online seller of books and many other goods. Plaintiffs entered into several online agreements to sell the book. The plaintiff joined Amazon's "Advantage Program," and was to accept the online membership agreement. The plaintiff could not have applied to the Advantage Program without clicking on a button that says "YES I AGREE." Plaintiff filed an action against Defendants for breaching obligations in the agreement about ordering, listing and selling the book on Amazon.com

Analysis:

The court determined the enforceability of the forum selection clause and determined that it does apply to this case, regardless of plaintiffs' lack of filing an opposition to the motion. The lack of filing has led to the lack of plaintiff satisfying their burden of demonstrating unreasonableness. Therefore, the court found the venue of the forum selection valid and dismissed the claims.

CONCLUSION

The court granted the motion to dismiss. Based upon the validity of the forum selection clause.

Vallavista Corp. v. Amazon.com, Inc.
Trademark Infringement

***Vallavista Corp. v. Amazon.com, Inc.*, 657 F. Supp. 2d 1132 (N.D. Cal. 2008).**

ISSUE

Whether summary judgment should be granted here if there is no genuine dispute of material fact.

RULE

A court may grant summary judgment for a claim if the opposing party does not provide any supporting evidence to prove harm was caused and may deny summary judgment when there is a genuine dispute of material fact between the parties.

CASE DETAILS

Facts

Plaintiff has right to the word "Taxi Wallet" and is the registered owner of the trademark for a logo. Target sold taxi wallets that did not have the label taxi wallet on it or on the bar code.

Analysis

There is a genuine issue of material fact in determining if the term "taxi wallet" is generic. A reasonable fact-finder may not find the mark "taxi wallet" as famous and the plaintiff does not provide any evidence otherwise to support dilution of the mark. A genuine issue of material fact is established in determining if Target willfully infringed on the plaintiff's marks.

CONCLUSION

The court grants Target's motion for summary judgment pertaining to dilution because no evidence was provided by the plaintiff and denies the motion for summary judgment for all other claims and damages because there is a genuine dispute of material fact between the parties.

Vance v. Amazon.com, Inc.
Workers Compensation and Employees Rights; Procedure – Motion for Judgment on the Pleadings

---

***Vance v. Amazon.com, Inc. (In re Amazon.com, Inc.),* No. 3:14-md-2504, 2016 U.S. Dist. LEXIS 48650 (W.D. Ky. Mar. 30, 2016)**

ISSUE

Whether the court should grant defendant's motion for judgment on the pleading where federal law resolves the state law claims.

RULE

"After the pleadings are closed – but early enough not to delay trial – a party may move for judgment on the pleadings." Fed. R. Civ. P. 12(c). A motion for judgment on the pleadings is weighed under the same standard as a motion to dismiss for failure to state a claim under Rule 12(b)(6). *Wee Care Child Ctr., Inc. v. Lumpkin*, 680 F.3d 841, 846 (6th Cir. 2012).

CASE DETAILS

Facts

The plaintiffs are a group of hourly-paid workers at Amazon.Com. Inc.'s (Amazon) fulfillment center in Shepherdsville Kentucky. Workers there are assigned specific shifts and must clock in and out. At the ends of their shifts, employees are given a security screening. The security screening purpose is to deter theft. These screenings can take between ten and thirty minutes. Both parties agree that the employees are not paid for the time they are being screened.

Plaintiffs originally pursued their claims for unpaid time under both federal and Kentucky Law. However, the Supreme Court decided a case that also resolved plaintiffs state law claims.

Analysis

The court finds that the plaintiffs do not have a sufficient claim under Kentucky law. Even though Kentucky has its own wage and hour law, the state statute closely resembles the FLSA. Neither the statute or the FLSA defines the word "work." The court finds that in order to define the term "work," that Kentucky courts will look to federal cases interpreting the FLSA to decide what activities constitute "work." In the *Busk* case, the Supreme Court held that the the Portal-to-Portal Act excludes post-shift security checks, and Kentucky courts will use *Busk* to fill the state's statutory void. Therefore, the court will grant the defendants motion for judgment on the pleadings.

CONCLUSION

The court finds that if the state of Kentucky looks to federal law to determine what is work under its wage and hour laws, that it cannot find reason to ignore federal law explaining what is not work. For the foregoing reasons, the court holds that the defendants' motion for judgment on the pleading is granted. The plaintiff's Kentucky, state law claims are dismissed.

Vantage Point Technology v. Amazon.com Inc.
Patent Infringement; Procedure

***Vantage Point Tech., Inc. v. Amazon.com, Inc.*, 2015 U.S. Dist. LEXIS 675 (E.D. Tex. Jan. 6, 2015).**

ISSUE

Whether the court should grant the defendants' Motion to Stay?

RULE

The consumer suit exception in the first-to-file rule is an exception to the general rule that favors the forum of the first-filed action. *Tegic Commc'ns Corp. v. Bd. of Regents of Univ. of Tex. Sys.*, 458 F.3d 1335, 1342 (Fed. Cir. 2006). The main question under this exception "is whether the issues and parties are such that the disposition of one case would be dispositive of the other." *Katz v. Lear Siegler, Inc.*, 909 F.2d 1459, 1463 (Fed. Cir. 1990).

CASE DETAILS

Facts:

Vantage Point filed numerous patent infringement lawsuits against two types of defendants: companies that design and manufacture chipsets and companies that utilize chipsets in their products. Defendants have requested a stay based on the consumer-suit exception to the traditional first-to-file rule.

Analysis:

The court divided the defendants into three groups based on their factual similarities. The court grouped Amazon and Sharp together, as they are both of which are alleged customers with manufacturers that only have pending cases in the Eastern District of Texas. Their requests for stay are also substantially similar to each other. There are no second filed cases in different forums. Instead both the consumer and manufacturer have pending cases for pretrial matters. Amazon and Sharp have also not agreed to be bound by the findings of the first trial. The first-to-file exception is not warranted for Amazon and Sharp.

CONCLUSION

The court denied Amazon's and Sharp's requests for a Motion to Stay.

Vantage Point Technology v. Amazon.com Inc.
Patent Infringement; Procedure

***Vantage Point Tech., Inc. v. Amazon.com, Inc.*, 2015 U.S. Dist. LEXIS 8335 (E.D. Tex. Jan. 26, 2015).**

ISSUE

What definitions the court should apply to the disputed terms within the patent at issue here?

RULE

The court has the authority to construe various terms in patents in order to help encourage settlement after claim construction. *Intergraph Hardware Techs. Co., Inc. v. Hewlett-Packard Co.*, No. 6:04-CV-214 (E.D. Tex. Dec. 22, 2004). Claim construction is clearly an issue for courts of law to determine.

CASE DETAILS

Facts

Vantage Point filed numerous patent infringement lawsuits against two types of defendants: companies that design and manufacture chipsets and companies that utilize chipsets in their products. Amazon requested a stay based on the consumer-suit exception to the traditional first-to-file rule, which the court denied January 6, 2015. This case however discusses the definitions of disputed terms within the patent adopted by the court.

Analysis

The court adopts the following agreed upon definitions:

- "Associated with the first processor cluster" = "associated with only that processor cluster, not any other cluster"
- "Checking the tag memory to determine if a response to the request corresponds to data in the private processor cache associated with the first processor cluster" = "the tag controller determines whether the

information in a request from a second cluster matches a tag stored in the tag memory. If there is a match, the tag controller concludes that a response to the request would require data that is only stored in a private processor cache that is in the same cluster as the tag controller and tag memory"

- "external cache controller" = "hardware that is situated apart from the private processor cache, which includes, but is not limited to, an external tag memory, a data-request monitor and a tag controller"

The Court additionally construed terms that the parties did not agree with as follows:

- " private processor cache, the contents of each such private cache being unknown externally to its associated microprocessor" = "a cache within and dedicated to a processor whose contents are unknown to any device external to that processor, including at least the external cache controller and external tag memory"
- "External tag memory" = " storage that is situated apart from the main memory and includes information about the status of the private processor cache"
- "external tag memory non-hardwired to the private processor cache" = "the private cache does not duplicate its status in the external tag memory and the private processor cache does not use the same logical address as the external tag memory"
- "deriving the status of the private processor cache associated with the first processor cluster by tracking evicted cache lines and data entering and exiting the first processor cluster" = "to get or obtain the status of the private processor cache associated with the first processor cluster by tracking: (1) all modified lines within the private processor cache of that same cluster, (2) all data that enters that same cluster, and (3) all data that exits that same cluster; and using at least that information to determine the status of each private processor cache in only the same cluster."
- "tag controller" = "a controller that manages the external tag memory"

- "when the processor bus is idling" = "when the processor bus is not being used by the processor or other connected device"
- "to identify if the data has been modified if the tag controller indicated that data is held within the private processor cache associated with the first processor cluster" to have its plain meaning
- "a snooper for snooping the private processor cache of the at least one microprocessor associated with the first processor cluster to identity if the data has been modified if the tag controller indicated that data is held within the private processor cache associated with the first processor cluster" to be indefinite
- "processor cluster" = "a set of one or more processors that share a common processor bus in a multiprocessor system"
- "instruction pipeline" = "of at least two structures, each consisting of a sequence of stages that process instruction"
- "master translation memory" to have its plain meaning
- "direct address translation unit" = "a common unit shared by all instruction execution pipelines that translates a virtual memory address and that also comprises the master translation memory"
- "storing the translation data for the virtual address from the master translation memory into the translation buffer" to have its plain meaning
- "whenever" = "every time that"

CONCLUSION

The court adopts the construction set forth for the disputed terms of the patents-in-suit.

Video Professor, Inc. v. Amazon.com, Inc. *Trademark Infringement; Lanham Act; Unfair Competition; Unfair Business Practices*

***Video Professor, Inc. v. Amazon.com, Inc.*, Civil Action No. 09-cv-00636-REB-KLM, 2010 U.S. Dist. LEXIS 29414 (D. Colo. Mar. 8, 2010)**

ISSUE

Whether the court has good cause to modify the discovery schedule where plaintiff has waited past the discovery deadline to seek additional discovery.

RULE

Pursuant to Fed. R. Civ. P. 16(b)(4), the discovery schedule may be modified only for good cause. Fed. R. Civ. P. 26(b)(1) specifies that parties may obtain discovery regarding any non-privileged matter that is relevant to any party's claim or defense. "Good cause to amend the scheduling order means that the scheduling deadlines cannot be met despite a party's diligent efforts.

CASE DETAILS

Facts

This is a trademark infringement case in which plaintiff claims for "false designation of origin and false representation" pursuant to the Lanham Act. Here plaintiff was making continued efforts to extend the discovery deadline. The parties had difficulty establishing agreeing on discovery scheduling and the matter was brought before the court three times.

Analysis

The court finds that plaintiff has not shown good cause for amendment of the deadline for discovery. Plaintiff's efforts to purse discovery were less than diligent, and plaintiff has not shown evidence that additional discovery is relevant to claims as they were stated in the complaint.

CONCLUSION

For the foregoing reasons, the plaintiff's motion to modify the discovery schedule is denied.

Video Professor, Inc. v. Amazon.com, Inc.
Procedure; Trademark Violations; Unfair Competition; Unfair Business Practices

---

***Video Professor, Inc. v. Amazon.com, Inc.*, 2010 U.S. Dist. LEXIS 39103 (D. Colo. Apr. 21, 2010).**

ISSUE

Whether the court should grant Amazon.Com Inc.'s (Amazon) motion for summary judgment.

RULE

Summary judgment is proper when there is no genuine issue as to any material fact and the movant is entitled to judgment as a matter of law. Fed. R. Civ. P. 56(c).

CASE DETAILS

Facts

Defendant Amazon.com, Inc. (Amazon), is an internet retailer that sells products on its website and allows third parties to sell its products on its website. Video Professor, Inc. (Plaintiff) markets and sells computer learning products, including CD's. Plaintiff sold its products to Amazon from December 13, 2003 until September 19, 2009. The vendor manual which contains the terms of the parties' agreements states that "[plaintiff] hereby grants to Amazon.com a non-exclusive, world-wide, perpetual, and royalty-free license to ... use all trademarks and trade names included in the Product Information." Plaintiff asserts 8 claims for relief: (1) false designation of origin and false representation; (2) trademark infringement; (3) violation of the Colorado Consumer Protection Act; (4) unfair competition; (5) tortious interference with business relationships; (6) common law trademark and trade name infringement; (7) accounting; and (8) constructive trust on illegal profits.

Analysis

The court finds that the trademark claims (claims1, 2, and 6), and the unfair competition claim (claim 4), can be analyzed together. The court states that the the language of the Vendor Agreement shows the intent of the parties and defines the scope of the license. The court holds that Amazon's use of the mark "video professor" was authorized, and thus plaintiffs second, fourth and sixth claims cannot succeed. Amazon is entitled to summary judgment on plaintiffs first, second, fourth, and sixth claims for relief.

As to tortious interference with a business relationship, the court finds that no reasonable fact finder could find for plaintiff on its claim. Here, Amazon used "video professor" as a sponsored link on Google and also portrayed Video Professor products along with competing products on Amazon's page. The court finds that these acts are both authorize under the terms of the trademark license in the vendor manual. Thus Amazon is also entitled to summary judgment on plaintiff's fifth claim for relief.

Plaintiff's seventh and eighth claims are for accounting and for a constructive trust on Amazon's allegedly illegal profits. The court finds that there is no basis for these claims because Amazon is entitled to summary judgment on the other 6 claims.

CONCLUSION

For the foregoing reasons the court grants summary judgment in favor of defendant Amazon.

Vivo Per Lei, Inc. v. Bruchim
Copyright Infringement, Patent Infringement, Trademark Infringement

---

Vivo Per Lei, Inc. v. Bruchim **Case No. 11cv05169 GW (JCGx). C.D. Cal., March 20, 2012.**

ISSUE

Whether information in a case should be determined confidential and protected.

RULE

A court may protect information if it would cause harm to either party or provide an unfair competitive edge to other companies

CASE DETAILS

Facts

Plaintiff alleges the defendants infringed its trademarks and copyrights in relation to the sale of certain products. Discovery may call for either side to disclose private information regarding trade secrets of third parties. The parties request to protect the third party's information from having their financial information published.

Analysis

It is likely that Amazon will have to provide information in discovery that would be potentially harmful if it were made available to its competitors.

CONCLUSION

The court granted the protective order to keep the requested information confidential and required both parties to sign a non-disclosure agreement.

Voltstar Tech. v. Amazon.com
Patent Infringement: Procedure

***Voltstar Techs., Inc. v. Amazon.com, Inc.*, 2014 U.S. Dist. LEXIS 102306, 2014 WL 3725860 (N.D. Ill. July 28, 2014)**

ISSUE

Should the court grant summary judgment in favor of the plaintiff or the defendant?

RULE

Pursuant to the Federal Rules of Civil Procedure Rule 56 "Summary judgment shall be rendered when the pleadings, depositions, answers to interrogatories, and admissions on file, together with the affidavits, if any, show that there is no genuine issue as to any material fact and that the moving party is entitled to judgment as a matter of law."

CASE DETAILS

Facts

Plaintiff, Voltstar Technologies, filed suit against defendant, Amazon.com for patent infringement of patent 192, entitled "Electrical Charger". The mini charger manufactured by Voltstar was sold on Amazon.com and was used to charge Amazon products.

The parties then filed cross motions for summary judgment pursuant to the Federal Rules of Civil Procedure 56.

Analysis

The court compared the two devices and found that there were significant differences. Additionally, the differences were so severe that the court found they were "sufficient to grant summary judgment without examining the prior art in the eyes of many district courts."

The court then looked to the prior art and held that, "an ordinary observer, familiar with the prior art, would be not deceived into thinking that the Amazon design was the same as the Voltstar design.

CONCLUSION

The District Court denied the plaintiffs cross motion for summary judgment and granted the defendant's motion for summary judgment.

Volstar Techs., Inc. v. Amazon.com, Inc.
Procedure

***Voltstar Techs., Inc. v. Amazon.com, Inc.*, 2015 U.S. App. LEXIS 6008, 599 Fed. Appx. 385 (Fed. Cir. 2015)**

ISSUE

Whether the lower court judgment denying summary judgment to the plaintiffs and granted to the defendants should be affirmed.

RULE

A court may affirm a lower court judgment after reviewing all the related material and hearing the case and determining the lower court did not err in making the judgment.

CASE DETAILS

Facts

This is an appeal from the United States District Court for the Northern District of Illinois.

Analysis

The court heard and considered the case and subsequently affirmed the lower court judgment.

CONCLUSION

The court affirmed the lower court judgment after hearing the case and determining the lower court did not err.

Walker Digital, LLC v. Facebook Inc.
Patent Infringement; Procedural

***Walker Digital, LLC v. Facebook, Inc.*, 852 F. Supp. 2d 559 (D. Del. 2012).**

ISSUE

Whether the court should grant Defendants' motion to dismiss for failure to state a claim.

RULE

Federal Rules of Civil Procedure 12(b)(6) allows the court to dismiss a case with prejudice for failure to state a claim. Additionally, in a motion to dismiss filed under Fed. R. Civ. P. 12(b)(6), the court must accept all allegations made by the non-moving party as true and draw reasonable inferences in their favor.

CASE DETAILS

Facts

Walker is a Delaware limited liability company with its principal place of business in Connecticut. Amazon is a Delaware corporation with its principal place of business in Washington. Plaintiff alleges that Amazon "has and continues to directly infringe one or more claims of the patent" by selling, using, offering for sale, and making products.

Timeline

On April 11, 2011, Walker Digital filed a patent infringement litigation against multiple defendants including Amazon. Walker filed a first amended complaint on July 29, 2011. Amazon, along with Zappos, moved to dismiss with prejudice the claims against them in the plaintiff's first amended complaint under FRCP 12(b)(6).

Analysis

The court determined that at least at the time for the filing of the complaint, Amazon was aware that it was infringing on the patent and continued to do so.

The complaint sufficiently identified the patent at issue and the infringing conduct, defendant's receipt of the complaint and decision to continue its conduct despite the knowledge gleaned from the complaint satisfies the requirements of *Global Tech.* The court denied the defendants' motions to dismiss.

CONCLUSION

The court denied the defendant's motion to dismiss.

Walker Digital, LLC v. Facebook Inc.
Patent Infringement; Procedural

***Walker Digital, LLC v. Expedia, Inc.*, 2013 U.S. Dist. LEXIS 148983 (D. Del. Oct. 16, 2013).**

ISSUE

Whether a settlement agreement transferred all rights to patents, terminating the right to pursue litigation such that this case should be dismissed for lack of standing.

RULE

A court may determine a party has no constitutional right to litigation after looking at a settlement agreement as a whole.

CASE DETAILS

Facts

Plaintiff filed actions against the defendants alleging infringement and the defendants filed motions to dismiss. The parties entered into a confidential settlement and license agreement transferring ownership rights of a patent to eBay.

Analysis

The settlement agreement clearly transferred ownership rights of the patent to eBay. The court grants the defendant's motion to dismiss for lack of standing.

CONCLUSION

The court grants the defendant's motion to dismiss, the plaintiff has no right to litigation because all rights to the patent were transferred to the defendant.

Warner Bros. V. Jimenez
Copyright Infringement; Procedure

***Warner Bros. Home Entm't v. Jimenez*, 2013 U.S. Dist. LEXIS 97139 (C.D. Cal. July 8, 2013).**

ISSUE

Should the court enter default judgment against Jimenez, an Amazon seller?

RULE

The Federal Rules of Civil Procedure 55(a) provides that, "when a party against whom a judgment for affirmative relief is sought has failed to plead or otherwise defend, and that failure is shown by affidavit or otherwise, the clerk must enter the party's default."

CASE DETAILS

Facts

Plaintiff, Warner Bros. filed suit against defendant Jimenez, an Amazon.com seller for copyright infringement. Defendant, copied, reproduced distributed and sold unauthorized copies of TV programs. Plaintiff alleged that the plaintiff acted "in willful disregard of laws protecting copyrights and that plaintiff has and will continue to sustain substantial damage to the value of its creative works, specifically including the TV programs."

The defendant was properly served by leaving the complaint with her family member/co-occupant on December 21, 2012 and did not file a response to the complaint. On February 5, 2013, the clerk entered a default judgment against the defendant.

Analysis

The court looked to the possibility of prejudice to plaintiff and found the plaintiff would suffer prejudice if default judgment is not entered because plaintiff would be denied the right to judicial resolution of the claims presented, and would be without other recourse for recovery."

The court then looked to the merits of plaintiff's substantive claims and the sufficiency of the complaint. The court found that the plaintiff had established ownership of the copyrights by submitting copyright registration certificates for the TV Programs. Additionally, the court found that the plaintiff adequately alleged that the defendant violated the plaintiff's exclusive rights under the Copyright Act. Therefore, the court found that "plaintiff need not demonstrate access to establish copying because of the high degree of similarity between the TV Programs and the infringing products."

When the court looked to the amount of money at stake, the court found that, the amount in damages would be a substantial burden on the defendant. The court then looked to the possibility of a dispute concerning material facts and found that it was unclear whether there would be any genuine dispute over material facts. When the court looked to whether the default was due to excusable neglect, the court found that this waived in favor of default judgment. On the issue of the strong policy favoring decisions on the merits, the court found that the entry of default judgment was appropriate.

CONCLUSION

The court concluded that a judgment should be entered in favor of plaintiff Warner Bros. and awarded damages in the amount of $66,000.00.

Wax v. Amazon Techs., Inc.
Trademark Violation

***Wax v. Amazon Techs., Inc.*, 500 Fed. Appx. 944 (Fed. Cir. 2013).**

ISSUE

Whether the decision of the Trademark trial and Appeal Board, denying the registration of the mark Amazon Ventures to plaintiff was proper.

RULE

"The Patent and Trademark Office (PTO) may refuse to register a trademark if it is so similar to a registered mark as to be likely, when used on or in connection with the goods of the applicant, to cause confusion, or to cause mistake, or to deceive" *Coach Servs., Inc. v. Triumph Learning LLC*, 668 F.3d 1356, 1366 (Fed. Cir. 2012) (citing 15 U.S.C. § 1502).

"We determine likelihood of confusion by focusing on the question whether the purchasing public would mistakenly assume that plaintiff's services originate from the same source as, or are associated with defendant. *In re Majestic Distilling Co., Inc.*, 315 F.3d 1311, 1315-16 (Fed. Cir. 2003).

CASE DETAILS

Facts

Plaintiff, Wax is a patent attorney who helps startups obtain venture capital funding. In 2000 he filed an intent to use application in order register Amazon Ventures for "investment management, raising venture capital for others, ... and capital investment consultation." Defendant, Amazon Technologies, Inc. (Amazon) opposed the registration because several registered Amazon.Com marks have filing dates prior to plaintiff's application and because Amazon has common law priority over use of plaintiff's mark. The PTO found that Amazon established priority and that there was a likelihood of confusion between the Amazon Ventures and Amazon.Com marks. This case is the appeal to the PTO decision.

Analysis

As to priority the court concludes that the PTO did not err in its priority analysis because Amazon has established priority on the basis of its registered marks. Amazon's failure to register Amazon.Com for financial services does not negate the priority of its marks for advertising services, business management, credit card services, and other services with respect to plaintiff's application.

As to the likelihood of confusion, the court finds no error in the PTO's decision. The court finds that the record shows that "Amazon" and "Amazon.com" are used interchangeably to refer to defendant's services. This supports the PTO's finding that "Amazon" is the dominant feature of the mark.

CONCLUSION

After consideration of plaintiff's remaining arguments, the court concludes they lack merit and affirms the decision of the PTO; plaintiff may not register his Amazon Ventures trademark.

Westermajer v. Nutrex Research, Inc.
Procedure

***Westermajer v. Nutrex Research, Inc.*, 2015 U.S. Dist. LEXIS 167245 (D.N.J. Dec. 15, 2015).**

ISSUE

Whether defendant Vitamin Shoppe was fraudulently joined in an effort to destroy diversity jurisdiction such that the case should NOT be remanded to state court.

RULE

A district court has "original jurisdiction over matters in which there is complete diversity of citizenship between the parties and the amount in controversy exceeds $75,000." 28 U.S.C. § 1332. "When a non-diverse party has been joined as a defendant, then in the absence of a substantial federal question the removing defendant may avoid remand only by demonstrating that the non-diverse party was fraudulently joined." *In re Briscoe,* 448 F.3d 201, 217 (3d Cir. 2006) (quoting *Batoff v. State Farm Ins. Co.,* 977 F.2d 848, 851-52 (3d Cir. 1992)). "Joinder is fraudulent if there is no reasonable basis in fact or colorable ground supporting the claim against the joined defendant, or no real intention in good faith to prosecute the action against the defendant or seek a joint judgment. *Briscoe,* 448 F.3d at 216 (quoting *Abels v. State Farm Fire & Cs. Co.,* 770 F.2d 26, 32 (3d Cir. 1985)).

CASE DETAILS

Facts

This case concerns two dietary supplements known as "Hemo Rage" and "Lipo 6," both which contain a compound called DMAA. In April 2012, the FDA published a warning letter stating that DMAA is not a natural compound and could not be the active ingredient in a dietary supplement under the apllicable regulatory laws. Plaintiff, purchased and consumed these products between 2011 and 2013 and was ultimately diagnosed with symptoms associated with their use. Plaintiff claims that as a result of use of these products he now requires daily use of a catheter. Plaintiff further alleges that defendants did not recall DMAA supplements because they had made investments in these products and wanted to sell off the remaining inventory. Defendant Vitamin Shoppe was joined, and defendants argue that this was fraudulent joinder used only as an attempt to defeat diversity jurisdiction. Plaintiff claims that he did not fraudulently join Vitamin Shoppe, that he often used cash and only sometimes used his Vitamin Shoppe membership card.

Analysis

The court holds that defendant Vitamin Shoppe was not fraudulently joined and the case can be remanded. The court finds that the defendants have not established that Vitamin Shoppe's membership information is a complete record of all of plaintiff's purchases from their store. Plaintiff claims that he purchased both products at issue from Vitamin Shoppe's retail store, and that he made most of his purchases with cash and without giving his membership information. Defendants also have not shown that Vitamin Shoppe's customer information profile included cash purchases or sales to customers who did not provide membership information. Therefore, a genuine issue of material fact remains as to whether plaintiff purchased a product containing DMAA from Vitamin Shoppe.

CONCLUSION

The court holds that Vitamin Shoppe was not fraudulently joined. The court grants plaintiff's motion to remand.

Whitsitt v. Amazon.com
Procedure

***Whitsitt v. Amazon.com*, 2014 U.S. Dist. LEXIS 58780, 2014 WL 1671502 (E.D. Cal. Apr. 25, 2014).**

ISSUE

The issue here is whether the plaintiff's amended complaint satisfies the legal requirements for properly stating a claim under Federal case law and the Federal Rules of Civil Procedure.

RULE

In order to avoid dismissal for failure to state a claim, a complaint must contain more than "naked assertions." "labels and conclusions" or "a formalistic recitation of the elements of a cause of action." *Bell Atlantic Corp v. Twonbly*, 550 U.S. 544, 555-557 (2007). Although the federal Rules adopt a flexible pleading policy, a complaint must give fair notice and state the elements of the claim plainly and succinctly. *Jones v. Community Redev. Agency*, 733 F.2d 646, 649 (9th Cir. 1984). Plaintiff must allege with at least some degree of particularity overt acts which defendants engaged in that support plaintiff's claim. *Id.*

CASE DETAILS

Facts

Plaintiff in his original complaint, failed to file a clear, concise complaint that gave fair notice and stated the elements of the claim plainly and succinctly, but the court used its discretion and allowed plaintiff to file the amended complaint at issue here.

Plaintiff's claims were for violations of the ADEA and IIED. Plaintiff was told what the requirements for stating these types of claims were. However, plaintiff's amended complaint still did not meet the requirements for a sufficiently stated complaint.

Analysis

Here, plaintiff's filed a 20 page amended complaint. According to the court the plaintiff's amended complaint made no attempt to concisely state his claims. The amended complaint had duplicative sections that were virtually cut and pasted from the original. The amended complaint also contains 35 lines per page, but the rule has a 28 line per page limit.

CONCLUSION

The court concludes that: (1) Plaintiff's motion to exceed the page limit for filing and amended complaint is denied; (2) Plaintiff's amended complaint is dismissed; and (3) The plaintiff now has 30 days to file a second amended complaint. The court set forth the rules and requirements for plaintiff's second amended complaint.

Whitsitt v. Amazon.com
Worker's Compensation and Employee Rights

***Whitsitt v. Amazon.Com*, 2014 U.S. Dist. LEXIS 62652 (E.D. Cal. May 6, 2014).**

ISSUE

Whether the court should dismiss plaintiff's complaint for failure to state a claim and for stating a frivolous claim.

RULE

The federal in forma pauperis statute authorizes federal courts to dismiss a case if the action is legally "frivolous or malicious," fails to state a claim upon which relief may be granted, or seeks monetary relief from a defendant who is immune from such relief. 28 U.S.C. § 1915(e)(2). "A claim is legally frivolous when it lacks an arguable basis either in law or in fact. *Neitzke v. Williams*, 490 U.S. 319, 325 (1989). The court may, therefore, dismiss a claim as frivolous where it is based on an indisputable meritless legal theory or where the factual contentions are clearly baseless. *Neitzke*, 490 U.S. at 327.

CASE DETAILS

Facts

In this case, plaintiff seeks to proceed in forma pauperis under 28 U.S.C. § 1915. Plaintiff was ordered to show why this action should not be dismissed for false statements he made on the in forma pauperis affidavit. The court accepts plaintiffs excuse of mistake and discharges the order to show cause. The court must now determine if the claim is frivolous or malicious.

Analysis

The court finds that the allegations in plaintiff's complaint are so vague and conclusory that it is unable to determine whether the current action is frivolous or fails to state a claim for relief. The court holds that the claim does not meet the sufficiency requirements found in Fed. R. Civ. P. 8(a)(2). Because plaintiff has failed to comply with the Federal requirements, the complaint must be dismissed. The court however allows time for the plaintiff to file an amended complaint.

CONCLUSION

For the foregoing reasons the court dismisses plaintiff's complaint. However, plaintiff is allowed 30 days to file an amended complaint that complies with the Federal Rules of Civil Procedure.

Wireless Recognition Tech v. A9.com Inc.
Patent Infringement

Wireless Recognition Tech. v. A9.com, Inc., 2012 U.S. Dist. LEXIS 130159 (N.D. Cal. Sept. 11, 2012).

ISSUE

Whether the court should grant defendant's motion to stay this action pending the reexamination of the patent at issue.

RULE

Pursuant to 35 U.S.C. Section 302, "Any person at any time may file a request for reexamination by the PRO of any claim of a patent on the basis of any prior art consisting of patents or printed publications."

Following the rule found in *Telemac Corp. v. Teledigital, Inc.*, a court will stay a case pending reexamination by looking to see, "whether discovery is complete and whether a trial date has been set; whether a stay will simplify the issues in question and trial of the case; and whether a stay would unduly prejudice or present a clear tactical disadvantage to the non-moving party".

CASE DETAILS

Facts

Plaintiff, Wireless Recognition Tech. filed suit against defendants; A9.com, Amazon.com, Google Inc., Nokia Corp., Ricoh Innovations, Inc., and Ricoh Company, Ltd claiming that the 287 patent was infringed. The United States Patent and Trademark Office (PTO) issued a rejection on the 474 patent claiming it was too obvious. The defendants then sought a stay of this action pending the final exhaustion of the 474 reexamination. Wireless Recognition Tech claims that a stay pending final exhaustion of reexamination procedures is not an appropriate action because, "MicroStrategy, not defendants, initiated the *inter partes* reexamination."

Analysis

The court found that because of the likelihood of the reexamination resulting in invalidation of some or all of the 474 claims weigh in favor of a stay. Additionally the court looked to see if the non-moving party would suffer undue prejudice as a result of the stay and found that the undue prejudice weighs in favor of a stay. Finally, the court looked to equitable factors being, first, that defendants did not initiate inter partes reexamination; and to consider a statement made by the defendants where they agreed to negotiate a joint schedule for the cases. In considering the equitable factors, the court found that no equitable factors would defeat a stay.

CONCLUSION

The United States District Court granted the defendant's motion for a stay of this case.

Worldslide, LLC v. Amazon.com, Inc.
Procedure

***Worldslide, LLC v. Amazon.com, Inc.* Case No. 2:11-cv-03352-GEB-CKD. United States District Court Eastern District of California, March, 2012.**

ISSUE

Can the court consolidate the four different lawsuits that Worldslide has filed?

RULE

The court can consolidate cases if they are similar or the same claims, the same transaction or event, similar questions of fact or the same question of law or the include the same defendants. The court will consolidate as a result of saving judicial efforts and convenience for the parties.

CONCLUSION

The court held that the cases are closely related and therefore should be consolidated for purposes of efficiency.

Wreal LLC, v. Amazon.com, Inc.
Trademark Infringement

***Wreal, LLC v. Amazon.com, Inc.*, 2014 U.S. Dist. LEXIS 160160 (S.D. Fla. Nov. 14, 2014).**

ISSUE

Whether the parties should disclose the names of non-testifying consulting experts who receive the most-confidential type of discovery?

RULE

Fed. R. Civ. P. 26(c) gives court the discretion to grant protective orders concerning dissemination of sensitive information and to decide when a protective order is appropriate and what degree of protection is required. *Seattle Times Co. v. Rhinehart*, 467 U.S. 20, 36 (1984).

CASE DETAILS

Facts

In this case, plaintiff Wreal claims they have provided a streaming video service, "Fyre TV" to consumers long before Amazon began its "Fire TV" set-top box service. Amazon filed a motion to disclose the non-testifying consulting experts who receive highly confidential information despite the protective order. Wreal argues that revealing these identities is unnecessary. Additionally, Wreal has made discovery requests to obtain Amazon's financial, business and marketing strategies, which Amazon claims would cause substantial harm if made known to competitors. Wreal filed a lawsuit and five months after starting the lawsuit, filed a motion for preliminary injunction, to compel Amazon to stop providing the "Fire TV" service. Wreal argues that consumers will easily mistake that Wreal's "Fyre TV" is associated with Amazon or that Wreal is the infringer. The parties have agreed to a protective order to protect their trade secrets and sensitive information.

Analysis

When courts are considering the grounds for a protective other, they should "balance the interests of those requesting the order." *McCarthy v. Barnett Bank of Polk City*, 876 F.2d 89,91 (11th Cir. 1989). The party must demonstrate good cause for the order, and then the burden shifts to the opposing party to explain why it is not warranted. *Am. Standard Inc. v. Pfizer*, 828 F.2d 734, 741 (Fed. Cir. 1987). Additionally, Rule 26(b)(3)(B) does not prevent the disclosure of the identity of a non-testifying expert.

CONCLUSION

The court held that Amazon has demonstrated a good cause to have the requested provision to reveal the identities of experts included in the protective order and therefore granted the motion.

Wreal LLC v. Amazon.com Inc.
Trademark Infringement

***Wreal LLC v. Amazon.com, Inc.*, 2015 U.S. Dist. LEXIS 176382 (S.D. Fla. Feb. 3, 2015).**

ISSUE

Should the court grant the plaintiff's motion for preliminary injunction?

RULE

15 U.S.C. Section 1116(a) provides that "in order to obtain a preliminary injunction, the party must demonstrate, (1) a substantial likelihood of success on the merits; (2) irreparable harm should the injunction not be granted; (3) that the threatened injury to the plaintiff outweighs any potential harm to the defendant; and (4) that granting the injunction would not be adverse to the public interest."

CASE DETAILS

Facts

Plaintiff, Wreal LLC, filed suit against defendant, Amazon.com. Amazon, with knowledge of the trademarked protection for "Fyre TV" used the name "Fire TV" for its video streaming service. Amazon claimed that the two televisions were dissimilar because Fyre TV dealt specifically with pornographic content.

Amazon filed a preliminary injunction motion several months after the launch of the Fire TV product. Wreal filed a preliminary injunction.

Analysis

When the court looked to the distinctiveness of mark it found this issue weighed in favor of Amazon. When the court looked to the similarity of the marks, the court found that the marks were not similar enough to cause this factor as favoring Wreal. When the court looked to the similarity of the products they again waived in favor of Amazon. When looking to the similarity of sales outlets and customer base, the court found this waived in Amazon's favor. For the similarity of advertising, this waived in favor of Amazon. For the defendant's intent, the court found this waived in neither party's favor. The actual confusion weighed in favor of Amazon.

For irreparable harm, the court found that Wreal failed to establish irreparable harm. Additionally, the court found the balance of hardships was not proven by Wreal. Finally, the court found that the public interest did not favor issuing an injunction to reward Wreal.

CONCLUSION

The Magistrate Judge recommended that the District Court deny plaintiff's motion.

Wreal LLC v. Amazon.com, Inc. (S.D. Fla., 2015)
Procedure

***Wreal LLC v. Amazon.com, Inc.*, 2015 U.S. Dist. LEXIS 35082 (S.D. Fla. Mar. 20, 2015).**

ISSUE

The issue here is whether plaintiff's use of an expert opinion in connection with its motion for preliminary injunction, but not as a designated expert at trial is sufficient to allow the court to grant Amazon a subpoena for that expert.

RULE

An expert's participation in preliminary injunction proceedings is separate and apart from whether that expert is a testifying expert for purposes of trial, as contemplated by Federal rule 26. "[A] plaintiff would not be prejudiced by an order disallowing [an] expert's deposition because the expert will not testify at trial, and therefore there is no need to depose her in preparation for cross examination. *Estate of Manship v. United States of America*, 240 F.R.D. 229, 237 (M.D. La., 2006).

CASE DETAILS

Facts

Here, plaintiff Wreal used expert opinion twice in connection with its motion for preliminary injunction. In both instances the expert testimony challenged surveys performed by Amazon experts. Amazon has requested a subpoena for issuance of two categories of documents: (1) All questions, responses, reports and results of any survey or study involving plaintiff's expert; and (2) All non-privileged documents and communications in possession by the expert that relate to this case.

Analysis

The court finds that at the "moment," that the subpoena cannot be granted. Although the expert testimony was used at the preliminary injunction phase of this claim, at the present moment, plaintiff has not designated that expert for use *at trial* of the case. According to the Federal Rules, these types of disclosures are not yet required under the timeline of this case. The court notes that the plaintiff is generally the "master of its own case," and at this time has not designated its expert testimony for use at trial. This fact alone is enough for the court to hold that the expert is simply a consulting, non-testifying expert, regardless of his role in the preliminary injunction phase of this case.

CONCLUSION

The court ultimately concludes that barring discovery relating to the expert testimony will not prejudice Amazon because the expert testimony will not be used at trial. Thus Amazon will not need to prepare for a cross examination of the expert at trial. If plaintiff later designates this expert testimony for use at trial Amazon will be free to renew its subpoena.

Yasin v. Q-Boro Holdings, LLC
Unlawful Use of Images, Privacy Violations

***Yasin v. Q-Boro Holdings, LLC*, 27 Misc. 3d 1214(A) (N.Y. Sup. Ct. 2010).**

ISSUE

Whether the court should grant plaintiff's motion for permanent injunction which would force defendants to cease use of her photograph.

RULE

New York does not recognize a common-law right to privacy (see Messenger v. Gruner & Jahr Print & Publ., 94 NY2d 436, 441, 727 N.E.2d 549, 706 N.Y.S.2d 52 [2000]. Instead, a limited statutory right to privacy is created by Civil Rights Law §§ 50 and 51. Under Civil Rights Law § 50, it is a misdemeanor to use a person's name, portrait or picture for advertising or trade purposes without having first obtained the written consent of such person. Civil Rights Law § 51 in turn, provides for civil and equitable redress. The elements of a cause of action under Civil Rights Law § 51 are (1) the use of a person's name, portrait, picture (2) for advertising purposes or for the purpose of trade, (3) without written consent (see Molina v. Phoenix Sound, 297 AD2d 595, 597, 747 N.Y.S.2d 227 [2002].

CASE DETAILS

Facts

The Plaintiff, Tasleema Yasin, alleges unlawful use of her photo without her consent on the cover of a book published by Q-Boro Holdings, LLC and Urban Books, LLC entitled Baby Doll. This fiction book is published by defendants, and it is commercially distributed by retailers including Borders, Barnes & Noble, and Amazon.com.

Yasin requests a permanent injunction to prohibit the further sale, display, and use of her image by defendants and for an award of partial summary judgment on the issue of liability. The Defendants move to dismiss Yasin's complaint.

Analysis

It is undisputed that there is no relationship between Yasin's picture and the subject matter contained in the book; which is admittedly a pure work of fiction that neither references Yasin by name or otherwise identifies her as a character in the book. In view of the foregoing, the defendants unauthorized use of Yasin's image on the front cover of the Baby Doll book violates her statutory right to privacy pursuant to Civil Right's Law § 51. Accordingly, plaintiff Yasin's motion for a permanent injunction is granted and the defendants are prohibited from further selling, displaying, or using her image.

CONCLUSION

The court held that the use of plaintiff's image violated her statutory fright to privacy and thus her motion for a permanent injunction was granted.

Zaretsky v. Maxi-Aids, Inc.
RICO Violations

***Zaretsky v. Maxi-Aids, Inc.*, 2012 U.S. Dist. LEXIS 84291, 2012 WL 2345181 (E.D.N.Y. June 18, 2012).**

ISSUE

Was there a clear error on the face of the Report?

RULE

Pursuant to the Federal Rules of Civil Procedure, Rule 72 (b) permits magistrate judges to conduct proceedings on dispositive pretrial matters without the consent of the parties. In order for a district judge to accept the magistrate judge's recommendation, they only need to be satisfied that there is no clear error apparent on the face of the record.

CASE DETAILS

Facts

Feige Berlin and Aaron Berlin (plaintiffs) filed an action against defendants pursuant to the Racketeer Influenced and Corrupt Organizations Act. The Magistrate Judge found in the report that the Berlin's motion for an extension of time should be denied and defendants Citibank, N.A.; European American Bank; and JP Morgan Chase Bank motion to dismiss should be granted. The District court now reviews this report.

Analysis

The Federal Rules of Civil Procedure, Rule 72 (b) permits magistrate judges to conduct proceedings on dispositive pretrial matters without the consent of the parties. In order for a district judge to accept the magistrate judge's recommendation, they only need to be satisfied that there is no clear error apparent on the face of the record. The court here found there was no error on the face of the report.

CONCLUSION

The District Court held that since there was no error on the face of the report, the plaintiff's motion for an extension of time is denied and the defendant's motion to dismiss is granted.

Zaretsky v. Maxi-Aids, Inc. (2nd Cir., 2013)
Rico Violation

***Zaretsky v. Maxi-Aids, Inc.*, 529 Fed. Appx. 97 (2d Cir. N.Y. 2013).**

AMAZON is a listed party, but did not play a substantive role in this case.

ISSUE

The issue here is whether the lower court abused its discretion in dismissing appellants' complaint for failure to comply with a court order and for failure to prosecute. Here, appellants failed to object to the court order within the time allotted by statute which normally bars appellate review.

RULE

The general rule is that a party's "failure to object timely to a magistrate's report operates as a waiver of any further judicial review of the magistrates' decision" if the report "explicitly states that failure to object to the report within [fourteen] days will preclude appellate review." *Small v. Sec'y of Health and Human Servs.*, 892 F.2d 15, 16 (2d Cir. 1989).

There is an exception to the rule that allows the reviewing court to use their discretion and can excuse a party's failure to objet "in the interests of justice." *Roldan v. Racette*, 984 F.2d 85, 89 (2d. Cir. 1993).

CASE DETAILS

Facts

Here, the appellants failed to follow a court order requiring them to object to a magistrate's report or recommendation within 14 days.

Analysis

The court held that appellants failed to object to the order after receiving notice that they were required to file objections and that a failure to do so would result in a waiver of their right to appellate review. This means that appellants have legally waived their right to appellate review.

The court stated that even if they were to excuse appellants' failure to object that the lower court still acted within its discretion in dismissing the claim because they followed the magistrate's recommendation.

CONCLUSION

Here, the decision of the lower court was affirmed. Dismissal of a claim is proper when a party fails to comply with requirements set forth by a court.

Made in United States
Orlando, FL
04 November 2026

90198159R00433